Holocaust Denial as an International Movement

HOLOCAUST DENIAL AS AN INTERNATIONAL MOVEMENT

Stephen E. Atkins

PRAEGER

Westport, Connecticut
London

Library of Congress Cataloging-in-Publication Data

Atkins, Stephen E.
    Holocaust denial as an international movement / Stephen E. Atkins.
        p. cm.
    Includes bibliographical references and index.
    ISBN 978–0–313–34538–8 (alk. paper)
1. Holocaust denial literature—History and criticism. I. Title.
D804.355.A85 2009
940.53'1818—dc22   2008052834

British Library Cataloguing in Publication Data is available.

Library of Congress Catalog Card Number: 2008052834
ISBN: 978–0–313–34538–8

First published in 2009

Praeger Publishers, 88 Post Road West, Westport, CT 06881
An imprint of Greenwood Publishing Group, Inc.
www.praeger.com

Printed in the United States of America

The paper used in this book complies with the
Permanent Paper Standard issued by the National
Information Standards Organization (Z39.48–1984).

10 9 8 7 6 5 4 3 2 1

Contents

Introduction

Holocaust denial may have started in Europe after World War II but now in the early twenty-first century, it has become an international movement. It has spread from Europe throughout the world with Holocaust deniers active in almost every country. Several books appeared in the late 1980s and early 1990s that traced the state of Holocaust denial in that era. Deborah Lipstadt's *Denying the Holocaust: The Growing Assault on Truth and Memory* appeared in 1993, and it made a major impact in the study of Holocaust denial. Gill Seidel's *Holocaust Denial: Antisemitism, Racism and the New Right* (1986) and Kenneth S. Stern's *Holocaust Denial* (1993) were two others that made major contributions to the understanding of the Holocaust denial movement. It has been more than a decade since these books appeared, and there has been no attempt to bring the Holocaust denial movement up-to-date. The importance of an update is in keeping with Stern's conclusion in 2001.

> Holocaust denial, in fact, may be the single most potent ideological force tying together a variety of extremists from around the globe—including old Nazis, neo-Nazis, anti-Israeli Arab governments, American black separatists and others.[1]

My intent in writing this book is to trace the state of the international Holocaust denial movement in the early 2000s with appropriate attention to the development of Holocaust denial in the past.

Holocaust denial has been stimulated by three factors: a desire to rehabilitate Adolf Hitler and the Nazi regime so that it would be possible to reestablish a neo-Nazi state, a renewal of the ancient scourge of antisemitism, and a way of denying the legitimacy of the state of Israel. Each of these factors has its own partisans, but sometimes there has been crossover when these partisans found out they share the same goals. Few neo-Nazis have any love for

Israel. Nor does the Arab hatred for Israel avoid spilling over into antisemitism. This sharing has penetrated even to the radical Left in Europe and the United States. Holocaust denial allows its partisans with separate ideologies and religious views to share a common goal.

The Holocaust denial movement has never been a mass movement. It has never had more than 250 active participants, but they have been able to convert thousands of fellow travelers. Almost all of the active participants come from the antisemitic right wings in their respective countries. The exception is that Holocaust denial has become more acceptable to the European extreme Left as a means to attack Israel. Following Part I, which outlines the current understanding of the background to the Holocaust and the Holocaust itself, this book intends to concentrate on the leaders of the Holocaust movement. Because Holocaust deniers are true ideologues, my intention is not to try to convince them that they are wrong about the Holocaust. Rather it is to promote an understanding on the nature of the Holocaust and how the deniers have distorted the historical record. A corollary is to trace the history of the Holocaust denial movement and its current practitioners.

Holocaust deniers come in a variety of types. These types are not exclusive as certain Holocaust deniers may belong to more than one type. Nevertheless, it is useful to denote the various types and the individuals who belong to a particular type.

The most famous and influential are the academic research stars. These individuals are the ones who have specialized on detailed research topics to disprove one or more aspects of the Holocaust. The most famous of these are France's Robert Faurisson, Italy's Carlo Mattogno, Germany's Germar Rudolf, and America's Fred A. Leuchter, Jr. They have adopted a pseudoscience approach to denying the Holocaust. These academic research stars have considerable prestige in the Holocaust denial movement because of their expertise in challenging aspects of the Holocaust. Because they have specialized on such narrow topics, Holocaust scholars have had to redirect their research to answer sometimes trivial issues, or unanswerable ones.

Second in importance to the academic research stars are the media stars. These Holocaust deniers demand publicity because it promotes their agenda. They also publicize the research conclusions of the academic research stars. The most famous examples of this type are Great Britain's David Irving and Australia's duo of John Bennett and Fredrick Töben.

Following closely behind the other two types are the distributors of Holocaust denial materials. Their role is to provide these materials around the world, and especially in countries with laws against Holocaust denial, such as Germany and Austria. They also make a good living selling these materials. The best examples of distributors have been America's Gary Lauck and Canada's Ernst Zündel. Both have encountered legal troubles in Germany because of the distribution of their materials there. The Internet has simplified the problem of distribution, so in the future the risks will be less and the profits better.

Another type is the Holocaust deniers who do it for political reasons. They subscribe to Holocaust denial because it advances a political agenda. The best examples of this type are France's Maurice Bardèche, who wanted to rehabilitate the Vichy Regime, General Otto Ernst Remer, who wanted to reestablish Nazism, and the Americans Willis A. Carto and Mark Weber, both of whom have used Holocaust denial for political reasons.

There are also opportunists who have become Holocaust deniers as out-growths of their antisemitic views. To them Holocaust denial is an instru-ment to further their hatred of the Jews. The best example of this type was the French novelist Louis-Ferdinand Céline. He advanced Holocaust denial only because it could be a weapon against the Jews.

Next, there are the true believers. These individuals have adopted Holo-caust denial after reading its literature, or hearing about it from others. They communicate their Holocaust denial views to friends, colleagues, and some-times students, but are careful to avoid publicity. Some of them held anti-semitic views before exposure to Holocaust denial materials, and others had not. The best examples of the true believer type are the Canadians James Keegstra and Malcolm Ross. Both Keegstra and Ross were school-teachers before their Holocaust denial advocacy led them to lose their jobs.

Finally, the last and largest type of Holocaust denial adherents is the fellow travelers. The fellow travelers have been exposed to Holocaust denial, and they believe in it. They are careful not to communicate their views to others unless to other Holocaust deniers. These fellow travelers are the solid base of the movement because they are the ones who buy the materials that provide the financial support for the movement. The best example of this was the $7.5 million given by Jean Farrell, the grandniece of the famous inventor Thomas Alva Edison, to Willis A. Carto and the Institute for Historical Review to promote Holocaust denial studies.

Holocaust deniers have had the freedom to operate because of the reluc-tance of academic specialists in the field of Holocaust studies to challenge them. When Holocaust denial first made its appearance, "its claims seemed so absurd that historians and journalists dismissed it as a temporary aberra-tion, an eccentricity on the lunatic fringe of opinion," but this attitude has changed.[2] Academics are still reluctant to enter the fray. The response of these academics is not to belittle themselves in answering challenges to what they consider to be a historical fact. To them the Holocaust is an established fact of history with only the need for more intensive study to round out the details of history. Somewhere in the neighborhood of between 5.1 and 6.2 million Jews died in the Holocaust. Enough survivors from the work camps have been able to testify about the general workings of the system. German concentration camp administrators have further confirmed the policy of extermination of the Jews. Eberhard Jäckel, the German authority on Hitler, stated the problems.

> Perhaps for no other problem of such magnitude in modern history is the documentation so poor. There are various reasons for this. The operation was ultrasecret. Consequently as little as possible was written down. Much was transacted orally, particularly on the highest level. Of the few relevant documents, many were destroyed before the war ended. And of those that survive, many contain code names and terms that further hamper the task of clearly establishing their contents. Moreover, many of the persons directly involved died before they could be interrogated. Of those who survived, most answered evasively. But even those who were ready to talk were often not questioned precisely enough, for their interrogators were not interested in the kinds of details that historians would want to clarify. Many were then executed, and their knowledge disappeared with them.[3]

The problem is that there are always internal inconsistencies about eyewitness testimony. People hear things and sometimes elaborate on them. I have personal experience with this in my tour of duty with the U.S. Army in South Vietnam in 1968. Rumor control was often inaccurate in the details, but in general it was the way an enlisted man found out how things functioned. Orders came from the top without explanation, but human nature wants to know more. I never found out the military or political situation, but I knew how to function in the personal realm. It is much the same way with survivors of the Holocaust. German authorities never gave them explanations, but the Jewish concentration camp survivors learned how to survive. It is pure sophism to maintain as proof that gas chambers did not exist because there were no gas chamber survivors. There were no gas chamber survivors because those entering a gas chamber died.

Holocaust denial is a new variation of antisemitism, and it should be viewed as such.

> "Denial, or "revisionism" as the deniers cynically call it, plays on classical anti-Semitic stereotypes: Jewish conspiracy and Jewish control of the media. It is unabashedly anti-Israel. It is well organized. And it exploits a true historical phenomenon: history is always reexamined by later generations, especially histories of wars, since the victors do indeed put their "spin" on events.[4]

Historians, journalists, and others have had difficulty communicating with Holocaust deniers as they speak from such completely different perspectives. But it is dangerous to ignore the deniers. Eric Zorn of the *Chicago Tribune* places the problem in context.

> Ignore the revisionists and their pronouncements float unchallenged. Answer them in general but refuse to debate head-to-head, as mainstream historians and Jewish groups have, and you risk seemingly afraid of confrontation. Respond to their allegations one by one and you appear to dignify arguments, perhaps making it seem

to the uninformed as though the existence of the Holocaust is a question serious people consider seriously, when, in fact, the revisionists have failed to make their case with virtually every active scholar in the field.[5]

Finally, the Holocaust is difficult to comprehend because it verges on unreality. The scale and numbers are almost mind-boggling. Even survivors have had trouble comprehending it all.

> The very extremity of Auschwitz and related Nazi murder renders it close to unreality. A distinguished European physician, who had struggled with Nazi brutality for years—first as an inmate of Auschwitz and other camps and then as an authority on medical consequences of that incarceration—said to me very quietly at the end of a long interview, "You know, I still can't really believe that it happened—that a group of people would round up all the Jews in Europe and send them to a special place to kill them." He was saying that the Auschwitz 'other world' is beyond belief. The wonder is that there is not an even greater tendency than actually exists to accept the directly false contention that Nazi mass murder did not take place.[6]

I also am aware of the limitations of any scholar attempting to probe the depths of the Holocaust. Robert Jay Lifton's interview with a survivor of the Holocaust puts it in perspective.

> The professor would like to understand what is not understandable. We ourselves who were there, and who have always asked ourselves the question and will ask it until the end of our lives, we will never understand it, because it cannot be understood.[7]

Holocaust deniers prefer to be call revisionists. Revisionist historians have made a proud record of revisionism by questioning historical orthodoxy. They have made major contributions into the understanding of past events. This does not mean, however, that most revisionist treatments are persuasive. A. J. P. Taylor's revisionist theory on the origins of World War II may be intriguing, but it has never convinced most historians to change their opinion about Hitler's aggressive war policy. What is most objectionable is mindless revisionism based solely on political motives. Hatred of Franklin Delano Roosevelt does not make him guilty of advanced knowledge of the Pearl Harbor attack. Holocaust denial is another form of antisemitism, so it is difficult to qualify it to be considered revisionism. Consequently, I use the term "Holocaust deniers" throughout the book and refer to revisionism only when that term is used by others, and on the occasional case where there is an attempt at real historical revisionism.

The reason for this book comes from my study of extremism around the world. Since my area of specialty is extremists and extremist groups, Holocaust denial became a part of that research. Holocaust deniers have never espoused violence, but they create an environment that encourages modern antisemitic and neo-Nazi movements to envisage the return of regimes that have promoted violence against ethnic groups. Consequently, my decision to tackle Holocaust denial is part of my study of extremism.

The book is organized into four parts. Part I is a general treatment of the growth of antisemitism, Hitler's role in the development of the Holocaust, and how the Nazis implemented the Final Solution. This background is necessary to establish the current state of knowledge about the Holocaust. It is also important to show that historians are still debating aspects of the history of the Holocaust but that the Holocaust is a fact of history. Part II has chapters on European Holocaust denial divided by country. Part III has three chapters on American and Canadian Holocaust deniers. Part IV has two chapters on Holocaust denial throughout the rest of the world.

Varieties of spelling need to be explained. Scholarly opinion differs on the use of the term Anti-Semitism and antisemitism. Antisemitism seems to be the preferred term among modern scholars, but in the course of the book both versions will appear, particularly in quotations. Both terms mean the same thing: hatred of the Jews.

I believe it is important to establish my personal relationship to the topic. The American history professor John Weiss contends that it is important that "the reader should know the ethnic and religious backgrounds of those who write about it (the Holocaust), if only to be alerted to possible intellectual manipulation in the service of a hidden agenda."[8] I subscribe to this view. Unlike many scholars in the field, I am not Jewish, nor is any member of my family. Although I was brought up in a variety of Protestant churches, I now am a member of the Unitarian-Universalist Church. I think that it is important for non-Jews to be active in Holocaust research because the Holocaust transcends ethnic, nationality, and/or religious lines. Both sides of my family arrived in the American colonies prior to 1690, and they lived in rural areas in Virginia, Kentucky, and Tennessee before ending up in Missouri. My contact with Jews during my youth was limited to a couple of acquaintances in Fort Worth, Texas. In college, I dated a Jewish woman at the University of Missouri–Columbia, but she dumped me when I went away to graduate school at the University of Iowa. My academic advisor on my Ph.D. in French history at the University of Iowa was more Marxist than Jewish. Dr. Alan Spitzer is one of the most brilliant men that I have ever had the good fortune to meet. That is the sum of my experience with Jews.

My association with Holocaust deniers is even more limited. After I became a librarian, my jobs at the University of Illinois at Urbana-Champaign and Texas A&M University exposed me to extremist literature. In 1996, a Jewish professor of English specializing in Holocaust literature came to Evans Library at Texas A&M University to complain about the library acquisition of Holocaust denial material from the Institute of Historical Review. The then dean of the library, Dr. Fred Heath, and I met with the professor and discussed the problem. Our solution was to place

Holocaust denial materials under a special Library of Congress category of controversial literature and then place these materials back into the collection.

What is important is my training as a historian. My B.A. and part of my M.A. were in German history with a specialty of the Nazi period. Dr. William Sheridan Allen was the German history historian at the University of Missouri–Columbia. The other part of my M.A. was under Dr. David Pinkney at the University of Missouri–Columbia. My Ph.D. in modern French history was under Dr. Alan Spitzer at the University of Iowa. Among my professors at the University of Iowa was Dr. Ulrich Trumpener, a German who had served in the Hitler Youth. My academic training exposed me to research on the Nazi extermination policy before it became known as the Holocaust. For the last two decades my research has been on American, European, Latin American, and Middle East extremism and terrorism leading to three books on the subjects.

Just for the record I also served in the U.S. Army in South Vietnam during most of 1968. Beginning as an enlisted infantryman in Co. C., 6th Battalion, 31st Infantry, I later became a historian with the 19th Military History Detachment in Dong Tam, South Vietnam. Besides the award of the Combat Infantryman's Badge for performance under fire, I received a Bronze Star and an Army Commendation Medal. Only after I left the U.S. Army did I finish my Ph.D.

I do want to give thanks to my many students in my history classes at Texas A&M University. Although most of my academic career has been as a librarian, I have been teaching a history course entitled Extremism and Terrorism in the Contemporary World for several years. This is a survey course on extremism and terrorism from 1945 to the present in five regions of the world: Europe, Latin America, the Middle East, South Asia, and the United States. They asked many stimulating questions, some of which I had to delve deeper into my research to answer them. This book is a product of the first lecture in this course.

PART I

The Holocaust

Background Leading to the Holocaust

INTRODUCTION

An understanding of the motivation and scope of the Holocaust is necessary before placing this event into Holocaust denial. The Holocaust actually happened, but where the differences occur are in the interpretations of aspects of it by historians. Various historians have attempted to estimate the number of European Jews exterminated by the Nazi regime during World War II, citing a variety of methods of execution from gas chambers, mass executions, summary executions, and maltreatment. At the Wannsee Conference, the German administrators of the Final Solution concluded that there were more than 11 million Jews in areas under their control. This figure may be disputed, but it is in the ballpark of between 9 million and 11 million Jews in Eastern Europe and the Soviet Union in 1939. Among these estimates of Jews killed during the Final Solution are Gerald Reitlinger's 4,578,800 (1953), Raul Hilberg's 5,109,822 (1961), Israel Gutman and Robert Rozett's 5,859,622 (1990), and Wolfgang Benz's 6,269,097 (1991).[1] The total number of victims has increased over the years as more research provides data that are more accurate. The opening of the Russian archives has also improved the accuracy of the calculations of the number of Jews killed. Even the Nazi government was shaky on its estimates. A Nazi physician, Dr. Wilhelm Hoettel, testified on November 26, 1945, at the first Nuremberg Trial on the number of victims with the following words:

In the various concentration camps approximately four million Jews had been killed, while about two million were killed in other ways, the majority of these having been killed by the action squads of the security police. Himmler had not been satisfied by the report, since in his opinion the number of Jews killed must have been greater than six million. Himmler had declared that he would send Eichmann, a man from his Office of Statistics so that he could make a new report, on the basis of Eichmann's sources, in which the exact number would be worked out.[2]

What has mystified scholars of the Holocaust since then is that "never before had there been an attempt to systematically destroy an entire people simply on the basis of their birth and apparently for no practical reason."[3] Complicating the logic is the effort to wipe out the Jews hindered the German war effort by diverting critical resources at crucial times. Critical troop and military supply trains were delayed to allow the transportation of Jews to the death camps in Poland. Members of the Schutzstaffel (SS) hindered war production by killing key slave workers in critical industries. Moreover, the SS took photographs as official policy. Heinrich Himmler told Dr. Felix Kersten the reason.

> Do you know why the S.S. guards were ordered to photograph all the tortures inflicted in the camps? It is so that a thousand years from now people will know how the real Germans fought the accursed Jewish race and the enemies of the German Führer. And future generations will admire these pictures of the century of Adolf Hitler. They will be grateful to him for all eternity.[4]

What is important to understand is the point made by Enzo Traverso.

> The Shoah (Holocaust) marked the victory of a quite new, alledgedly scientific ideology: biological racism. The extermination had no other social-economic, or political end in view than that of eliminating the "Jewish race" and of asserting the superiority of the "Aryan race". Auschwitz had shown once and for all that economic and industrial progress is not incompatible with human and social regression.[5]

To understand how this happened there needs to be some background to understand how it came to be that the Nazis considered their Jewish neighbors undesirable and candidates for extermination.

THE ARYAN MYTH AND ANTISEMITISM IN THE NINETEENTH CENTURY

Another factor in the growth of antisemitism in the nineteenth century was the construction of the so-called "Aryan Myth." European scholars defined race as a concept in the first half of the nineteenth century out of their study of the linguistic relationship between Sanskrit and European languages.[6] Popularizers of the concept of Aryanism in the 1850s were the French writer Ernest Renan and the German scholar Christian Lassen.[7] Scholars began to divide what they classified as the newly discovered races along the lines of "Aryans," "Semites," and "Hamites."[8] They also established a hierarchy with the Aryans being elevated as the superior race, Semites inferior to the Aryans, and Hamites as little more than half animals.[9] Exactly where those races not matching these three categories resided was left unsaid but with the understanding that they, too, were also inferior racially to the Aryans.

The belief in the superiority of the Aryan race soon became tied to the Social Darwinism that had also become popular in scientific and political circles in late nineteenth century Europe and the United States. Social Darwinism became closely identified with the phrase "survival of the fittest."[10]

> The basic premise of Social Darwinism was that natural selection had, over geological time, ensured that those organisms which were best adapted to the environment would survive and pass on their inherited advantages, while the weak and maladaptive would die and, in doing so, fail to reproduce.[11]

Social Darwinism also attracted "anti-democratic elements and their campaign against liberalism, parliamentarism, egalitarianism and internationalism because they believed these 'isms' were violations of natural law and symptoms of degeneracy due to racial mixture."[12] German Social Darwinists came to believe that natural selection of evolution was essential to human progress and the state's duty was to promote the biologically valuable elements in society. Whereas American and English Social Darwinists tended to be optimistic, the German Social Darwinists were more pessimistic because they feared degeneration of the race because "medical care for 'the weak' had begun to destroy the natural struggle for existence,'" and "because the poor and misfits of the world were beginning to multiply faster than the talented and fit."[13] Both in Europe and the United States social planners used Social Darwinism to justify the idea that "many humans were not only less worthy, many were actually destined to whither away as a rite of progress" and that "to preserve the weak and the needy was, in essence, an unnatural act."[14]

Soon after the acceptance of race as a determinant factor for humans, efforts were made in both Europe and the United States to make racial studies scientific by the construction of lists of common physical traits of the races. An attempt to make "Jewish hatred" more scientific was Wilhelm Marr's justification for the use of the new term that he named antisemitism.[15] Marr's attempt was followed by Eugen Dühring's 1881 book *The Jewish Question as a Question of Race, Custom and Culture. A World Political Response (Die Judenfrage als Racen-, Sitten- und Culturfrage. Mit einer Weltgeschichtlichen Antwort)* in which he scientifically classed races with Jews at the bottom of the heap.[16] Once the idea of racial superiority was accepted by elements among the academic and political elites, then it was easy for racist ideologues and propagandists to translate social Darwinism and biological superiority into popular forms and slogans.[17] Once these racial ideas had been popularized, then political movements followed. As MacMaster so aptly put it:

> It (antisemitism) was able to provide a total explanation for every conceivable ill in modern society through the "diabolical causality" of a great Jewish conspiracy that was, from behind the scenes intent on achieving global domination through the control and manipulation of entire national economies and political systems.[18]

POLITICAL ANTISEMITISM IN FRANCE AND RUSSIA

Antisemitism became a political force in the late nineteenth century with two countries—France and Russia—displaying the most active antisemitic movements. There had always been antisemitic beliefs current among the French aristocracy and upper classes since the French Revolution, but this antisemitism of the elite began to extend to the middle and lower classes in the late nineteenth century. Count Arthur de Gobineau, an unsuccessful mid-ranking French diplomat with aristocratic pretensions, published his book *The Inequality of Human Races (Essai sur l'inégalité des races humaines)* between 1853 and 1855, but again it appealed mostly to an elite audience. Gobineau's thesis that race was the determining factor in world history received only a lukewarm reception in France and elsewhere.[19] The first popular antisemitic work was Edouard Drumont's *Jewish France (La France juive)* in 1886.[20] Drumont was a journalist and his book was a combination of "Catholic, populist, quasi-socialist and frankly racist motifs in a pot-pourri of scandal, gossip and pointed denunciations of social and political corruption which appealed to a mass audience."[21] Following the appearance of his book, Drumont formed the Antisemitic League of France in 1889, and he then started the antisemitic newspaper *Free Speech (La Libre Parole)* in 1892. Helping spur the French antisemitic cause was the participation of several prominent Jewish financiers in the Panama Canal scandal in the early 1890s. Finally, and most significantly, the Dreyfus Affair polarized French public opinion making antisemitism almost patriotic. This affair allowed France's aristocracy and upper classes to find constituencies among the middle and lower classes. Dreyfus's various trials and convictions spurred antisemitic feeling in France that lasted long after the pardon for Dreyfus in 1899 and his acquittal in 1906. Antisemitism became a permanent part of the worldview of the French right wing that has lasted for more than a century. Besides becoming a part of the French political right-wing landscape, anti-Jewish stereotypes appeared in French literature that depicted Jews "as strangers, intruders, cosmopolitan financiers, as rapacious parasites, unscrupulous parvenus, or as base, immoral, cowardly, treacherous, and dishonest."[22] These types of stereotypes continued well into the twentieth century.

The Zionist movement was a by-product of the Dreyfus Affair. Jews in Western Europe had increasingly become assimilated into the societies of their individual countries, but the Dreyfus Affair and the antisemitic outcry caused Jewish leaders to reexamine assimilation as a policy. Theodor Herzl, a Jewish journalist from Vienna, came to the conclusion during the Dreyfus Affair that assimilation as a policy for Jews was a failure.[23] Earlier Herzl had read the antisemitic book of Eugen Dühring and had begun to think about the need for a homeland for the Jews.[24] Herzl decided that the only solution was to establish a Jewish state where Jews could live without fear of repression. Exactly where this state would be was a problem, but that was for future negotiations. His ideas first appeared in the booklet *The Jewish State* in 1896. His writings and speeches led to the creation of the Zionist movement with the intent to found an independent Jewish state.

Of even a more immediate impact on the formation of a future Jewish state was the Balfour Declaration of November 2, 1917. This declaration proclaimed the support of the British government for a national homeland for the Jews in Palestine. Arab intellectuals and political leaders protested the prospect of a Jewish homeland in Palestine with vague promises of the use of force. For the antisemitic movement the idea of a Jewish homeland "reinforced anti-Semitic notions of Jewish dual loyalties and fed the conspiracy myths of an insatiable Jewish lust for domination."[25]

Russian antisemitism was more of the scapegoat type. It has been described as "a combination of simple primitive hatred for the Jews 'as aliens' and of Christian orthodox religious prejudice which regarded the Jewish people as deicides."[26] The Russian Jewish population was the largest in the world with around 5 million Jews living in the Pale of Jewish Settlement by the late nineteenth century. Because Russia's Jewish population had been relegated to certain areas, it made the Jews readily identifiable and easy to target. Throughout the late nineteenth century there were Russian government sponsored pogroms against the Jews, beginning seriously after the assassination of Czar Alexander II in 1881.[27] Regardless of the inspiration, large-scale pogroms against the Jews occurred in Russia during 1881–1882 and 1903–1906. Only in the second pogrom did a secret organization, the Union of the Russian People, or the Black Hundreds, appear to orchestrate it by presenting political unrest as a Jewish plot and to get Jews massacred to show how real the plot was.[28] The purpose of these pogroms was to increase the involvement of Jews in Russian radical movements. There is evidence that high-ranking members of the government approved and participated in the pogroms.

To justify its antisemitism, the Russian secret service (Okhrana) produced *The Protocols of the Learned Elders of Zion*. This work combined religious hatred of Jews and fear of their economic influence with the idea of an international Jewish conspiracy.[29] Russian secret service agents under the leadership of Pyotr Ivanovich Rachkovsky plagiarized two works—Hermann Goedsche's *Biarritz* (1868) and Maurice Joly's *A Dialogue in Hell: Conversations between Machiavelli and Montesquieu about Power and Right* (1864)—to produce the final version of *The Protocols of the Learned Elders of Zion* sometime between 1897 and 1899.[30] Rachkovsky had made a career of concocting forgeries.[31] The first appearance of the *The Protocols of the Learned Elders of Zion* was in the antisemitic newspaper *The Banner* (*Znamya*) in St. Petersburg in 1903.[32] Shortly thereafter Sergei Alexandrovich Nilus, a former Russian businessman, landowner, and judge, assumed control of the document and began publishing it in various publications. Nilus was a confirmed antisemite, but he recognized that the work was a forgery and he so stated.

> You know my favorite quotation from St. Paul?—"The power of God works through human weakness." Let us admit that the *Protocols* are spurious. But can't God use them to unmask the iniquity that is being prepared? Didn't Balaam's ass prophesy? Can't God, for the sake of our faith, change dog's bones into miracle-working relics? So he can put the announcement of truth into a lying mouth![33]

This work was widely distributed and its international sales in the 1920s and 1930s have been described as "astronomical."[34]

> The *Protocols* gained in popularity everywhere in Europe precisely because roughly the same forces of reaction were engaged in roughly the same crusade to justify themselves in their fight against the republic, the soviet, the bourgeoisie and the proletariat, socialism and capitalism, liberalism and Bolshevism.[35]

The identification of the Bolshevik government with Jews intensified anti-semitism in Russia. Lenin believed antisemitism was an outgrowth of class conflict, and it would disappear in a classless society. Jews flocked to the new Soviet government because it offered them opportunities lacking before. Careers were open to talent, but Soviet legislation targeted Jewish institutions from synagogues to the Zionist movement. In the interwar years, the white Russian exiles constantly attacked the Bolshevik regime as part of a Jewish conspiracy. This identification of Bolshevikism with Jews was accepted by the emerging Nazi movement of Adolf Hitler, and it appears full-fledged in his book *Mein Kampf*.

POLITICAL ANTISEMITISM IN GERMANY AND AUSTRIA

German and Austrian antisemitism lacked both an event, such as the Dreyfus Affair, and government sponsorship, such as in the pogroms of Russia, but political antisemitic movements developed nevertheless. Neither

Germany nor Austria had a particularly large Jewish population, and a significant portion of that population had been assimilated into German and
Austrian society. This fact had little impact in the growth of political antisemitism first in Austria and then in Germany. Part of the problem was the
growing visibility of Jews in German society as they fled pogroms in Russia,
but more so was the emergence of the assimilated Jews in academic, business, and cultural life.[36] Besides achievements in these areas of life,
the assimilated Jews were allied with political and economic liberalism at a
time when the traditional German and Austrian elites were becoming more
conservative and nationalistic.[37] Enzo Traverso placed this dilemma into
context.

> Thanks to the emancipation the Jews could be accepted as citizens, but
> remained excluded from nationality. Assimilation had dissolved the Jewish
> "nation" and confessionalized its members within German society, but the for-
> mer nationality was never replaced by Germanity. Whether consciously or not,
> assimilated Jews inhabited a no-man's land.[38]

He added that "Jews could live like but very rarely with middle-class
Germans; they could become imbued with the values of the host society
but strong counterforces prevented them from merging with it; they could
recognize themselves there, but were not recognized."[39]
    The identification of German Jews with the emerging modern world made
them subject to attacks, being accused of being anti-German or of not being
participants in German culture. German leaders of the Völkisch movement
cast them as outsiders. The German historian Karl Dietrich Bracher put it
this way:

> Even in the preracist stereotype, the Jew was thought to be incapable of creativ-
> ity and spirituality. He was the embodiment of everything negative, which,
> under the heading "civilization," was counterposed to the higher value of true
> "culture." ... The growing conflict between the reality of an industrial urban
> world and the poetic glorification of rural virtues of the simple life, of irrational
> life forces was linked to the repellent figure of the urban, commercial Jews.[40]

A leader in the attack on Jewish assimilation was the German composer
Richard Wagner. He had become the archenemy of assimilated Jews in the
arts and society. In his 1850 book *Jewishness in Music* (*Das Judentum in der
Musik*), Wagner charged the Jews' entry into German life "as the infiltration
of a wholly alien and antagonistic group whose success symbolizes the spiritual and creative crisis of German and European culture."[41] In Wagner's eyes
artistic creativity was an outgrowth of race, and he considered Jews as enemies
of the German spirit because they lacked German volkish soul.[42] Wagner
actively promoted the racial theories of the French author Gobineau, and they
became close friends after meeting with him in Rome in 1876.[43] Among

Wagner's other anti-Jewish views was his advocacy of the de-Jewification of Christianity, the deportation of German Jews to Palestine, and open opposition to mixed marriages and the assimilation of Jews into German society. Wagner's antisemitic views had an impact on the development of the German antisemitic movement and ultimately on Adolf Hitler. Wagner's political writings were Hitler's favorite reading material during his early years in Vienna.[44] Later, Hitler became a close friend of the Wagner family.

Perhaps the most influential German antisemite in the late nineteenth century was Paul de Lagarde. Lagarde was an eminent Orientalist and Bible scholar, but he was also a German nationalist. His scheme to revitalize Germany was for it to have a Germanic Christianity that would have Germany free of Jews. He warned about a worldwide Jewish conspiracy against Germans and Germany.[45] Among his other charges was that Jews controlled German capitalism, making it a necessity for the state to seize credit and banking institutions to free them from the Jews.[46] His hatred for Jews led him to advocate extermination. From his writings comes the following statement:

> With trichinae and bacilli one does not negotiation, nor are trichinae and bacilli subjected to education; they are exterminated as quickly and as thoroughly as possible.[47]

Lagarde was also an avid imperialist advocating the colonization of the Eastern lands as an integral part of Germany's divinely assigned mission.[48] After Lagarde's death in 1891, his reputation grew in German right-wing circles both before and after World War II. It is not surprising that Lagarde was one of the Nazi regime's favorite thinkers, and in 1943 the Nazi government republished all of his writings.

Another important figure in the growth of German antisemitism was the author Gustav Freytag. He wrote a novel *Debt and Credit (Soll und Haben)* in 1855 glorifying German bourgeois virtues.[49] Freytag made the villain of the book a rapacious Jew by the name of Veitel Itzig. Itzig's personal characteristics contained elements that included "repellent, ugliness, slimy ambition, blood-sucking and megalomania" that combined with a lack of scruples.[50] This book was a best seller, becoming the most successful German novel of the nineteenth century with a readership in the hundred of thousands.[51] German critics praised the book for its realism.[52] Novels of this type contrasting honest Germans and dishonest Jews became a widespread practice among popular German novelists in the late nineteenth and early twentieth centuries.[53]

Certain German and Austrian politicians capitalized on the growing resentment against Jews. Foremost among these was the Lutheran court minister Adolf Stoecker, who started a German antisemitic party, the Christian Social Workers Party, in 1878 in an attempt to win over the German working class to the conservative Right. Stoecker, the son of a sergeant in the Prussian army, used his status as a military chaplain during the Franco-Prussian War to be elected royal chaplain to the court of Kaiser Wilhelm I. At first his political party had trouble resonating with the German populace until Stoecker turned to antisemitism. He was able to transform attacks on Jews into political force in German politics. His antisemitic campaign was so successful among the lower middle class Germans that it attracted support from the German Chancellor Otto von Bismarck.[54]

A number of German and Austrian political figures used antisemitism as a political tool. One such influential antisemitic politician was the German populist leader Otto Böckel.[55] He founded the Anti-Semitic People's Party in 1889, and by 1914 this party had around 350,000 members.[56] In Austria, Karl Lueger, the mayor of Vienna, also found antisemitism a political tool for political success.[57] Part of the impetus for these radical antisemitic parties was the growing identification of Jews in the promotion of liberal ideas, radicalism, and Social Democracy in Germany and Austria.[58] Jews were attracted to socialism and communism that promised emancipation because as a disadvantaged minority they desired progress toward full equality.[59] This identification with liberal causes led German conservatives to identity with antisemitism. Such feelings even extended into academia where the conservative nationalist historian Heinrich von Treitschke wrote an anti-semitic article in the 1880 *Prussian Yearbook* (*Preussische Jahrbücher*) with the title *A Word about Our Jewish Folk* (*Ein Wort über unser Judentum*) in which he coined the phrase "The Jews are our Misfortune" (Die Juden sind unser Unglück).[60]

> He (Treitschke) attributed the Jewish influence to all the negative consequences of Germany's industrialization and economic modernization, and not least the negative effects on the nation's intellectual and spiritual life of a "materialism" which was at best uncreative, at worst destructive, and which he characterized almost as a Jewish onslaught on the German mind.[61]

This article later appeared in pamphlet form, and it gave prestige to the anti-semitic movement.

By the end of the nineteenth century, antisemitism had become the credo of German conservativism. It combined with other beliefs as outlined by Christopher Browning.

> To be a self-proclaimed anti-Semite in Germany was also to be authoritarisn, nationalist, imperialist, protectionist, corporative, and culturally traditional.[62]

The leading figure in tying antisemitism with Social Darwinism was Houston Steward Chamberlain. This expatriate Englishman became more German than the Germans, and he worshiped Richard Wagner. In 1908, he married Eva Wagner, the daughter of Richard and Cosima Wagner.

Earlier in 1899, he had written the book *The Foundations of the Nineteenth Century (Die Grundlagen des neunzehnten Jahrhunderts)*. In this best-selling work, Chamberlain elevated the Germanic peoples to a level of supe-riority over all other peoples. He also charged that the greatest threat to the Germanic peoples was the Jews. His antisemitism also included Christianity because it was a Jewish religion. Chamberlain's influence was such that German church leaders ignored even this attack on Christianity.[63] The popularity of Chamberlain's racial antisemitism helped spread it through the German educated middle class and made it part of the intellectual climate at the turn of the century. Hitler and Chamberlain met at least twice before Chamberlain died in 1927, and Chamberlain regarded Hitler as Germany's future savior. Hitler's association with Chamberlain gave him status, and it encouraged Hitler's sense of mission.[64]

Despite the active participation of Jews in the German army in World War I, political antisemitism grew after the defeats of Germany and Austria. The "stab in the back" myth accusing the Jews of undermining the war effort gained currency in right-wing circles in the interwar period. However, more important was the general economic and social dislocation of German soci-ety and the need for scapegoats. Antisemitism filled that role. Helping spur the antisemitic feeling was the influx of more than 75,000 Jews fleeing from Russia and Eastern Europe.[65] The appearance of a sensational best-selling, antisemitic, and quasi-pornographic novel in 1918 by Artur Dinter, *Sin Against the Blood,* further inflamed feelings against Jews.[66] Adding to Ger-man antisemitism was the appearance in Germany of *The Protocols of the Learned Elders of Zion* in January 1920. It became an immediate best seller, but at first its survival depended on a subsidy from German aristocratic circles.[67] After several printings in 1920, the sale of *Protocols* reached 120,000 in that year alone.[68] The German novelist Jakob Wassermann con-cluded in 1921 that "Judeo-phobia was the German national hatred."[69] He added that "Germans were emotionally resistant to accepting Jews as their equals and given to scapegoating them for every crisis, setback, or defeat."[70]

INFLUENCE OF *THE PROTOCOLS OF THE LEARNED ELDERS OF ZION*

Interpreters both pro and con of *The Protocols of the Learned Elders of Zion* faced a dilemma in the early 1920s. The key question was whether or not this work was authentic, or a clever forgery. Jewish critics had the unenviable prospect of producing a negative proof.[71] Most others accepted *Protocols* on face value, but questions kept popping up as to its source, and versions of its origin kept changing. Speculation continued until Philip Graves, a *Times* (London) correspondent in Istanbul, demonstrated in

August 1921 in three long articles that *The Protocols of the Learned Elders of Zion* was a forgery. Despite the success of these articles and other articles demonstrating further proof, the myth of the Jewish conspiracy in *The Protocols of the Learned Elders of Zion* lived on and spread around the world.

The popularity of *The Protocols of the Learned Elders of Zion* soon extended to the United States. Among its early fans was Henry Ford, the popular American businessman.[72] He was already receptive to antisemitism from his background and limited education. Ford used his wealth to publicize *Protocols* to American readers in his authorized four-volume treatise *The International Jew: The World's Foremost Problem* published first in his newspaper, the *Dearborn Independent,* beginning in early 1920 and later in book form in October 1920.[73] The importance of this work is best described by Leo P. Ribuffo as its "perverse accomplishment was to combine Anglo-Saxon chauvinism, anti-Semitic beliefs common during the Progressive era, and the comprehensive conspiracy theory sketched in the *Protocols.*"[74]

In book form *The International Jew* was an international best seller. It appeared in most European countries and in South America. By 1933, it had undergone 29 printings in Germany alone.[75] Even the verdict in a Bern trial in Switzerland on May 14, 1935, that *The Protocols of the Learned Elders of Zion* was "a forgery and a work of plagiarism" did not deter its popularity.[76] Frank P. Mintz places the document in perspective by stating that "the Protocols were a fraudulent concoction, but they satisfied the needs of ideologists who expounded a plot theory of history that pointed to collusion between high finance and the forces of rebellion and subversion."[77] Another feature of *Protocols* was its generality because it "left room for elaborations to fit local circumstances."[78] Almost as much as politics the economic situation during the Depression stimulated antisemitism and the acceptance of *Protocols*. In Germany *Protocols* was especially popular particularly among the antisemitic right wing and Adolf Hitler.

EUGENICS MOVEMENT

By the beginning of the twentieth century Social Darwinism and racist ideology combined to produce the eugenics movement. Francis Galton, a famous nineteenth century British scientist and Darwin's cousin, coined the term eugenics after the Greek work "eugenes, namely good stock, hereditarily endowed with noble qualities."[79]

> This (eugenics), and the allied words, eugeneia, etc, are equally applicable to men, brutes, and plants. We greatly want a brief word to express the science of improving stock, which is by no means confined to questions of judicious mating, but which, especially in the case of man, takes cognizance of all

influences that tend to the suitable races of strains of blood a better chance of prevailing speedily over the less suitable than they otherwise would have had.[80]

This theory led to the idea that, if some races are superior, why not take measures to improve the human racial stock. After all, selective breeding had made strides in improving physical characteristics of animals. Ethical reasons might impede selective breeding of humans, but efforts could be made to restrict breeding rights of those considered defective.

> Together with his friend Karl Pearson, he (Galton) called for a national effort to breed a superior race of people by encouraging the fittest to procreate and by discouraging by sterilization if necessary, the procreation of feeble, incompetent, and sickly types.[81]

Galton always believed in the positive side of eugenics and this form of eugenics concentrated on "suggesting, facilitating, predicting and even legally mandating conducive marriages."[82]

The eugenics movement soon developed the negative side of eugenics. Both extreme Social Darwinists and eugenicists were concerned that advances in health care were preventing the operation of natural selection by not eliminating the unfit.[83] The fear that the white race was in danger of becoming overwhelmed by lesser races and the unfit led to the convening of the July 1912 International Eugenic Congress at the University of London.[84] Dr. Woods Hutchinson, Clinical Professor of Medicine at the New York Polyclinic, proposed the implementation of what he termed "negative eugenics," or "the prevention of ill-bornness."[85] This concern produced a flurry of alarmist books in the early 1920s, including Leon Whitney's *The Case for Sterilization* and Madison Grant's *The Passing of the Great Race*.

Negative eugenics had a series of consequences. One of the indicators of physical and mental degeneracy was masturbation and its impact on both the abuser and the abuser's descendants.[86] Other indicators were "nervous prostration, sick headaches, neurasthenia, hysteria, melancholia, St. Vitus' Dance, epilepsy, syphilis, alcoholism, pauperism, criminality, prostitution, and insanity."[87] Birth control and forced sterilization programs were the preferred method of controlling the defective. Those defectives that could not be prevented needed to be isolated and prevented from reproducing. A 1927 U.S. Supreme Court decision sanctioned compulsory sterilization laws by an 8 to 1 vote.[88] One scholar of the eugenics movement, Nancy Ordover, characterized it as follows:

> American eugenicists, armed with charts, photographs, and even human skulls, were there to provide the visual and mathematical support that rendered racism scientifically valid and politically viable.[89]

Eugenicists were active in lobbying for the passage of restrictive immigration laws in both 1917 and 1924, because they wanted to preserve white breeding stocks from inferiors. While Eastern European Jews were not singled out, they were included in the so-called inferior racial stock flocking to America.

Although eugenics was most popular in the United States, it soon had its adherents in Europe. It became especially popular in Germany, especially negative eugenics. In Germany eugenics became closely allied to a nationalist form of Social Darwinism. An early adherent of negative eugenics in Germany was the physician Gustav Boeters whose early travels in the United States in the late 1890s showed him how the eugenic sterilization system worked.[90]

Ernst Häckel, a German zoologist, was the major proponent of the theory of National Social Darwinism in the late nineteenth and early twentieth centuries. His book, *The History of Creation* (*Natürliche Schöpfungsgeschichte*), first appeared in 1868, but it was republished in several editions well into the twentieth century. In this work, Häckel advanced Sparta as a model because it had slain the weak, sickly, or physically deficient children and thereby improved the race.[91] He also translated Darwinism into a struggle between national states. Since Häckel believed that the Aryan race was the highest form of human evolution, he accepted in principle the extermination of lower forms of humanity that he termed the biologically weak.[92]

A popular proponent of negative eugenics was Jörg Lanz von Liebenfels. He had been a Cistercian monk at the Heiligenkreuž monastery, but he left the order in 1899.[93] Before World War I he had founded a movement called Ariosophy. This movement asserted the divinity of Aryan man and celebrated him.[94] Lanz von Liebenfels proposed the selective breeding of Aryans to produce a race of Aryan supermen.[95] To preserve the Aryan race Lanz von Liebenfels believed it imperative "to clear society of degeneracy."[96] He proposed that inferior races were to be exterminated, deported or enslaved to preserve the Aryan race.[97] His attitude toward the Jews was also harsh believing that sterilization, or castration, would solve the Jewish question.[98] His ideas appeared in his journal *Ostara: Newsletter of the Blond Champions of Man's Rights* (*Ostara: Briefbücherei der Blonden und Mannesrechtler*). The journal was named after the Germanic goddess of spring. The goal of this journal founded by Lanz in 1905 was to improve the Nordic race.

> The *Ostara* is the first and only periodical devoted to investigating the heroic racial characteristics and the law of man in such a way, by actually applying of ethnology, we may through systematic eugenics...preserve the heroic and noble race from destruction by socialist and feminist revolutionaries.[99]

This journal received wide distribution throughout Germany and Austria. It is known that Hitler was also a frequent reader of Jörg Lanz von Lieben-fels's journal *Ostara.*[100] The young Hitler also visited Lanz several times at his Werfenstein castle.[101] At least one of these visits was to obtain back issues of *Ostara,* which Lanz provided free of charge.[102] The German histo-rian Karl Dietrich Bracher tied the ideas of Lanz von Liebenfels with Hitler in the following analysis:

> Lanz's works disseminated the crass exaggerations of the Social Darwinist theory of survival, the superman and superrace theory, the dogma of race con-flict, and the breeding and extermination theories of the future SS state. The scheme was simple: a blond, heroic race of "Areheroes" was engaged in battle with inferior mixed races whose annihilation was deemed a historico-political necessity; "race defilement" was not to be tolerated, and the master race was to multiply with the help of "race hygiene," polygamy, and breeding stations; sterilization, debilitating forced labor, and systematic liquidation were to offer a final solution.[103]

Alfred Ploetz was the leader of the German racial hygiene movement. He was a physician and had traveled in the United States in the mid-1880s. His concern was to improve the biology of the human species, and his big fear was that the high rate of reproduction of the unfit would harm German society. In 1895, Ploetz published the multivolume book *The Foundations of Racial Hygiene* (*Grundriss der Rassenhygiene*) that introduced the German public to his ideas on racial and social health. Consequently, Ploetz founded in 1904 the *Journal of Racial and Social Biology* (*Archiv für Rassen- und Gesellschaftsbiologie*). He followed this up by being one of the co-founders of the German Society for Racial Hygiene (Gesellschaft für Rassenhygiene) in 1905. Both the journal and the society had the goal of sponsoring research to improve the German race. As the society expanded in Germany, its lead-ers opted to appeal for an international scope by changing its name to the International Society for Racial Hygiene (Internationale Gesellschaft für Rassenhygiene) in 1907. After World War I, the German Society for Racial Hygiene grew rapidly so that by 1930 it had 1,200 members in 16 branches.[104] Although Ploetz was not an antisemite, he did consider the white race as superior to all other races.[105] Once the Nazi regime was in place, Ploetz and his racial ideas were incorporated into Nazi ideology. Ploetz received numerous honors, and he joined the Nazi Party in 1937. Nazi leaders considered him so highly that they nominated him for the Nobel Peace Prize for his work in racial hygiene.[106]

Perhaps the most popular of the racial eugenics proponents was Hans F. K. Günther. His books *The Racial Characteristics of the German People* (*Rassenkunde des deutschen Volkes*) (1922) and *The Racial Characteristics of the Jewish People* (*Rassenkunde des jüdischen Volkes*) (1930) had both been best sellers. Although both books were popularized works, they combined the racist ideology of the late nineteenth and early twentieth centuries with the appeal that the conclusions had a scientific basis. He had taught at various German universities—Berlin and Freiburg—before his appointment to the chair of racial science at the University of Jena in 1930. His appointment was highly controversial with most of the opposition coming from the faculty.[107] Hitler had displayed interest in Günther's career so he placed pressure on university officials to approve his appointment.[108] After joining the Nazi Party in 1932, Günther became the regime's official race theoretician. He utilized this entree into the Nazi Party to gain admittance into the Nazi ruling elite. His antisemitism was based on his idealization of Nordic racial purity and his fears of the perils of Jewish racial contamination.[109] Günther defined race as "a group of people which is distinguished from all other groups of people by a combination of endowed physical features and spiritual characteristics and which repeatedly reproduces only its own kind."[110] Consequently, in Günther's scheme of things, there is no Jewish race.

> From the standpoint of the definitions above, the Jews cannot be viewed as a race. Rather, they constitute a nation of mixed races. If popular usage is reluctant to give up the term "race" in the case of Jews, the reason lies in the Jewish people physical and spiritual hereditary endowments of non-European peoples are predominant and these are quite noticeable when seen among the differently composed racial mixtures of the European population and especially that of northwestern Europe.[111]

This distinction that Jews do not constitute a race was never accepted by the Nazi leaders, but they still considered Günther as one of theirs. Besides his close contacts with Nazi leaders, Günther's writings became popular with the German public.

CONCLUSION

Considerable space has been given to outlining the growth of antisemitism, Social Darwinism, negative eugenics, and racial biology because this was the intellectual environment that existed in Germany when the National Socialists took power in 1933. It was a lethal mixture of pseudoscience, prejudice, insecurity, and hatred. The ideology of National Socialism incorporated all of these factors. Benno Müller-Hill, a German professor of genetics at the University of Cologne, summarized it best in 1984.

> The ideology of the National Socialists can be put very simply. They claimed that there is a biological basis for the diversity of Mankind. What makes a Jew a Jew, a Gypsy a Gypsy, an asocial individual asocial, and the mentally abnormal mentally abnormal is in their blood, that is to say in their genes. All these individuals, and perhaps others, are inferior. There can be no question of

equal rights for inferior and superior individuals, so, as it is possible that inferior individuals breed more quickly than the superior, the inferior must be isolated, sterilized, rejected, and removed, a euphemism for killed. If we do not do this, we make ourselves responsible for the ruin of our culture. The murder of others is the secret mystic message. It is an ideology of destruction, of mystery, and of worship of the blood.[112]

2

Hitler's Antisemitism and Its Impact on the Antisemitic Policies in Germany during the Third Reich

ORIGINS OF HITLER'S ANTISEMITISM

The key figure in the development of the idea and the implementation of the Holocaust is Adolf Hitler. Questions about his abilities, beliefs, and motivations remain an open book that has been studied by scholars for over 60 years. Hitler spent much of his youth in Linz, Austria, but he lived most of his formative years in Vienna, Austria. The one trait that his friend August Kubizek remarked upon was that Hitler had a rigid personality and once he seized upon an idea, he almost never changed it.[1] It was in Vienna where Hitler absorbed the cultural and intellectual atmosphere of the early years of the twentieth century. His biographer, Joachim C. Fest, claimed that Hitler "merely picked up the kind of ideas current in the newspapers he found in cheap cafes, in the books and pamphlets on the newsstands, in operas, and in the speechifying of cynical politicians."[2]

One of those ideas that Hitler was receptive to was antisemitism. There is evidence from Hitler's childhood friend, August Kubizek, that Hitler held antisemitic views picked up in Linz before leaving for Vienna.[3] Already in his youth Hitler had become a devoted fan of Richard Wagner and read works on Wagner's life and ideas.[4] If Hitler already had antisemitic views before Vienna, his stay in Vienna then reinforced them. There was a lively antisemitic movement in Vienna led by Karl Lueger, who was Vienna's mayor from 1897 to 1910. Another active antisemitic movement in Austria was that of the Pan-German Georg von Schönerer. These antisemitic movements were responding to the influx of Jews from Eastern Europe beginning in the early 1870s. Resentment had increased among Austria's Germans because Jews had flocked into academic, banking, business, and journalism positions that they believed belonged to them.[5] Hitler had Lueger and Schönerer to provide a lesson on how to use antisemitism "as a method of mobilizing the masses against a single, highly visible and vulnerable enemy."[6] There is evidence that Hitler had Jewish acquaintances, some of whom he liked, but at the same time he blamed the Jews for his personal misfortunes.[7] But it is instructive that the only organization that Hitler joined during his lengthy stay in Vienna was the League of Anti-Semites (Antisemitenbund). He joined that league sometime before he left for Munich, Germany, in 1913. Hitler's brand of antisemitism has been described as "emotional," because "he seized eagerly on every pseudo-scientific 'doctrine' of modern antisemitism which provided him with a legitimate justification for his feelings of hatred."[8]

Hitler carried his brand of antisemitism to his new home in Munich, Germany, shortly before the outbreak of World War I. Hitler's enthusiasm for Germany led to his joining a Bavarian unit in the German army in the early days of the war. His wartime experiences had little impact on his antisemitic views, but Hitler was wounded twice and temporarily blinded by a British gas attack. Although he made it to the military rank only of lance corporal, Hitler received the Iron Cross—First and Second Class. He was in a hospital suffering from the aftereffects of a gassing attack when the war ended. It was the chaotic events of 1918–1919 that reinforced his antisemitism as he blamed the Jews for Germany's defeat and postwar troubles. Hitler's first articulation of his antisemitism was in a written statement on September 16, 1919, to Captain Karl Mayr, his superior officer in the Enlightenment Department of Bavarian Group Command IV, in 1919.

> Anti-Semitism on purely emotional grounds will find its ultimate expression in the form of pograms. The anti-Semitism of reason, however, must lead to the planned judicial opposition to and elimination of the privileges of the Jews … Its ultimate goal, however, must absolutely be the removal of Jews altogether. Only a government of national power and never a government of national impotence will be capable of both.[9]

In Hitler's view, Jews must be removed from positions of authority, but this can be accomplished only by a strong German government willing to accept responsibility. He reinforced this antisemitic outlook in his first major speech for the National Socialist German Workers' Party (Nationalsozialistische Deutsche Arbeiterpartei, or NSDAP) on August 13, 1920, by reference to "scientific anti-Semitism."[10] By this time Hitler's worldview incorporated two laws of nature that he never relinquished throughout the rest of his life.

One was the law of racial purity, racial endogamy, whose violation through interbreeding leads to decadence and eventual extinction. The other was the law of selection, or the elimination of the weak in combat or through a deliberate eugenic policy.[11]

Sometime in the early 1920s Hitler was exposed to the book by Wilhelm Bölsche, *From the Bacillus to the Apeman* (*Vom Bazillus zum Affenmenschen*), that had first appeared in 1899. Bölsche's thesis was that there was "a struggle for dominance between the zoological species of 'Man' and the 'lowest form of organic life.'"[12] Werner Maser attributed Hitler's anti-Jewish references to parasites as coming from his reading of Bölsche's book.

> To Bölsche may be attributed, not only Hitler's ideas about Jews and his manner of expressing them, but also his monstrous anti-Jewish policy which culminated in his destroying them like vermin with the pesticide Cyklon B.[13]

This contention by Maser may be hard to prove, but Hitler's speeches against Jews throughout the 1920s and later are filled with biological references implying that Jewish blood had been and continued to pollute German blood.[14] Because in Hitler's view the Jews represented evil, and in his eyes "if radical evil has been exposed to be at the root of things, squatting like a Jewish 'maggot in a rotting corpse,' as Hitler put it, then radical measures are needed to remove the cancerous abscess" upon the German politic.[15] A further indication of the depth of his antisemitism was his 1922 statement to Josef Hell, a German journalist and former officer in the German army in World War I, in response to Hell's question what Hitler would do to the Jews once he came to power.

> Once I really am in power, my first and foremost task will be the annihilation of the Jews. As soon as I have the power to do so, I will have gallows built in rows—at the Marienplatz in Munich, for example—as many as traffic allows. Then the Jews will be hanged indiscriminately, and they will remain hanging until they stink; they will hang there as long as the principles of hygiene permit. As soon as they have been untied, the next batch will be strung up, and so on down the line, until the last Jew in Munich has been exterminated. Other cities will follow suit, precisely in this fashion, until all Germany has been completely cleansed of Jews.[16]

Among Hitler's early heroes was Henry Ford. Ford was famous as an American industrialist, but Hitler was more impressed with Ford's antisemitism. Hitler openly expressed his gratitude to Ford for his publication of *The International Jew: The World's Foremost Problem*.[17] He later gave Ford a Nazi award in a public ceremony in Germany for his achievements.

Despite the proven evidence that it was a forgery, Hitler believed in the authenticity of *The Protocols of the Learned Elders of Zion* and its alleged plan for Jewish world domination. He had contact in the early 1920s with *The Protocols of the Learned Elders of Zion* and believed in its outline of an international Jewish conspiracy.[18] Hitler disclosed to Hermann Rauschning, then a Nazi and president of the Danzig Senate, in 1934 that he had read *The Protocols of the Learned Elders of Zion,* and he did not care "whether the story was historically true" or not because "its intrinsic truth was all the more convincing to him."[19] In Hitler's eyes "the Jews personified the devil, the vampire, the parasite upon the nations."[20] Tie these ideas with Aryan supremacy, Social Darwinism, and negative eugenics and there is little wonder that Hitler's antisemitism was so prevalent.

There is also strong evidence that Hitler was aware of American negative eugenics and racist thought. While in a Munich prison for leading the attempted Munich Beer Hall Putsch against the Weimar Republic, Hitler spent time studying eugenic textbooks.[21] He sent letters to the president of the American Eugenics Society (AES), Leon F. Whitney, and the author of *The Passing of the Great Race,* Madison Grant, thanking them for their work.[22] In his letter to Grant, Hitler described Grant's book as his bible.[23] In his book Grant had written in favor of sterilization and euthanasia.

> Mistaken regard for what are believed to be divine laws and a sentimental belief in the sanctity of human life tend to prevent both the elimination of defective infants and the sterilization of such adults as are themselves of no value to the community. The laws of nature require the obliteration of the unfit and human life is valuable only when it is of use to the community or race.[24]

Hitler also concentrated his energies in prison reading German eugenics literature. He read among others the second edition of the German book *Foundation of Human Heredity and Race Hygiene (Grundriss der menschlichen Erblichkeitslehre und Rassenhygiene)* authored by three of Germany's leading eugencists—Erwin Baur, Fritz Lenz, and Eugen Fischer.[25] This book depended heavily upon American eugenic principles and examples, including its racist and negative eugenics orientation. In this and in other writings by German eugenicists, Jews were considered "eugenically undesirable."[26]

In *Mein Kampf,* Hitler expressed his antisemitism and his adherence to racial negative eugenics openly, and there is no evidence that he ever changed his views. Hitler dictated this work to Rudolf Hess while in prison in a stream of consciousness fashion. Few of the ideas in *Mein Kampf* are original, but it shows the state of Hitler's mind at the end of a distressing episode—the failure of the Munich Beer Hall Putsch. The problem is that the ideas showcased in the book remained with Hitler for the rest of his days. This is the thesis of his biographer Joachim C. Fest.

> Inadequate and clumsy *Mein Kampf* may have been. But it set forth, although in fragmentary and unorganized form, all the elements of National Socialist ideology. Here Hitler spelled out his aims, although contemporaries failed to

recognize them... Nationalism, anti-Bolshevism, and anti-Semitism linked by a Darwinistic theory of struggle, formed the pillars of his world view and shaped his utterances from the very first to the very last.[27]

Hitler's unwavering belief in antisemitism and Aryan superiority were constants until his death in 1945. Because of Hitler's belief in the iron law of racial biology, there was no place for redemption for the Jews. Before the advent of Nazism, Jews could be redeemed by renouncing Judaism and converting to Christianity, but this was looking at Judaism as a religion, not a race. Robert S. Wistrich gave the best explanation for the Nazi position.

> For Hitler and the Nazis, in contrast to the traditional teachings of Christianity, no spiritual redemption of the Jews was possible—their racial characteristics were eternal and unchanging. Jewish influence meant the triumph of antinature over nature, of disease over health, of intellect over instinct. This mystical, biological and naturalistic racism was later to be used to sanction final measures against all Jews, whatever their social background, beliefs or political convictions.[28]

Assimilated or not, Jewishness was eternal; there was no escape for them from Hitler and the Nazis' biological racism. In fact, Christianity had been tarnished in Hitler's eyes because it had evolved from Judaism. This view was later articulated by the Nazi philosopher Alfred Rosenberg in his 1934 book *The Myth of the Twentieth Century* when he characterized "Christianity as an effeminate, race-destroying dogma invented by Jews which was sapping the pristine Germanic values of honour, freedom, independence and virility."[29]

Hitler was a shrewd charismatic politician, but he was by no means an intellectual. He did, however, have some intellectual talents.[30] But once Hitler seized upon an idea, he never deviated from that idea. Central to this mind-set was the idea that the Jews had stabbed the German army in the back in November 1918 and that this was never going to happen again.[31] He identified the Russian Revolution and the Bolshevik regime in Russia as a product of the machinations of the Jews.[32] Lucy S. Dawidowicz placed Hitler's identification of the Bolshevik regime and the Jews in these words.

> Hitler's association of the Jews with Russian Bolshevism—an idea fostered and insisted on by Rosenberg—was, in its delusional conclusion, more original than his other ideas about Jews and race that derived from the ample sources of European anti-Semitism and racial doctrine. That the Jews were the revolutionaries par excellence, the masterminds of the Bolshevik Revolution—that was nothing new. The reality of Leon Trotsky and the forgery of the *Protocols* documented that charge to the satisfaction of most anti-Semites. But Hitler went beyond this and "penetrated" beneath the surface of the conspiracy: "In Russian Bolshevism we must see the attempt undertaken by the Jews in the twentieth century to achieve world domination." All Russia, he believed had somehow become captive of the Jews.[33]

Hitler believed that Germany was "the object of a world-wind conspiracy, pressed on all sides by Bolshevists, Freemasons, capitalists, Jesuits, all hand in glove with each other and directed in their nefarious projects by the 'bloodthirsty and avaricious Jewish tyrant.' "[34] The Jews also stood in the way of Hitler's goal of making the German people the "chosen people."[35] Hitler told Rauschning in 1934 that "there cannot be two Chosen People," because "we (the Germans) are God's People."[36] He also believed that the Aryan race was in danger of extinction. If a letter to Madison Grant, the American author of *The Passing of the Great Race,* is to be believed, Hitler had read his book and its thesis of the growing threat to the white race by writing that "the book was his bible."[37]

Several times Hitler went so far as to classify Jews as less than human. In a speech in May 1923 in the Krone Circus in Munich, Germany, Hitler stated,

> The Jews are undoubtedly a race but not human. They cannot be human in the sense of being an image of God, the Eternal. The Jews are the image of the devil. Jewry means the racial tuberculosis of the nations.[38]

Later in his conversations with Rauschning in 1934 Hitler further outlined his hatred of the Jews in these words:

> Two worlds face one another—the men of God and the men of Satan! The Jew is the anti-man, the creature of another god. He must have come from another root of the human race. I set the Aryan and the Jew over against each other; and if I call one of them a human being I must call the other something else. The two are as widely separated as man and beast. Not that I would call the Jew a beast. He is much further from the beasts than we Aryans. He is a creature outside nature and alien to nature.[39]

Rauschning concluded that Hitler truly believed that the Jews were a danger to Germany.

> Hitler, however, believes in the natural wickedness of the Jews. For the Jew is evil incarnate. He has made capital out of it; but behind this is a manifestly genuine personal feeling of primitive hatred and vengefulness.[40]

Hitler confessed that "anti-Semitism was beyond question the most important weapon in his propagandist arsenal, and almost everywhere it was of deadly efficiency."[41]

Yet, despite his avowed hatred of the Jews, Hitler grudgingly admired some of their characteristics. Hitler found "their racial exclusiveness and purity seemed . . . no less admirable than their sense of being a chosen people, their implacability and intelligence."[42] He came to regard them akin to "negative supermen," and this was what made the Jews so dangerous to

Germany and his nationalistic agenda.[43] They endangered the special mission entrusted to him to lead Germany to its world prominence.

Jews had also become a symbol of Germany's modernization, and Hitler led an antimodern counterrevolution. Besides racial inferiority, the Jews were corrupting German society. Hermann Graml placed the Nazi movement in context of this counterrevolution.

> The Nazis transformed uneasiness with industrial society to radical hostility producing anti-urban blueprints for a healthy and harmonious social order, in which the whole nation would be transformed into a people of warriors and landowners. The flight from the reality of the twentieth century into a mythical medieval pat was the most consistent element of their propaganda. Their romantic agrarian view of society, which postulated a sort of refeudalization process had little to do with the industrial nations. They were also basically indifferent to the great conflict between capitalism and socialism.[44]

This vision of German society had no role in it for Jews. In the view of Hitler and the Nazi movement, Jews were parasites on the German body politic. In Robert S. Wistrich's view the reason that Hitler ordered the Holocaust was because his antisemitism was an "apocalyptic vision of the future of civilization and of the 'Aryan' destiny that necessitated the complete eradication of a rival Jewish messianism."[45]

> It was the Judeo-Christian ethic that had alienated humanity from the wholeness of the natural order in pursuit of the "lie" of a transcendent God. Judeo-Christianity in its secularized form had, he (Hitler) believed, given birth to contemporary teachings of pacifism, equality before God and the law, human brotherhood, and compassion for the weak, which the Nazis were determined to uproot. They no longer made any secret of their contempt for Christian ideals of charity, meekness, and humility, inimical as they were to the Germanic warrior ethos.[46]

Hitler's racist views also extended to the idea of providing space for Germany to expand. In his eyes Germany's greatness depended on its ability to reproduce itself more prodigiously than inferior races.[47] This philosophy meant that Germany had to find living space (Lebensraum) in Eastern Europe at the expense of the lesser races living there. Lack of space for a revitalized Germany would mean that Germany's ability to be a world power would be endangered. Hitler wanted a breed of "hard, callous, obedient and determined youth that would delight in war and conquest" to subjugate and rule over the population there.[48]

Hitler and leaders of the Nazis made secret plan to seize political power in Germany and carry out Hitler's dream of ridding Germany of Jews. In November 1931, the Frankfurt police released captured secret Nazi documents, the so-called "Bornheimer Papers," on how the Nazis planned on using a national emergency to establish a Nazi dictatorship.[49] These documents had been found at a farm, the Bornheimer Hof, in Hesse. In the documents the Nazis outlined procedures to be used to gain control of the state, and on how Jews were to be eliminated by "mass starvation and expulsion."[50] Hitler disavowed knowledge of these plans, and the author, Werner Best, was able to escape legal charges by a friendly interpretation of the law by the Reich Supreme Court (Reichsgericht).

IMPLEMENTATION OF HITLER'S ANTISEMITISM CAMPAIGN

Once in power Hitler was an active participant in the implementation of the Nazis' anti-Jewish program. His vehement rhetoric about the Jews and their impact on German society meant that he had to satisfy his antisemitic constituency. The slogan of the Nazi Party as proclaimed by Julius Streicher and widely distributed was "Without a solution of the Jewish question no Salvation for the German People" (Ohne Lösung der Judenfrage keine Erlösung des deutschen Volkes).[51] Yet in the early days of his regime, Hitler was also concerned about the impact of anti-Jewish steps to Germany's foreign image and its exports. But the Thousand Year Reich would be possible only if the German politic could be purified by ridding it of what he considered Jewish parasites. Moreover, the confiscation of Jewish property could fund German rearmament, a goal close to Hitler's heart.

The first tentative step toward the Jews was a one-day boycott of Jewish businesses called for on April 1, 1933. Justification for this boycott was that "a clique of Jewish men of letters, professors, and profiteers inciting the world against us, while millions of our own Volksgenossen are unemployed and degenerating."[52] Perhaps a better explanation was that Hitler was responding to criticism from militants in the Nazi Party eager for action against the Jews. The boycott was somewhat effective, but Nazi leaders noted that it had received little open support from the German public.[53] Foreign reaction, however, was uniformly negative.

Hitler did use the Law for the Restoration of the Professional Civil Service on April 7, 1933, to rid Jews from the German bureaucracy, the courts, and the universities. The only exception was for Jewish veterans of World War I, those serving in the German army since August 1, 1914, or those whose fathers or sons were killed in action.[54] This exception toned down the implications of this legislation, and it was intended to reassure President Paul von Hindenburg and the conservative coalition partners that the Nazi government could be reasonable. After Hindenburg's death, the veterans' exception was no longer a factor as Jews were universally banned from government service. With this legislation more than 2,000 non-Aryan scientists and professors, including a number of world-famous scholars, lost positions.[55] This ridding of Jews from civil positions was popular in certain circles even among non-Nazis. Part of this was because Jews had been excluded from the German civil service and the military until 1914, so Jews had been active in both the civil service and the military for only a generation.[56] German medical doctors also approved of the exclusion of Jews "as a means of rectifying what was presented as Jewish hegemony in the field of medicine."[57] Two weeks later a companion piece of legislation, the Law Against the Overcrowding of German Schools and Institutions of Higher Learning, banned most Jewish students from schools and universities. Although this measure was an antisemitic attack on Jews, it was also directed against massive overcrowding in German universities. These pieces of legislation were the first part of nearly 400 laws and decrees directed against Jews during the Third Reich.

The Nazi government had been surprised by the number of Jewish military veterans, so it made Jewish military service a target. Legislation in the form of the Military Service Law of May 21, 1935, restricted military call-ups to Aryans and ended promotions for Jewish officers and noncommissioned officers. Another law of July 25, 1935, banned the drafting of non-Aryans for active service. These military service laws and other legislation based on racial distinction produced confusion among German civil servants because of an absence of definitions of what constituted a race.

The next significant legislation was the Nuremberg Race Law of September 15, 1935, that disenfranchised German Jews from German life. Hitler asked his subordinates to prepare legislation regulating German-Jewish "blood" relationships that led to this law.[58] This legislation banned marriages between Germans and Jews, and it outlawed extramarital intercourse between German and Jews.[59] Implementation of this law was left to the German bureaucracy to designate who was considered a Jew, and it took several weeks for them to do so. An administrative ruling defined a Jew to be anyone with at least three Jewish grandparents, or anyone with two Jewish grandparents who was either married to a Jew or still adhered to the Jewish religion. Germans of mixed blood (Mischlinge) were further defined as first-degree Mischlinge and second-degree Mischlinge according to the number of Jewish grandparents.[60] A complex chart was drawn up to illustrate Jews from Mischlinge and the subcategories. Although German Jews at first thought that these laws were the Nazis final anti-Jewish effort, the Nuremberg Laws proved to be a serious deterioration in the political and social situation of most Jews and only the beginning of even more restrictive legislation.[61]

Almost a part of the Nuremberg Laws but distinctly separate was the Reich Citizenship Law of September 15, 1935, that established criteria for German citizenship excluding Jews from citizenship. Hitler had also requested this legislation. Wilhelm Stuckart, Secretary of State in the Ministry of Interior, and Hans Globke, a ranking member of the Minister of Interior, interpreted the Reich Citizenship Law in a 1936 commentary *Civil Rights and the Natural Inequality of Man:*

Only he who is a racial comrade can be a citizen. Only one who is of German blood, no matter what his religious faith can be a racial comrade. Therefore no Jew can be a racial comrade. Anyone who is not a citizen can live in Germany only as a guest and is subject to special legislation for foreigners. The right to determine the leadership and legislation of the state may be granted only to citizens. We demand, therefore, that every public office, regardless of its importance, and whether in the Reich, in the Land, or in the municipality be occupied only by citizens.[62]

Reich citizenship was thus bestowed upon the racially pure Germans and those Germans who were politically subservient. Stuckart and Globke borrowed heavily from the works of Hans F. K. Günther and his ideas on race.[63]

These anti-Jewish laws encouraged Jewish emigration, but such emigration came at a high cost. Around 170,000 Jews immigrated to other countries between 1933 and 1938.[64] Most left after the conclusion of the Haavara Agreement between Zionists and the Reich Ministry of Economics in August 28, 1933. Jews had to surrender business interests and almost all of their property to participate in this program. Expropriations of Jewish property allowed leading Nazis to enrich themselves by buying ex-Jewish property at low rates.[65] These restrictions limited the ability of most German Jews to leave Germany. Because the German authorities considered the Haavara Agreement as a boost to the German economy and exports and at the same time a discouragement to a worldwide Jewish boycott of German goods, this agreement received the approval of Hitler.[66]

Hitler was aware of the anti-Jewish violence against the Jews in the November 1938 Kristallnacht (Crystal Night). The Nazi government used the assassination of Ernst vom Rath, the German embassy counselor in Paris, by Herschel Grünspan, a young German Jew distracted over the treatment of his parents by the Germany government, on November 7, 1938. Grünspan's parents and two surviving sisters had been deported to the Polish border by the Gestapo in late October and left there in limbo.[67] After the news of vom Rath's death on November 9, Hitler let it be known to Joseph Goebbels, the Nazi propaganda chief, that anti-Jewish demonstrations were not to be organized by the party, but neither were they to be discouraged if they broke out spontaneously.[68] Hitler approved of the anti-Jewish riots because he wanted to appropriate Jewish businesses.[69] Hitler ordered Heinrich Himmler to keep the Schutzstaffel (SS) completely out of the riots.[70] Himmler followed instructions, but he gave the order to arrest between 20,000 and 30,000 Jews to be sent to concentration camps.[71] Goebbels briefed Hitler during the course of the riots, but Hitler "preferred to distance himself, preserving an attitude of aloof detachment" for public consumption.[72] On November 12, 1938, Joseph Goebbels, Hermann Göring, and Reinhard Heydrich each received a letter written on Hitler's orders to solve the Jewish question "one way or the other."[73] This letter was a virtual blank check for the implementation of more severe measures against the Jews. Although the 1938 pogram had been a success in Hitler and his inner circle's eyes, secret reports indicated that German public opinion had not approved of the level of violence, and international public opinion had been appalled. These leaders decided that future operations against the Jews needed to be conducted "in secrecy and in a more 'orderly manner.'"[74] In the meantime, Hermann Göring, whom Hitler had put in charge of Jewish policy in Germany, was busy expropriating Jewish property. This expropriation impoverished German Jews, but it left the German state much richer. Hitler was not willing to go much further on the Jewish question because the Jews were Germany's best protection from foreign powers intervening in German affairs during the delicate days of rearmament.[75] The Nazi actions during the Kristallnacht were the beginning of a new state of Nazi prosecution of the Jews that had progressed from depriving Jews of their civil and political rights; the expropriation of their property; social isolation; and, finally, the possibility of the annihilation of the Jews as both possible and desirable.[76]

NAZI RACIAL HYGIENE

Negative eugenics had already become a part of popular culture in Germany and Austria by the 1920s, and it had adopted the academic name of Racial Hygiene. Hitler was an early convert to both positive and negative eugenics and National Social Darwinism.[77] Soon after the establishment of the Nazi state both positive and negative eugenics became part of state policy. Glorification of the monogamist family was stated as the highest goal. Hermann Paull stated this policy in his 1934 book *German Race Hygiene* (*Deutsche Rassenhygiene*).

> Thus the family is the most important instrument of eugenics. It will become even more clear later that the eugenic concept of "family" in its deepest essence is synonymous with the Christian concept of a "religious-moral family"; which rests upon the twin pillars of "premarital chastity,"and "conjugal fidelity."[78]

The Nazi goal was for a "healthy, clean, hardworking, athletic Aryan man married to a woman of the same race who produced many children for him," and anything that deviated from this model was to be eliminated.[79] Abortions were prohibited by law except for the so-called racial emergencies—for mixed marriages or for possible hereditary defects.[80]

Among German eugenicists there was an added dimension and a further qualifier of racism that became "racial negative eugenics." In contrast to the idealized view of improving the race by positive eugenics was the theory of eliminating the unfit of racial negative eugenics. The Nazi authorities called forth to articulate and implement so-called "scientific racism were physical anthropologists, geneticists, and racial theorists but especially medical doctors."[81] An early target of racial eugenics was the Gypsies since the Nazis considered them antisocial misfits.[82]

GERMANY'S STERILIZATION PROGRAM

The first effort in the negative eugenics program was forced sterilization of the unfit. An early exponent of sterilization in Germany was Fritz Lenz. He was a physician-geneticist with a doctorate from the University of Freiburg in 1912. Lenz had been appointed the editor of the influential racial hygiene journal *Journal of Racial and Social Biology* since 1917, giving him considerable clout in influencing German medical and public opinion. It was about this time that he began openly advocating sterilization to preserve the Nordic race.[83] Lenz's massive two-volume book with co-authors Erwin Baur and Eugen Fischer, *Outline of Human Genetics and Racial Hygiene* (*Grundriss der menschlichen Erblichkeitslehre und Rassenhygiene*) first appeared in 1921, and it and subsequent editions were the most important work on racial hygiene. This work was important in the scientific world, but it also became popular enough that Adolf Hitler read it while he was in Landsberg Prison after the failed Munich Beer Hall Putsch.[84] His drive in the 1920s was for a widespread compulsory sterilization to be implemented by the German government.[85] Lenz's growing influence led him to be appointed a professor at the University of Munich in 1923 as its first chair of racial hygiene. Lenz and other advocates of forced sterilization of the unfit looked to research from the United States to justify this policy—the William L. Dugdale's study of the Juke family and Henry Herbert Goddard's Kallikaks study.[86] Later in 1937, Lenz joined the Nazi Party where he continued to agitate for a sterilization program.

NAZI STERILIZATION PROGRAM

The Nazi government instituted such a sterilization program beginning with a sterilization law in July 1933. Up until this date, sterilization of patients was illegal for any reason whatsoever. But the Law for the Prevention of Genetically Diseased Offspring (Besetz zur Verhütung erbkranken Nachwsuchese) of July 14, 1933, set up a sterilization program. This law was intended to be "eugenic rather than punitive—that is, persons ordered sterilized were not to be considered perpetrators of a crime for which they were receiving punishment."[87] Among the diseases included in this program were mental deficiency, schizophrenia, epilepsy, Huntington's chorea, hereditary blindness, hereditary deafness, grave bodily malformation, and hereditary alcoholism that involved 410,000 people.[88] Special Hereditary Health Courts—a government medical officer, a physician, and a district judge—administered the program. It took a majority vote to approve sterilization, so for all intents and purposes the physician always cast the deciding vote.[89] There was an appeals court of prominent physicians to handle any appeals. By the end of 1934, 181 genetic health courts and appellate genetic health courts had been formed to carry out the law.[90] Regardless of the merits of the cases, more than 90 percent of the cases taken to the special courts in 1934 ended up with the sterilization of the person in question.[91] Despite the fact that these courts operated in secrecy, Robert Jay Lifton concluded after examining the research that somewhere between 200,000 and 350,000 Germans were sterilized during the Nazi regime.[92] Those Germans deemed eligible for sterilization who refused to submit were generally sent to concentration camps.[93] Hitler's interest in sterilization led him to acquire the book by Leon F. Whitney of the American Eugenics Society, *The Case for Sterilization*, in 1934.[94] While the original sterilization law was not directed against German Jews, Hitler did intervene in secret and have the offspring of black French occupation troops and native Germans be sterilized.[95] The sterilization program was not without its dangers as between 1934 and 1936, 367 women and 70 men died as a result of the sterilization procedure.[96] There had been some opposition to the sterilization policy by the hierarchy of the Catholic Church, but ultimately Catholic institutions cooperated.[97]

NAZI EUTHANASIA PROGRAM

A new dimension in the negative eugenics debate appeared in the topic of euthanasia. Germany had a history of interest in mercy killings. As early as 1895 Adolf Jost had written a book *The Right to Death (Das Recht auf den Tod)* in which he maintained that the state had the right to kill the incurably ill to keep "the social organism alive and healthy."[98] Two German university professors, Karl Binding and Alfred Hoche, went the next step in the 1920 book *Permission to Destroy Life Unworthy of Life (Die Freigabe der Vernichtung lebensunwerten Lebens)*. Binding, a jurist at the University of Leipzig, and Hoche, a professor of psychiatry at the University of Freiburg, included in the unworthy the likes of "not only the incurably ill but large segments of the mentally ill, the feebleminded, and retarded and deformed children."[99] They advocated a three-person panel—a general physician, a psychiatrist, and a lawyer—to decide euthanasia cases.[100] Hoche argued that besides such deaths being medically ethical, they removed an economic burden from society.[101]

Adding to the debate in Germany was a book by a French doctor advocating euthanasia. Dr. Alexis Carrel was a French-educated medical doctor who had won the Nobel Prize for medicine in 1912. Carrel had immigrated to the United States in 1904, and he held a prominent position at the Rockefeller Institute for Medical Research in New York City. Carrel's book *Man the Unknown* was published in 1935 in both France and the United States. In his book Carrel proposed mental defectives and criminals "should be humanely and economically deposed of in small euthanistic institutions supplied with proper gases."[102] His book was a nonfiction best seller, but it received negative critical acclaim.[103] A German translation of Carrel's book appeared in Germany in 1937.

Hitler was already a convert to euthanasia before he seized power in 1933.

> If Germany would have a million children annually and eliminate seven to eight hundred thousand of the weakest, the result in the end might be an increase in her energies.[104]

Hitler decided that in wartime the "Reich must be rid of useless consumers of food, who were also a burden on hospitals and their staff" because if German soldiers died on the battlefield "then those of inferior racial heritage must not survive."[105] He made similar remarks to his personal doctor, Dr. Karl Brandt, as early as 1933 that one day he would try to eliminate the mentally ill.[106] Then, in comments to Dr. Gerhard Wagner at the Nuremberg Party rally of 1935, Hitler reiterated his intent to eliminate the "incurably ill."[107] Hitler advanced this idea because he had a "deep emotional hatred for the handicapped" that rivaled his hatred for Jews.[108]

After discussion by Hitler and Nazi medical authorities, the decision was made to proceed in the event of war in 1939. An advisory committee, Committee for the Scientific Treatment of Severe, Genetically Determined Illness (Rechtsausschuss zur wissenschaftlichen Erfassung von erb- und anlage bedingter schwerer Leiden), was established to set up a euthanasia program in May 1939.[109] This committee called on the German medical establishment to report the birth of all defective babies and defective children up to the age of three.[110] Questionnaires were sent to doctors and nurses all over Germany to find candidates for the program. Again a three-doctor panel modeled on the Binding-Hoche recommendation was set up to decide individual cases.

The first phase of the euthanasia program was to be rid of defective children up to age three. Children selected by panels of the Committee for the Scientific Treatment of Severe, Genetically Determined Illness were ordered into institutions where they were put to death. Methods of killing ranged from injections of morphine and cyanide gas to starvation and exposure.[111] It has been estimated that as many as 5,000 children died in the first phase of this program.[112]

The next phase was adult euthanasia. Authorization for the adult phase of euthanasia came down from Hitler via an oral order in July 1939. Procedures used in the children euthanasia program were adopted for the adult program. A total of six medical facilities were built or remodeled for this program—Gas Chambers and crematoria—at Grafeneck, Bernburg, Sonnenstein, Hadamar, Brandenburg, and the castle at Hartheim near

Linzwere selected as the sites. Carbon monoxide was the preferred method of death, but later Zyklon B replaced it.

Nazi officials became nervous about the legal ramifications of the euthanasia program. Reich Minister Hans Heinrich Lammers warned Dr. Leonardo Conti, the head of the euthanasia program, on the need for a law to protect physicians and hospital staff against prosecution. Conti's insistence on a law led to Hitler authorizing the killing of the incurably ill in a letter with two typewritten lines on Hitler's private stationary that was marked "Secret."[113] This October 1939 letter, backdated to September 1, 1939, entrusted Reich Leader Philipp Bouhler and Dr. Karl Brandt with the responsibility of heading a euthanasia program with the following words:

> Reich Leader Bouhler and Dr. Brandt are charged with the responsibility for expanding the authority of physicians, to be designated by name, to the end that patients considered incurable in the best available human judgment, after critical evaluation of their state of health, may be granted a merciful death.[114]

Hitler's allowing of the killing of the sick and disabled was hidden under the code name Aktion T4.[115]

> T4 doctors decided who would live and who would die; economic status was one of the common criteria—individuals unable to work or able to perform only "routine" work could be put to death.[116]

Hitler received briefings on the progress of the euthanasia program, and he approved the use of carbon monoxide as the killing method.[117] Gassing of handicapped patients began in January 1940 at the psychiatric hospital in Brandenburg near Berlin.[118] A witness, August Becker, a chemist employed by the Reich Criminal Police Office, witnessed the first gassing by carbon monoxide of 18–20 people and their subsequent cremation.[119] Another observer, Maximilian Friedrich Lindner, described the process:

> Did I ever watch a gassing? Dear God, unfortunately yes. And it was all due to my curiosity.... Dwnstairs on the left was a short pathway, and there I looked through the window ... In the chamber there were patients, naked people, some semi-collapsed, others with their mouths terribly wide open, their chests heaving. I saw that, I have never seen anything more gruesome. I turned away, went up the steps, upstairs was a toilet. I vomited everything I had eaten. This pursued me days on end.[120]

German authorities kept meticulous records so that the total killed in this program was 70,273.[121]

Despite attempts at secrecy, news of the deaths at insane asylums had become public knowledge by mid-1940. The distinctive gray buses with curtained windows and the constantly smoking chimneys of the "euthanasia" crematoria were noticed by the German population.[122] Since every death certificate had to be falsified, mistakes happened. Parents complained about the deaths of their children when discrepancies appeared in the official death notices. One example was that patients were reported to have died of appendicitis even though their appendixes had been removed years earlier. Since large numbers were being euthanized, the paperwork had become sloppy, leading to errors like this. People had also begun to notice the disappearance of the elderly. Legal charges against doctors at the euthanasia facilities were contemplated until it was learned that Hitler had authorized the program.[123] Since Hitler had signed the order for the euthanasia program, he came under criticism from church leaders, especially from the Catholic Church, and in the German press, making him even more reluctant from then on to issue written orders.[124] Cardinal Adolf Bertram lodged an official protest against the policy of euthanasia with the head of the Reich Chancellery, Lammers, on August 11, 1940.[125] Then Bishop Count von Galen preached against euthanasia of mental patients in Münster on August 3, 1941, in a sermon in the St. Lambert Church in Münster, increasing public pressure against the program and irritating Hitler and the Nazi hierarchy.[126] Hitler's verbal order ended the official liquidation of the incurably ill and handicapped on August 24, 1941. The program was quietly shifted to the individual hospitals, and the euthanasia program continued throughout the remainder of the Nazi regime on a reduced scale.[127] The major difference was that the patients were no longer killed by gassing but by starvation and drugs.[128] This change of policy by Hitler showed that internal opposition could at times curtail what Hitler wanted to do, but it could not force a course of action upon him.[129]

Jews had not been targeted in the original euthanasia program, but they ultimately became a part of it. In April 1940, orders came down from the Reich medical authorities to include Jewish patients. The first gassing of Jewish patients began in June 1940.[130] In the fall of 1940 there was a shift in Jewish policy when Jewish patients were ordered to be sent to Poland in freight cars to various destinations. Most of these patients ended up in German death camps in Poland.

The German medical community had little difficulty with either the sterilization or euthanasia program because of its commitment to negative eugenics, or what it called racial biology. An ability to adjust to the notion that biological inferiors could be sacrificed to the cause of the German race had the obvious potential to be extended to others. Jews were an obvious case. Proctor maintained that "by the late 1930s German medical science had constructed an elaborate world view equating mental infirmity, moral depravity, criminality, and racial impurity" on the Jews.[131] If Jews were racial inferiors and a danger to the German Aryan race, then they were a cancer that needed to be eradicated. This was the next step, and Hitler and the Nazi regime were willing to take it.

The outbreak of the war provided the final justification for the euthanasia program. It also provided the secrecy necessary for the program to proceed without public controversy.

> The "euthanasia" of Germany's "less fit elements" was defended as a measure that would balance the counterselective effects of the war and free up beds for the German war effort; the cloak of war also provided the secrecy necessary for the massive programs of human destruction.[132]

Among the first victims of the outbreak of the war in 1939 was the killing of institutionalized mental patients in Poland and the incorporated territories of Danzig–West Prussia. German special forces began killing Polish patients by shooting them in nearby forests.[133] Soon these killings of mental patients by this method extended to German patients in Pomerania and East Prussia.[134] The method of execution changed in December 1939 with the construction of a gas chamber that used carbon monoxide.[135] It was also at this time that Herbert Lange developed a mobile gas van that also used carbon monoxide to kill patients.[136] A German scholar has estimated the number of Polish-German patients killed using these methods at around 7,700.[137]

ROLE OF HITLER IN THE DEVELOPMENT OF THE HOLOCAUST

Debate still rages among historians on the exact role of Hitler in the final implementation of the Holocaust. Two historical schools have emerged: intentionalists and functionalists.[138] Those in the intentionalist school maintain that Hitler had a clear plan from the beginning of the Third Reich and probably even before for the destruction of European Jews and this plan was carried out by representatives of his regime. To the intentionalists the Final Solution was "a methodical plan conceived, prepared, and finally implemented at Hitler's command."[139] This interpretation is based on the totalitarian nature of the Nazi state, which had a monolithic and hierarchical structure with Hitler at the center.[140] One of the most outspoken adherents of this school of thought was Lucy S. Dawidowicz.

Functionalist adherents claim that Hitler's antisemitism played a role but the final plan for the destruction of European Jews was improvised. In a regime where decisions were made by conflicting authorities, Hitler was not able to determine policy but was driven into decisions by his subordinates. Functionaries claim that it was the implicit approval of Nazi leaders from Hitler downward that caused the implementation of the Final Solution, but that Hitler was not the sole instigator. In this theory Hitler was a weak dictator instead of a strong one. German historians Martin Broszat and Hans Mommsen have been the foremost proponents of the functionist thesis.

While this debate between the intentionalists and the functionalists has never been resolved, there is a growing consensus that both views have elements of truth to them. Bernhard Jäckel, an author of several works on Hitler, tried to give a balanced assessment of the two schools.

> It is my opinion that the controversy is based on a profound misunderstanding on both sides. It would have been a misunderstanding if the so-called intentionalists had assumed that we can explain Hitler's acts by demonstrating that he had intentions. They would have neglected the fact that men can act only under certain conditions of support or compliance and that these conditions have to be demonstrated as well. On the other hand, it is a misunderstanding if the functionalists assume that in a polycractic regime the decisions are necessarily made in a polychromic way, that is, by conflicting authorities. There is abundant evidence that all the major decisions in the Third Reich were made by Hitler, and there is equally abundant evidence that the regime was largely anarchic and can thus be described as polycracy. The misunderstanding is to suppose that the two observations are contradictory and that only one of them can be true.[141]

The issue remains whether or not Hitler ordered the Final Solution. Jäckel's position is that Hitler gave not one but several orders that concerned the Final Solution over an extended period of several months and that covered a wide variety of methods and victims.[142] What is certain is that Hitler never put an order down on paper for the extermination of the Jews.[143] This habit of not having written orders was a characteristic of Hitler. It was characteristic for Hitler to issue vague instructions without written orders. Richard Breitman noted this habit:

> Many charges against him cannot be proved, partly because Hitler was not the sort of person to put things on paper, but also partly because he did not always involve himself in the details. Others brought plans to him for his approval which he gave orally.[144]

Hitler was even reluctant to write anything down whatsoever. He stated that "it is an old maxim of life: whatever one can discuss orally one should not write down."[145] This lack of paperwork was in keeping with the Nazi goal of secrecy because "it is undeniable that those planning the 'final solution' tried, as far as possible, to implement it under conditions of utmost secrecy."[146] Moreover, Hitler was by nature a secretive person. He did not like even his intimates to know exactly what he was thinking, and this trait led to his refusal to put his ideas down on paper. This obsession about avoiding paperwork, however, did not extend to his frequent oral outburst heard by his inner circle and to an occasional outsider. Since Hitler had no desire to be tied to any hierarchical system, he passed his orders to the largest possible number of major and minor authorities in a calculated policy of preventing the emergence of a possible rival to power.[147] In the Nazi dictatorship Hitler's will had the force of law.[148] It was also a fact that any promise made in Hitler's Reich was valid only so long as Hitler did not utter an opposing opinion.[149] Albert Speer noted this because of his frequent interaction with Hitler. Both historical schools allow that Hitler meant his threat in a January 30, 1939, Reichstag speech.

> Today I want to be a prophet once more: If international finance Jewry inside and outside of Europe should succeed once more in plunging nations into another world war, the consequence will not be the Bolshevization of the earth and thereby the victory of Jewry, but the annihilation of the Jewish race in Europe.[150]

This speech has withstood a variety of interpretations by historians on whether or not this was a promise to annihilate the Jewish race in Europe in the event of a world war or merely a boast or grandstanding. Philippe Burrin's interpretation provides the best insight.

> It would seem that what Hitler was announcing was that, even if it was not within his power to decide on a victorious end to a possible world war, it would be within it at least to make sure that the Jews would not emerge as victors.[151]

Joseph Goebbels in his diary on December 14, 1942, gave even more credence to Hitler's intent with these remarks.

> The Jewish race has prepared this war; it is the spiritual originator of the whole misfortune that has overtaken humanity. Jewry must pay for its crime just as our Fuehrer prophesied in his speech in the Reichstag; namely, by the wiping out of the Jewish race in Europe and possibly in the entire world.[152]

Otherwise Hitler's rhetoric has been described as "murderously ambiguous," but it is beyond doubt that he was committed to "getting the Jews out of Germany" regardless of the costs.[153] Field-Marshal Wilhelm Keitel, military associate of Hitler, further confirmed Hitler's way of operating with oral orders in a handwritten memorandum dated October 7, 1945, by stating that Hitler employed "semantic conventions (eine Sprachregelung) to communicate with his closest political aids."[154] Gerald Fleming, an American historian, concludes that "by observing the agreed upon 'semantic convention'—that is, code language—in his spoken responses to Himmler's briefings on the Jewish question (responses that Himmler at least once committed to paper) and by deliberately misleading those in his midst, including some of his intimate collaborators, Hitler threw a mantle of secrecy over his undeniably personal responsibility for the Final Solution of the Jewish question."[155] Besides, Hitler had no need to issue orders as Christopher Browning explained.

Within the polycratic regime, Hitler did not have to devise a blueprint, time-table, or grand design for solving the "Jewish question." He merely had to proclaim its continuing existence and reward those who vied in bringing forth various solutions. Given the dynamics of the Nazi political system, a ratchetlike decision-making process permitted bursts of radicalization periodically alternating with tactical pauses but never moderation or retreat. In the end "final solutions" would become the only ones worthy of submission to Hitler.[156]

The nature of the Nazi administrative structure was a key in how Hitler ruled. Karl Dietrich Bracher outlined how extensive Hitler's authority extended during the Third Reich.

> The omnipotent power of the Führer, abrogating all state and legal norms and sanctioning all deeds, was the basic law of the Third Reich. The creation of the system of terror and extermination and the functioning of the police and SS apparatichiks operating that system rested on this overturning of all legal and moral norms by a totalitarian leader principle which did not tolerate adherence to laws, penal code, or constitution but reserved to itself complete freedom of action and decision-making. Political power was merely the executive of the Leader's will.[157]

Hitler ruled as the sole authority in Nazi German, but he pursued a policy of divide and rule making certain that no one could challenge him for control of the state. This policy led Joachim C. Fest to describe the Third Reich as "authoritarian anarchy."[158]

> Cabinet ministers, commissioners, special emissaries, officials of party affiliates, administrators, governors, many of them with assignments kept deliberately vague, formed an inextricable knot of interlocking authorities with Hitler alone, with virtually a Hapsburgian grasp of puppet mastery, could supervise, balance, and dominate.[159]

Because of this structure, access to Hitler and his attention determined policy in the Nazi state. Hitler encouraged rivalries among his associates partly because such friction was useful for consuming energy, which might be a threat to him. Despite this tactic, Hitler came to depend on a number of close associates; Martin Bormann, Joseph Goebbels, and Heinrich Himmler are the most obvious examples.

This desire to get rid of the Jews led Hitler to authorize the 1938–1939 negotiations for a massive evacuation of Jews from Germany and Austria in return for international aid in their relocation and certain financial benefits for Germany. Hitler already had ideas about moving populations, and he said so in a 1934 conversation with Hermann Rauschning, the Nazi president of the Danzig Senate who later defected to the Allies; Hitler is quoted saying,

We are obliged to depopulate, ..., as part of our mission of preserving the German population. We shall have to develop a technique of depopulation. If you ask me what I mean by depopulation, I mean the removal of entire racial units. And that is what I intend to carry out—that, roughly, is my task. Nature is cruel, therefore, we, too, may be cruel. If I can send the flower of the German nation into the hell of war without the smallest pity for the spilling of precious German blood, then surely I have the right to remove millions of an inferior race that breeds like vermin! And by "remove" I don't necessarily mean destroy; I shall simply take systematic measures to dam their great natural fertility.[160]

Hitler and German officials knew that the transfer of Jews to other countries was a forlorn hope because of the failure of the 32 nations of the world at the July 6–July 13, 1938, Evian Conference to accept more Jews. None of the major powers was willing to accept German or Austrian Jews. This conference proved once and for all time that there was no place to transfer German and Austrian Jews let alone any others that the Germans might acquire by conquest. This type of deal was no longer feasible once fighting broke out, because until the war Hitler had been able to use the Jews as hostages to control the behavior of the Western powers.[161] Hitler never signed off on the deal because of the lack of outside funding and a final place to relocate the Jews.[162]

After the defeat of France in May 1940, the idea of using the island of Madagascar as a place to send Jews surfaced. Justification for this plan was that Germany could use 4 million Jews as a counterweight to control the political behavior of the Jews in the United States.[163] But this idea was more the figment of a plan than a serious proposal.[164] Joachim C. Fest considered that this scheme negated Hitler's intentions.

For if Jewry really was, as he (Hitler) had repeatedly stated and written, the infectious agent of the great world disease, then to his apocalyptic mind there could be no thought of providing a homeland for that agent, no course but to destroy its biological substance.[165]

Thus, Hitler's attitude toward the Jewish problem became more extreme particularly as he was planning for the war with the Soviet Union. Since efforts at deportations and blackmailing the Western powers were no longer possible, Jews became expendable. Viktor Brack, a high official in the German euthanasia program, testified at Nuremberg about an alternative approach that he had proposed.

In 1941, it was an "open secret" in higher party circles that those in power intended to exterminate (ausrotten) the entire Jewish population in Germany and occupied territories. I and my co-workers, especially Drs. Hefelmann and Blankenburg, were of the opinion that this was unworthy of party leaders and humanity more generally. We therefore decided to find another solution to the Jewish problem, less radical than the complete extermination of an entire race . . . . We drew a plan (to send Jews to Madagascar) along these lines and presented it to Bouhler (head of the Party Chancellery). This was apparently not acceptable, however, and so we came up with the idea of sterilization might provide the solution to the Jewish question. Given that sterilization is a rather complicated business, we hit upon the idea of sterilization by X-rays. In 1941 I suggested to Bouhler the sterilization of Jews by X-rays; this idea was also rejected, however. Bouhler said that sterilization by X-rays was not an option, because Hitler was against it.[166]

More than one German historian has questioned the extent of Hitler's direct intervention into the decision making of the Final Solution. Martin Broszat has been the leading proponent that, without denying Hitler's responsibility for or approval of extermination plans, has maintained that his subordinates had planned and initiated the killings in advance of Hitler's orders. Eberhard Jäckel has countered this argument.

Until that date (spring of 1941), with the exception of the killings during the invasion of Poland in 1939, all officials in charge of the Jewish question, from Göring and Himmler to Heydrich and Eichmann, were fully involved in emigration, evacuation, or deportation, and there is no evidence that any one of them proposed or envisaged a different procedure. On the other hand, there is a great deal of evidence that at least some of them were shocked or even appalled when the final solution went into effect. To be sure, they did not disagree with it. But they agreed only reluctantly, referring time and again to an order given by Hitler. This is a strong indication that the idea did not originate with them.[167]

Hitler had entrusted then Chief of Security Police Reinhard Heydrich, through Hermann Göring, on January 24, 1939, with the authority to solve the Jewish problem. Heydrich, a member of the SS, was a subordinate of Reichführer SS Heinrich Himmler, so Heydrich had to include Himmler into his operations. This was in part because Himmler was already in control of the Nazi concentration camp system. In May 1940 Hitler received a secret six-page document from Himmler entitled "Some Thoughts on the Treatment of Foreign Populations in the East" that had as its main point the recommendation for the destruction of the Eastern peoples to make room for German settlement.[168] Himmler kept this document secret and available to only a handful of his closest collaborators.[169] Jews were to be eliminated by means of major deportations, or by neglect. The problem with deportation is that there was no place to send them since earlier plans to send the Jews to Africa had fallen through. Himmler confided to Hitler's masseur, Felix Kersten, that he was happy because Hitler had approved his plans for the German occupied Eastern Territories.[170]

Himmler then delegated authority to Heinrich Heydrich to carry out the Final Solution. Eichmann placed this delegation in German context.

The final solution itself—I mean, the special mission given to Heydrich—to put it bluntly, the extermination of the Jews, was not provided for by Reich law. It was a Führer's Order, a so-called Führer's Order. And Himmler and Heydrich and Pohl, the head of the Administration and Supply—each had his own part in the implementation of this Führer's Order. According to the then prevailing interpretation, which no one questioned, the Führer's orders had the force of law. Not only in this case. In every case. That is common knowledge. The Führer's orders have the force of law.[171]

Hitler's attitude toward the Jews remained hostile. A report of Hitler's remarks to Nazi leaders on December 12, 1941, the day after Germany declared war on the United States, confirmed this.

Hitler returned once more to his famous prophecy of destruction, uttered nearly three years earlier about what would happen "if the Jews again provoked a world war." He solemnly warned that these were not "vain words," since the war had now arrived and the "destruction of the Jews must be the necessary result." There was no room for sentimentality regarding the Jews since the German people had "already sacrificed 160,000 dead on the Eastern front."[172]

It appears that the famous Wannsee Conference held in Germany on January 20, 1942, was more an organizational meeting by mid-level officials to work out details of the Final Solution rather than a decision-making meeting. Because of this, most of the time was spent in allocating resources and responsibilities for the Final Solution.[173] But it was also an opportunity for the SS to gain "formal control of the measures they had already embarked upon."[174] This explains the tone of the meeting because no participant questioned any aspect of the issue except how to implement it. Although the Final Solution was a carefully guarded secret, news shortly thereafter reached the Allies through a German industrialist, Eduard Schulte, that the implementation of the Final Solution was under way in July 1942.[175]

What is certain is that Hitler and the other Nazi leaders considered Jews to be beneath humanity. Bernard Lewis placed the Nazi view of Jewishness in this context.

Jewishness for the Nazis, was not a religious or cultural quality, it did not consist in belonging to a community or a people. It was an attribute of race, inherited and immutable, and so potent that even one grandparent out of four belonging to this race transmitted an indelible taint which put its inheritor beyond the pale of humanity.[176]

After the implementation of the Final Solution Hitler did nothing to hinder it because in his eyes the extermination of the Jews was a necessity. Shortly after the Wannsee Conference that formulated the administration of the Final Solution, Hitler made a statement at the end of February 1942 that summarized his attitude.

> The discovery of the Jewish virus is one of the greatest revolutions which has been undertaken in the world. The struggle we are waging is of the same kind as, in the past century, that Pasteur and Koch. How many diseases can be traced back to the Jewish virus! We shall regain our health only when we exterminate the Jews.[177]

Hitler's knowledge of the direction of the Final Solution is confirmed by an entry in the diary of Joseph Goebbels on February 14, 1942.

> World Jewry will suffer a great catastrophe at the same time as Bolshevism. The Fuehrer once more expressed his determination to clean up the Jews in Europe pitilessly. There must be no squeamish sentimentalism about it. The Jews have deserved the catastrophe that has now overtaken them. Their destruction will go hand in hand with the destruction of our enemies. We must hasten this process with cold ruthlessness. We shall thereby render an inestimable service to a humanity tormented for thousands of years by the Jews. This uncompromising anti-Semitic attitude must prevail among our own people despite all objectors. The Fuehrer expressed this idea vigorously and repeated it afterward to a group of officers who can put that in their pipes and smoke it.[178]

Goebbels at least was under no illusions about the deadliness of the Final Solution when he added to his diary on March 27, 1942, the belief "that about 60 per cent of them (Jews) will have to be liquidated whereas only about 40 per cent can be used for forced labor."[179]

In July 1942, the Germans began to put pressure on the Finnish government for it to turn over Finnish Jews to Germany. Dr. Felix Kersten reported that Himmler told him that it was Hitler who wanted this.

> Hitler wants the Finnish Jews to be taken to Maidanek (death camp) in Poland. Hitler believes that the German victory is not far off and wishes to have one of his principal aims assured: the complete extermination of all Jews. At the peace conference Hitler's first condition will be that all the Jews of the world be handed over to Germany. The moment is favorable to induce Finland to yield in this matter. Her supplies of grain will be exhausted by the middle of September; she is in desperate need of a delivery of grain, about thirty thousand tons, from Germany. We will not make this delivery until Finland has surrendered up her Jews.[180]

Whenever Hitler wanted to know the progress of the Final Solution, Martin Bormann, the secretary of the Nazi Party and the Führer's deputy, would make pointed inquiries. These inquiries had the force of law, and they made Himmler and his subordinates nervous. On occasion, Bormann would notify Himmler that not enough was being done, or it was not fast enough.[181] Besides making Himmler nervous, these inquiries and spurs to action infuriated Himmler, and he passed his displeasure on to his subordinates.[182] Evidently, Odilo Globocnik, the commandant at the Chelmno death camp, made a personal report to Hitler on the progress of the Jewish extermination program, and Hitler had remarked "Faster, get the whole thing over faster."[183] Exactly when this meeting took place is uncertain, but it probably was sometime in 1942. In April 1943, Himmler responded to a request for a report on the status of the Final Solution. He had statistics compiled by a professional statistician, the Chief Inspector of the Statistical Bureau of the SS Dr. Richard Korherr, for such a report—"The Final Solution for the Jewish Question in Europe." This lengthy report concluded that something in excess of 4 million Jews had been lost as of December 31, 1942. Himmler sent the report to Bormann, who returned it with instructions to remove the words "liquidation" and "special treatment" from it and shorten it. Himmler had the word for the special treatment of the Jews changed to "shifted through." This six-page revised report was resubmitted to Bormann in June 1943, but it was never read by Hitler because "the head of the Party Chancellery felt that at this point the Führer did not wish to receive the report."[184] Most of Hitler's attention at this stage was on the conduct of the war, which was deteriorating rapidly. Nevertheless, it is possible that Bormann gave Hitler a verbal report. There is no confirmable report that he did so.

Hitler never gave up in his war against the Jews even as the war approached its end. In the last days as the Soviet army was closing in on Berlin in April 1945, Hitler continued to rail against the Jews. He still blamed the Jews for the outbreak of the war and for his final defeat. In his final Political Testament composed shortly before he committed suicide, Hitler included a plea to continue policies against the international Jew.

> Above all, I enjoin the government and the people to uphold the race laws to the limit and to resist mercilessly the poisoner of all nations, the international Jewry.[185]

CONCLUSION

Considerable effort and space has been devoted to showing Hitler's direct complicity in the idea and then implementation of the extermination of the Jews and what Hitler and the Nazis classified as undesirables. His upbringing and the political environments in both Germany and Austria were conducive to his acceptance of antisemitism and negative eugenics. These ideas were out there for Hitler to absorb, and he did so because they gave direction to his hatreds. Because Hitler and the leading Nazi leaders were aware of the possible political consequents of the Final Solution of the Jewish question, efforts were made to keep its implementation secret. The problem for them was that no operation that size could be kept a secret for long. Consequently, word slowly made its way to the German public mostly by word of mouth from German soldiers and ultimately to the world at large. Since the Final Solution was to be secret, Hitler never acknowledged it by a written order. Written orders were simply not his way of doing things, especially since he had been burned so badly by the publicity about the euthanasia program. Hitler's preferred method of issuing an order was by verbal instruction. All Nazis believed that the "wish of the Führer had the force of law. After all, Hitler was both the civilian and military leader of Germany.

Another factor that assisted Hitler was the doctrine of command responsibility. Both the German army and the Nazi administrative hierarchy depended on the concept of command responsibility. In this doctrine the legal responsibility for a command resided on the individual who issued the command. Consequently, an illegal command would fall exclusively on the issuer of the order. This was the philosophy of "Orders are orders" (Befehl ist Befehl) that permeated both the German army and the Nazi regime. There was no legal concept that a German solider or a Nazi could refuse to obey an order, either lawful or unlawful. At the time of World War II no military power anywhere in the world had such a provision for disobeying an unlawful order. It was only much later did this right to disobey an unlawful order make its way into the American military and the Uniform Code of Military Justice. Consequently, once Hitler gave the order or expressed the desire that it be done, there was no impediment for the Final Solution taking place. It was Hitler's command responsibility, and his subordinates never questioned the legality, morality, or the wisdom of the order. After all, orders are orders. Any person who might question the order or refuse to obey it would have suffered severe consequences ranging from being thrown into a concentration camp to possibly execution. Even if there was no such retribution, the individual would suffer sanctions that would ruin his career, and to the ambitious this was the worst fate. This was the dilemma that Germans faced and most failed the test as the Nuremberg Trials after the war proved. Ultimately, even in German eyes Hitler is responsible for the Holocaust, but the German system of obedience to orders made its implementation possible.

Implementation of the Final Solution

INTRODUCTION

Even before the implementation of the Final Solution the Nazis showed their determination to rid their conquered lands in Poland of undesirables or of potential threats to German occupation. Using Einsatzgruppen troops and Polish Germans (Volksdeutsche), the Germans targeted "Polish intelligencia, nationalists, Catholic priests, Jews, 'Gypsies,' and even Catholic Germans, ethnic Germans married to Poles, and anyone else denounced by at least two Volksdeutsche for whatever personal reasons."[1] Some of these individuals were sent to concentration camps, but others were executed. While there are no accurate statistics on the number of those executed in Poland by the end of 1939, Browning quotes a source that fixed the number at around 50,000.[2]

Adolf Hitler's goal was to provide room for ethnic Germans to settle on former Polish lands. This goal necessitated the transfer of a staggering amount of people. Germans tried to force as many Jews as possible into the Soviet zone. Hitler approved the plans to transfer all Jews to the Lublin District of the General Government, but the difficulties of organization and transport caused this plan to be only partially implemented. Next, the Germans concentrated the Jews in ghettos in Lodz and then Warsaw as a temporary expedient. German authorities wanted to use the Jews for forced labor, but the Germans never supplied the Jews in the ghettos with enough food, leading to malnutrition and starvation. Thousands of Jews died in

these ghettos from lack of food. The experience in Poland of massive transfers of population and the difficulties administrating the Jewish ghettos led
the Germans to conclude that in many cases it was "easier to murder than
resettle."[3]

OPERATION BARBAROSSA

Even before the June 1941 invasion of the Soviet Union, Hitler envisaged
that the war with the Soviet Union was to be a war to the death. Hitler
equated the war against Bolshevikism with the war against Judaism since
he believed that Jews, communism, and the Soviet state were allied. The
war against the Soviet Union allowed him to strike against communism
and Jews and at the same time clear space for Germans to expand into the
fertile agriculture areas of west Poland and the Soviet Union. Hermann
Graml, a German historian, believes that Operation Barbarossa and the
Final Solution of the Jewish problem were obviously connected from the
beginning.[4]

Unlike in earlier operations in Poland and France, Hitler issued a series of
directions that detached the German army from responsibility for the rear
areas in their areas of operation. He assigned to Heinrich Himmler the
responsibility to administer special operations. Then, just prior to the invasion of the Soviet Union in June 1941, Hitler issued a secret decree that guar-
anteed "his armed forces immunity from subsequent prosecution for
shooting enemy civilians 'even if the action is also a military crime or misde-
meanor.' "[5] While this decree never mentioned Jews, it opened a hunting
season on Polish and Russian Jews. Reinhard Heydrich informed the
commanders of the Einsatzgruppen and Einsatzkommandos that "Judaism
in the east was the source of Bolshevikism and must therefore be wiped out
in accordance with the Führer's aims."[6] Four Einsatzgruppen battalions
numbering around 3,000 troops operated behind the German lines murder-
ing more than 1 million Jewish men, women, and children in the first
18 months after the German invasion of Russia in June 1941.[7] Most of the
victims died of gunshot wounds, and they were buried in mass graves previously dug by the victims. The most famous of these mass killings was at Babi
Yar near Kiev, where 33,771 Jews died in late September 1941.[8] In a legal
fiction, reports about the deaths of Jews included the phrase that the executions had taken place in reprisal for some hostile action by the Jews.[9]

The extent of the killings began to take a psychological toll on the German
soldiers. Other methods of killing were investigated to cure this problem.[10]
German doctors noted that Einsatzgruppen personnel suffered psychological
disorders that were more severe and lasted longer than the combat reactions
of ordinary German soldiers.[11] Moreover, news of the mass murders had
become widespread throughout the German army, causing considerable dis-
quiet.[12] Attempts to lessen the strain on German soldiers led to the

introduction of mobile gas vans, but this method of killing was even more unpopular because the soldiers found "the unavoidable cruelty 'morally intolerable' from their own point of view."[13] Consequently, in late 1941 personnel experienced in killing by poison gas from the euthanasia program and their apparatuses were transferred to concentration camps in Poland to deal with the growing Jewish and other nationalities' populations.[14] The complicity of the chancellor's office (Hitler was chancellor) is apparent from an October 18, 1941, letter from Dr. Wetzel, an official in Alfred Rosenberg's Ministry for the Occupied Eastern Territories, to Heinrich Himmler.

> With reference to my letter of 18 October 1941, I should like to inform you that Oberdienstleiter Brack of the Führer's Chancellery has said that he is prepared to collaborate in the provision of the necessary accommodation and appliances for gassing people. For the time being the appliances in question are not available in sufficient numbers so they must first be assembled. Since, in Brack's opinion, the assembly of these appliances would cause far greater difficulties in the Reich than in the places where they are to be used, he believes that the most expedient course would be to send his people to Riga, in particular his chemist, Dr. Kallmeyer, who will arrange everything. Oberdienstleiter Brack has indicated that the process in question is not without its dangers, so that special protective measures are necessary . . . In the present situation, there are no objections to doing away with those Jews who are unfit for work with the aid of Brack's resources.[15]

What followed was the transfer of personnel from the euthanasia program to the German death camps in Poland. Proof of this is a letter from Dr. Friedrich Mennecke, a psychiatrist who worked in the Eichberg Mental Hospital, to his wife.

> The day before yesterday, a large contingent from our euthanasia programme has been moved under the leadership of Brack to the Eastern battle-zone. It consists of doctors, office personnel, and male and female nurses from Hadamar and Sonnenstein, in all a group of 20–30 persons. This is all top secret. Only those who, for the most pressing of reasons, cannot be spared from our euthanasia programme are not coming along.[16]

ROLE OF HEINRICH HIMMLER IN THE FINAL SOLUTION OF THE JEWISH QUESTION

The person charged by Hitler to carry out the Final Solution of the Jewish question was Heinrich Himmler. At the time of its implementation Himmler was the Reich Führer SS, the highest rank in the elite SS (Schutzstaffel), and a key member of the inner circle surrounding Hitler. He literally worshipped Hitler, consulting him on all matters pertaining to the SS.[17] Himmler's intimate relationship with Dr. Felix Kersten led Kersten to believe in Himmler's unquestioned loyalty to Hitler.

> Himmler was no great judge of men, and he was completely devoid of critical faculty in his judgments of Hitler, whom he worshipped almost as a god. Had Hitler told him to hang himself at twelve o'clock sharp on a certain day he would have done so, and kept the appointment with death to the split second of time. If someone had passed by and tried to prevent the act or to query his reasons for it, he would have replied: "The Fuehrer's will is supreme law. He knows why he vies a command; all I have to do is to carry it out in every detail." Then he probably would have added, "Heil Hitler!" as he knotted the rope around his neck.[18]

In return, Hitler highly valued Himmler's "devotion, discretion and reliability."[19] Himmler was the perfect bureaucrat with strong organizational skills and obedience to orders. Most of Himmler's acquaintances characterized him as "colorlessly average and dependent, but devoid of feeling and overeager in the 'carrying out' of all plans."[20] Despite his closeness to Hitler, Himmler was always in a cold panic when summoned by Hitler, and "Hitler seldom treated him other than as an industrious, but not particularly intelligent, pupil."[21] Albert Speer was a rival to Himmler, and he had a less flattering opinion of Himmler.

> Himmler was a cross between a sober realist who single-mindedly pursued his goals and a visionary of often grotesque proportions. I still find it inexplicable today that this inconspicuous man could achieve and know how to maintain such power. It will always be an enigma to me. Himmler strove to impress people with the importance of his title or with the flashy uniforms of the men surrounding him—or with the princes and counts that he attracted. Yet, oddly, he seemed like a philistine who had suddenly been catapulted to the top, an utterly insignificant personality who, in some inexplicable manner, had risen to a high position.[22]

Just what was Himmler's role in the Holocaust. There is room for conjecture on whether Hitler gave a direct oral order for the Final Solution, or whether Himmler took it on himself to carry out Hitler's wishes.[23] It was a characteristic of Himmler that "when the Führer wanted something, Himmler was usually eager to bring it about—even without express instructions."[24] On the other hand, Himmler rarely attempted anything big, or sometimes little, without running it by Hitler during one of his frequent meetings. A German general reported Himmler saying to army commanders in Koblenz on March 13, 1940, that "I do nothing which the Führer does not know."[25] Himmler followed this comment by stating that "he was prepared in some things that perhaps appeared incomprehensible to take responsibility for the Führer before the people and the world, because the person of the Führer cannot be connected with these things."[26]

Himmler also served as a conduit for others. Adolf Eichmann described a way that directives came down to him in 1939.

> The war had reduced the possibility of emigration. On the other hand, the Gauleiters, the Propaganda Ministry, and Office of the Führer's Deputy, in other words, Bormann—were putting every possible pressure on us. They did not communicate directly with men of my rank. They addressed themselves to Himmler. He was the kind of man who always wanted to oblige the high placed—then highly placed—leaders. It was considered the right to meddle in Jewish affairs. No sooner had Hitler made a speech—and he invariably touched on the Jewish problem—then every party or government department felt it was up to them to do something. And then Himmler authorized each one to attend to it. He'd pass the order on to Heydrich, head of the Security Police and the SD, who would pass it on to [Heinrich] Müller, and then it came to me.[27]

Further proof that Himmler was responding to Hitler's wishes is the testimony of Obersturmbannführer Dr. Otto Bradfisch who asked Himmler in Minsk in August 1941 "who was taking responsibility for the mass extermination of the Jews," and "Himmler answered me in a fairly sharp tone that these orders had come from Hitler as the supreme Führer of the German government, and that they had the force of law."[28] Albert Speer, who was no friend of Himmler, added his opinion.

> The dichotomy in the man (Himmler), who was in charge of total mass murder and yet who constantly opposed extermination policies, leads me to suspect that he was not the driving force in the murder of the Jews. I would point instead to Hitler, Joseph Goebbels, and that hate-filled mover Martin Bormann.[29]

Complicating Himmler's role in the Holocaust was his desire to build a SS industrial empire. Albert Speer claimed in his 1981 book that the extermination of the Jews interfered with Himmler's plans to build an industrial empire for the SS based on Jewish manpower and concentration camp inmates.[30] Along these lines SS authorities tried to improve living conditions at the labor concentration camps, but, of course, there was no need to do so at the death camps.[31] Ultimately the goals of building an industrial empire and extermination were incompatible.

Once the decision was made to exterminate the Jews, the code name "the Final Solution" came into play. Richard Breitman placed the phrase Final Solution in context.

> The phrase "Final Solution of the Jewish question" allowed Nazi officials to avoid dirtying their lips with words like "mass murder" or extermination." The program known as the Final Solution was an attempt to eliminate the Jewish "race" from the earth. This was to be accomplished by means of mass murder, through working people to death and allowing some privileged

categories of elderly Jews to die out were also significant parts of the process. But the exceptions only highlighted the general practices of executions and gassings.[32]

Himmler was already in the concentration camp business before the implementation of the Final Solution. He had established the first concentration camp on March 22, 1933, at Dachau to house political prisoners. Himmler had the authority to establish a concentration camp from an emergency decree on February 28, 1933, "For the Protection of People and State" that allowed people to be sent to a concentration camp on suspicion of anti-State activity.[33] Dachau was located on the northern outskirts of Munich at a former munitions factory in a swampy area that was almost always moist and foggy. From the first the inmates were treated as scum. The commander of the SS unit in charge made the following statement in late March:

> Comrades of the SS! You all know what the Führer has called upon us to do. We haven't come here to treat those swine inside like human beings. In our eyes, they're not like us, they're something second-class. For years, they've been able to pursue their criminal devices. But now we've got the power. If these swine had taken over, they'd have made sure our heads rolled in the dust. So we know no sentimentality. Any man in our ranks who can't stand the sight of blood doesn't belong here, he should get out. The more of these bastards we shoot, the fewer we'll have to feed.[34]

Its first commandant was SS-Obersturmführer Hilmar Wäckerle, but he lasted only a short time because of "his partiality for murder under the guise of punishment."[35] His successor was Theodor Eicke, who did not have a much better reputation for brutality than his predecessor, but he was a better disciplinarian.[36] Many of the commandants in later concentration camps received their training from Eicke. Eicke impressed on his men that "any compassion for an enemy of the state was unworthy of an SS man."[37] His goal was to "break down and dehumanize the 'enemies' within."[38] Attempts to investigate deaths at Dachau ran into opposition from Himmler, and they were quashed never to be attempted again.[39] Concentration camp commandants had unlimited authority to run their camps in any way they wanted, subject only to the approval of Himmler.

Other concentration camps opened in other parts of Germany in 1933, but by early 1934 Himmler had control of all of them. Many of the early concentration camps were the so-called "wild concentration camps." These camps were impromptu facilities established by the SS and the Sturmabteilung (SA) to take care of what they considered to be enemies of the regime. At one time there were several hundred of these impromptu camps, but most of them were subsequently closed down when Himmler took over all control of the concentration camp system.

Hitler approved the creation of the concentration camps, and he ignored complaints about their excesses. In 1934, Hitler responded to complaints with the following statement:

> I forbid you to change anything. By all means, punish one or two men, so that these German Nationalist donkeys may sleep easy. But I don't want the concentration camps transformed into penitentiary institutions. Terror is the most effective political instrument. I shall not permit myself to be robbed of it simply because a lot of stupid, bourgeois mollycoddles choose to be offended by it. It is my duty to make use of every means of training the German people to severity, and to prepare them for war.[40]

Hitler then added that "these so-called atrocities spare me a hundred thousand individual actions against disobedience and discontent," because "people will think twice before opposing us when they hear what to expect in the camps."[41]

The first victims of concentration camps were Communists, Social Democrats, and labor leaders, but Jews and other social undesirables were soon added. In 1937, Himmler rounded up 2,000 criminals and sent them to concentration camps where some of them became Kapos (foremen of work details).[42] By 1937 there were men at Dachau, Sachsenhausen, and Buchenwald, and women at Lichtenburg. Then in 1938, three new camps were set up at Flossenbürg, Mauthausen, and Geisen near stone quarries for convict labor.[43] Himmler was always looking to find more categories of people to send to concentration camps. Jews became a special target after 1938. Gypsies and other social undesirables were also targeted. By 1939, the various categories of prisoners and their colored patches were red triangles for political prisoners, green for criminals, pink for homosexuals, black for the antisocials, purple for Jehovah's Witnesses, and yellow for Jews.

Himmler was a relatively late convert to using extreme measures against the Jews. Like most of his Nazi peers, Himmler held antisemitic views even before he joined the Nazi Party, but his personal ambitions to succeed were far greater than his hatred for the Jews. He operated at the fringes of the negotiations for the transfer of Jews in 1938, and again his involvement in the deal was more for SS financial benefit than his own ideology. Himmler's attitude toward the Jews became more extreme after the outbreak of the war in 1939. Hitler's increasing violent diatribes against the Jews influenced him. In a meeting with Hitler prior to the invasion of the Soviet Union in June 1941, Himmler received a verbal order to begin implementation of the extermination of Europe's Jewish population. In his briefing of Rudolf Höss, the commandant of Auschwitz, in the summer of 1941 to turn Auschwitz into a death camp, Himmler cited Hitler's order with the statement that "the Führer has ordered the Final Solution of the Jewish question."[44] Himmler followed with his justification for the Final Solution:

The Jews are the eternal enemies of the German people and must be exterminated. All the Jews within our reach must be annihilated during the war. If we
do not succeed in destroying the biological foundation of Jewry now, then one
day the Jews will destroy the German people.[45]

Himmler's chief assistant was Reinhard Heydrich, and he had been
assigned by Himmler to handle Jewish issues for the SS. Since Hermann
Göring was technically in charge of Nazi Jewish policy, it was Göring who
produced the decree of July 31, 1941, that appointed Heydrich in charge
of the Final Solution. Heydrich may have received his mandate from Göring,
but he was still subordinate in the SS hierarchy to Himmler. The order from
Göring did make it easier to gain cooperation from other segments in the
Nazi administration, particularly transportation.

Heydrich was both able and intimidating. Those who met Heydrich found
it uncomfortable to be around him. Even Himmler was intimidated by
Heydrich, although Heydrich was always correct and obliging with him.[46]
One of Heydrich's so-called Jewish experts, Adolf Eichmann, was sent to
Vienna shortly after the Anschluss (the unification of Germany and Austria)
in 1938 to expedite the immigration of Jews. Eichmann used a combination
of persuasion and force to rid Vienna of 50,000 Jews.[47]

Eichmann described his reaction to Heydrich's statement about the Final
Solution in late summer of 1941:

> The Führer has ordered the physical extermination. These were his (Heydrich's)
> words. And as though wanting to test their effect on me, he made a long pause,
> which was not at all his way, I can still remember that. In the first moment,
> I didn't grasp the implications, because he chose his words so carefully. But then
> I understood. I didn't say anything, what could I say? Because I'd never thought
> of a ... of such a thing, of that sort of violent solution.[48]

ADMINISTRATIVE OPERATIONS OF THE CONCENTRATION
CAMP SYSTEM

The administrative head of the German concentration camp system was
Oswald Pohl. He was a former naval officer recruited into the SS for his
administrative abilities. He became the head of the SS Business Administrative Office (Wirtschafts-Verwaltungshauptamt, or WVHA).[49] It was his
responsibility to administer the 700,000 concentration camp inmates who
worked in the German war economy.[50] The SS business credo was articulated by a SS lawyer—Leo Volk.

> Why does the SS pursue business? The question is thrown at us especially by
> those who think in purely capitalist terms and look unfavorably on public enter-
> prise or at least on enterprises that have a public character. The time of liberal
> economics promoted the primacy of business. That is, first comes the economy

and then the state. In contrast, National Socialism stands by the point, the state commands the economy; the state is not there for the economy, but the economy is there for the state.[51]

Pohl and his subordinates operated in a dual system with their concern on managing production in contrast to the prison SS administration's running of the camps. Eicke and his successors as head of the Death's Head units of prison guards gradually lost control of the administrative side of running the camps because they "idealized military bearing, discipline, and the decisive act; as a corollary they disdained desk work as the pursuit of idlers and do-nothings."[52] This dichotomy of function led to conflict.

> Pohl's men prided themselves as modern administrators. When it came time to manage prison industries, they clashed with camp guards who, true to their self-conception as punishers, often beat and killed prisoners even when this undermined productivity within the SS's own corporations.[53]

Over the 12-year existence of the Third Reich, the number of concentration camps and its affiliates blossomed. There were 23 main concentration camps, but there were thousands of subcamps. Among these were 900 forced labor camps for Jews in Eastern Europe, labor-education camps, camps for criminals, transit camps, collection camps, and at least 500 forced ghettos of Jews.[54] The largest of these forced ghettos of Jews was the Warsaw Ghetto. A German scholar has estimated the total number of camps of all types at 10,006.[55]

By the end of 1941, the German SS administrators had organized the concentration camp system in final form. There were three categories of concentration camps: Category I, Category II, and Category III. Category I contained those concentration camps that were exclusively work camps.[56] Most of the concentration camps had brickworks or were near stone quarries since there were shortages of bricks and decorative stones for Hitler's future building program. The SS formed a company, German Excavation and Quarrying Company Ltd., to control production, distribution, and profits of the slave labor.[57] Later, war industries were set up near the concentration camps to take advantage of the free and available labor. Conditions in these camps were brutal, and deaths did occur from mistreatment, malnutrition, executions, and medical experimentations, but in comparison to the concentration camps in the other categories the survival rate was fairly high. These camps had a mixture of criminals, homosexuals, political prisoners, social undesirables, and German Jews.

The best example of a Category I concentration camp was Dachau. While Dachau had a gas chamber and crematorium constructed in 1943, the gas chamber was never used, unlike the crematorium, which was heavily used.[58] Thousands of sick and invalid inmates were gassed, but not at Dachau. Those gassed were transported to the gas chambers at Hartheim near Linz,

Austria.[59] The total number of prisoners incarcerated at Dachau from 1933 to 1945 was 206,206.[60] Estimates of the number of deaths at Dachau range from 27,839 to 29,438, excluding those sent elsewhere to be killed.[61] Much of the labor at Dachau was work made to torment the inmates, but later work in the munitions factories meant better treatment and an escape from the "capricious and thoughtless beatings from the SS guards."[62] It was at Dachau that German doctors experimented with inmates on survival rates of downed German air force pilots. Deaths accelerated in late 1944 and 1945 because of overcrowding as a result of massive transfers of inmates from other concentration camps and a bad outbreak of typhus in the winter of 1945.[63] Not surprisingly concentration camp officials and guards continued to prosper at the same time inmates were dying.

Category II concentration camps were also work camps, but conditions in them were harsher and the camp officials were less concerned with the survival of the prisoners. These camps served two purposes: punish enemies of the Third Reich and work the inmates to death. German authorities tended to send those they considered the most dangerous prisoners to Category II camps, but this was not always the case.[64] Manual labor in both Category I and II camps was more for punishment than productive uses, and the mortality rate for sickness alone was between 8 and 11 percent per month by 1942 and even higher in the winter.[65] Both Category I and Category II camps were exclusively in Germany and Austria. During most of its existence, Buchenwald was a Category II camp, but it was considered the worst concentration camp of its type. It was at Buchenwald where some of the worst cases of medical experimentation took place in Block 46.

Category III concentration camps were the death camps. They were all set up outside of Germany in Poland, and operations remained a state secret. These camps were Auschwitz-Birkenau, Belzec, Chelmno, Majdanek, Sobibor, and Treblinka. Both Auschwitz-Birkenau and Majdanek were different because they were both extermination camps and slave labor camps. The others were exclusively death camps operating for a short existence under Operation Reinhard. Methods of killing differed from camp to camp between gas chambers, gas vans, and shootings. Somewhere between 3.1 million and 4.8 million died in the six death camps with a majority of the victims being Jews, but a goodly number of them were Polish and Russians. Nobody will ever know the exact ethnic or national breakdown of all of the victims. Attempts by some German bureaucrats to save some of the skilled Jews for war work in the General Government of Poland were turned down with the response that "economic considerations are not to be taken into account in the settlement of the problem."[66]

The Theresienstadt concentration camp was a special case. It was a model concentration camp northwest of Prague, Czechoslovakia, that the Germans showed to the outside world, special visitors, and Red Cross inspectors.

They also used it as a transit camp, and most of its inmates eventually ended up in Auschwitz-Birkenau.

The exception to the regular German concentration camp system was those camps that were part of Operation Reinhard. Three camps were part of Operation Reinhard: Belzec, Sobibor, and Treblinka. Instead of the regular concentration camp chain of command, these camps fell under the command of Odilo Globocnik, and he reported directly to Heinrich Himmler and through him to Hitler's Reich Chancellery Office in Berlin.[67] Odilo Globocnik administered the three camps, and he was notorious for his carrying out of orders regardless how distasteful. Operation Reinhard had close ties to the T4 euthanasia program, and it recruited personnel from it to build and run the camps. These camps existed solely for the killing of large numbers of Jews with as few SS and its allies participating as possible. At each of these camps only between 20 and 35 SS were present at any one time, but there were others there helping process Jews. The most SS officers serving at Belzec and Sobobor were 7, and only 4 were ever present at any one time at Treblinka.[68] Jews were shipped to these camps in railway freight cars, and they were killed as soon as possible. To do this the camps were camouflaged in various ways, mostly as train stations. Justification for Operation Reinhard came from Hans Frank, the head of the General Government of Poland, in a December 16, 1941, speech at Krakow, Poland.

> We must destroy the Jews wherever we meet them and whenever the opportunity offers so that we can maintain the whole structure of the Reich here . . . . The Jews batten on to us to an exceptionally damaging extent. At a rough estimate we have in the General gouvernment about 2.5 million people (Jews)—now perhaps 3.5 million who have Jewish connections and so on. We cannot shoot these 3.5 million Jews, we cannot poison them, but we can take measures that will, one way or another (so oder so), lead to extermination, in conjunction with the large-scale measures under discussion in the Reich.[69]

EARLY EXPERIMENT LEADING TO THE IMPLEMENTATION OF THE FINAL SOLUTION

All the top leaders in the Nazi hierarchy were antisemitic, but the measures to be taken to solve the so-called "Jewish Problem" evolved in the period from June to September 1941. Violent acts against Jews in the following three months of the invasion of the Soviet Union in Operation Barbarossa were in mostly individual executions, or Aktions by the German military, SS units, or collaborators.[70] At the time in the period before the invasion on June 1941, there was a vague idea of a Final Solution of the Jewish problem, but historians have been unable to find an order that demanded the killing of all Jews in Occupied Territories.[71] Mass executions of Jews took place in Soviet territories without prior approval, but these executions received postaction approval from the SS high command. Only gradually did these excesses become official policy, mostly because in the early days of these executions Nazi leaders were leery of the response from the German elites and the German public at large. An example was the report by Walter Stahlecker, the head of Einsatzgruppe A on June 23, 1941, on Kaunas, Lithuania.

> Similarly, within a few hours of our entering the city (Kaunas), local anti-Semitic elements were induced to engage in pogroms against the Jews, despite the extremely difficult conditions. In accordance with orders the security police were bent on solving the Jewish question with extreme firmness using all the ways and means at its disposal. It was thought a good idea for the security police not to be seen to the involved, at least not immediately, in these unusually tough measures, which were also bound to attract attention in German circles.[72]

Despite efforts at secrecy, news about the killings slowly made its way to Germany. Once it became apparent that there would be nowhere near the outcry about the killing of Jews that had happened during the euthanasia campaign, then it was easy to proceed toward the next step of mass annihilation of the Jews. After all, the Nazis were in the process of killing Soviet prisoners of war either by execution or neglect.

Once Hitler and the Nazi leadership decided on the necessity for the extermination of the Jews, the only decision left was how to do it. The experiences of the Einsatzgruppen soldiers in the early days of Operation Barbarossa proved that the traditional method of mass shootings and burials had shortcomings. The massacre at Babi Yar outside of Kiev took two days and several units to kill and bury 33,771 Jews.[73] It was time-consuming in both shooting and burying the victims, and the psychological impact on the executioners endangered the morale of the soldiers. Gustave Fix, a member of Sonderkommando 6, reported the psychological impact on the German executors.

> I would also like to mention that as a result of the considerable psychological pressures, there were numerous men who were no longer capable of conducting executions, and who thus had to be replaced by other men. On the other hand, there were others who could not get enough of them and often reported to these executions voluntarily.[74]

Himmler showed concern about the psychological effect the killings might have on the SS because it could endanger the SS's elite status.[75] An example is the account of executions by SS enlisted man Felix Landau on July 12, 1941.

> Twenty-three have to be shot, including the women I mentioned before. They are remarkable. They even refuse to accept a glass of water from us . . . Presently

there were only six of us, and we looked for a suitable spot for the shooting and burial. After awhile we found one. The condemned were given shovels in order to dig their own grave ... After they had all been lined up together in a clearing, the two women were taken to the edge of the grave to be shot ... Six of us had to shoot them, divided so that three of us aimed at the heart and three at the head. I took the heart. The bullets struck and the brain mass burst through the air.[76]

This report does not distinguish whether or not the victims were Jews or Russian partisans, but it matters little because executions of this type involving Jews took place regularly in 1941 and 1942 in Russia. Einsatzgruppen Operational Situation Report No. 126, dated October 27, 1941, indicated that the traditional way of liquidating Jews was too slow and sloppy, with word getting out so Jews in the city disappeared before they could be rounded up.[77] Another problem was that these executions were too labor-intensive because of the large number of SS personnel required.[78] There was even an attempt to expedite the process by using explosives, but the experiments were unsatisfactory.[79]

Experiments with mobile gas vans proved impractical in the field because it was too inefficient in handling the numbers targeted for death. Germans did commit 15 mobile poison gas vans to the German-occupied Soviet territory.[80] There were also psychological problems in the handling of the dead according to August Becker.

Apart from that I gave orders that all men should stand as far away as possible from the van during the gassings, so that their health would not be damaged by any escaping gases. I would like to take this opportunity to draw your attention to the following: some of the Kommandos are using their own men to unload the vans after the gassing. I have made commanders of the Sonderkommandos in question aware of the enormous psychological and physical damage this work can do to the men, if not immediately then at a later stage.[81]

These types of operations were almost impossible to keep secret. Jews learned about what was happening and began joining partisan forces to fight against Germany military forces. News also reached Germany. One SS officer, SS-Untersturmführer Max Täubner, violated orders by taking pictures of the executions and showing them to his wife and friends in Germany.[82] In his court-martial, Täubner was not punished for killing Jews because "the Jews have to be exterminated and none of the Jews that were killed is any great loss," but because of excessive cruelty "unworthy of a German man and an SS officer," for the unwarranted killing of the commander of the Ukrainian militia, and for taking and showing pictures to the German public about the executions.[83] Despite the limitations of this extermination campaign, the Einsatzgruppen operations killed over 1 million victims buried in mass graves in Ponar near Vilna, Fort IX at Kovno, Rumboli near Riga, Babi Yar at Kiev, Drobitzki Valley near Kharkov, in the Crimea, and in numerous other sites in areas of German occupation in the Soviet Union.[84]

While there had always been executions by hanging, firing squads, or by individual shootings in the concentration camps, the extent of the killings made necessary by the Final Solution made these methods impractical. Despite some experiments in the field of using carbon monoxide, the experience gained in the euthanasia program of mass gassings using carbon monoxide in the T4 program was a ready-made solution for the killing of masses of people because the technical apparatus was already in place. Even before the mass extermination of the Jews began, Nazi authorities had already started gassing of Jews in psychiatric hospitals as early as June 1940.[85] In early 1941, the leader of the T4 program, Philipp Bouhler, loaned T4 personnel and facilities to Himmler to eliminate the sick, lame, and mentally ill from German concentrations camps under the code name of 14f13.[86] This program operated officially at Dachau, Mauthausen, Ravensbrück, and Sachsenhausen, but it may have been implemented in other German concentration camps. Only a perfunctory physical examination led to the classification of inmates into the 14f13 program.[87] Those initially targeted were the mentally ill and the handicapped, but it soon moved to political prisoners, Jews, Poles, draft dodgers, social misfits, and finally criminals.[88] Jews were given special consideration for inclusion in the 14f13 program, but the German authorities extended it in 1944 to rid the concentration camps of overcrowding.[89] Of the probably 30,000 victims of the 14f13 program most were gassed at the gas chambers at Hartheim.[90] The success and secrecy of the 14f13 program allowed the Germans to consider expanding it to the German concentration camps in Poland. In the summer of 1941, Dr. Ernst-Robert Grawitz, chief SS doctor, recommended to Himmler the use of the carbon monoxide method to kill large numbers of people in an orderly way.[91] It was the decision by the commander of Auschwitz-Birkenau to use the pesticide Zyklon B only at Auschwitz-Birkenau.

AUSCHWITZ-BIRKENAU AS SYMBOL AND REALITY

Auschwitz-Birkenau was the largest of the German death camps in Poland, but it was also a large slave labor camp. The commandant of Auschwitz-Birkenau from May 1940 to December 1, 1943, was Rudolf Höss. The original intent of the Auschwitz camp was to serve as a transient quarantine camp for Polish prisoners on their way to prisoner-of-war camps in Germany.[92] It had been the site of an artillery barracks for the Polish army. Before long, orders came down to Höss to turn Auschwitz into a camp for holding captured members of the Polish resistance movement.[93] Höss supervised the building of the camp to hold 20,000 inmates. Evidence shows that nothing in the original conceptual sketches of the crematoria or in the blueprints that date from January 1942 suggest homicidal gas chambers or their use in the Final Solution, but this was to change.[94]

When Himmler visited Auschwitz in the spring of 1941, he ordered Höss to enlarge the camp to handle the greatest possible numbers.[95] His next order was to build a camp of 100,000 in Birkenau. Around 12,000 Soviet prisoners of war (POWs) arrived in Auschwitz in the winter of 1942–1943 during the time the Germans were building the subcamp Birkenau.[96] This expansion was originally planned to handle an influx of Soviet prisoners of war, but the Nazi SS hierarchy had other plans. Eastern European Jews were rounded up and some of them arrived at Auschwitz. In the summer of 1940 executions of concentration inmates picked up, but the executions were sporadic.[97] At this time, most of the executions were by gunshot. To keep the noise of the executions down, an SS officer adapted a small-bore file with a silencer for these executions.[98] Wieslaw Kielar reported that in the summer of 1940 the sick and disabled persons were shipped probably to Dresden where they were alledgedly killed by poison gas.[99] This testimony is confirmed by the statement from Commandant Karl Otto Koch of the Buchenwald concentration camps that secret orders had come down from Heinrich Himmler that all feebleminded and crippled inmates of Germany's concentration camps were to be killed.[100]

Then Höss received a direct order from Himmler to start the mass executions of Jews. Himmler explained to Höss that there were other extermination camps already in operation, but they were too small to carry out the large-scale action of extermination.[101] In his memoirs Höss remembered the Himmler meeting in Berlin in the summer of 1941 in the following account:

In the summer of 1941, I am unable to recall the exact date, I was suddenly ordered by Himmler's adjutant to report directly to the Reichsführer SS in Berlin. Contrary to his usual custom, his adjutant was not in the room. Himmler greeted me with the following: "The Führer has ordered the Final Solution of the Jewish question. We the SS have to carry out this order. The existing extermination sites in the East are not in a position to carry out these intended operations on a large scale. I have, therefore, chosen Auschwitz for this purpose. First of all, because of the advantageous transport facilities, and secondly, because it allows this area to be easily isolated and disguised. I had first thought of choosing a higher-ranking SS officer for this job so as to avoid any difficulties with someone who doesn't have the competence to deal with such a difficult assignment. You now have to carry out this assignment. It is to remain between the two of us. It is a difficult job which requires your complete commitment, regardless of the difficulties which may arise. You will learn the further details through Major (Adolf) Eichmann of the RSHA (Reich Security Headquarters), who will soon visit you. The administrative department involved will be notified by me at the appropriate time. You are sworn to the strictest silence regarding this order. Not even your superiors are allowed to know about this. After your meeting with Eichmann I want you to immediately send me the plans of the intended installations."[102]

Later, Höss met with Eichmann to discuss the details of turning Auschwitz into a death camp. Eichmann explained the size of the roundup of the Jews, and they decided that gassing was the only practical method to handle the huge numbers.[103] Mobile gas vans already in use were determined to be insufficient to handle the large number of Jews available.[104] Although Eichmann and Höss selected Birkenau, which was adjacent to Auschwitz, to be the extermination site, they were unable to decide on the type of gas to use. A group of Soviet POWs were killed with the pesticide Zyklon B, and this demonstration of its killing proficiency convinced Höss that it could be used on the incoming Jews.[105] In 1946, an American psychiatrist, Leon Goldensohn, asked Höss a series of questions about the Auschwitz-Birkenau death camp.

> I (Goldensohn) asked how many people were executed at Auschwitz during his time. "The exact number cannot be determined. I (Höss) estimate about 2.5 million." Only Jews? "Yes." Women and children as well? "Yes."[106]

Subsequent research has concluded that Höss's estimate is much too high. The actual figure was somewhere less than 1.1 million.[107] In a later statement Höss said that he could account for only 1,125,000 deaths.[108] Goldensohn continued with his interview.

> Did you ever protest? "I (Höss) couldn't do that. The reasons Himmler gave me I had to accept." In other words, you think it was justified to kill 2.5 million men, women, and children? "Not justified—but Himmler told me that if the Jews were not exterminated at that time, then the German people would be exterminated for all time by the Jews."[109]

Finally, Goldensohn asked Höss about the gas chambers.

> Did you (Höss) supervise the gas chambers murders? "Yes, I had the whole supervision of the business. I was often, but not always, present when the gas chambers were being used."[110]

IG Farben had a slave labor factory complex adjacent to Auschwitz. This factory manufactured synthetic oil and rubber, and its executives had picked Auschwitz largely because of its access to labor and to the local coal and water resources. Early in 1943 other companies came to Auschwitz— Krupp's fuse plant, Hermann Göring Works' coal mining, Siemens-Schuckert's electrical parts, and the Speer ministry's pursuit planes. The biggest problem of these companies was keeping their work forces intact, but the factory managers did little to improve conditions for the inmate laborers. Consequently, work efficiency was never high. SS-Unterscharführer Pery Broad stated that "barbarous hygienic conditions, insufficient food rations and hard work, together with other torments, meant that the majority of the people sent to Auschwitz met a sad end after a few weeks or a few months at most.[111] Dr. Miklos Nyiszli, an inmate at Auschwitz, agreed with Broad that even the "healthiest individual was given three or four weeks to collapse from hunger, filth, blows and inhuman labor."[112] Broad also reported that it was not unusual for Jews to be driven to suicide by the conditions.[113]

This combination of death camp and slave labor facility made the Germans have to deal with a mass of incoming Jews of all ages and physical conditions. Actual gassings began on September 3, 1941. Incoming train-loads of Jews would arrive to be met by the SS guards. A doctor would select those healthy enough to work to go to the right, and the rest would sent to the left and the gas chambers.[114] In his diary Dr. Johannes Paul Kremer mentioned participating in these selections (Sonderaktion). Dr. Josef Mengele also participated in the selection process after he arrived at Auschwitz in 1943.[115] These gas chambers used Zyklon B gas to kill those not selected for slave labor—old, infirm, children, and mothers who went with their children.[116] There were other mass gassings of other groups. One such was the gassing of women from the women's camp in September 1942. Kremer described it at a hearing on July 18, 1947, in Krakow, Poland—the gassing of about 800 women prisoners on September 5, 1942.

> The action of gassing emaciated women from the women camp was particularly unpleasant. Such individuals were generally called Muselmänner [Moslem]. I remember taking part in the gassing of such women in daylight. I am unable to state how numerous that group was. When I came to the bunker they sat clothed on the ground. As they were wearing worn-out camp clothing they were not let in the undressing hut but were made to undress in the open air. I concluded from the behaviour of these women that they had no doubt what fate awaited them, as they begged and sobbed to the SS men to spare them their lives. However, they were herded into the gas chambers and gassed. As an anatomist I have seen a lot of terrible things, I had had a lot of experience with dead bodies, and yet what I saw that day was like nothing I had ever seen before.[117]

The gas chambers represent a horror that almost is indescribable but is the example of modern technology gone completely mad. Trying to describe this process in a meaningful way is Philippe Burrin's treatment.

> Both methods (shooting or gassing) testify to an industrial-type rationalization of massacre, accompanied by a dehumanizing representation of the victims, but the gas chamber represented the more advanced state of that rationalization and, above all, dehumanization. What it reduced its victims to in their last moments testified to an ultimate dehumanization. Whereas death by shooting

afforded the martyrs at least the possibility to offer each other a measure of mutual comfort and to feel something like a sense of solidarity in their trials, the gas chamber camouflaged as a shower room ruled out anything of the kind. The sudden darkness provoked terror, suffocation increased this to panic, and families clinging together were swept apart in a wild rush for the door. Next, everyone tried to find oxygen to breathe up close to the ceiling. The strong trampled on the weak—relatives, loved ones and friends no longer mattered. Human beings found themselves reduced to the most elementary of all impulses, the desire to survive, which can dissolve.[118]

In one of those ironies of German bureaucracy those selected for death in the gas chambers required no death certificate, but those killed later did, so the SS doctors signed false death certificates for them.[119]

German concentration authorities relegated the dirty tasks to special inmates. These prisoners were the Sonderkommandos. The handpicked healthy men and women earned the nickname "commando of the living dead."[120] In exchange for special privileges, food, and civilian clothing, they ran the crematoria at Auschwitz.[121] The 860 Sonderkommandos were never permitted to leave the crematorium grounds, and every four months the Germans liquidated them.[122] During the history of the Auschwitz death camp, there were 14 cycles of Sonderkommandos. All the dirty work at the gas chambers had been left to the Sonderkommandos, but the actual gassing was done by two German officers—a SS officer and the Deputy Health Services Officer.[123]

Only once was there resistance by the Jewish prisoners. Before entering the gas chambers the prisoners were forced to undress. One young Jewish woman refused to undress in front of the SS. When SS-Oberscharführer Schillinger tried to force her to undress, in the struggle she gained control of his gun and killed him.[124] She also wounded another SS officer. Instead of gassing this group, the enraged SS shot all of them.

The first crematoria were unable to handle the load, so in between March and April 1943 four new installations went into operation in the Birkenau section of Auschwitz. The two larger crematoria each had nine ovens with four wells each.[125] Two smaller crematoria each had a reduced capacity with eight ovens.[126] With the addition of these four, there were five operating crematoria at Auschwitz. Each of the wells had the capacity of holding three bodies. These ovens were kept running at full capacity because it took about twenty minutes to cremate a body.[127] Accelerating the process was important to the SS so that sometimes as many as four bodies were loaded into one oven well at a time.[128] This meant at maximum capacity several thousand individuals could be cremated in a day. Ashes from the crematoria were then dumped into the Vistula River only a mile away.[129]

This process remained uninterrupted until the Sonderkommando revolt on October 6, 1944. It was at the end of the Sonderkommando cycle, but this time they had smuggled in arms to resist the SS. When the SS attempted to implement the changeover, violence broke out.[130] In the course of the fighting, 70 SS officers and enlisted men died, and 850 Sonderkommandos also died.[131] Other casualties of the battle were Number 3 crematorium, which burned to the ground, and Number 4 crematorium, which was rendered useless as a result of damage to its equipment.[132]

It was also at Auschwitz that Dr. Josef Mengele conducted his medical experiments. He was a doctrinaire Nazi eugenicist who had earned his medical degree at Munich University studying under a noted antisemite.[133] Mengele specialized in the study of twins, and at Auschwitz there were enough twins for him to study their reactions to various experiments and the freedom to kill them for autopsies to study the results of the experiments.[134] Of the 1,500 sets of twins, only 200 or so twins survived to report on Mengele's experiments.[135] An important eyewitness was a doctor inmate, Miklos Nyiszli, who served as an assistant to Mengele and survived to testify against him.

Despite the efforts of the Germans to retain secrecy, rumors began to spread to other countries about the atrocities in the concentration camps. Some of these tales were spread by German soldiers. Olga Lengyel, a Jewish surgical assistant in Cluj, Transylvania, reported that a friendly German major in the Wehrmacht told her about conditions in concentration camps.

> He (the major) told us about motor vans, constructed expressly to gas prisoners. He spoke of huge camps devoted solely to the extermination of civilian minorities by the millions. My flesh crawled. How could anyone believe such fantastic tales?[136]

In another case, two German soldiers told Elizabeth Mermelstein in Pesach, Czechoslovakia, to escape "because there was really such a thing as a concentration camp and they were actually killing the Jewish people."[137] Again Mermelstein was unable to believe them. Her later experiences proved that the warning was real, but she was lucky enough to survive.

The mass killings at Auschwitz ended abruptly. There were no more mass killings after the uprising in Auschwitz in October 1944 because two of the gas chambers had been destroyed.[138] But the real reason was that Himmler was busy negotiating to save his life, and the death camps were shut down to show good faith with the Allies.[139] Orders arrived at Auschwitz on November 17, 1944, to end the killing of any more prisoners.[140] There were approximately 100,000 survivors of Auschwitz, but many were too weak to live long.[141] Many of these survivors were able to testify about how the extermination process operated.

OPERATION REINHARD DEATH CAMPS IN POLAND

The Operation Reinhard death camps in Poland were Belzec, Sobibor, and Treblinka; they operated from March/July 1942 until the winter of 1943. These camps had no other purpose than to exterminate Jews residing in the General Government of Poland. This operation was named in honor of SS-Obergruppenführer Reinhard Heydrich, who had been attacked in Czechoslovakia on May 27, 1942, and later died on June 4. Himmler gave Odilo Globocnik verbal orders to begin the extermination of the Jews in Operation Reinhard because Himmler, like Hitler, opposed giving written orders or any documentation of his involvement in activities against the Jews.[142] Unlike other concentration camps the number of personnel handling operations always remained small. Belzec and Treblinka had 60 to 80 officials and guards, not all of them Germans.[143] Altogether Globocnik had an organization of around 450 men with 92 of them transferred from the euthanasia program.[144]

Belzec started out as a slave labor camp in April 1940 before it was turned into a death camp beginning in November 1941. It was located in the Lublin District of the General Government of Poland about 47 miles north of the city of Lvov. The slave labor camp was dismantled at the end of 1940, but in November 1941 it was reconstituted as a death camp as part of Operation Reinhard (Aktion Reinhard). Actual operations started on March 17, 1942, with Jews shipped in from Lublin and Lvov. During the first stage of the gassings, two to three transports arrived with 150 Jews each, and they were soon killed.[145] SS Colonel General Christian Wirth, a former police officer and a veteran of the T4 euthanasia program, was Belzec's first commandant.[146] Wirth utilized his experience with the euthanasia program to devise ways to improve the killing process. After rejecting the use of Zyklon B, Wirth developed a system of extermination based on carbon monoxide from gasoline and diesel fuel. At first gas vans were used, but later a small gas chamber was torn down and replaced by a much bigger facility.[147] By late spring 1943, the Germans began dismantling the camp. It was the first of Operation Reinhard's camps to close. In June 1943, the camp was dismantled, and the site was ploughed over and disguised as a farm. Somewhere in the neighborhood of 434,500 Jews were killed at Belzec, along with an unknown number of Poles and Gypsies.

Sobibor was an Operation Reinhard death camp designed to kill as many Jews as possible in the shortest time possible. It was built in March 1942 near the small village of Sobibor in the eastern section of the Lublin District of the General Government of Poland. Operations commenced in May 1942. It was the smallest of the death camps, but it gassed in the neighborhood of 260,000 Jews.[148] The head of administration at Sobibor, Hans-Heinz Schütt, explained that it was not always easy to force the Jews into the gas chambers.

Getting the detainees into the gas-chambers did not always proceed smoothly. The detainees would shout and weep and they often refused to get inside. The guards helped them on by violence. These guards were Ukrainian volunteers who were under the authority of the members of the SS Kommando. Members of the SS held key positions in the camp, i.e. one SS man oversaw the unloading (transports), a further SS man led the detainees into the reception camp, a further SS man was responsible for leading the detainees to the undressing area, a further SS man oversaw the confiscation of valuables and a further member of the Kommando had to drive the detainees into the so-called tube which led to the extermination camp. Once they were inside the so-called tube, which led from the hut to the extermination camp, there was no longer any escape.[149]

Sobibor was also the place where 300 or so Jews revolted on October 14, 1943, and overpowered the German and Ukrainian guards and escaped. Few of the escapees survived (47 survived the war), but it caused the Germans to close the camp as soon as possible. The site was torn down, and the area was planted over with trees to disguise it as a farm.

Treblinka opened as a death camp in July 1942 as part of Operation Reinhard. It was the largest and because it was constructed last as a death camp, it had all the improvements learned from the construction of earlier camps. The location of Treblinka was on the Bug River about 65 miles northeast of Warsaw. Its first commandant was SS-Obersturmführer Irmfried Eberl. He was a medical doctor and a veteran of the euthanasia program. The camp had been built under the supervision of an engineer from the T4 euthanasia program, and most of the SS personnel had been active in that program. Eberl proved to be a failure because he was unable to organize the killings at the level that his superiors wanted. Until the construction of larger gas chambers and a better way to dispose of the bodies, there was chaos at Treblinka.

> Because the gassing facilities were prone to technical breakdowns, the camp was unable to cope with such an enormous number of people. Those who could not be forced inside the chambers were shot in the reception camp. More and more prisoners and more and more ditches were needed to bury all those who had been shot, in addition to the thousands who had died during the journey to Treblinka. An excavator from the gravel pit in the nearby Treblinka punishment camp was used for digging additional mass graves.[150]

After an inspection a few weeks after the first transportations of Jews on June 22, 1942, he was fired in August 1942 for inefficiency.[151] His successor was SS-Obersturmführer Franz Stangl. Treblinka operated at peak efficiency only until early January 1943 when the number of transports of Jews began to decline. Himmler visited Treblinka in late winter 1943, and he ordered the gradual closing of the camp and the wholesale burning of all corpses. In the process of the liquidation of the camp, there was a revolt of the Jewish prisoners on August 2, 1943, with a number of prisoners managing to escape.[152] The camp was finally shut down in November 1943, and a farm was built to camouflage the site.[153]

Because none of the Operation Reinhard camps had crematoria, a major problem was always the disposal of bodies. Most common was the burial of the bodies in large burial pits near the death camp. Disposal of so many bodies caused this system to malfunction. Only later did the SS realize that these mass burial pits would leave too much evidence to the advancing Soviets. Orders came down to open the burial pits and burn the bodies.

INDEPENDENT DEATH CAMPS IN POLAND

Chelmno was by far the oldest of the death camps with its establishment in November 1941. It was located about 9 miles from the town of Kolo, Poland, in the General Government of Poland and around 40 miles from Lodz on the main railway line from Lodz to Poznan. The first extermination operation started on December 1, 1941, with Jews from the Kolo neighborhood. As the earliest death camp, it was used for experiments to test the best methods to kill inmates. The first commandant was SS-Obersturmführer and Criminal Police Inspector Herbert Lange, and he experimented with techniques of gassing.[154] Lange used large vans that killed by use of carbon monoxide. His original van had the sign "Kaiser's Coffee Company" on it.[155] Hauptsturmführer Hans Bothmann succeeded Lange as commandant of Chelmno. He continued the use of gas vans as the execution method. Eichmann described the gassing of Jews at Chelmno in the autumn of 1941.

> I saw the following: a room, perhaps, if I remember right, about five times as big as this one here (medium sized room). There were Jews in it. They had to undress and then a sealed truck drove up. The doors were opened, it drove up to a kind of ramp. The naked Jews had to get in. Then the doors were closed and the truck drove off.... I drove after the truck.... And there I saw the most horrible sight I had seen in my life. It drove up to a fairly long trench. The doors were opened and corpses were thrown out. The limbs were as supple as if they'd been alive. Just thrown in.[156]

The vehicle used at Chelmno was one of three special vehicles designed for operations of this kind and still in operation in June 1942. A German civil servant from the Reich Security Head Office noted on June 5, 1942, that these three special vehicles had "processed" 97,000 persons since December 1941.[157] Ultimately 30 such special vehicles, or gassing vans, were delivered to Chelmno and other death camps.[158] According to the estimates of the Reich Security Head Office, these 30 gassing vans could have exterminated the estimated 11 million Jews in six years.[159] This estimate may have been on the high side, and, anyway, the Germans did not have six years to accomplish their extermination of the European Jewish population. At first the bodies were buried in large common graves, but in the spring of 1942 the Germans built two large crematoria to burn the bodies. They also dug up the bodies of previous victims and burned them. It is impossible from the data available to know the exact number of Jews killed at Chelmno, but the best estimate is in the 340,000 range. In the autumn of 1944 the Germans began to dismantle the Chelmno camp and destroy evidence of its existence. The German gas vans were sent back to Germany. The camp closed for good on January 17, 1945, but there were executions by shooting even that night. Only 3 of the estimated number of 152,676 Jews survived the experience of Chelmno. These three, Michel Podchlebnik, Shimon Srebrnik, and Mordechai Zurawski, testified against the SS officers in trials after the war.[160]

Majdanek was another independent death camp. Unlike the other death camps, Majdanek was in an urban area only about three miles from the city center of Lublin, Poland, in the General Government of Poland. It was established in October 1941 as a SS prisoner of war camp. The first commandant of Majdanek was Karl Otto Koch, who had formerly been the commandant at Buchenwald. At first the Germans used the facilities there to house Soviet prisoners of war after the June 1941 invasion of the Soviet Union. Mass transports of Jews began arriving at the Majdanek camp beginning in April 1942. They were killed in gas chambers using Zyklon B poison gas. These executions continued until July 1944. Unlike other death camps, the Waffen-SS ran the camp. Majdanek's Jews were also used for slave labor for munitions works and the Steyr-Daimler-Puch weapons factory. The death toll for Majdanek was around 360,000, but many of the victims were Soviet POWs and Poles, so it is difficult to isolate the number of Jews killed there. It has been estimated that around 125,000 Jews died in Majdanek. The Soviet army found Majdanek only partially destroyed and thousands of inmates still alive when it occupied Lublin after the Germans had deserted it in July 1944.

END OF THE CONCENTRATION CAMP SYSTEM

As the Soviet army advanced from the east and the American, British, and French forces moved in from the west, the SS began to consolidate the concentration camps. Efforts were made to destroy evidence as this consolidation took place. The last two crematoria at Auschwitz were torn down, and the remaining Sondercommandos were executed. Special units of the SS were sent to old mass graves to dig up the bodies and burn them. SS soldiers burned incriminating documents and evidence of the gas chambers. German units drove surviving slave labor in long forced marches to concentration camps within Germany. Besides the harsh conditions of the forced marches, on arrival at camps such as Dachau there was insufficient food and shelter for the new arrivals.[161]

Dachau had been a Category I concentration camp, but conditions there had become desperate by the spring of 1945. The liberation of Dachau in Bavaria took place on April 29, 1945, by elements of the 3rd Battalion, 157th Infantry Regiment, of the U.S. 45th Division. By this time most of the SS guards had fled, leaving only a few hundred SS guards. The temporary commander, Waffen SS-Obersturmführer Heinrich Skodzensky, attempted to surrender the camp but was killed in the confusion. A total of 560 German guards and Waffen SS were killed in summary executions by U.S. forces or camp inmates in a display of revenge.

LEGACY OF THE HOLOCAUST

There was a slowness to recognize the awesome dimensions of the Holocaust. Scholarly attention remained directed on other aspects of the Nazi regime and on the personality and role of Hitler. Survivors' accounts began to trickle out, but there was reluctance to come to grips with what had happened. A concentrated effort to record testimony from survivors came from the Central Historical Commission of Liberated Jews that started in early 1945. This committee was about to record testimony from 2,550 Jewish survivors from 12 different countries that had been under German occupation.[162] Despite efforts of this type, people wanted to forget and resume their lives. Isaac Schipper at the Maidanke concentration camp stated it succinctly.

> Who will believe our stories? No one will want to believe because our misfortune is that of the whole civilized world. We will have the thankless task of proving to the world turning a deaf ear that we are Abel, the murdered brother.[163]

Another explanation came from a survivor of the Dachau concentration camp, the Catholic priest Johannes Neuhaüsler, when commenting on the widely different estimates of the number of inmates that died at Dachau.

> Why this great lack of certainty and the enormous difference between estimates? Is it due to a lack of willingness to speak the truth, to feel and confess guilt, to be accurate and honest? I do not believe so. The root of the evil seems to me to be much deeper in the great secrecy which surrounded the concentration camp at Dachau from the very beginning to the end, as was the case with all concentration camps and all other such extermination centres of the Third Reich.[164]

While this debate over the role of Hitler and the Nazis in the Holocaust continues in historical circles, the ambiguity has given considerable ammunition to the Holocaust denial movement. What is also certain is the Nazi leadership made certain that there would be uncertainties about the Holocaust. Primo Levi, a survivor of the Holocaust, described it best when the SS militiamen told the concentration camp inmates the following story:

> However this war may end, we have won the war against you; none of you will be left to bear witness, but even if someone were to survive, the world will not believe him. There will perhaps be suspicions, discussions, research by historians, but there will be no certainties, because we will destroy the evidence with you. And even if some proof should remain and some of you survive, people will say that the events you describe are too monstrous to be believed: They will say that they are the exaggerations of Allied propaganda and will believe us, who will deny everything, and not you. We will be the ones to dictate the history of the Lagers.[165]

Even in the latter stages of World War II Nazi leaders began a cover-up of the extermination policy of the Final Solution. Himmler ordered the destruction of the death camps in Poland before the Soviet army arrived. He also wanted as few survivors as possible. These measures also included the destruction of written records. His personal secretary, Erika Lorenz, traveled in May 1945 to the SS castle in Fischhorn with the mission to destroy SS secret files, which she promptly did.[166] What prevented the record of German actions from being completely wiped out was the confusion caused by the disintegration of the Nazi regime. Buildings were easier to blow up than destroy all of the written records or kill off all of the survivors. The problem for Holocaust scholars was the spotty survival record of documents and the relatively small number of survivors with factual knowledge about how the system operated. Robert Jan van Pelt explained how witness testimony has been inconsistent.

> Reliable testimony presupposes first of all an accuracy of perception, and many witnesses of Auschwitz made their observations under the most difficult circumstances: suffering from hunger and fatigue amid utter squalor, shorn of their former identity, at best demoralized and more usually at the edge of absolute despair, these people lived without any ability to control even the smallest part of their existence in a completely unintelligible world marked by random violence. As a result, even within valuable testimonies one often finds a range of credibility, ranging from the obviously factual through the plausible to the implausible.[167]

This void of information has been partially filled with accounts from captured concentration camp officials, but again the number of those captured was small. Then, both the death camp sites and many of the documents were unavailable for inspection because they were behind the Iron Curtain. Finally, many former Nazis found it convenient to have memory losses because of the possibility of legal taken against them. What followed was a kind of nationwide collective memory loss. This memory loss also had the sanction of the West German government.

> This "deliberate forgetfulness" which made any dialogue with the survivors of the genocide impossible was to become one of the pillars of postwar Federal Germany's political consensus and stability.[168]

Consequently, the sum total of this is the record has always been incomplete on the Holocaust.

Besides these handicaps, Holocaust deniers have also stacked the decks by instituting roadblocks. Holocaust deniers have adopted a series of requirements that it is difficult to even discuss the Holocaust on their terms. The French scholar Pierre Vidal-Naquet has enumerated them.

1. Any direct testimony contributed by a Jew is either a lie or a fantasy.

2. Any testimony or document prior to the Liberation is a forgery or is not acknowledged or is treated as a "rumor."

3. Any document, in general, with firsthand information concerning the methods of the Nazis is a forgery or has been tampered with.

4. Any Nazi document bearing direct testimony is taken at face value if it is written in coded language, but unacknowledged (or underinterpreted) if it is written plainly . . . . On the other hand, any manifestation of wartime racism in the Allied camp (and they were not lacking, as may be imagined) is taken in the strongest sense.

5. Any Nazi testimony after the end of the war—in trials either in the East or the West, in Warsaw or Cologne, Jerusalem or Nuremberg, in 1945 or 1963, is considered as having been obtained under torture or by intimidation.

6. A vast pseudotechnical arsenal is mobilized to demonstrate the material impossibility of mass gassings.

7. Formerly, God's existence was proven by the notion that existence was contained in the very concept of God. Such was the famous "ontological proof." It may be said that for the "revisionists," the gas chambers did not exist because nonexistence was one of their attributes. Such is the nonontological proof.

8. Finally, anything capable of rendering this frightening story acceptable or believable, of establishing its evolution or furnishing terms for comparison is either unacknowledged or falsified.[169]

PART II

European Holocaust Denial

INTRODUCTION

Postwar Neo-Nazism and the Development of Holocaust Denial

Holocaust denial has played an important role in the revitalization of the neo-Nazi movement. National Socialism had been discredited as a mass ideology by the death of Hitler and the German defeat in World War II. Its cousin Italian Fascism had suffered a similar fate with the ignominious fall of Benito Mussolini. Despite these setbacks, both Nazism and Italian Fascism retained a base of solid supporters in Germany and Italy. There was a smaller but nonetheless vocal number of supporters in other Western European countries and the United States. Fear of an expansionary Soviet Union caused the Allies' denazification program to end prematurely in Germany, leaving former members of the Nazi Party in positions of trust.

These neo-Nazis realized that a Hitlerite regime was impossible, but a reasonable facsimile was possible in the future. For the present, "Hitler's defeat robbed antisemites of the prerequisites for political victory: it stripped them of their legitimacy, destroyed their symbols, elevated their racial enemies, and left them without a viable institutional alternative to the liberal state."[1] This state of affairs was intolerable to the former followers of the Nazi regime. These neo-Nazis and their allies realized that any rehabilitation of Nazism could be accomplished only by discrediting the Holocaust.[2] After all Karl Jaspers, the German philosopher, placed the Holocaust in context.

> Anyone who on the basis of such a judgment plans the organized slaughter of a people and participates in it, does something that's fundamentally different from all crimes that has existed in the past.[3]

This discrediting strategy meant that three types of evidence had to be tarnished or demolished: victim's testimony, challenge of the number of Jews killed during the Holocaust, and rejection of the Nazi use of gas chambers in the concentration camps. Victim's testimonies became suspect because "each testimony is tinged by the limitations of memory and also by the fact that its content has, perforce, been organized retrospectively."[4] It has been difficult to find out the exact number of the dead because much of the information was unavailable because of wartime destruction and so much of it had been behind the Iron Curtain. Finally, it has taken decades of research to reconstruct the gas chambers because the Nazis blew them up to prevent them from discovery by the advancing Soviet army. Nevertheless, the gas chambers become a key issue as Richard J. Green and Jamie McCarthy point out.

> The argument goes that what is physically impossible cannot be true, no matter what testimonial evidence, documentary evidence, or physical evidence is amassed to demonstrate it. No number of witnesses suffices to prove that water can run uphill, and likewise all evidence regarding the Holocaust could be wiped away, if deniers could only prove that gassings were physically impossible.[5]

A corollary argument was that the Allied bombings of German cities, especially Dresden, constituted as serious a war crime as the Holocaust. A prominent French classicist and critic of Holocaust denial has characterized those involved in this campaign as "assassins of memory."[6] Memory of the Holocaust is crucial, and it is best explained by Alain Finkielkraut:

> Memory seeks to know about the genocide while recognizing it as unknowable to guarantee the genocide's presence against oblivion and its distance against reductive discourses, to make the event graspable while keeping it out of our reach, to welcome it without assimilating it.[7]

Holocaust denial has an undeniable relationship with antisemitism. This relationship is best related by Walter Reich in a book review article for the *New York Times*.

> The primary motivation for most deniers is anti-Semitism, and for them the Holocaust is an infuriatingly inconvenient fact of history. After all, the Holocaust has generally been recognized as one of the most terrible crimes that ever took place, and surely the very emblem of evil in the modern age. If that crime was a direct result of anti-Semitism taken to its logical end, then anti-Semitism itself, even when expressed in private conversation, is inevitably discredited among most people. What better way to rehabilitate anti-Semitism, make anti-Semitic arguments seem once again respectable in civilized discourse and even

make it acceptable for governments to pursue anti-Semitic policies than by convincing the world that the great crime for which anti-Semitism was blamed simply never happened—indeed, that it was nothing more than a frame-up invented by the Jews and propagated by them through their control of the media? What better way, in short, to make the world safe for anti-Semitism than by denying the Holocaust?[8]

It can also be stated that there is more than one category of Holocaust denier. There are the so-called "hard" and "soft" Holocaust denier schools. The hard-liners completely deny the existence of the Holocaust with no reservation. They consider the Holocaust to be propaganda initiated by Jews and Zionists to punish the Germans. In contrast, the adherents of the soft line accept the fact that there was a large loss of life among Jews during World War II, but these deaths were not part of a systemic plan of the Nazi government to commit genocide. Despite these differences in outlook, they agree on certain essential tenets as outlined by Pierre Naquet-Vidal. (1) "There was no genocide and the instrument symbolizing it, the gas chamber, never existed." (2) "The 'final solution' was never anything other than the expulsion of the Jews toward eastern Europe." (3) "The number of Jewish victims of Nazism is far smaller than has been claimed." (4) "Hitler's Germany does not bear the principal responsibility for the Second World War." (5) "The principal enemy of the human race during the 1930s and 1940s was not Nazi Germany but Stalin's Soviet Union." (6) "The genocide was an invention of Allied propaganda, which was largely Jewish, and specifically Zionist."[9]

The existence and use of gas chambers in the concentration camps is the critical issue to both the Holocaust and Holocaust deniers. This is the reason for the intense debate in recent years over the existence and operation of gas chambers. Raul Hilberg expresses it best:

You built a gas chamber with a view to killing a mass of people. Once you have a gas chamber, you have a vision, and the vision is total annihilation. In a gas chamber, you don't see the victim. So the gas chamber in that sense is more dangerous, the gas chamber is more criminal. The gas chamber has wider implications. So when you deny the gas chamber, you deny not just a part of the event, you deny one of the defining concepts. Auschwitz has become the synonym for the Holocaust. And of course you deny, apart from anything else, the death of several million people.[10]

French Holocaust Denial

INTRODUCTION

The Holocaust denial movement started soon after the end of World War II. French antisemitism before 1945 was the traditional right-wing antisemitism common in most European countries. It had its roots in the late nineteenth century, and the turmoil surrounding the Dreyfus Affair only magnified its appeal to the right-wing conservatives. Throughout the early twentieth century antisemitism continued to be identified almost exclusively with the French right wing. The Great Depression and the Stavisky Affair in January 1934 caused antisemitism to grow among right-wing groups seeking to overthrow the Third Republic. Antisemitism reached a high point in 1936 with the Popular Front and its Prime Minister Léon Blum.

The first regime in France that made antisemitism part of its program was the Vichy regime. Collaboration with the Germans in turning over French Jews for the death camps made the Vichy regime a partner in the Holocaust. The Vichy regime passed laws against Jews even without pressure from the Germans. The first deportation of foreign Jews in France to Auschwitz began in March 1942, and it was soon followed by the deportation of French Jews.[1] In total between 80,000 and 90,000 Jews were deported to Auschwitz from March 1942 to August 1944 with most of them dying there.[2]

The revival of antisemitism in France since 1945 has had to face the specter of the Holocaust. Right-wing groups have been forced to confront the Holocaust before there could be a successful rehabilitation of the Vichy regime. Old-style political antisemites still exist in France, but most of them have embraced Holocaust denial, or as the French call it, "negationism," to be influential. What has helped them is that little more than a third of the French accept that between 5 and 6 million Jews died during the Holocaust.[3]

France was slow to recognize the Holocaust because most of its attention was on the returning of French deportees and prisoners of war. Because left-wing and resistance circles gave such little attention to the Holocaust, it became easier for antisemitic propagandists to reappear and claim that the Jews had suffered no more than others.[4] Despite the slowness of antisemitism to reestablish itself as a political force in France, the French have been the most active of the Europeans in Holocaust denial. They started out sooner, and for several decades most of the significant Holocaust denial writings came out of France. The initial impetus for Holocaust denial in France was the Louis Darquier de Pellepoix interview in the French weekly *L'Express* on November 4, 1978, during which he stated that the gas chambers and the Holocaust itself were creations of satanic Jewish propaganda.[5] Shortly afterward antisemitic and Holocaust denial tracts began appearing in increasing numbers. Already active long before 1978 were the two most important of the early French Holocaust deniers—Paul Rassinier and Maurice Bardèche. They had been prominent Holocaust deniers long before this controversy, and they came out of different political traditions.

Before surveying the prominent individuals and their impact in French Holocaust denial, there are three factors that make the French unique. First, Holocaust denial has penetrated into French academia more so than any other country. Henry Rousso has demonstrated this fact in his report on the University of Lyon III.[6] Second, Holocaust denial has found a home on both the extreme Right and the extreme Left.[7] Third, Islamist groups in France have embraced Holocaust denial to challenge the justification for the foundation of Israel.

PAUL RASSINIER AND THE BEGINNING OF THE INTERNATIONAL HOLOCAUST DENIAL DEBATE

The first important figure in the early days of French Holocaust denial was Paul Rassinier. He was born on March 18, 1906, in Beaumont, a small village near Montbéliard. His training was as an educator, and before World War II he taught first as a grade-school teacher and then as a history and geography teacher at the secondary school in Faubourg Montbéliard.

Rassinier had a checkered political past both before and after World War II. His pre–World War II political orientation had been first as a Communist joining the French Communist Party soon after its founding in 1922. Leaving the Communist Party in 1932, Rassinier migrated to the Socialist Party (SFIO), joining in the mid-1930s. Rassinier belonged to the pacifist wing of the SFIO, and he supported wholeheartedly the Munich Agreement with Hitler in 1938. He also violently protested the German-Soviet Pact in 1939. During World War II, he joined the French resistance against German occupation. He was the editor of the resistance journal *La IVe République*. After his arrest in October 1943, the Gestapo tortured him for information before deporting him to a German concentration camp. Most of his time in the German concentration camps of Buchenwald and Dora was spent in the infirmary.[8] After release from a concentration camp at the end of the war, Rassinier returned to France on a stretcher and was considered a total invalid. He won election as a Socialist deputy for Belfort in the Second Constituent Assembly. Defeated in the first postwar election for the Legislative Assembly in 1946, Rassinier retired from politics and left Belfort for Paris.

In postwar France Rassinier had begun to reexamine his experiences in the concentration camp. Rassinier had come to identify more with the SS guards than he did the Communists who ran the camp internally. He blamed the Communists for the harsh conditions at Buchenwald and Dora. Conditions at Buchenwald and Dora were harsh and deaths did occur on a daily basis, but neither camp was a death camp where wholesale exterminations took place. Executions took place, but gas chambers were not used at Buchenwald. What Rassinier never accepted was that the death camps had been situated in Poland deliberately to isolate them from the German populace to avoid publicity and discontent. Moreover, Rassinier was a political prisoner and not Jewish, so he avoided much of the negative attention directed by prison guards against Jews. Despite his different experiences, he also became suspicious of survivors' accounts of life in the camps.

> With my argument concerning the bureaucracy of the concentration camps in which I clarified this bureaucracy's determining role in the systemization of the horror it is the new light I've shed on the gas chambers which has the most seriously damaged sacred images of the concentration camps [. . .]. I am therefore justified in saying that all those who, like David Rousset or Eugen Kogon, have offered detailed and heart wrenching descriptions of their operation, based these descriptions solely on gossip. This—let me be precise in order not to have any new misunderstandings—doesn't mean in any way that there had not been extermination by gas. The existence of the installation is one thing, its purpose is another, and a third is its actual utilization. In the second instance it is remarkable that, in all the publications about concentration camps or at the Nuremberg trials, no document could be produced proving the fact that the gas chambers had been installed in the German prison camps by government order with the purpose of having them used for the massive extermination of detainees. Witnesses, for the most part officers and non-commissioned officers and seven simple SS soldiers, most certainly did say that they had carried out exterminations by gas and that they had received orders to do so. None of them was able to produce the order they were hiding behind and none of these orders [. . .] has been found in the archives of the camps at the time of the

Liberation. It was thus necessary to take these witnesses at their word. Who can prove to me that they did not testify in this way in order to save their lives in the atmosphere of terror, which began to take hold in Germany the day after it, had been crushed.[9]

Over the years Rassinier had become more convinced in questioning the Holocaust, and he began to write books on the subject.

His slide into revisionism and denial came when he made the shift from inter-preting these accounts as the normal confabulation and confusion that occurs in all eyewitness testimony, to speculating that these people might be deliber-ately lying. From this assumption he extrapolated that the number of Jewish victims must also have been exaggerated and published his own estimate that only about one and half million died.[10]

In 1948, he wrote the book *Crossing the Line* (*La Passage de la ligne*) in which he began his defense of the Nazis and his attack on the Jews.[11] His thesis was that it was the fault of the prisoners, not the Nazi guards, for bad conditions in the camps.[12] Rassinier also repudiated survivor testimony about concentration camps. At first, Rassinier allowed that the Germans had used gas chambers with the stipulation that there were not as many of these gas chambers as had been reported, but later he denied their existence.[13] Pierre Vidal-Naquet added by stating that Rassinier's book was

Excellent as testimony by the author of what he experienced, interesting when criticizing other witnesses of Buchenwald and Dora and revealing those in charge of a political apparatus run principally by communist deportees, it becomes frankly absurd, even heinous, when dealing with what the author had no knowledge of: the extermination camps, and principally Auschwitz.[14]

Rassinier's writings attracted the support of the anarcho-Marxist editor Pierre Guillaume and his publishing house La Vieille Taupe (The Old Mole). He decided in 1950 to publish his next book *The Lie of Ulysses* (*Le Mensonge d'Ulysse*).[15] This book continued his attacks on the testimony of concentration camp survivors. By this time the former Communist and Socialist had made the political transition to the French radical right wing. Rassinier's former Socialist allies had expelled him from the SFIO in April 1951.[16] His association with other French right-wingers and his growing antisemitism led him to become critical of the Holocaust. Rassinier began to associate with notorious French antisemites such as Henry Coston.[17] In his 1964 book *The Drama of the European Jews* (Le Drame des Juifs Europeéns), Rassinier defended the Nazis against charges of using gas cham-bers against concentration camp Jews.[18] Rassinier had come to blame the Zionists for perpetuating a hoax.[19] He, in particular, attacked Raul Hilberg, the Jewish author of *The Destruction of the European Jews,* which had appeared in 1961, for his research conclusions on the Holocaust.[20] Rassinier maintained that the Final Solution of the Jewish problem was a massive shift of the Jewish population and only between 500,000 and 1 million Jews died.[21]

By the mid-1960s Rassinier had become the leader of the French Holocaust denial movement, and at the same time his views became accepted abroad. The American revisionist historian Harry Elmer Barnes became acquainted with Rassinier's views and broadcast them to an American audience through his writings.[22] Deborah Lipstadt characterized Rassinier's books as "a mixture of blatant falsehoods, half-truths, quotations out of context, and attacks on the 'Zionist establishment.' "[23] Rassinier continued to move to more radical positions until his death in 1967.

Rassinier has a unique status in the Holocaust denial movement. As a survivor of the German concentration camp system, he was acclaimed as an authority that no other Holocaust denier can match. His writings have achieved the pinnacle of believability in the Holocaust denial movement so that his mocking of Holocaust survivors has been accepted without questioning. But in France his death in 1967 went almost unnoticed.[24] His death also ended the first phase of the French Holocaust denial movement.

LOUIS-FERDINAND CÉLINE AND THE DEVELOPMENT OF HOLOCAUST DENIAL

The famous French writer Louis-Ferdinand Céline was an early Holocaust denier, and in his case it was a natural outgrowth of his virulent antisemitism. He was born in 1894 in Paris of parents from Brittany. His birth name was Louis-Ferdinand Destouches. Céline, a wounded veteran of World War I, was a convinced antisemite. His original antisemitism had been augmented by his exposure to Henry Ford's brand of antisemitism during his stay as a doctor in the Ford Motor Company in Detroit, Michigan.

Céline began to write novels, and he became an overnight literary sensation. He became famous for his first book *Journey to the End of the Night* in 1932, and he had it followed by a best seller *Death on the Installment Plan* in 1936. Then, he had a book that appeared in 1937, *Trifles for a Massacre* (*Bagatelles pour un massacre*), which was a diatribe against Jews and their influence on French society. Later, Céline wrote two other novels, *The School of Cadavers* (*L'Ecole des cadavers*) and *The Fine Mess* (*Les beaux draps*), that had antisemitic themes. Nicholas Fraser described Céline's views in the following light:

> Céline's racism, for instance, was of the deepest, blackest kind based on his conception of culture. He believed that civilization, if it meant anything at all, should be founded on the difference between groups or individuals. Céline was sufficiently well educated to understand that the race theories implied by

German anti-Semitism were nonsense—indeed he found the seriousness of Germans ridiculous. But culture was important to him, and he believed that a culture could die as easily as any other organism. Looking around him, Céline announced that France was mortally threatened. The last vestiges of Frenchness would be extinguished in the next war. The "bagatelles" of which he wrote were a form of consolation offered before the imminent prospect of Armageddon, and they consisted of telling Fellow French that it remained the obligation of every Frenchman to hate Jews.[25]

Céline's antisemitism grew more intense as war with Nazi Germany appeared imminent. In the late 1930s, Céline campaigned for a French alliance with Hitler because he feared that the Jews would drag France into a war.[26] His hatred for the Jews extended to his challenging the German author Ernst Jünger during World War II, questioning why the Germans were not killing every Jew.[27] His relationship with the Nazis occupying France was rocky because of his eccentric behavior and radical views. He was tolerated because of his literary reputation. This tolerance ended with the German evacuation of Paris and the installation of the Charles de Gaulle government.

Céline fled to Denmark in 1945, and the French government sentenced him to death in absentia. These charges were dropped, however, after he returned to France in 1950. Céline never repudiated his antisemitic views, and he made public statements denying the Holocaust.[28] His antisemitic books remain banned in France and have not been republished for over 50 years, and they have never been translated into English. Many European Holocaust deniers and neo-Nazis consider Céline and his virulent antisemitism to be a precursor to their ideas, and they claim him as one of them.

MAURICE BARDÈCHE AND HOLOCAUST DENIAL

Another prominent early Holocaust denier was the neo-Fascist leader Maurice Bardèche. Born into a family of civil servants in a small town near Bourges, Bardèche attended Lycée Louis-le-Grand in Paris, where his best friend was Robert Brasillach. Under Brasillach's leadership Bardèche became active in the prewar antisemitic extreme right wing.[29] He decided to pursue an academic career completing a thesis on Honoré de Balzac. After a brief stay as a temporary professor at the Sorbonne, Bardèche found a job at the University of Lyons in 1942. His commitment to right-wing causes led him to become a supporter of the Vichy regime of Marshal Philippe Pétain. Bardèche had married Brasillach's sister, Suzanne, in 1934, and he was outraged by Brasillach's execution for crimes against the French state on February 6, 1945.

After a brief arrest in September 1944 for writing three literary articles in the Vichyite *Je suis partout*, Bardèche spent the next few years defending the actions and policies of the Vichy regime by publishing in 1947 the book *Letter to François Mauriac* (*Lettre à François Mauriac*). Then in 1948 Bardèche wrote another book, *Nuremberg or the Promised Land* (*Nuremberg ou la terre promise*), defending the German army and attacking the Nuremberg Trials for placing German generals on trial. As part of his defense of the Nazis, he contended that the Holocaust never happened.[30] Bardèche outlined the general position of subsequent Holocaust deniers by advocating certain principles: (1) Jews are responsible for World War II, (2) eyewitnesses are not reliable, (3) horrors of the communist regime should not be forgotten, (4) atrocities committed in the camps are committed by the deported, (5) after the first defeats of the Germans, things became more difficult in the camps, (6) at no time did the National Socialist regime want to exterminate the Jews, and (7) if there was gas at Auschwitz, it was to prevent disease.[31] This work landed him in legal difficulties with French authorities, but, after a lengthy trial, he served only several days in jail in July 1954 and a fine.[32] Other of his works defended both Hitler and Nazism as bulwarks against Communism.

Holocaust denial became a crusade for Bardèche. Most European neo-Nazis wanted to rehabilitate Hitler to reestablish a facsimile of a Nazi regime, but Bardèche and other French neo-Fascists had a different agenda. Bardèche and others believed that it would be impossible to refurbish the reputation of Marshal Philippe Pétain and whitewash the Vichy regime without denying the Holocaust. Consequently, he and his colleagues made every effort to deny the existence of the extermination camps for the Jews because the Vichy regime had been active in transporting French Jews to Germany.

Besides defending Nazis and promoting Holocaust denial, Bardèche became active in the establishment of the Pan-European Movement. In 1951, he helped form the European Social Movement (Mouvement Social Européen, or MSE). Then in 1952, Bardèche launched the journal *Defense of the West* (*Défense de l'Occident*) with the idea of promoting an independent Europe free from the influence of either the Soviet Union or the United States. Later this journal began publishing articles by Holocaust deniers. At the same time that his publications supported neo-Nazism and Holocaust denial, Bardèche established a reputation as a French literary scholar. Bardèche was also active in the French New Right, and he was a devotee of the Group for the Research and Study for a European Civilization (Groupement de recherche et d'études pour la civilisation européenne, or GRECE) of Alain de Benoist. His overt Fascist orientation made him a controversial figure in Holocaust denial circles then and now, but his political viewpoint has not prevented Holocaust deniers from borrowing many of his ideas.[33] Bardèche remained active in the Holocaust denial movement until his death in 1998.

FRANÇOIS DUPRAT—HOLOCAUST DENIAL'S FIRST MARTYR

François Duprat was a young French historian and politician who was murdered for his advocacy of Holocaust denial. He was born on October 26, 1940, in Corsica. His academic achievements at Bayonne and Toulouse earned him acceptance into the prestigious Lycée Louis-le-Grand in Paris. He earned a diploma of higher studies in history in 1963. He worked as a schoolteacher. His first political orientation was as a Trotskyite, but this political belief lasted only a short time.

Duprat became active in French right-wing politics. His patron was the French Fascist Maurice Bardèche. In 1960, he was one of the co-founders of the Federation of Nationalist Students (Fédération des étudiants nationalists). His commitment to French Fascism and Holocaust denial made him the natural successor and spiritual heir to Bardèche.[34] He also began a career as a revisionist historian with the publication of his book in 1967 entitled *History of the SS* (*Histoire des SS*). Duprat's antisemitism led him to become a vigorous defender of the Palestinian cause after the Israeli victory in the 1967 Six-Day War. In the early 1970s, Duprat began an association of like-minded neo-Fascists in an organization called New Order (Ordre Nouveau). This group wanted to establish a right-wing revolutionary part to change the French political scene.

Duprat was one of the co-founders and chief theoreticians of the National Front (Front National) in October 1972. Jean-Marie Le Pen soon took over leadership of the National Front after the directors of the party appointed him to be its president. Duprat's co-founders Alain Robert and François Brigneau soon left the Front National over ideological and personal reasons, but Duprat remained to become one of its leaders. Duprat's goal was a political career that would take him to the forefront of French politics.[35] At the same time, Duprat was active both as an anti-Zionist and as a Holocaust denier, and he brought these issues into the National Front. Nicolas Lebourg placed Duprat's ideas in context.

> In sum, one sees the resurgence of the idea of Drumont, enriched by all the antisemitic-anticapitalist-anti-Zionist discourses. It is the return to legitimacy— the neo-fascists can thus finally situate themselves besides the oppressed and not the oppressor, to make reborn "the fascism of the left," but also against the Jews. The first means of domination will be, Duprat believes, the "myth of the Shoah", thus he becomes the principal negativist propagandist.[36]

Duprat was active in the Front National. He participated and was on the editorial board of the journal of the Front National, *Le National*. His campaigning for Le Pen in the May 1974 presidential election solidified his position in the party. In 1977 and early 1978 Duprat was active in organizing Le Pen's next run for the presidency.

Duprat was also active as a historian. He was editor of neo-Fascist journals *The European Action* (L'Action Européenne) and the *Review of the History of Fascism* (*Revue d'Histoire du Fascisme*). Besides writing a book on American Fascism, *American Fascism 1924–1941* (*Les Fascismes Americanes 1924–1941*) with a colleague, Duprat was active in publicizing the works of Paul Rassinier. He also translated into French the Richard Verrall (Richard E. Harwood) book *Did Six Million Really Die?* His research into the Holocaust began with an article "The Mystery of the Gas Chambers." By the mid-1970s Duprat was considered the chief theorician of the French extreme Right.[37]

The murder of Duprat on March 18, 1978, was gruesome. He and his wife were traveling to Normandy when his automobile blew up. Besides killing Duprat instantly, it blew off both of his wife's legs. Shortly before this attack, in 1977 his name and address had been publicized by the Jewish leader Patrice Chairoff. A couple of Jewish extremist groups claimed responsibility for the bombing, but French authorities were never able to find the culprits. Duprat had built a reputation as a neo-Fascist and Holocaust denier when his career came to an abrupt end. Since his death Duprat has been cited repeatedly as the first martyr of the Holocaust denial movement.

AMBIGUOUS POSITION OF JEAN-MARIE LE PEN AND THE FRONT NATIONAL

Jean-Marie Le Pen has kept the Front National away from overt displays of antisemitism, but the extreme Right of the party has continued to flirt with antisemitism and Holocaust denial. The Front National originated out of the French extreme Right's New Order (Ordre Nouveax). Its founders, Alain Robert, François Brigneau, and François Duprat, wanted to establish a grand gathering of the French extreme Right in order to form a national political party. Soon after the founding of the Front National on October 8, 1972, the six members of the directors committee selected Le Pen as its president. Robert and Brigneau soon left the party, but Duprat remained. Duprat's advocacy of Fascism and Holocaust denial made him the leader of the party's extreme Right. Duprat's death in 1978 removed him as a potential threat to Le Pen's leadership of the party.

Le Pen has been careful that no leader would appear to challenge his position as the head of the Front National. Yet it is certain that Le Pen holds antisemitic views and they surface on occasion.[38] Most famous was his 1987 remark that gas chambers during the Holocaust were a "detail" in the history of World War II. This remark caused him to come into conflict with the Fabius-Gayssot law on negationism. A French court condemned him to pay 183,200 euros for this offense. He compounded the issue in a December 1996 press conference in Germany during which he reaffirmed that the gas chambers were merely a "detail." This act led a Munich court in June 1999 to fine Le Pen for his remarks that minimized the Holocaust. He also in 1988 played a word game on the surname of the French Jewish politician Michel Durafour and the French word for crematory.

Le Pen is aging and there is competition to replace him as head of the Front National. Le Pen's daughter, Marine Le Pen, is one of the challengers for succession. Her goal is to make the party broader and make it a serious participant in the competition for national office. The other challenger is Bruno Gollnisch, a former right-wing professor from Lyon III.[39] Gollnisch is violently anti-semitic, and in October 2004 he openly acknowledged his Holocaust denial views.[40] Le Pen has backed Gollnisch against his daughter, so the issue is still open as to where the Front National is going. One problem that remains is that the Front National's anti-immigrant platform prevents it from cultivating Muslims who share the party's views on Israel and Holocaust denial.

ROLE OF ROBERT FAURISSON

Robert Faurisson is the leading French Holocaust denier in Europe. He was born in 1929 in Shepperton, England. His father was French and his mother Scotch. Faurisson began his schooling in Singapore, and the family did not arrive in France till 1936. He attended several religious schools before entering the prestigious Lycée Henri-IV in Paris. A fellow student at the lycée, Pierre Vidal-Naquet, did not remember him fondly.[41] While at the lycée, Faurisson already showed his admiration for Maurice Bardèche and his neo-Fascist and Holocaust denial ideas. He entered the University of Paris at the Sorbonne where he studied comparative literature. In 1974, he received his doctorate from the Sorbonne with the thesis "Psychology in the Novel of Marivaux" ("La Psychologie dans le roman de Marivaux"). His academic specialty was in his words in revealing "the real meaning of texts."[42] He named this process the "Ajax method" because "it scours as it cleans as it shines."[43] After years of teaching at a girl's lycée in Vichy, he was offered a lectureship in contemporary literature at the right-wing University of Lyon III. His literary work there was controversial. His two books, *A-t-on lu Rimbaud?* (*Has Anybody Read Rimbaud?*) (1961) and *A-t-on lu Lautréamont?* (*Has Anybody Read Lautreamont?*) (1972), produced a major controversy in French literary periodicals. Despite political controversy, Faurisson remained at the University of Lyon III until his retirement in 1990.

While at the Sorbonne, Faurisson became a convert to Holocaust denial after reading a letter by Martin Broszat in *Die Zeit* in August 1960. Broszat stated in this letter that there were no gas chambers at German concentration camps within Germany.[44] Of course, this is true because the death camps with the gas chambers were in Poland. Next, he read the writings of Paul Rassinier, which reinforced his belief that the Holocaust was a myth.[45] Faurisson began a correspondence with Rassinier, and Rassinier offered

encouragement for him to deny the Holocaust. Armed with this encouragement, Faurisson openly joined the ranks of the Holocaust deniers on July 27,
1974, by publishing a letter in the weekly newspaper *Le Canard enchaîné*
(Paris) in which he challenged the claim that the Nazis had planned the geno-
cide of the Jews He followed this up with a 1980 book *Testimony in Defense:
Against Those Who Accuse Me of Falsifying History: The Question of the
Gas Chambers* (*Mémoire en défense: Contre ceux qui m'accusent de falsifier
l'histoire: La question des chambers à gaz*) published by Guillaume's La
Vieille Taupe. This book is most famous for the introduction by Noam
Chomsky.

Faurisson's Holocaust denial arguments led to him facing a series of trials
that lasted from 1979 to 1983 for falsification of history. During those years,
Faurisson continued to maintain that Hitler never authorized the elimination of the Jews and that the Holocaust is an invention of the Zionists.[46]
He wrote a number of anti-Holocaust works that had been published by
La Vieille Taupe and its editor Guillaume. He escaped from these trials paying only minor fines and after receiving considerable financial and moral
support from both the French extremist Right and the extremist Left. His
most serious run-in with the French government was over his remarks in
an article in *Le Monde* on June 30, 1981, in which Faurisson stated,

> The alleged Hitlerian gas chambers and the so-called genocide of the Jews form
> a single historical lie whose principal beneficiaries are the State of Israel and
> international Zionism and whose principal victims are the German people, but
> not its leaders, and the Palestinian people in its entirety.[47]

Faurisson's high profile made him unpopular among elements in French
society. He suffered verbal abuse on many occasions, but he was always able
to hold his own. In September 1980, he was assaulted by alleged Jewish
assailants near his home in Vichy, France, and he suffered a badly shattered
jaw.[48] Faurisson survived his assault, and it did little to stop him from asserting his Holocaust denial views.

Throughout the 1980s Faurisson established closer working relationships
with the international Holocaust denial circle and in the process became
more radical in his views. By this time, Faurisson had established his methodology of challenging the evidence of gas chambers at Auschwitz and other
Holocaust documents by applying textual exegesis to history.[49] His association with the neo-Nazi movement and the German-Canadian neo-Nazi
Ernst Zündel became close.[50] He testified as a defense witness at both the
1985 and 1988 Zündel trials in Canada. At the 1985 trial the Crown pros-
ecutor asked him to explain the missing 6 million Jews and "Faurisson
acknowledged that he did not know what happened to them but urged surviving Jews to give him the names of family members they had lost so he
could try to locate them."[51] Of course, Faurisson never carried out this

promise. Faurisson also became the champion of *The Leuchter Report* that allegedly proved scientifically that the Germans had not used chambers.[52] By this time Faurisson had become affiliated with Willis A. Carto's Institute for Historical Review. Then he supported the appearance of the French Holocaust denial journal *Annals of Revisionist History (Annales d'histoire Révisionnniste)*. Faurisson's anti-Holocaust activities caught up with him in 1983. The Paris Court of Appeal convicted him on April 25, 1983, for the falsification of history for the following statement:

> The alleged Hitlerian gas chambers and the so-called genocide of the Jews formed a single historical lie whose principal beneficiaries are the State of Israel and the International Zionism and whose principal victims are the German people but not its leaders, and the Palestinian people in its entirety.[53]

Partly because of his notoriety and age, Faurisson retired from the University of Lyon III in 1990. Then later in 1990 French Parliament passed a law against "criminal revisionism." In March 1991 Faurisson was convicted of violating this law.[54] Since then, Faurisson has not let legal troubles, injuries, or negative publicity prevent him from traveling in France and Europe, lecturing on his Holocaust denial views. His most recent appearance of note was at the Iranian government's sponsored conference "Review of the Holocaust: Global Vision" held December 11–12, 2006, in Tehran, Iran.

The influence of Faurisson cannot be exaggerated. He had an academic reputation before becoming a Holocaust denier. But his real importance is in establishing a pseudoscientific basis for Holocaust denial

> One the other hand, the interest of the Faurisson pieces, like those of Anglo-Saxon negationists translated in the 1970s, lies in the fact that they develop a pseudo-scientific jargon different from the texts of Maurice Bardèche or of Paul Rassinier. This offers them the possibility of removing their ideas from the clandestine where they were developed and voicing them on a larger, more public stage. There they can be transformed from simple ideological topoi which are hardly noticed into objects of scientific "debate" founded on "objective" facts and leading to "arguable" theories.[55]

FAURISSON'S LEFT-WING ALLIES

Much of the popularity of Faurisson's ideas in France has come from support from his left-wing Marxist supporters. Pierre Guillaume, the owner of the book store La Vieille Taupe (the Old Mole) and an intransigent Marxist, decided in the early 1950s to publish books by Paul Rassinier. What attracted Guillaume and his small group of anarcho-Marxists was Rassinier's strong anti-Stalinist bent.[56] Alain Finkielkraut's masterful study of the issue in his book *The Future of a Negation: Reflection on the Question of Genocide* (1982) explains the ideological background of Guillaume's version of

Marxist. Exactly how this ideology led Guillaume and his compatriots to accept Holocaust denial is explained in Finkielkraut's words:

> And needless to say, these militants participate in the falsification with a good faith that is beyond suspicion. No task is too daunting for them when it comes to conforming the face of history to the unflinching restrictive idea they make of it. They *know* that the gas chambers are a myth in the same way that Wilhelm Liebknecht knew that Dreyfus was guilty. Auschwitz serves their enemy's purpose, hence their fervor to contest the evidence of its reality by every means possible, including the most fraudulent. For the evidence of genocide is just so many deceptions, so many traps laid for anticapitalist radicality, designed to force it into dishonest compromise and eventual loss of resolve.[57]

This resolve to support Holocaust denial by publishing and republishing books with Holocaust denying themes on the part of Guillaume and his fellow Marxists has never wavered since the early 1970s. These left-wing Marxists are not advocates of antisemitism, but rather consider it a system of the capitalist system that they are combating. What they find offensive is that the Jews have claimed a crime worse "than the wrong to which the working class is subjected daily."[58]

> The attraction of the theories of Rassinier and later Faurisson for groups such as the Vieille Taupe can be explained by a greater receptiveness to theories of conspiracy, to "cryptohistory" and "hypercriticism," but also by their inability to admit that the extermination of the Jews did not arise from a materialist logic. Their inability to admit this carried them to the point of denying the existence of the Holocaust because it did not conform to the logic of class struggle. Their negationism, like that of Rassinier, also derived from a rabid anti-Stalinism that led them to minimize Nazi crimes.[59]

This philosophy led Guillaume in 1978 to back Faurisson and his theory denying the Holocaust by publishing Faurisson's works.

Most of the extreme leftists have turned their hostility toward Israel. They characterize Israel in the following terms:

> Yet the stereotypes of Jews that are found in the literature of the political left are extremely negative, reflecting as they do a built-in visceral hatred of Israel and Zionism. Thus the Israelis are invariably militarist, aggressive, expansionist, fascist oppressors; colonizers who ruthlessly confiscate other people's lands; blackmailers who try to silence criticism by playing on the Holocaust; and, worst of all, modern practitioners of "genocide" against the Palestinian people.[60]

SERGE THION

Serge Thion is a Holocaust denier with close connections to Pierre Guillaume and La Vieille Taupe. He was born in 1942. He studied sociology, anthropology, history, and linguistics at the University of Paris–Sorbonne. After seven years of study, he received a doctorate in sociology in 1967 with a dissertation on the South African political system of Apartheid. Later, his revised dissertation appeared under the title *Le pouvoir pâle, ou le racisme sud-africain* in 1969. After a stint of teaching in Vietnam and Cambodia in the years between 1967 and 1970, Thion returned to France where he found a position in 1971 as a research fellow with the National Center for Scientific Research (CNRS) in Paris. Most of his research activities at the CNRS concerned Cambodia, Vietnam, and Africa.

Thion became a convert to Holocaust denial. He collaborated with Robert Faurisson in the book *Historical Truth or Political Truth?* (*Vérité historique ou vérité politique?*). In this book Thion expressed the views of Holocaust deniers on the authenticity of the confessions of Nazi leaders.

> Once one is prepared to imagine the situation of those defeated men, gambling with their own lives between the hands of their jailers, a paltry game in which truths and lies are the basic tokens in a tactic of survival, one will not be prepared to accept all their declarations as valid currency.[61]

His Holocaust denial activities led the CNRS to fire him in November 2000. One of his critics was the writer Didier Daeninckx. Thion's attacks on Daeninckx led a Correctional Tribunal Court of Appeal to condemn him on December 4, 2002, for defamation and fined him.

Since his firing, Thion has become even more active in the Holocaust denial movement. He was prominent at the Iranian Holocaust Denial Conference on December 11, 2006, in Tehran, Iran, sponsored by Iran President Mahmoud Ahmadinejad. Like many of his leftist colleagues, Thion champions Holocaust denial as an expression of freedom of speech and an attack on the capitalist system.

HENRI ROQUES AND HIS CONTRIBUTION TO HOLOCAUST DENIAL

Henri Roques made headlines in the 1980s because of his advocacy of Holocaust denial in his critique of an early German reporter of the Holocaust. He was born in 1920 in Lyon, France. Most of his career Roques worked as an agricultural engineer. He also had been a member of the antisemitic and neo-Nazi French Phalange (Phalanges Française) serving as its secretary general. Beginning in the mid-1950s and continuing to Rassinier's death in 1967, Roques maintained a correspondence and friendship with Rassinier. Roques's antisemitic and neo-Nazi background made it easy for him to become a Holocaust denier.

Roques decided in the late 1970s to attack the testimony of former Waffen-SS officer Kurt Gerstein. Gerstein had been the head of the Technical

Disinfection Department of the Waffen-SS charged with the task of improving the efficiency of the gas chambers in German concentration camps. This
mission meant that Gerstein had to visit all the death camps, and what he
saw there horrified him. Gerstein had never been a dedicated Nazi because
of his religious views and the euthanasia of his sister, but the inhumanity
of the mass executions in the gas chambers sickened him. Instead of ignoring
what was happening, Gerstein risked his life to pass information about the
Final Solution to the Allies. After the war, Gerstein turned over a detailed
report on the murders at Belzec and Treblinka. He died in a French military
prison on July 25, 1945, under mysterious circumstances. Because of his
report, Gerstein has long been an obstacle to the thesis of the Holocaust
deniers that the gas chambers never existed in the German concentration
camp system, so he was a tempting target. Rassinier had told Roques that
Gerstein was the most damaging witness to the existence of gas chambers
at German concentration camps.[62]

Roques decided that his mission as a Holocaust denier was to discredit
Gerstein and his report. His intention was to write a dissertation on Gerstein
that would discredit him. Roques searched the report for discrepancies in an
effort to discredit Gerstein. Acceptance of his findings by a dissertation committee would give credence to his dissertation and its charges. The problem
was to find French historians who would buy into his dissertation and its
thesis. He marketed it to the University of Paris IV, but he could not find
enough support. Roques found a right-wing medieval literature professor
at the University of Nantes to serve as an advisor. Roques received his degree
for his dissertation *The Confessions of Kurt Gerstein: Comparative Study of
Different Versions: Edition Critical* (*Les confessions de Kurt Gerstein, étude
comparative des différentes versions: Édition critique*).

The ensuing controversy of Roques and his dissertation divided French
academia. Roques had supporters who defended academic freedom, but
other academics found his methods and his research repugnant. There were
charges that there were irregularities in the examining jury, including the
charge that a signature of an absent member of the jury had been falsified.[63]
These irregularities led the French government to look into the controversy.
This investigation did prove that there were irregularities in the granting of
Roques's degree.

First, Roques transferred from the University of Paris to Nantes in March 1985,
three months after the deadline for student enrollment had passed and without
authorization from the University rector. Second, he did not have the necessary
qualifications or title for presenting a thesis in literature or history. Third, the
mandatory oral examination did not take place. Fourth. he wrote the thesis in
two months rather than the two years required minimum registration period.
Finally, the signature of one of the examiners said to have been present at the
presentation of the thesis was forged.[64]

The Minister of National Education, Alain Devaquet, annulled the thesis on July 2, 1986. Finally, 200 facility members of the University of Nantes signed a declaration deploring the Roques degree process. This decision to revoke Roques's degree received final confirmation by the Council of State in 1992. These setbacks have not prevented Roques from having his dissertation published in book form in English as *The Confessions of Kurt Gerstein* by the Institute for Historical Review. He then expanded his earlier work with *When Alain Decaux Recounts the History of SS Kurt Gerstein (Quand Alain Decaux raconte l'histoire du SS Kurt Gerstein)* with the help of Vincent Reynouard.

HOLOCAUST DENIAL AND LYON III

The University of Lyon III has long been a hotbed of French right-wing politics and Holocaust denial research. Officially the university is named the Université Jean Moulin after the martyred French Resistance leader. It was in 1973 that the University of Lyon III broke with the University of Lyon II because of political differences arising out of the conflicts associated with May 1968.[65] French students have also called it the "Fascist university" because so many of its professors belong to far-right French political parties. This university gained this title when a number of scholars with ties to right-wing parties created the Institute of Indo-European Studies in 1981. In the years since 1981 the university has undergone a number of controversies.

The first controversy was over a doctoral committee that granted highest distinction to a thesis denying the existence of gas chambers in Polish concentration camps. Jean-Paul Allard, one of the founders of the Institute of Indo-European Studies and a German studies professor, served on that dissertation committee. He was forced to defend his actions, but even after the Ministry of Education nullified the dissertation in 1986, Allard remained on the faculty.[66]

Next was the Notin Affair. Bernard Notin was a senior lecturer in economics at the University of Lyon III when he wrote a 1989 article in the journal *Économies et Sociétés* in which he challenged the existence of the gas chambers.

> The real passes in judgment before the unreal. The historical theme of the homicidal gas chambers is quite revealing of this process. The proofs to demonstrate their existence evolved according to circumstances of time and place, but issued forth from a Pandora's box having three drawers; at the bottom, the visit to the site (slightly credible); in the middle, the assertion of the victors (=the gas chambers existed); on top, rumor (story of the man who saw the man who saw the man who ...). The existence [of the gas chambers] has been postulated in toto, no matter the reality of this reality.[67]

Notin's article and the uproar that followed led to his suspension from teaching at the University of Lyon III for three years. When the university tried to reinstate him in February 1993, students of the French Union of Jewish Students demonstrated against him. Notin never returned to the University of Lyon III and took a position abroad.

Another scandal about a Holocaust denier also surfaced in 1999 at the University of Lyon III in the form of the Plantin Affair. Jean Plantin had been a graduate student at the university in 1990. His master's thesis that earned him a master's degree cum laude in history was a laudatory work on a Holocaust denier. He followed with another work that advanced the thesis that it was typhus, not gas chambers, that caused the deaths at German concentration camps.[68] Scholars had long known about the typhus outbreaks at the various concentration camps, but the deaths were insignificant compared to the number murdered. After graduation, Plantin operated a right-wing bookstore in Lyon. News of his Holocaust denial research reached French authorities, and he was arrested in 1999. The university reluctantly revoked his degree after a civil court had condemned him for these works. Although he had been convicted and fined, a French appeals court threw out his sentence because the statute of limitations had passed.

In 2001 students at Lyon III protested against the political orientation of the university. The students requested that France's Ministry of Education appoint an independent commission to examine right-wing influence at Lyon III. Although the president of the university, Gilles Guyot, claimed that only three professors had clear affiliations with extreme-right groups, a representative of the students countered with the names of some 20 extreme-right members of the faculty.

> Other critics of Lyon-III say the school's importance to far-right parties—particularly the anti-Semitic and xenophobic National Front—cannot be determined by mere head counts. Its value, they say, lies more in the theoretical and institutional legitimacy the school lends to Holocaust denial, which in the past has served as a key campaign strategy for the National Front.[69]

These demonstrations led the French government to set up a commission in 2002 to shed light on racism and negationism that might have found expression within University of Lyon III.[70] The eminent historian Henry Rousso was appointed to head the commission. After nearly a two-year investigation, the commission issued its report in October 2004. Almost immediately the report was attacked by Bruno Gollnisch, a professor of Japanese at the University of Lyon III, a European deputy from the Far Right, and one of the contenders to replace Jean-Marie Le Pen as head of the Front National. Gollnisch accused Rousso of allowing his Jewish bias to color the report.[71] Gollnisch's attack earned him a five-year suspension of teaching at the University of Lyon III. In actuality, the report was objective, but it did note the right-wing orientation of Lyon III and the large number of Holocaust deniers coming out of it.

GARAUDY AFFAIR

Roger Garaudy is the latest of a long line of French Holocaust deniers. Garaudy was born on July 17, 1913, in Marseille, France. He grew up as a French Protestant. After graduation from the University of Marseille with a degree in philosophy, he served in the French army in 1940. Escaping prisoner-of-war status, Garaudy joined the French Resistance. His resistance activities led to his internment in a French prison camp in Algeria. After World War II, Garaudy joined the French Communist Party becoming one of the party's leading Marxist theoreticians. Later, he won a seat in the National Assembly and then a seat in the Senate. Although he had earned a reputation as a staunch Stalinist, his pro-Czechoslovakian stance in 1968 led to a reprimand from the party's leadership.[72] His continued intransigence finally caused the leaders of the Communist Party to oust Garaudy from his leadership posts in February 1970.[73] Shortly thereafter, Garaudy left the Communist Party. By this time, Garaudy had become increasingly interested in religion, and he joined the Catholic Church.

Garaudy found Christianity lacking, so in 1982 he became a Muslim after marrying a Palestinian woman. From this time onward, Garaudy became the champion of the Palestinian cause against the Israeli state. He found a publisher in 1985 for his book *The Founding Myths of Modern Israel*. In this book Garaudy challenged the existence of the Holocaust and the justification for the state of Israel.

> Comparing Menachem Begin's racism to Hitler's and insisting that there is no real difference between the two, Garaudy goes on to argue that the "myth" of the Holocaust is essential to Israel in order to justify its own form of aggression—"Zionist colonialism"—and its oppression of the Palestinians. Israeli power, in turn, serves the global ambitions of the United States, which seeks to subjugate the Third World and appropriate and control the flow of all Middle Eastern oil. Broadening his attacks on Euro-American racism, Garaudy also asserts that what Hitler did to "whites" was no different than what European and American colonists did to people of color for centuries.[74]

His book caused a sensation in French intellectual circles and in France in general because of his celebrity status.[75] Pierre Vidal-Naquet, however, dismissed both Garaudy and his arguments with the following statement in a 1996 interview in *Le Monde*:

> Here is a man, agrégé in philosophy who has multiple conversions, at first Protestantism, then Communism, then Catholicism, then Islam. It is not exactly an example of intellectual stability.[76]

Garaudy's publications led him into direct conflict with the 1990 Fabius-Gayssot law.[77] This law makes it a crime to challenge crimes against humanity as defined by the Nuremberg Tribunal of 1945–1946. On February 27, 1998, a Parisian court found Garaudy guilty and gave him a nine-month suspended jail sentence and a fine of around $29,500. Unable to have the verdict overturned in French courts, Garaudy appealed to the European Court of Human Rights. In a news release on July 7, 2003, this court answered:

> Having analyzed the book concerned the Court found that, as the domestic courts had shown, the applicant had adopted revisionist theories and systematically disputed the existence of the crimes against humanity which the Nazis had committed against the Jewish community.[78]

The Garaudy Affair might have ended little more than another Holocaust denial case except for the intervention of Abbé Pierre. Abbé Pierre was a Roman Catholic priest famous for both his piety and for his war record. Under his secular name of Henri Antoine Groués, he had served in the French Resistance in World War II, saving many Jews from deportation to Germany and concentration camps. After renouncing his family's fortune, Abbé Pierre had become the beloved conscience of France by his defense of the poor and downtrodden, including poor African and Arab immigrants. Over the years he had become friends with Garaudy.[79] Shortly after the publication of Garaudy's book, Abbé Pierre came out and defended his friend in the left-wing daily *Libération*. He also called for a debate over the Holocaust. In the ensuing controversy, Abbé Pierre backtracked and under pressure from Catholic Church and Jewish leaders withdrew his support for Garaudy.[80] He later confessed that he had not read Garaudy's book. This silencing of Abbé Pierre was only temporary as he was later quoted making antisemitic remarks.[81] Abbé Pierre's death at age 94 on January 14, 2007, ended his role in the controversy, but Garaudy is still around.

FRENCH MUSLIMS AND HOLOCAUST DENIAL

The influx of Muslims from North Africa and other countries of the Middle East have added a new strain to antisemitism and Holocaust denial in France. They are violently hostile to Israel and question the justification for the state of Israel. Roger Garaudy's book attacking the justification for the Israeli state is popular among French Muslims as it is in the Arab world. It has not hurt that Garaudy had converted to Islam and is married to a Palestinian woman. Holocaust denial to French Muslims is just another weapon to be utilized against Israel in the ongoing Israeli-Palestinian conflict. There is little likelihood that things will change as long as there is no peace between Israel and the Palestinians.

Anti-Zionism and Holocaust denial have been combined to be used as a weapon. Young, second or third generation Muslims in France and elsewhere in Europe have been exposed to "hate preachers from the Arab world" who constantly seek to radicalize them.[82] The result is that Muslim youth have been active in antisemitic attacks on Jews. They are also a ready market for Holocaust denial.

German Holocaust Deniers

INTRODUCTION

Holocaust denial adherents were initially harder to find in Germany because of decades of severe legal restrictions by the German federal government against denying the Holocaust or uttering neo-Nazi statements. Immediately after World War II the German Parliament passed laws against the dissemination of Nazi materials, or advocacy of a return to the Nazi regime. Consequently, attacks on the Holocaust, be they verbal or in print, brought quick criminal charges, fines, and/or imprisonment. A counter strategy was undertaken with a campaign by former Nazis to downplay Hitler's responsibility for World War II and at the same time glorifying the German soldiers.[1]

The earliest Holocaust deniers were former members of the Schutzstaffel (SS) and/or members of veterans' associations. But the threat of and the initiation of court cases shut most of them up.[2] This crackdown, however, did not prevent underground literature downplaying the Holocaust or justifying Nazi policies from being passed around among former Nazis. Two former Nazi leaders, Dr. Heinrich Malz, a one-time SS police aide in Berlin and postwar neo-Nazi lawyer, and Dr. Karl Henrich Peter, a former director of Dr. Walter Frank's antisemitic Reich Institute for the History of the New Germany (Reichsinstitut für Geschichte des Neuen Deutschlands) at Frankfurt, started preliminary research to deny the Holocaust, and they produced a memorandum entitled "The Big Swindle of the Six Million."[3] In this manuscript they contended that "millions of Jews were hidden in current world census figures and were not exterminated."[4] They were able to avoid prosecution because this memorandum was never published, but it made the rounds in neo-Nazi circles both in Germany and abroad. Elements of the story reached the United States when Malz and Peter sent the pamphlet *The Jewish War against the German People* to a German-American, Frederick Charles Weiss, a leader in the American National Renaissance Party in New York City in June 1955.[5] This version incorporated most of the charges of the previous underground manuscript.

Other books by German authors began to circle around Holocaust denial without actually stating it. Among these was a book by Peter Kleist, an assistant to National Socialist Foreign Minister Joachim von Ribbentrop. Kleist's book, *You Took Part Too* (*Auch du warst dabei*) (1952), tried to whitewash Nazi Germany by charging that Allied leadership had been supported by international Jewry to attack Germany.[6] Helping the growth of German Holocaust denial was the Grabert publishing house in Tübingen, Germany. Herbert Grabert, who had been part of Alfred Rosenberg's Ministry for the Occupied Eastern Territories during the war, founded his publishing house in 1953.

Holocaust denial began to gain some German converts in the 1960s with the appearance of works that justified the actions of the Nazi regime. One of these was the publication of the American historian David Hoggan's *The Forced War* in Germany in 1961. This work absolved Hitler from responsibility for starting World War II by blaming the English, American, and Polish governments for its outbreak.

Then in 1967, an Austrian antisemitic academic, Franz Scheidl, published the book *History of the Defamation of the Germans* (*Geschichte der Verfemung der Deutschen*) that claimed that World War II was a war between Germany and the Jews.[7] Because international Jewry had declared war on Germany, it was responsible for the atrocities.[8] Scheidl carefully avoided mentioning the death camps or Auschwitz, but the implication was there that the Jews were responsible for them also.

A number of Holocaust denial books and pamphlets began to appear in the 1970s. They appeared because neo-Nazis and right-wing Germans agreed upon a common thesis.

> Denying the Holocaust and responsibility for the Second World War has been instrumental in enabling the far right to attain growing political strength and impetus. The thesis works on the notion that if concentration-camps could be recast as ordinary penal colonies, if Hitler could be painted an ordinary dictator, and if German fascism had not been unique, then the stain could be removed. If denying the Holocaust could be successful, then fascists could more easily become an accepted force in political, legal and above all moral terms.[9]

Among these were Thies Christophersen's *Die Auschwitz-Lüge* (*The Auschwitz Lie*) in 1973, Wilhelm Stäglich's *Der Auschwitz Mythos* (*The Auschwitz*

Myth) in 1979, and Udo Walendy's *Forged War Crimes Malign the German Nation* in 1979.

The leading Holocaust denial institute is the German-Austrian Institute for Contemporary History. Its role is similar to the American Institute for Historical Review and there is interaction between them. Most of its scholarship is devoted to proving that the Holocaust was a hoax concocted by Jews to win financial support from Germany.[10]

Another Holocaust institute is the Research Institute for Contemporary History (Zeitgeschichtliche Forschungsstelle). Alfred Schickel founded this institute in 1981. He has remained head of this institute that is headquartered in Ingolstadt, Germany.[11] Schickel has been careful to avoid German legal restriction against attacking the Holocaust, so he has concentrated on so-called Allied atrocities against the Germans during and after the war. He has also frequently written in the extreme right journal *Young Freedom* (*Junge Freiheit*). Schickel has cautiously incorporated the Auschwitz lie thesis in his writings.[12]

GENERAL OTTO ERNST REMER AND EARLY HOLOCAUST DENIAL

Former Nazi leaders were not above challenging the Holocaust. Among these was General Otto Ernst Remer. Remer was born on August 18, 1912, in Neubrandenburg, Germany. After entering the German army in 1930, he served as a junior officer on both the Western and Eastern Fronts. After suffering a wound, he was transferred to an army post in Berlin as commander of the Bodyguard Brigade of Hitler's headquarters. Hitler made him a hero of the Third Reich for crushing the conspiracy against Hitler in Berlin after the July 20, 1944, assassination plot against Hitler failed. Hitler promoted him from major to general for his actions. He commanded a Panzer brigade at the Battle of the Bulge until American troops captured him. He spent most of the next two years as an American prisoner of war. Leaving the prison camp in 1947, Remer remained an unreconstructed Nazi.

Remer became an important figure in postwar German right-wing political circles. He was one of the co-founders of the Socialist Reich Party in 1950. Remer remained an important leader of this party until it was banned in 1952 for its neo-Nazi position. His antisemitism led him to deny the Holocaust. His remarks at a SS reunion in Bavaria led to a six-month prison term. A reporter from the German magazine *Stern* recorded the incident.

From the right-hand pocket of his suit, [Remer] removed with a grand gesture a gas-filled cigarette lighter. He held it under his nose, pressed carefully on the release so that the gas escaped slowly. "What is that?" he asked, sniffing it, and then he gave the reply: "A Jew nostalgic for Auschwitz."[13]

In his newsletter *Remer Dispatch (Remer Despeche)* Remer continuously hammered away that there were no gas chambers and no Holocaust.[14]

Remer's neo-Nazi activities and Holocaust denial activities landed him in trouble with West Germany authorities several times. First, it was his leadership of the Socialist Reich Party in the early 1950s. Later, it was because of his Holocaust denial remarks and writings. Before his 1991 trial, he persuaded the young German chemist Germar Rudolf at the Max Planck Institute to do an update of *The Leuchter Report*. The report, *The Rudolf Report: Expert Report on Chemical and Technical Aspects of the 'Gas Chambers' of Auschwitz,* again charged that gas chambers did not exist at Auschwitz, but again scientists have repudiated the report as unscientific.[15] In 1985, a West German court convicted Remer of defaming the dead with his denial of the Holocaust. This verdict was overturned by an appeals court on procedural grounds, but in a subsequent trial he was convicted for inciting and spreading racial hatred. His sentence was for a 22-month jail term, but Remer was able to avoid jail time.

Again Remer left Germany for Spain in February 1994. The Spanish government and the high court of Spain refused to extradite Remer. In his last years Remer was the grand old man of the neo-Nazi movement. Among his other activities Remer attended as a special guest the Eighth Holocaust Denial Convention in Irvine, California, in 1987, sponsored by the Institute for Historical Review. Remer spent the last few years of his life living in Egypt and Syria. In an interview with the Egyptian paper *Al-Sha'b Remer* in Cairo during one of his visits to Egypt, Remer outlined his beliefs on the Holocaust.

> He (Remer) cites *The Protocols of the Elders of Zion* as an accurate indication of Jewish plans and intentions. The Jewish Mafia, he says was the one force which truly benefited from the world wars. Refering to America's massive financial support of Israel, Remer expresses his anger "as a German" at the amount of money that Germany pays annually to Israel, especially given that the Holocaust is nothing but a fallacy, a Jewish invention."[16]

He died in 1997. Remer mentored a generation of German right-wingers, neo-Nazis, and Holocaust deniers.

THIES CHRISTOPHERSEN AND HOLOCAUST DENIAL IN GERMANY

Thies Christophersen started the rebirth of public Holocaust denial in West Germany. He was born in 1918 in Schleswig in northern Germany. Until the outbreak of World War II, Christophersen worked as a farmer. Entering the German army in 1939, he was badly wounded in the face during the May 1940 campaign in Western Europe. Christophersen was no longer able to be a combat soldier; he received specialized agriculture training as a second lieutenant in the SS. His agricultural specialty was the cultivation of a variety of dandelion (kok-saghyz) to produce a form of natural rubber.[17] Rubber was a scarce commodity because most of it had to be imported. He spent most of the war in German-occupied Ukraine working with the dandelions. Ordered out of the Ukraine because of the advance of Soviet troops, Christophersen was assigned in January 1944 to the labor camp of Raisko, a satellite of Auschwitz concentration camp. He supervised about 300 workers in the cultivation of dandelions. He remained in this area until December 1944 when he was transferred out again.

After the war, Christophersen returned to his farming. For nearly three decades, he remained quiet about his experiences, but gradually he decided to enter the West German political arena. His goal was to revive the legal status of the German National Socialist Worker's Party. He started a small publishing house, Nordwind, that published the quarterly magazine *The Farming Community* (*Die Bauernschaft*) and the *Critic* (*Kritik*). It was this press that published his pamphlet *The Auschwitz Lie* (*Die Auschwitz-Lüge*) in 1973. Christophersen claimed that he had visited Birkenau several times, and he had seen no evidence of mass extermination there. He claimed that Auschwitz-Birkenau resembled a resort where prisoners were well treated. This book created a sensation in West Germany, and it has been a favorite of Holocaust deniers since its publication.

Christophersen's publication of his book started his legal troubles with West German authorities that continued throughout the rest of his life. Although he was never prosecuted for *The Auschwitz Lie,* he was placed in legal jeopardy for other of his writings. Christophersen moved to Belgium to avoid West German criminal charges, but the Belgium police arrested him and turned him over to the West German police. He served a year in prison in West Germany beginning in 1983 on the charges of "contempt against the state" and defamation of the Jews for these writings.[18] Trying to avoid further criminal charges, Christophersen moved to Denmark where he continued to publish Holocaust denial materials in his Nordwind Press. In March 1988, Christophersen traveled to Toronto, Canada, to testify in the trial of Holocaust denier Ernst Zündel. After negative publicity about his Holocaust denial in Denmark, Christophersen traveled to Switzerland and then to Spain seeking asylum for his political views. German authorities canceled his stated medical insurance and stopped payment on both his state retirement and military service pensions. Complicating his problems was the fact that Christophersen was caught on videotape "confessing that he had lied about the gas chambers because of loyalty to the SS and his desire to protect Germany's honor."[19] Christophersen finally returned to Germany in time to die on February 13, 1997, at Molfsee, Kiel, in north Germany. Despite his discrediting, Holocaust deniers still consider Christophersen a reliable witness and quote him frequently.

WILHELM STÄGLICH AND THE AUSCHWITZ MYTH

The next significant German Holocaust denier was Wilhelm Stäglich. He was a West German judge. During World War II, he served in the German army as an officer with an antiaircraft unit near Auschwitz concentration camp. After becoming a judge in Hamburg, his remarks on Auschwitz led to disciplinary action against him in 1965. Refusing to change his views, he published a Holocaust denial article in the magazine *Nation Europa* in 1973. By this time, Thies Christophersen's pamphlet denying mass gassings at Auschwitz had appeared. Again disciplinary proceedings were undertaken, but this time Stäglich decided to retire from the bench. In his free time he undertook research for his book *The Auschwitz Myth: A Judge Looks at the Evidence* that appeared in 1979. In this book Stäglich examined trial testimony, affidavits, and eyewitness accounts and found them unreliable because they were given under duress. He also interpreted the idea of the Final Solution to be a policy to remove Jews from the German sphere of influence in Europe through emigration.[20] Stäglich also denied that there were gas chambers at Auschwitz, and he maintained that those rooms had been gas-tight air-raid shelters.[21]

Stäglich's book produced a firestorm of controversy in West Germany, leading to the passage of a German law to criminalize Holocaust denial. In retaliation, the University of Göttigen withdrew his 1951 Ph.D. Stäglich also had to suffer from police raids on his home to seize forbidden literature. Although banned in Germany, the Institute for Historical Review published a translation of *The Auschwitz Myth* in the mid-1980s.

UDO WALENDY AND HOLOCAUST

Udo Walendy is another of the early German Holocaust deniers. He was born in 1927 in Berlin. Most of his youth was during the early years of the Third Reich. He served in the German army during the later stages of World War II. After the war, Walendy studied history at the Hochschule für Politik in West Berlin from 1950 to 1956. After receiving his degree of specialized study, he worked as a teacher for the German Red Cross. Walendy also became a leading member of the neo-Nazi German National Democratic Party (Nationaldemokratische Partei Deutschlands, NPD).

Beginning in the early 1960s, Walendy began questioning German war guilt and the Holocaust. In 1964, he published the book *Truth for Germany: The Guilt Question of the Second World War* (*Wahrheit für Deutschland— Die Schuldfrage des zweiten Weltkrieges*). This book was a defense of Germany's actions in World War II. Then in 1965, Walendy founded in Vlotho, West Germany, the publishing firm Verlag für Volkstum und Zeitgeschichtsforschung. He used this publishing firm to start publishing pro-Nazi and Holocaust denial materials. His most famous translation into

German was Arthur R. Butz's book, *The Hoax of the Twentieth Century.*
Walendy also started publishing a series of booklets in West Germany—
Historical Facts (Historische Tatsachen)—that had Holocaust denial
themes. A major concentration has been on disproving the authenticity of
German atrocity photographs of World War II. He published the book
Faked Atrocities in which he analyzes what he considers blatant forgeries
of photographs. Walendy's activities led the Institute for Historical Review
to make him a member of its Editorial Advisory Committee from 1980 to
2002. His stature in the Holocaust denial movement led him to advise
and testify for Zündel at both his 1985 and 1988 Holocaust denial trials
in Canada.

Walendy's Holocaust denial activities landed him in legal troubles with
West German authorities. German police conducted a raid of Walendy's business and residence on February 7, 1996, seizing incriminating materials. A district court in Bielefeld sentenced Walendy on May 17, 1996, to a 15-month
prison term. Then on May 6, 1997, a Herford court added an additional sentence of 14 months for "publishing 'one-sided' history that did not give suffi-
cient attention to alternative interpretations."[22] Finally, a district court in
Dortmund fined Walendy 20,000 marks (approximately $38,000) for posses-
sion of 12 copies of Adolf Hitler's *Mein Kampf.* Despite having serious health
problems, Walendy spent more than two years in prison. After his release from
a German prison, Walendy has resumed his Holocaust denial activities.
He has, however, been more circumspect with his challenges of German law.

GERD HONSIK AND AUSTRIAN HOLOCAUST DENIAL

Gerd Honsik is the leading Austrian Holocaust denier. He was born on
October 10, 1941, in Vienna, Austria. Honsik has been variously described
as a writer, journalist, and poet. In the 1980s, he began to publish Holocaust
denial materials, including the *Acquittal for Hitler? 36 Unheard Witnesses
against the Gas Chamber Lie (Freispruch für Hitler?36 ungehörte Zeugen
wider die Gaskammer)* in 1988. In this book Honsik presented interviews
with former Nazis who denied the Holocaust and the existence of gas chambers.[23] Beginning in 1980, Honsik published the newsletter *Halt* that specialized in Holocaust denial material. In November 1987, Honsik published the
so-called Lachout Document in *Halt.* This document was purported to be a
legally notarized memorandum written by a Lieutenant Lachout to prove
that there had never been any gassings in the Mauthausen concentration
camp, or in 12 other concentration camps in Germany. The problem was that
this document was easily proven to be a forgery because Lachout had never
been a member of the nonexistent Military Police Service of the Allied Military Command.[24] This investigation led the Austrian Resistance Archives
(Dokumentationsarchiv des österreichischen Widerstandes) to launch judicial proceedings against both Honsik and Lachout in 1990.

Honsik spent the next two years answering charges of forgery and distributing neo-Nazi materials. After convictions in both Austria and Germany on these charges, he fled to Spain in 1992 to avoid an 18-month prison sentence. Honsik has established a good working relationship with Pablo Varela of CEDADE (Círculo Español de Amigos de Europa) in Spain. Most of his activity in Spain is in publishing the newsletter *Halt* and sending it back to Austria. Several times the German government has tried to have him extradited to Germany to face criminal charges, but Spanish authorities refused to cooperate. This situation changed in April 2007 when action by the European Union enabled the Spanish government to arrest Honsik on August 23, 2007, in Málaga, Spain. Then on October 4, 2007, the Spanish government deported Honsik to Austria to face charges of promoting Holocaust denial.

STRANGE CAREER OF BELA EWALD ALTHANS

Bela Ewald Althans joined the Holocaust denial movement in the 1980s. He was born in 1966 in Hanover, West Germany into a middle-class family. After a Jewish uncle told him about the Nazi regime, Althans became attracted to the German right-wing movements.[25] He met Michael Kühnen, the then head of the National Socialist Action Front (Aktionsfront Nationaler Sozialisten), and Kühnen appointed him director of the local Hannover branch of his group. After Kühnen's jailing for neo-Nazi political agitation, Althans made contacts with other prominent right-wing politicians. He also became a convert to Holocaust denial. A supporter of Ernst Zündel paid Althans's way to Zündel's 1988 trial in Canada.[26] After his return to Germany, Althans began to distribute Zündel's Holocaust denial and neo-Nazi materials in Germany. He also founded a youth organization, Deutsche Jugendbildungswerk, to spread Zündel's materials among German youth. Althans stated at a Holocaust denial meeting held on April 20, 1990, that "the [H]olocaust is a fabrication, the pictures of the dead, of gas chambers, of mass murder are filmed by Hollywood, narrated by Trevor Roper, and directed by Hitchcock."[27]

Althans decided that he wanted to be a leader in the extremist movement in Germany. He attempted in 1991 to hold a Leuchter-Kongress in Munich. Among those invited were the French Holocaust denier Robert Faurisson, the British historian David Irving, the author of *The Leuchter Report*, Fred A. Leuchter, the Austrian Holocaust denier Gerd Honsik, and Zündel. This conference collapsed after the city of Munich charged him with false booking, but a memorial service on the steps of the Deutsches Museum was allowed.[28] This failure did little to boost Althans's standing among German right-wingers.

Althans continued to advance Holocaust denial and the restoration of the Nazi regime until he ran into legal troubles in the early 1990s. His intemperate remarks advocating the relegalization of the Nazi Party attracted attention from German authorities, but it was his role in a German documentary that led to his prosecution for sedition, insulting the memory of the dead, and insulting the State.[29] Althans had performed as the leading character in Winfried Bonengel's film *Profession Neo-Nazi* (*Beruf Neonazi*) that had appeared in 1993. A German court in Berlin found him guilty of the charges in 1995, and Althans received a prison sentence of three and a half years.

The trial and the prison sentence were a turning point for Althans. During the course of the trial, Althans repudiated his former views. It also came out that he had approached the Office for the Protection of the Constitution (Verfassungsschutz) and attempted to sell the names and addresses of rank-and-file German neo-Nazis for a substantial sum of money.[30] Althans already had a shaky reputation in the Holocaust denial movement because of his erratic actions and the fact that he was openly gay. After leaving prison, Althans disappeared from the Holocaust denial and neo-Nazi scene. He was last reported to be living in Belgium under an assumed name.[31]

GÜNTER DECKERT AND HOLOCAUST DENIAL

Günter Deckert is another significant German Holocaust denier. He was born in 1940 in Germany. While in high school, Deckert began to question the official version of World War II. Deckert received a teaching degree, and he worked as a schoolteacher in Heidelberg until the German government banned him in 1988 because of his right-wing political activities.

Deckert started his career in German extremist politics at an early age. He joined the youth wing of the right-wing German Free Democrats, and he remained in this party until 1964 when the party recognized the Oder-Neisse Line as the western border of Poland.[32] His next move was to join the Far Right National Democratic Party of Germany. Deckert left this party in 1982 only to rejoin it in 1991. Party leaders made him head of the National Democratic Party of Germany in 1991, and he remained its head until 1996.

Throughout his political career since 1970 Deckert has been active in the German Holocaust denial movement. His closest collaborator has been another German Holocaust denier, Udo Walendy.[33] Together they organized Holocaust denial meetings, including the annual Kurpfälzer Forum. David Irving spoke at the Kurpfälzer Forum in 1990. The next year the featured speaker was Fred Leuchter. Deckert also translated Holocaust denial and Far Right works by Alain de Benoist, David Hoggan, and Henri Roques into German.

Deckert's Holocaust denial activities landed him in political difficulty. Irving and Leuchner's speeches at the Kurpfälzer Forum led to Deckert's conviction on the charge of seditions, defaming the memory of the dead, and incitement to racial hatred in 1993, but he received only a small fine. The laxity of the sentence caused the German authorities to demand a retrial, and Deckert again was fined only a small amount. Further enraged by the results of this second trial, the Federal Court overturned this sentence, and in yet another retrial Deckert was sentenced to a two-year prison term. Deckert's three trials gave him and Holocaust deniers in Germany considerable publicity, and it gave him prestige within the international Holocaust denial movement.[34] Since his release from prison in October 2000, Deckert has resumed his Holocaust denial activities but in a much more subdued manner.[35]

GERMAR RUDOLF AND GERMAN HOLOCAUST DENIAL

One German has challenged the German legal system by publishing a Holocaust denial book—Germar Rudolf. Rudolf was born on October 29, 1964, in Limburg an der Lahn in West Germany. After his schooling in Remscheid in 1983, Rudolf started undergraduate training in chemistry in 1983 at the University of Bonn where he finished a certification as a chemist in 1989. Fulfilling his military service in the German air force in the years 1989–1990, he worked on his Ph.D. in chemistry at the Max Planck Institute for Solid State Research in Stuttgart from 1990 to 1993.

Even before finishing his education, Rudolf began an involvement in German right-wing politics. He joined the extreme right-wing Republican Party (Republicaner Partei) in 1985. He had trouble adjusting to the party, leaving in 1986 only to rejoin it again in 1989. Rudolf also wrote for the right-wing publication *Junge Freiheit* (Berlin).[36] By this time, Rudolf had become a full-fledged Holocaust denier. Later, Rudolf attributed his conversion to Holocaust denial because of the writings of Paul Rassinier, Armin Mohler, and Fred A. Leuchter.[37] He had established contacts with the neo-Nazi German Nationalist Party and with the Holocaust denier Günter Deckert.[38] Fearing that his controversial views might reflect badly on the Republican Party, Rudolf resigned from it for the final time in mid-1991.[39]

Rudolf's claim to fame in the Holocaust denial movement is his *Rudolf Report (Rudolf Gutachten)*. He began research on this report in 1991 by preparing a report for the legal defense of the former Nazi war hero General Otto Ernst Remer.[40] It was part of a strategy by Holocaust deniers to provide quasiscientific documents to be used in court trials.[41] He traveled to Auschwitz and illegally removed material from the gas chamber ruins for chemical inspection.[42] His chemical analysis proved to him that the claims made in *The Leuchter Report* were accurate.[43] In 1993, the wrote the final version of his research in the *The Rudolf Report: Expert Report on Chemical and Technical Aspects of the 'Gas Chambers' of Auschwitz (Gutachten über die Bildung und Nachweisbarkeit von Cyanidverbindungen in den*

'*Gaskammern*' *von Auschwitz*) in which he maintained that the gas chambers at Auschwitz and Birkenau were not used to murder prisoners.[44] He based much of his final analyses on the findings of the by then discredited *Leuchter Report*. His final argument was that because the gassing of the Jews did not exhibit the German passion for "precision work," this was proof of its nonexistence.[45]

Rather than let his report withstand scientific scrutiny on its merits, Rudolf turned to subterfuges. To make his work appear more impressive Rudolf used pseudonyms of scientists and historians to portray himself as an unbiased scientist in the pursuit of the truth.[46] He also produced three versions of the work to appeal to different audiences in Germany.[47] Rudolf attempted to publicize his report by sending it to German Chancellor Helmut Kohl and to 1,400 addresses.[48] He also tried to serve as an expert witness at the May 1992 trial of David Irving in Munich, and General Otto Ernst Remer's trial in October 1992 in Schweinfurt, but both times the judges denied him this status.

> Although the "Rudolf-Report" has been rejected as a legal document Whenever presented in court, financing this costly document must have seemed worthwhile to its publishers. The fact is, that it is widely distributed and used by Holocaust deniers to "prove" the non existence of gas chambers in Auschwitz/Birkenau.[49]

This work violated German law prohibiting distribution of Holocaust denial materials. Shortly after the appearance of his report, the Max Planck Institute expelled him for the unauthorized use of the institute's letterhead to have the chemical samples from Auschwitz analyzed. Rudolf sued for wrongful dismissal, and the institute made an out-of-court settlement, which gave Rudolf no compensation, but designated the dismissal as a termination of his contract by mutual agreement.[50] Later, the University of Stuttgart rejected his dissertation.[51] Rudolf was arrested and brought to trial in Stuttgart on November 22, 1994, and he was convicted in 1995 for violation of this law. Avoiding a prison sentence of 14 months and before his appeal was denied, Rudolf fled first to Spain and then to Great Britain before finally ending up in the United States. While living in Great Britain, Rudolf contacted David Irving and right-wing extremists in the National Front and the British National Party.[52] He also started the Holocaust denial publishing company Castle Hill Publishers in 1997.[53] His publishing company specialized in publishing Holocaust denial books and a journal. Landing in Chicago, Rudolph sought political asylum in the United States.

Much like other Holocaust deniers, Rudolf had a series of secret financial supporters. His chief financier has been the rich paper industrialist Hans-Joachim Dill.[54] Besides Rudolf, Dill has financially supported Otto-Ernst Remer and other Holcaust deniers.

Rudolf has maintained a high level of respect in the Holocaust denial movement. He is unique because of his training in chemistry, but it is more that he has avoided the infighting so prevalent among Holocaust denial leaders.[55] Rudolf has successfully cultivated close ties with the American Institute for Historical Review and Bradley Smith's Committee for Open Debate on the Holocaust. In 2000, Rudolf was appointed to the Editorial Advisory Committee of the *Journal of Historical Review*, and he remained on it until the journal's demise in 2002.[56] His most recent publication is the anthology *Dissecting the Holocaust: The Growing Critique of 'Truth' and 'Memory'* (2003), which is published by the Institute for Historical Review's Theses & Dissertations Press.

Rudolf's cultivation of American Holocaust denial circles was unable to prevent his return to Germany. On October 19, 2005, he was arrested in Chicago on a German government warrant for his 1995 conviction in Germany. American authorities deported him to Germany on November 14, 2005, and German authorities arrested him on his arrival at Frankfurt, Germany.[57]

OUTSIDE INFLUENCES PROMOTING HOLOCAUST DENIAL IN GERMANY

Translations of the works of American Holocaust deniers began to appear in Germany in the 1970s. Most important of these books was Arthur R. Butz's *The Hoax of the Twentieth Century: The Case Against the Presumed Extermination of European Jewry*. It became a hit in German right-wing circles. Less influential was the translation of David Hoggan's book *The Forced War (Der Erzwungene Krieg)*. Hoggan's book had a poor reception because of "his poor style and even worse translation."[58]

David Irving has played a key role in reviving Holocaust denial in Germany. He made several trips to West Germany before landing into legal troubles with West German authorities. He has had a receptive audience particularly with Gerhard Frey's German People's Union (Deutsche Volksunion, DVU). In January 1982, Irving gave a speech before a DVU audience in Hamburg during which he broached his doubts about the Holocaust.[59] Later, in March 1982 Irving made 10 more speeches at DVU rallies.

Almost as important on the growth of the Holocaust denial movement in Germany as Irving has been Ernst Zündel. Although a native German and a German citizen, Zündel was able to flood Germany with Holocaust denial and neo-Nazi materials from his home in Toronto, Canada. His German representative in the late 1980s and early 1990s was Bela Ewald Althans.[60] Althans distributed Zündel's materials from an office in Munich, Germany, until his arrest in 1994. He was later disowned by Zündel, making it necessary for him to find another distributor. Later after Zündel launched his

Web site Zündelsite, he no longer had to worry about a distributor because his materials could be spread more easily over the Internet.

A significant portion of Holocaust denial materials have come from outside Germany, mostly from the United States. Gary Lauck, a German-American from Lincoln, Nebraska, has made a career and a good living from publishing Holocaust denial and neo-Nazi materials and sending them to Germany. Lauck's activities landed him in legal difficulties in Germany in 1996. He received a prison sentence of four years, and he served most of his sentence. Since then, he has restricted his activities to the Internet and his Web site.

CONVERSION OF HORST MAHLER

One of the newest recruits to the world of Holocaust denial is Horst Mahler, a former member of the Red Army Faction. He was born on January 23, 1936, in the town of Haynau in Silesia. His father was a dentist, who held right-wing political views. His family fled from Silesia in 1945 to Naumburg, West Germany. After his father's death in 1949, his mother brought Mahler and her two other children to West Berlin. Mahler entered the Free University in West Berlin to study law. While there he joined a right-wing-oriented dueling fraternity. Then he joined the Social Democratic Party, becoming a leader in its youth organization. After graduation, he joined a well-known Berlin law firm specializing in business. His increasing interest in left-wing causes led him to represent leftists in legal trouble. He was one of the founders of the radical leftist Socialist Lawyers Collective. Mahler defended students against charges of attacking Vice President Hubert Humphrey in April 1967.[61] Among his other clients were Rudi Dutschke, Andreas Baader, and Gudrun Ensslin.

Mahler's association with Baader and Ensslin resulted in his joining the Red Army Faction. Several times Mahler found himself in legal difficulties because of his activities with the Red Army Faction, but it was his conviction on the charges of conspiracy to commit aggravated robbery and participation in the same that led to a sentence of 12 years in October 1972. During his time in prison, the German legal profession disbarred him in 1974. He remained in prison until 1980. His friends in the legal profession helped him regain his license to practice law in 1988. Mahler used the years after his release to begin a legal practice in Berlin again.

In the years since his release from prison Mahler reevaluated his former beliefs and became a fervent German nationalist and antisemite. In August 2000, he joined the German neo-Nazi NPD. Mahler soon became one of the NPD's chief spokespersons. His radical neo-Nazi views led him to justify the September 11, 2001, attacks on the United States, and his anti-American statements landed him in legal troubles on the charge of approving of crimes and inciting violence.[62] He has also been active in making antisemitic remarks about Jews and the international Jewish conspiracy. Because of the strict German laws against extremist speech, Mahler has been circumspect about his views denying the Holocaust. Nevertheless, he has been quoted stating that "it is a lie that we (Germany) systematically murdered six million Jews."[63] Mahler is now counted among the growing number of extremist intellectuals in Europe who have adopted Holocaust denial as a weapon against Israel.

6

British Holocaust Denial

INTRODUCTION

British Holocaust denial in the period from 1945 until 1980 was a pale reflection of French Holocaust denial. Michael Shermer and Alex Grobman suggest, however, that the first Holocaust denier may have been the Scotsman Alexander Ratcliffe, a Protestant antisemite who suggested as early as 1943 in the pamphlet *The Truth about the Jews* that German atrocities were a Jewish invention.[1] This pamphlet received little attention because most Europeans and the British, in particular, devoted all of their energies to ending the war. One of the reasons was that there was little impulse among the British to rehabilitate Hitler and the Nazis. British neo-Nazis were fragmented and busy fighting among themselves.

RICHARD VERRALL AND THE 6 MILLION CONTROVERSY

The most prominent early British Holocaust denier was Richard Verrall. He was born in 1948 in England. After a standard British education, Verrall obtained a history degree from Westfield College, now a part of the University of London. After a stint as a member of the Conservative Party and a supporter of Enoch Powell, he left the party in the early 1970s to join the neo-Nazi National Front.

Verrall was an active member of the National Front. He was the editor of the neo-Nazi newsletter *Spearhead* from 1976 to 1980. He was a devoted follower of the National Front's leader John Tyndall. After Tyndall left for another party, Verrall stayed with the National Front.

It was during his stint as editor of the *Spearhead* that he began to question the Holocaust. Writing under the pen name of Richard Harwood, Verrall produced a series of Holocaust denial works beginning with the booklet *Did Six Million Really Die?: The Truth at Last* that first appeared in 1974. It was published by the neo-Nazi Historical Review Press.[2] In this work Verrall attempted to prove that it was statistically impossible for the Germans to kill 6 million Jews because he claimed that Nazi-controlled Europe never exceeded 2.5 million. The problem is that he based the size of the population of European Jewry on the wrong sources.[3] Most of the other material in the booklet was based on the misreading of survivor testimony or on outright distortions. In fact, the booklet was a rehash of an American book by David Hoggan entitled *The Myth of the Six Million*.[4] To make sure that his work received attention, Verrall had copies sent to academics, journalists, and politicians throughout Great Britain. Verrall followed with other booklets including *Six Million Lost and Found: The Truth at Last* in 1978, and then with *Nuremberg and Other War Crimes Trials: A New Look* in 1978. Gill Seidel has accused these pamphlets as being "virtual plagiarism" of French publications.[5] Verrall was a popularizer, not a historian, and his research techniques were sloppy.

MICHAEL MCLAUGHLIN AND HOLOCAUST DENIAL

Another important early British Holocaust denier was Michael McLaughlin. He was born in Liverpool and was employed there as a milkman. Active in Colin Jordan's British Movement, McLaughlin became its leader in 1975 after Jordan was forced to resign. He remained its head until the British Movement lost out to the British National Party in 1983.

McLaughlin's goal was for a revival of the Nazis, and the best method to do this was to discredit the Holocaust. His contribution to Holocaust denial was his booklet *For Those Who Cannot Speak* that appeared in 1979. Published by the neo-Nazi Historical Review Press, this work was more "virulently racist and antisemitic" than Verral's works.[6] McLaughlin defended Nazism from every conceivable angle, beginning with blaming the Jews for declaring war on Germany in 1933. He followed by claiming the Holocaust was a gigantic rip-off by the Jews, and there was no extermination of the Jews.[7] Besides praising Hitler, McLaughlin attacked the diary of Anne Frank as a fake. Finally, he argued for a restoration of a Nazi-like regime to save Europe. This pamphlet led to McLaughlin's brief imprisonment for crimes against race relations in 1979. After losing out in the competition for the loyalty of British neo-Nazis to the National Front in the 1980s, McLaughlin disbanded the British Movement. He then retired from politics and turned to running army surplus stores in England.

EMERGENCE OF DAVID IRVING AS A HOLOCAUST DENIER

David Irving is Great Britain's leading Holocaust denier. He was born in 1938 in Essex, England. His father was a Royal Navy commander who had fought at the Battle of Jutland in World War I and served on the HMS *Edinburgh* in World War II. After the war, he became a book illustrator. His mother was a commercial artist. Irving's family had limited financial resources after the father left the family in 1945.[8] Irving attended a minor private school before entering the Imperial College of the University of London. His career as a student was spotty. After failing a math exam, Irving lost his scholarship. He blamed the professor for this loss, characterizing him as a "known communist."[9] Irving considered joining the Royal Air Force (RAF) like his twin brother, but he failed the medical physical. Later he was suspended as editor of a student magazine, *Carnival Times,* for "printing racist cartoons" and soliciting funds from neo-Fascist organizations.[10] His editorials showed an appreciation for British Fascism and for the Apartheid regime in South Africa.[11] In the middle of his schooling, he traveled to Germany where he worked in a German steel mill in the Ruhr area.[12] After returning to the University of London, Irving completed his third year before leaving school. Irving later described himself as "a total failure" at the university and he blamed a professor for this failure.[13]

Irving decided to become a historian specializing in the history of World War II. Stimulated by his experiences working with Germans in the Ruhr, Irving's first book, *The Destruction of Dresden,* appeared in 1963. In this book Irving advanced a controversial anti-Allies thesis by maintaining that the bombing was unnecessary. The financial success of this book convinced Irving that he could make a living as a military historian without needing a college degree.[14] Irving's publisher was so happy over the success of his first book that he issued contracts for two further books.[15] A series of other books followed, giving Irving a fair reputation as a popular military historian by the early 1980s. His books were sensational, leading to several lawsuits in British courts with the most notable case involving the book about the destruction of Convoy PQ.17 in World War II. A British court awarded the captain of the convoy escort a £40,000 judgment against Irving.[16] This setback was only a bump in the road in an otherwise successful career in writing a series of popular books on modern German history.

Irving became controversial again with the appearance of a book in 1977 portraying Hitler in a favorable light. This book was *Hitler's War,* and Irving went to great lengths to defend Hitler and his policies.[17] Military historians bitterly attacked his conclusions in reviews without attacking him or his research. An exception was the prominent German historian Eberhard Jäckel in a two-essay series that was translated and entitled *David Irving's Hitler: A Faulty History Dissected* in which Jäckel criticized Irving's selective use of documents to prove Hitler's innocence in ordering the

Holocaust.[18] Another critic was the American-Hungarian historian John Lukacs. Lukacs found Irving's sources questionable, asserting that many of the "references and quotations are not verifiable."[19]

The most questionable point in Irving's book concerned his interpretation of Heinrich Himmler's handwritten telephone log of November 30, 1941, from Hitler's military headquarters bunker "Wolf's Lair." Irving interpreted the short message ("Jewish transport from Berlin. no liquidation, or Judentransport aus Berlin. keine Liquidierung"[20]) to mean that Hitler had learned about Himmler's role in the liquidations of Jews and ordered him to stop. Other historians examined the document and realized that Irving's quote had been truncated from a larger message ("Arrest Dr. Jekelius. Presumable Molotov's son. Transport of Jews from Berlin. No liquidation, or Verhaftung Dr. Jekelius. Angebl {ich} Sohn Molotovs. Judentransport aus Berlin. keine Liquidierung").[21] These historians have interpreted the message to mean to take Molovov's son, Dr. Jekelius, into custody before killing him with the Jews. There is evidence that everyone in that transportation had been liquidated before the message arrived. Lucy S. Dawidowicz posted a problem for Irving.

> Irving, wittingly or unwittingly, has in fact disproved his own theory. For if Hitler was indeed responsible for Himmler's call (there is no evidence that he was), then Irving has shown that Hitler did in fact know all about the murder of the Jews. And indeed, how else could it have been? The murder of the Jews was Hitler's most consistent policy, in whose execution he persisted relentlessly, and obsessiveness with the Jews may even have cost him his war for the Thousand Year Reich.[22]

Irving regained some of his academic respect in the *Der Stern* Affair. Sixty-two previously unknown volumes of *Hitler's Diaries* had come to light. After several academic historians had attested to the historical authenticity of the volumes, the magazine *Der Stern* had paid 3.8 million marks for the diaries. This would have been a spectacular find, but Irving had previously purchased documents from the same source, and he had concluded that they were forgeries.[23] Irving crashed the press conference proclaiming that the diaries forgeries, citing improbable events. Later, Irving recanted, accepting them as genuine shortly before a report came out stating that the diaries were forgeries and poor ones at that.[24] Much was made of Irving's early repudiation of the diaries, and his later recanting forgotten.

Irving moved from a defender of Hitler to a Holocaust denier in 1982. He made a series of speeches in Germany before receptive right-wing audiences in January and March 1982 outlining a thesis that Hitler had not ordered the extermination of Europe's Jews.[25] His point was that there was no written order from Hitler authorizing the Final Solution. As was pointed out in an earlier chapter, Hitler was reluctant to issue written orders for a variety of reasons;

mostly he did not have his orders down on paper so he could have deniability. Irving conveniently refused to acknowledge this habit of Hitler.

Irving made several speaking tours of Germany throughout the 1980s. His association with Gerhard Frey, the head of the right-wing German People's Union (Deutsche Volksunion, or DVU), was close, and Irving received substantial honorariums for speaking before the DVU.[26] At one such gathering before the DVU in 1989 Irving made Holocaust denying statements.

> We know and here I need only mention it as a footnote . . . that there were no gas chambers in Auschwitz! . . . . No gas chamber . . . no mass extermination . . . no guilt. So just as the gas chamber in Dachau was a dummy built in the first postwar years, the gas chambers that tourists now see in Auschwitz were built by present day Poland right after the Second World War. The evidence exists, the grounds have been chemically analyzed, and we have now published the facts all over the world.[27]

In 1983, he became affiliated with Willis A. Carto's Institute for Historical Review. This institution had become an international center of Holocaust denial. It was also a good place for Irving to raise funds by selling books. Over the next few years, Irving also gave lectures before William Pierce's neo-Nazi National Alliance.[28] In 1984, the Austrian government banned and then deported Irving because of his remark that Nazi leader Rudolf Hess deserved the Nobel Peace Prize.[29]

Besides his writings justifying Hitler as a German political and military leader, Irving also questioned the authenticity of the diary of Anne Frank. His charge that the diary was a fake led Otto Frank, Anne's father, to file a libel suit in British courts. Under this legal threat Irving withdrew his charge.

After achieving stature in the Holocaust denial movement, Irving participated in the 1988 trial of Ernst Zündel, a Canadian Holocaust denier, as a defense witness. In the documentary by Errol Morris on September 9, 1998, Ernst Zündel reported that before the trial Irving had seen *The Leuchter Report* and stated it was "a shattering document."

> The *Leuchter Report* is a shattering document. It is a stroke of genius by the defense. As a historian, anybody that will write history, the history of the Second World War that does not take into consideration what Fred Leuchter has found and unearthed, will henceforth do so at their peril because they will write propaganda. Not History.[30]

What he heard from Fred Leuchter's testimony at the trial reinforced his Holocaust denial views. After the trial, Irving maintained that *The Leuchter Report* proved that the Nazis had not used gas chambers to kill Jews at concentration camps.[31] This conversion led Irving to drop references to gas chambers from his revised edition of *Hitler's War*.[32] Irving formed the Clarendon Club in Great Britain, and its members' mission was to promote

Holocaust denial.[33] In 1991, Irving's comments before a Calgary, Canada, audience showed his attitude:

> I don't see any reason to be tasteful about Auschwitz. It's baloney. It's a legend. Once we admit the fact that it was a brutal slave labour camp and a large number of people did die, as large numbers of innocent people died elsewhere in the war, why believe the rest of the baloney? I say quite tastelessly in fact that more women died on the back seat of Edward Kennedy's car at Chappaquiddick than ever died in a gas chamber in Auschwitz. Oh, you think that's tasteless. How about this. There are so many Auschwitz survivors going around, in fact the number increases as the years go past, which is biologically very odd to say the least, because I am going to form an Association of Auschwitz Survivors, survivors of the Holocaust and other liars . . . A-S-S-H-O-L-S.[34]

In June 1992, German authorities arrested and fined him for violating the German law against "defaming the memory of the dead."[35] That same year he was also expelled from Canada.

Because of the controversy over his Holocaust denial stance, book publishers began rejecting his manuscripts on military and political history, causing him financial distress. Irving lost a $150,000 fee for a translation of the diary of Joseph Goebbels in 1992 due to protests against his advocacy of Holocaust denial.[36] Furthering his difficulties, Deborah Lipstadt, a professor at Emory University in Atlanta, Georgia, wrote a book entitled *Denying the Holocaust: The Growing Assault on Truth and Memory* in 1993. In this book she charged that Irving misused historical sources to conform to "his ideological leanings and political agenda."[37] This charge was a direct assault on Irving's scholarship, and it had serious financial and prestige implications for Irving. He complained at his trial that his "income, once in excess of £100,000 a year, has fallen sharply."[38] Irving had to self-publish his book *Goebbels: Mastermind of the Third Reich* in 1996 after a major publisher pulled out of the project because of negative prepublication reviews.[39] Irving began to advance the thesis that there was an international Jewish conspiracy aimed at suppressing his works.[40] His reaction to the actions of St. Martin's Press's rejection was to say, "I think that this kind of action by the organized Jewish community can only lead to an increase in anti-Semitism, because the general public will regard it as 'the Jews' throwing their weight around again."[41] After meeting with him in 1996, the author of a piece in the *New Republic* concluded his assessment of Irving in the following terms:

> IN SHORT, Irving's books cannot be divorced from the man and his historical mission. That mission is to normalize Hitler and Nazism so as to remove the unique stain of the Final Solution from Germany. The uniqueness of the stain has meant not only that postwar Germany has borne a special taint but that, since World War II, it has been taboo in the West to espouse anti-Semitism publicly. Irving's project is to smash this taboo.[42]

Even historians had expressed doubts about Irving's use of documents and his desire to exonerate Hitler from all blame. The eminent and conservative American-Hungarian historian John Lukacs took Irving to task in his 1997 book *The Hitler of History:*

> Because of Irving's tireless collecting of papers (mostly, though not exclusively, from people who had lived close to Hitler), his work has lately received some grudging recognition from military historians. But while some of Irving's "finds" cannot be disregarded, their interpretation is, more often than not, compromised and even badly flawed because of Irving's aim of rehabilitating Hitler. Anyone, of course, has the right to admire a historical personage, no matter how unpopular. But there exists no "fact" in history that is separable from its statement; and every statement, in turn, is inseparable from its purpose. Apart from (or, perhaps, in addition to) moral judgments, there are two main reasons why Irving's research on Hitler and the statesman and the strategist should be treated (and read) with considerable caution. The first is the evidence of his frequent twisting of documentary sources not only through their interpretation but through the inadequacy of their actual references. The other is that Irving's portrait of Hitler as statesman and strategist is achieved with undiscriminating strokes of his brush. He is satisfied with presenting the warrior Hitler as having been not only more able but also superior in character to all of his opponents. Consequently in Irving's works a discriminating historical reconstruction of Hitler's decisions and purposes hardly exists at all.[43]

When Penguin Books republished Lipstadt's book in Great Britain, Irving saw his chance to take legal action by suing Lipstadt and Penguin Books for libel. Libel laws in the United States protected Lipstadt from a lawsuit, but a looser definition of libel in Great Britain gave Irving a chance to recoup his finances and, more importantly, his reputation. It also gave him an opportunity to combat what he considered was an "International Jewish Conspiracy" against him.[44] The same day Irving also placed a libel charge against Gitta Sereny, another critic of his research.

The Lipstadt libel trial proved to be devastating to Irving. Irving decided to argue the case himself before a judge, not a jury. In a trial that lasted from January 11, 2000, to March 15, 2000, Irving attempted to refute the charges of sloppy and misleading scholarship before a team of historians. The central issue in the trial was the existence of gas chambers at Auschwitz. This fact was acknowledged on both sides and so stated by architectural historian Robert Jan van Pelt.

> Both sides agreed that Holocaust denial—revisionism, as Irving calls it, or negationism, as I prefer to call it—stood at the center of the case, and both parties accepted that at the center of Holocaust denial was Auschwitz, the largest of the extermination camps.[45]

Irving proved to be ineffective in his own defense, which was not helped by his overbearing manner.[46] Judge Charles Gray issued a verdict that Irving was both an antisemite and a Holocaust denier who had distorted evidence to fit his personal thesis. Irving's loss incurred a judgment of £2 million, which he promptly appealed. While Irving came out of the trial with his academic reputation in tatters and on the verge of bankruptcy, he is considered a hero among the supporters of Holocaust denial. He still attempts to bully and intimidate publishers and newspapers by threatening to sue them. Sometimes these tactics are successful because these publishers would have to pay costly court expenses without ever being able to collect damages from Irving.[47]

Beginning shortly after the Lipstadt Trial, Irving started traveling around the world speaking and attending book signings to improve his financial situation. Irving had frequently made tours of the United States to raise funds throughout the 1970s and 1980s. He had always found the Institute for Historical Review gatherings fruitful places to sell books. His speeches also garnered generous speaking fees. It also allowed him to make contact with other Holocaust deniers. During an October 1994 tour, Irving became friends with David Duke, the white supremacist leader. Irving even went so far as to give Duke editorial assistance in writing the Holocaust denial part of Duke's book *My Awakening*.[48] His supporters were busy raising funds for him. These supporters ranged from a former German U-boat commander, Henry Kersting, to American right-winger Albert W. Hess.[49] For a time it looked as if his financial problems were over when his friend Michèle Renouf introduced him to Prince Fahd bin Salman, the eldest nephew to former King Fahd of Saudi Arabia, but Salman died before he turned over the funds to Irving.[50] It is interesting that in 2002, of the 4,017 names on Irving's active contributors list, 2,495 were from the United States and Canada.[51]

On a speaking tour in Austria, however, Irving ran into legal problems. Stopped by the police in Styria, Austria, on November 11, 2005, Irving found himself in jail as a result of denying the existence of gas chambers and the murder of 6 million Jews in two speeches he had given in 1989. On February 20, 2006, Irving received a three-year prison sentence after an eight-man jury took less than two hours to deliver a unanimous verdict against him.[52] Irving had been eligible for a 10-year sentence, but he played to the jury by accepting that "there had been gas chambers in Auschwitz and that millions of Jews had indeed been killed by the Nazis."[53]

Irving was released from his Austrian prison in December 2006. Since then, he has continued his campaign of Holocaust denial by traveling around the world publicizing his views. It is his way to recover financially.

CONVERSION OF NICK GRIFFIN TO HOLOCAUST DENIAL

A recent convert to Holocaust denial is the head of the British National Party (BNP), Nick Griffin. He was born in 1959 in Barnet in north London, but he was raised in rural Suffolk, England. His father, a veteran of the RAF during World War II and a prosperous landowner, and his mother lived on a farm. Most of their income came from an electrical business in St. John's Wood. Griffin was educated at a minor public school of St. Felix in Southwold. While in school, Griffin became attracted to neo-Nazism, and in 1974 he joined the neo-Nazi National Front at the tender age of 14. After graduating from his public school, Griffin attended Cambridge University beginning in 1977. There he studied history and law. Besides his studies Griffin was also a boxer. He graduated from Cambridge with an honors degree in law.

Griffin turned his attention to British politics. He spent the next 18 years as an active member of the National Front. Griffin rose through the ranks quickly, becoming the national party organizer in 1978. His most significant contribution was founding the journal *Nationalism Today* in 1980. He earned notoriety for his participation in a political coup that overthrew Martin Webster, the then head of the National Front. This coup led to so much dissension among the National Front's leaders that Griffin resigned from the party in 1989.

Griffin turned toward another extremist group. He became a member in the Catholic extremist group International Third Position. This group had been founded by the Italian neo-Fascist Roberto Fiore, and its goal was advancing international Fascism. Again Griffin found himself in the middle of a power struggle, and again he lost out. During this period of uncertainty, Griffin had a firearms accident that cost him an eye and a lengthy stay in a hospital.

Griffin finally broke down and joined the British National Party in 1995. The veteran neo-Nazi John Tyndall recruited Griffin into the party to reaffirm its neo-Nazi roots.[54] Griffin entered the BNP firm in the conviction that the party needed to retain its neo-Nazi roots and advance an aggressive stance on Holocaust denial. Griffin assumed the editorship of the antisemitic quarterly *The Rune* to ensure the direction of the party. He then became editor of the BNP magazine *Spearhead* in 1996. In a 1997 article in *The Rune*, Griffin denied the Holocaust.

> I am well aware that the orthodox opinion is that 6 million Jews were gassed and cremated or turned into lampshades. Orthodox opinion once held that the earth is flat.... I have reached the conclusion that the "extermination tale is a mixture of Allied wartime propaganda, extremely profitable lie, and latter-day witch hysteria."[55]

This statement led a British court to sentence him to a nine-month prison sentence and a $3,200 fine, but the sentence was suspended for two years and he never served a day in prison. He followed this article in 1997 with a pamphlet *Who Are the Mindbenders?* In this pamphlet Griffin claimed that the minds of the British people are brainwashed because of Jewish control of the media.[56]

Griffin won a power struggle for the leadership of the British National Party in September 1999. Unlike his earlier extremism, Griffin decided to reposition the party to a more moderate stance to win electoral support.[57] He also toned down his antisemitic and Holocaust denial remarks, but he still continued to associate with David Irving. His new moderation provoked stiff opposition from other leaders in the party, causing Griffin to expel Tyndall from the party in 2002 for being a so-called "disruptive influence."[58] Since then there have been no challenges to Griffin's party leadership, and he was able to withstand charges of misuse of party funds. Griffin continues to direct his anger against Jews, Muslim fundamentalists, Pakistanis, and West Indians as a way to garner political support from Britain's alienated white population.[59] He has never repudiated his Holocaust denial views, and he is still outspoken about them.

> Back in the 1960s the Jews quietly shifted the alleged sites of the mass gassings from the no longer believable German camps such as Dachau and Belsen to the sites in Communist Poland such as Auschwitz and Treblinka. Now that the very idea of Zyklon-B extermination has been exposed as unscientific nonsense, they are once again re-writing bogus history, playing down gas chambers and the talking instead of "hundreds of hitherto unknown sites in the East where more than a million Jews were exterminated by shooting."[60]

Other European Holocaust Deniers

INTRODUCTION

Besides the centers of Holocaust denial in France and Germany, Holocaust deniers have appeared in a number of other Western European countries. None of these deniers have achieved the status of France's Robert Faurisson and Great Britain's David Irving, but they are working on it. Much as in other countries, the Holocaust deniers have divided themselves into the scholars and the distributors. The most prominent of the scholars has been Carl Mattogno in Italy. Most of the others have devoted their attentions to the distribution of Holocaust denial materials. These distributors have had more legal troubles because they have run up against anti-Holocaust denial laws in Belgium, France, and Germany in the course of their activities. Denmark has become a place where Holocaust denial materials can be published and distributed because of lax laws on Holocaust denial.

CARLO MATTOGNO AND ITALIAN HOLOCAUST DENIAL

Italy's foremost Holocaust denier is Carlo Mattogno. He was born in 1951 in Orvieto, Italy, into a respectable family. His specialty is in text analysis and critique, working as an independent scholar in Rome, Italy.

Mattogno is a prolific writer, producing both books and articles denying the Holocaust. In 1985, he wrote the book *The Myth of the Extermination of the Jews,* and later the same year the pamphlet *The Gerstein Report—*

Anatomy of a Fraud. Five of his articles have appeared in the *Journal of Historical Review.*

Mattogno has oriented his research on attacking the facts of the Nazi extermination program. His most recent confrontation has been with John C. Zimmerman over body disposal at Auschwitz.[1] From 1988 to 2002, Mattogno served on the Editorial Advisory Committee of the *Journal of Historical Review,* and he is a frequent participant in conferences of the Institute for Historical Review. In recent years, he has collaborated with the Swiss Holocaust denier Jürgen Graf on Holocaust denial topics.

DITLIEB FELDERER AND HOLOCAUST DENIAL

The most eccentric Western European Holocaust denier is Sweden's Ditlieb Felderer. He was born on April 23, 1942, in Innsbruck, Austria. His family had to flee German-controlled territory, so Felderer and his three brothers and sisters fled first to Italy and then to Sweden. He was educated in Swedish schools. After converting to Jehovah's Witnesses in 1959, he became active in the church, traveling on missionary work in Canada and the United States. Felderer remained a Jehovah's Witness until the 1970s until he wrote down his conclusions that challenged the Nazi persecution of the Jehovah's Witnesses. He was excommunicated from the church because of his writings. About the time of his dispute with the Jehovah's Witnesses, Felderer received a copy of Richard Verrall's (Richard Harwood) *Did Six Million Really Die?* In 1977, he decided to publish a Swedish edition of this work. He distributed around 10,000 copies in Sweden in the late 1970s. Since then, Felderer has been an active Holocaust denier.

Felderer has devoted the rest of his life to Holocaust denial. He founded a magazine, *Bible Researcher,* and publishing house, Bible Researcher. He traveled extensively to concentration camps in Germany and Poland attempting to discredit the existence of the gas chambers. Already convinced that the Holocaust was a hoax, Felderer found nothing at these sites that altered his preconceived beliefs. He published the book *Auschwitz Exit* in 1979 under the pen name Abraham Cohen. Felderer was also active in writing to discredit the diary of Anne Frank. Anne Frank had died of typhus at a German concentration camp, but the popularity of her diary and the discredit it brought on the Nazis disturbed Felderer and his colleagues in the Holocaust denial movement. Despite evidence to the contrary, Felderer claimed that the diary was an elaborate forgery.

By the middle 1980s Felderer had achieved status within the Holocaust denial community. The basis for his Holocaust denial was his virulent anti-semitism. He testified in Canada at the 1988 Zündel trial for spreading falsehoods. At that trial Felderer claimed that there was a swimming pool, a dance hall, and a concert auditorium for concentration camp inmates.[2]

Holocaust scholars have noted a pool, but it was not used for swimming, and there is no evidence of a dance hall and a concert auditorium. Felderer also cultivated a relationship with Willis A. Carto's Institute for Historical Review during those years. For a time he was on the editorial board of the *Journal of Historical Review*.

Felderer's activities led him into legal problems both in Sweden and abroad. In 1985, Felderer stood trial in Sweden and was convicted for sending the flyer "Please Accept This Hair of a Gassed Victim" to the staff of the Auschwitz Museum in Poland. He spent 10 months in prison for this offense. The following year, Felderer was convicted of libeling Mel Mermelstein in a Los Angeles Superior Court. Mermelstein had sued Felderer because of his attempts to intimidate Mermelstein during Melmelstein's suit against the Institute for Historical Review to claim the $50,000 reward for proving the existence of the Holocaust. Felderer had sent Holocaust denying pamphlets to Mermelstein. There were also hand-drawn cartoons along with a letter calling Mermelstein a racist and "exterminationist."[3]

Felderer's behavior has become more bizarre in the last decade. Swedish officials had ordered him to undergo court-ordered psychiatric treatment in April 1983. This treatment did little to slow him down. By the mid-1990s, he had begun to lose interest in Holocaust denial. He moved to the Canary Islands. The Institute of Historical Review dropped him from its editorial advisors list. His main interest has now become pornography.

AHMED RAMI AND HOLOCAUST DENIAL IN SWEDEN

Ahmed Rami is the leading Holocaust denier in the Muslim world, but he operates out of Sweden. He was born in 1946 in Tafraout, Morocco, into a prominent Berber family. He graduated from a high school in Tiznit in southern Morocco. Beginning in 1963, he was a teacher at schools in Casablanca. Then in 1966, he entered the military college in Meknès and graduated in 1968 with a military commission as a lieutenant. His first assignment was with an armored unit in Rabat. Rami's military career ended when he was implicated in two military coup-d'état attempts against the Moroccan government in 1971 and 1972. After going into hiding, Rami landed in Sweden in 1973.

Since his arrival in Sweden, Rami has become the leading spokesperson against the Moroccan government and Israel. He found friends in the Swedish neo-Nazi movement. Rami allied with David Janzon, a prominent neo-Nazi and member of the Swedish National Alliance (Sveriges Nationella Förbund) to establish Radio Islam in 1987. From this outlet Rami spread his anti-Israeli and antisemitic views. His attacks led to a six-month jail term in 1990. Rami has developed close ties to political authorities in Iran and the Lebanese Shi'ite organization Hezbollah. His advocacy of Holocaust denial

earned him acceptance from the leaders of the American Institute for Historical Review. He has also had contact and collaborated on occasions with
Robert Faurisson. Rami was one of the featured speakers at the 1992 Institute for Historical Review Conference, showing his importance in the Holocaust denial movement.[5] In 1996, Rami expanded his activities by forming a
Radio Islam Web site. The material on this Web site landed Rami in trouble
with French authorities. In October 2000, Rami was fined 300,000 francs
(approximately $25,000), in absentia, for inciting racial hatred.

SIEGFRIED VERBEKE AND BELGIAN HOLOCAUST DENIAL

Siegfried Verbeke is Belgium's leading Holocaust denier. He was born in
1941 and lived his life in the Flemish area of Belgium. His first appearance
in extremist circles came in 1977 when he co-founded the Flemish neo-
Nazi magazine *Haro* with Roeland Raes, later to be a leader in Vlaams Blok,
the extremist neo-Nazi Party. By this time he had become a member of the
militantly anti-immigrant Flemist group Vlaamse Militanten Orde (Flemish
Militants Order). After the Belgian government banned this group in 1981,
he turned to extremist publishing. Verbeke founded the Free Historical
Research Center (Vrij Historisch Onderzoek, or VHO) in 1983 to serve as
the organization to publish and distribute Holocaust denial materials. The
VHO had its headquarters in Antwerp. By the early 1990s, Verbeke became
infamous for distribution of Holocaust denial materials in Belgium to Jewish
citizens.[5] His activities led a Belgian court to sentence him to a one-year suspended prison sentence for distributing Holocaust denial materials. He also
lost his civil right for 10 years. Antwerp authorities then shut down
the VHO.

Banned from distributing Holocaust denial materials in Belgium, Verbeke
began sending these publications to the Netherlands and Germany.
He invited trouble in the Netherlands by cooperating with Robert Faurisson
in attacking the authenticity of the diary of Anne Frank in a book entitled
The "Diary" of Anne Frank: A Critical Approach (1991).[6] Responding to
a complaint by the Anne Frank Foundation, the Civil Court of Amsterdam
ruled in 1991 against the unsolicited distribution to Dutch libraries of
Verbeke's book, and it banned all publications that cast doubt on the
authenticity of Anne Frank's diary with the penalty of paying a $12,500
fine.[7] German authorities began in 1998 seeking his arrest on charges of
inciting racial hatred and denying the Holocaust. In 2004, a Belgium court
sentenced Verbeke to a year in prison and a fine of 2,500 euros ($3,000) for
his statements denying the Nazi genocide of Jews during the World War II.
This sentence also meant the loss of civil rights for 10 years. Efforts by
German authorities to have him deported to Germany were not honored by
Belgian authorities because he was still under sentence for the same charges in
Belgium and his appeal of his sentence was still outstanding. But his legal

troubles increased with his arrest on August 4, 2005, at Schiphol Airport in Amsterdam for deportation to Germany where a German arrest warrant awaited him. Verbeke remains unrepentant awaiting trail in Germany.

PEDRO VARELA AND SPANISH HOLOCAUST DENIAL

Pedro Varela is Spain's leading Holocaust denier. Antisemitism and its derivative Holocaust denial was slow to develop in Spain. José A. Llorens Borrás started a journal in February 1964 *Juanpérez: World Information Journal* that under its editor Narcisco Perales produced articles favorable to Nazi Germany, antisemitic in orientation, and containing an advocacy of Holocaust denial.[8] Then in 1966, a group of neo-Fascists and neo-Nazis from the Circulo Español de Amigos de Europa (Spanish Circle of Friends of Europe, or CEDADE).[9] Various prominent Spanish right-wing leaders led CEDADE from 1966 until 1978. Pedro Varela became CEDADE's president in 1978. He continued its neo-Nazi agenda by doing what CEDADE was best at: publishing books, journals, and promoting films. Next Varela tried to form a political party, Partido Europeo Nacional Revolucionario (European National Revolution Party), but nothing came of it because it lacked a voting constituency. Throughout this period CEDADE's publications were antisemitic and anti-Israel.

In the 1980s Varela brought CEDADE into the Holocaust denial camp. Its bulletin began covering Holocaust denial subjects, and CEDADE published Arthur R. Butz's *The Hoax of the Twentieth Century* in an abridged edition.[10] Members of CEDADE formed two associations promoting Holocaust denial in Spain: the Center of Revisionist Historical Studies (Centro de Estudios Históricos Revisionistas) in Alicante, and the Center for Revisionist-Oriented Studies (Centro de Estudios Revisionista Orientaciones) in Palma de Mallorca.[11] In 1992, Varela was arrested in Austria for delivering a speech praising Hitler. After serving three months in prison, Varela was acquitted in December 1992 by a court in Steyr, Austria. When Varela decided to leave CEDADA in 1993, the organization folded. Members flocked to other groups, but Varela headed toward the financial rewards of the publishing world.

Varela's publishing endeavors brought him to the attention of Spanish authorities. In April 1995, the Spanish House of Commons passed a bill making it a crime to deny the Holocaust. The Spanish legislature approved the bill, and it went into effect in May 1996. In the meantime, Varela had been active publishing and distributing Holocaust denial publications at his Europa bookstore in Barcelona. In December 1996, Catalonian police raided his bookstore, arrested Varela, and closed his bookstore after finding Holocaust denial materials there and some in the process of publication.[12] His inventory of 20,000 books was seized by the police and ordered to be burned.[13] Varela was released on provisional liberty until his trial. After a trial and his conviction on November 16, 1998, he received a five-year prison sentence and a fine of about $5,000. The international Holocaust denial movement responded with fury, and a drive to raise funds for Varela's appeal was launched. Varela's lawyer initiated an appeal on December 10, 1998. The provincial court of Catalonia suspended Varela's conviction on April 30, 1999, citing that Holocaust denial claims were constitutional protected free speech. His conviction was suspended and he was set free. Varela did not escape unscathed because a mob stormed his bookstore on January 16, 1999, and the mob destroyed office equipment and burned several hundred books.[14]

Subsequent attempts by the Spanish government to imprison Varela have run into opposition from the Spanish Constitutional Court. This court ruled in November 2007 that Varela's charges for Holocaust denial and possible imprisonment violated the right of freedom of expression in the Spanish Constitution. Subsequently, Varela invited David Duke, the American Holocaust denier, to tour with him around Spain to promote a Spanish edition of Duke's book, *Jewish Supremacism: My Awakening to the Jewish Question*. This tour led to charges in a Spanish court that Duke was inciting antisemitism.

GASTON-ARMAND AMAUDRUZ AND SWISS HOLOCAUST DENIAL

Gaston-Armand Amaudruz has been a longtime Holocaust denier. He was born in December 1920 in Lausanne, Switzerland. After earning a certificate of political sciences and social sciences, he became a language teacher. Shortly after the end of World War II, Amaudruz became a publisher.

Amaudruz was an early Holocaust denier. In 1946, he founded a French language monthly newsletter *Courier of the Continent* (*Le Courrier du continent*) with the intent to distribute right-wing and Holocaust denial materials throughout Europe. Then in 1949, he wrote the book *Ubu Justicier au Premier Procès de Nuremberg* in which he questioned the existence of Nazi gas chambers. From this era onward he championed Holocaust denial in all of his writings. In 1951, he was active in the founding of the New European Order. This organization had its headquarters in Zurich. Members of the New European Order based its ideology on the Italian neo-Fascist philosopher Julius Evola.

Despite his close identification to Holocaust denial, Amaudruz escaped legal sanctions until 2000. Several Jewish groups had complained to Swiss authorities about Amaudruz's writings violating the 1995 Swiss "anti-racism" law. On April 10, 2000, a Swiss court convicted Amaudruz for denying the existence of gas chambers in World War II German concentration camps. It cited his books and two 1995 articles in his newsletter *Le Courrier du continent*. Armaudruz had written the following:

> For my part, I maintain my position. I don't believe in the gas chambers. Let the exterminationists provide the proof and I will believe it. But as I've been waiting for this proof for decades, I don't believe I will see it soon.[15]

His sentence was one year in prison, $2,400 in fines, and court costs. An appeals court reduced his prison term to three months. Before starting his prison term, Amaudruz was back in court because of publishing a book about the trial that included the writings for which he had been convicted. This new offense earned him another three-month prison sentence. He entered prison on January 13, 2003.

AHMED HUBER AND HOLOCAUST DENIAL

Ahmed Huber is another Swiss Holocaust denier. He was born in 1927 in Freiburg, Switzerland, under the name Albert Friedrich Armand Huber. His parents were staunch Protestants. His first political involvement was by joining the Swiss Socialist Party. It was as a member of this party that Huber first made contact with Algerian rebels in their war against France in the late 1950s. He helped them acquire weapons to be used in the Algerian War of Independence. While in the process Huber became attracted to Islam as a religion, and he made a profession of faith (shahada) at the Islamic Center in Geneva.[16] He later renewed his profession of faith at Cairo's Al-Azhar University in February 1962.

After returning from the Middle East, Huber became active in right-wing politics. He became friends with the neo-Nazi Swiss banker François Genoud. His anti-American and anti-Israeli activities led to his expulsion from the Swiss Socialist Party. His contacts with the Muslim Brotherhood led to his involvement with the Al Taqwa Bank in Switzerland. This bank helped launder money for various Middle Eastern causes, including providing funds for the disposal of Osama bin Laden. Huber was vocal in his praise of bin Laden and the September 11 attacks in New York and Washington, D.C. Because of pressure from Western governments, Al Taqwa Bank changed its name to Nada Management Corporation, but it still channeled funds to Middle Eastern causes.

Because of his Muslim and neo-Nazi connections, Huber has also become a prominent Holocaust denier. He has been a sponsor of the Swiss Holocaust denier Jürgen Graf and the Swedish/Moroccan Holocaust denier Ahmed Rami. His contacts have also been close to the American Institute for Historical Review. Huber was one of the chief planners of the 2001 Lebanese Holocaust Denial Conference to bring together Western and

Muslim Holocaust deniers, but this conference never took place because of international pressure against it.

JÜRGEN GRAF AND HOLOCAUST DENIAL

Another prominent Swiss Holocaust denier is Jürgen Graf. He was born on August 15, 1951, in Basel, Switzerland. His father worked in a bank, and his mother was a housewife. Graf attended the University of Basel where he studied French, English, and Scandinavian philology. In 1979, he earned a master's degree in philology from the University of Basel. After finishing his education, Graf found a teaching position teaching languages at a school in Basel. From 1982 until 1988, he taught German in Taipei, Taiwan. After returning to Switzerland, he found a position teaching Latin and French in the small town of Therwil. He held this position until he was fired in March 1993 after the publication of his first Holocaust denial book. In October 1994, he found another job teaching German for foreign students at a private language school in Basel. Graf held this position until August 1998 when again he was fired for his writings on Holocaust denial.

Graf had converted to Holocaust denial in the early 1990s. Before his conversion, Graf already held anti-Zionist views. His family had been German, and he had been a Germanophile from early childhood. A friend, Arthur Vogt, a retired teacher of mathematics and biology, persuaded him to read the Holocaust denial works of Serge Thion, Arthur R. Butz, and Wilhelm Stäglich, and he decided on April 29, 1991, to become a Holocaust denier.[17] His first book was *The Holocaust under the Scanner* (*Der Holocaust auf dem Pruefstand*) that appeared in 1993. Next, Graf published *The Holocaust Swindle* (*Der Holocaust-Schwindel*) also in 1993. He made the acquaintance of a German-born engineer, Gerhard Förster, who agreed to publish more of Graf's Holocaust denial books. They collaborated on the next book, *Auschwitz. Perpetrator Confessions and Eyewitnesses of the Holocaust* (*Auschwitz. Tätergeständnisse und Augenzeugen des Holocaust*), that appeared in August 1994. In this book, Graf concluded that all the eyewitnesses at Auschwitz had lied.[18] Graf followed this book with a fictional treatment of the Holocaust, *Cause of Death: Research of Contemporary History* (*Todesursache Zeitgeschichtsforschung*) that appeared in October 1995. He began to work closely with the Italian Holocaust denier Carlo Mattogno. They wrote a book together, *Concentration Camp Majdanek: A Historical and Technical Study*) (*KL Majdanek: Eine historische und technische Studie*). Then in 1999, Graf and Mattogno published the book *Concentration Camp Stutthof and Its Function in National Socialist Jewish Policy* (*Das Konzentrationslager Stutthof und seine Funktion in der nationalsozialistischen Judenpolitik*). Besides these works, Graf decided to attack the scholarship of the Holocaust historian Raul Hilberg with the book *The Giant with Feet of Clay: Raul Hilberg and His Standard Work on the*

"Holocaust" (*Riese auf Tönernen Füssen. Raul Hilberg und sein Standard-werk über den Holocaust*) in 2000.

Graf's Holocaust denial writings led Swiss authorities to press charges against him for violation of the antiracism law. A July 1998 court in the Swiss town of Baden convicted him of violating the Swiss antiracism law, and he was sentenced to 15 months' imprisonment and a heavy fine. While out of jail awaiting the results of an appeal, Graf fled Switzerland and his jail term. After a trip that included stays in Poland, Russia, Ukraine, and Turkey, Graf ended up in Iran. A group of Iranian Holocaust deniers sheltered him in Tehran until Graf relocated to Moscow, Russia. There Graf married a Belarusian woman in 2001. He still resides in Moscow, working as a translator.

In the late 1990s Graf developed strong ties to the American Institute for Historical Review (IHR). He has attended several of IHR's conferences, and in 1997 the Institute for Historical Review extended to him an invitation to serve on the Editorial Advisory Committee of the *Journal of Historical Review.* He remained on this board until the journal folded in 2002.

ERIK HAAEST AND DANISH HOLOCAUST DENIAL

Denmark is one of the European states that has no law against Holocaust denial. This immunity from law has led Denmark to become an international center for the publication and distribution of Holocaust denial and Nazi materials.[19] Its convenient proximity to Germany has led various Holocaust denial leaders to stage operations from there.

Denmark's leading Holocaust denier is Erik Haaest. He is a self-styled journalist who is most famous for attempting to debunk the Danish author of military novels Sven Hassel. Haaest's father fought in the Danish Resistance, but the son has retained an admiration for German Nazis. In his writings, Haaest entered the ranks of the Holocaust deniers by asserting that there were no gas chambers and the number of Jews killed during the Holocaust was false.[20] He further claimed that the diary of Anne Frank is a forgery.

Haaest has been immune from prosecution but not from controversy. Twice Haaest received government grants from the Danish Arts Council (2004 and 2006) to conduct research on the Danish Freikorps on the Russian Front 1941–1945. News of these grants led to a controversy in 2007. Jewish groups protested that a notorious Holocaust denier would receive government grants to advance his viewpoints. The Danish government has been reluctant to intervene in the controversy.

NORMAN LOWELL AND POLITICAL HOLOCAUST DENIAL

The leading racist and Holocaust denier in the Republic of Malta is Norman Lowell. He was born on July 29, 1946, in Malta. Most of his life he spent as a banker. He lives in Attard, Malta. Besides his involvement in banking, he is a martial-arts expert of the Ch'uan Shu martial-arts school and an amateur artist. Lowell turned to politics in the late 1990s. He founded the Imperium Europa (Empire Europe) with the desire to unite all Europeans under a single flag celebrating a common racial heritage.

Lowell's political views are a mixture of different views. Critics have described him as a racist, antisemite, and neo-Nazi, but he has denied all these labels. Instead Lowell calls himself a racialist. Lowell says he is not against minorities, but his actions list Jews, black immigrants, and other non-Europeans as enemies. Efforts to classify him as a Fascist have led Lowell to call himself "a revolutionary conservative."[21] Among his other controversial views he has expressed admiration for Adolf Hitler and his book *Mein Kampf*. His attitude toward the Holocaust is that it is a "holy hoax" perpetrated by the Jews.[22]

Lowell has political ambitions. In the June 2004 election for the first European Parliament Lowell received less than 1 percent of the vote. He is nevertheless a popular figure in Maltese politics with his charming personality, white suit, and trademark walking stick.[23] Several times Lowell has run afoul of Maltese law because of his public statements and writings. In 2002, Lowell was banned from the Maltese media in response to his controversial comments on public television. Both in 2005 and 2006 Lowell was charged with incitement to racial hatred, but he has been able to escape conviction and jail. His demand for racial purity has put him in the forefront of Maltese agitation against West African immigrants landing in Malta. Lowell stated in January 2005 that "refugee boats should be prevented from docking and, after a warning, sunk if necessary."[24]

Lowell is a prime example of a charismatic politician using racism and Holocaust denial as political tools to advance his career. His plan is to turn Malta into the spiritual focal point of Europe. Lowell's ideas appear in his book *Credo: a Book for the Very Few* (1999). Unlike other Holocaust deniers, Lowell has not made contact with others in the Holocaust denial movement.

RUSSIAN AND EASTERN EUROPEAN HOLOCAUST DENIAL

Holocaust denial is a recent phenomenon in Russia and Eastern European countries. Even though there had been a lengthy history of antisemitism in Eastern Europe, these countries generally ignored the Holocaust while under the control of the Soviet Union. Nazi war crimes were glossed over and considered emblematic of capitalist society. Jewish losses in the Holocaust never became a topic of discussion because the Soviet and Eastern European authorities submerged the figures into the anti-Fascist campaign against the Nazis. This policy has been described as "state-organized forgetting."[25] Since the collapse of the Soviet Union, however, right-wing nationalists have emerged in Russia and Eastern Europe eager to advance their cause. They have embraced a revisionist history of their countries that incorporates a version of Holocaust denial. Randolph L. Braham has placed these actions into context.

> Revolting as the "revisionists" are, it is perhaps even more disturbing to witness the falsification of history by elites and public officials in power during the post-communist era. They are engaged in a "history cleansing" process, aiming, among other things, at the gradual rehabilitation of their countries' wartime leaders.[26]

Sometimes, however, the advocates of national revival go beyond revisionism to outright Holocaust denial. Leon Volovici reports this phenomenon.

> An extreme of the avoidance of facing the historical truth and neglecting to take responsibility for the past can be seen in the denial that the Holocaust took place, although this denial is less complete than what one finds sometimes in certain extreme circles, in the United State and Western Europe. Nearer to the "scene of the crime" debates in Eastern Europe center on "proving" the innocence of local authorities in the perpetration of the massacres, or seek to diminish substantially the number of victims.[27]

RUSSIAN HOLOCAUST DENIAL

Holocaust denial has been slower to develop in post-Soviet Russia. The Soviet hierarchy had been even tighter in Russia than in the Eastern Bloc countries to ignore the Holocaust and submerge it into the holy war to defeat Nazism. Any attempt to rehabilitate Nazism has to overcome the lasting memories of the heavy losses in the Great Patriotic War. Soviet historians have estimated Russian losses at around 20 million with the totals half civilian and half military, but Western historians agree at the 20 million and divide the totals at 13.6 million military and 7.7 million civilian.[28] Since much of the Holocaust denial is an effort to rehabilitate Nazism, it has had to be marketed in a different light.[29]

An early Holocaust denier was Konstantin Smirnov-Ostashvili. He was a leading member in the antisemitic right-wing Pamyat (Memory) Party. In an interview with Robert S. Wistrich in 1990, Smirnov-Ostashvili was vocal in his condemnation of Jews for what he called "the mass genocide of the Russian people," denied the Jewish Holocaust took place, and advocated a "Russo-German alliance to eliminate the 'dark forces' of Zionism from the world."[30] Smirnov-Ostashvili's antisemitic activities were so violent that the Gorbachev government arrested him in January 1990. On October 22, 1990, a Moscow court sentenced him to two years of hard labor for shouting antisemitic threats at a gathering at the Central House of Writers in January 1990. Smirnov-Ostashvili's career came to an abrupt end on April 26, 1991, when he committed suicide while in prison.

The leading active backer of Holocaust denial in Russia is Oleg Platonov. He is a nationalist antisemite economist with ties to the American Institute for Historical Review. Until the *Journal of Historical Review* shut down in 2002, Platonov was on its editorial advisory board since his appointment to it in 1997.[31] Rather than write Holocaust denial books or articles, Platonov publishes the works of prominent Holocaust deniers from Jürgen Graf to Carlo Mattogno. Holocaust denial themes, however, have appeared in one of his books, *Conspiracy of the Zionist Protocols* (*Zagadka sionskikh protokolov*).[32] He has also been quoted by Mark Weber in the *Journal of Historical Review* as follows:

> The myth of the Holocaust insults humanity because it portrays the Jewish peo-
> ple as the main victims of the last war, even though the Jews in fact suffered not
> more, but less than other peoples who were caught up in that murderous con-
> flict . . . Humanity paid for the war with 55 million human lives, in which the
> real—not the mythical—number of Jewish victims was not six million, but
> rather about 500,000, as the calculations of specialists show.[33]

The major attention of Russian scholarship is directed toward the history of the Soviet period of Russian history. Most historians are combing the archives and writing about Stalin and the Soviet period. The great fear is that Russian extremist groups will attach themselves to Holocaust denial for political reasons. So far the scapegoating of Jews has appeared "in main-stream politics, in the mass media and in academia, to a far greater extent than denial of the Holocaust."[34]

POLISH HOLOCAUST DENIAL

Holocaust denial has been less popular in Poland because of the existence of so many of the concentration camps there. This fact has retarded but not excluded the development of a Holocaust denial school in Poland. The extreme right nationalist party, the National Revival of Poland (Narodowe Odrodzenie Polski), under the leadership of Adam Gmurczyk, who had graduated with a degree in history from Warsaw Academy of Catholic Theol-ogy, launched a Holocaust denial campaign in 1994–1995 in its publication *The Sword* (*Szczerbiec*).[35] Among the first articles in this journal was David Irving's "Why I Don't Believe in the Holocaust."[36] This publication received a subsidy from the American organization Polish Historical Institute, which was headed by Miroslaw Dragan.[37] A number of Holocaust denial articles appeared, and the party published a book in 1997 entitled *The Myth of the Holocaust*. This book contained translated contributions from the most important Holocaust deniers in Western Europe and the United States.

Another Polish supporter of Holocaust denial was Tomasz Gabiś. He belonged to the right-wing Real Politics Party (Stronnictwo Polityki

Realnem). His role in the party is as editor for its journal *Stanczak,* but he has also been the author of several Holocaust denial articles.[38]

The first Polish Holocaust denial book appeared in March 1999 by Dariusz Ratajczak. Ratajczak was a historical researcher at the newly founded University of Opole when he wrote the book *Dangerous Topics* (*Tematy niebezpieczne*). He had been affiliated with the extreme right National Party (Stronnictwo Narodowe), and his book is extremely anti-semitic, with a chapter advocating Holocaust denial.[39] In this chapter Ratajczak did not explicitly endorse the Holocaust denial views of Paul Rassinier, Robert Faurisson, David Irving, and Ernst Zündel, but he did call Holocaust "eyewitness" testimony "useless" and described establishment Holocaust writers as "followers of a religion of the Holocaust" who impose on others "a false image of the past."[40] He also disparaged the 6 million Jewish death toll in the Holocaust, and he reduced it to 3 million.[41] Another Polish historian, Witold Kulesza, complained to Polish authorities that this book violated the 1997 law's "provision against those who deny crimes against humanity committed by the Nazi and Stalinist Communists on Polish territory."[42] A December 1999 court in Opole acknowledged that Ratajczak had broken the law, but it ruled his crime was "socially harmless."[43] Ratajczak appeared on a January 13, 2000, radio program on Radio Maryja with two other Polish historians, and they proceeded to advance Holocaust denial arguments. Administrators at the University of Opole reluctantly fired Ratajczak in the aftermath of the controversy about his remarks. Ratajczak avoided joblessness by taking a position at the private Higher School of Journalism at Warsaw.

Another Polish Holocaust denier is Bolesław Tejkowski. He is the leader of the neo-Fascist Polish National Fellowship. A lifelong antisemite, Tejkowski has claimed that "the Shoah (Holocaust) was actually a Jewish conspiracy to enable Jews to hide their children in monasteries during World War II so that they could be baptized and thereby take over the Church from within."[44] He followed that Pope John Paul II was actually a Jew.[45]

FRANJO TUDJMAN AND CROATIAN HOLOCAUST DENIAL

It is in this context that the late Croatian President Franjo Tudjman became a Holocaust denier. Many Croatians had cooperated with the Nazis in World War II. Tudjman had fought against the Nazis in the ranks of the partisans, but after the war he became an ultranationalist and an antisemite. Tudjman wanted to minimize the role of the Croatian Ustaše and the activities at the Croat concentration camp at Jasenovac.[46] Nazis and their Croatian allies killed approximately 800,000 Serbs, Jews, Gypsies, and anti-Fascists at Jasenovac. In earlier works Tudjman reduced the total killed at Jasenovac to 30,000. His book *Wastelands—Historical Truth* (*Bespuća povijesne zbiljnosti*) questioned the number of Jews killed during the

Holocaust. He wrote that the "estimated loss of up to 6 million dead is founded too much on both emotional based testimonies and on exaggerated data in the post-war reckonings of war crimes and squaring of accounts with the defeated perpetrators of war crimes."[47] Later, he wrote that the Israelis conducted "a genocidal policy towards the Palestinians that they can rightly be defined as Judeo-Nazis."[48]

ROMANIAN HOLOCAUST DENIAL

Holocaust denial has developed its own characteristics in Russia and Eastern Europe because most of the denial deals with historical figures in individual countries. The best example is Romania where Holocaust denial concerns the role of General Ion Antonescu in the deportation of Jews to German concentration camps. The leader of this rehabilitation campaign until recently was Iosif Constantin Drăgan, the second wealthiest man in Romania and an ultranationalist who controlled the right-wing weekly newspaper *Europa*.[49] Articles appeared in the summer of 1991 in *Europa* denying the Romanian Holocaust. The authors of these articles maintained that Antonescu is a national hero and there was no Holocaust in Romania.[50] His death on August 21, 2008, ended his influence as a Holocaust denier.

Most significant of these Romanian writers is Corneliu Vadim Tudor. Tudor had close ties to the former Romanian secret police—Securitate. He was a founder of the extreme right-wing weekly *Greater Romania* (*Romania Mare*) and the political party of the same name. Among his close associates were Eugen Barbu and Drăgan.[51] Several of his supporters were retired high-ranking army officers. Tudor continues to contribute articles to both *Europa* and *Romania Mare*. Beginning in 1990, antisemitic articles began to appear in both publications. Other right-wing publications joined in the attacks on Jews and their perceived allies. One, *Oblio*, issued *The Protocols of the Elders of Zion* in a serialized format.[52] In another, *Arena Magazin*, Holocaust denial articles began to appear. In a March 4, 1994, article in *Romania Mare* Tudor charged that the "Holocaust is a Zionist stratagem" and a "physical and technical impossibility" as "proven by English and American scholars."[53] He charged furthermore that the Holocaust was "nothing but" a Zionist scheme aimed at squeezing out from Germany about 100 billion Deutschmarks and to terrorize for more than 40 years all those who do not acquiesce to the Jewish yoke."[54] Romanian nationalists remain active in their efforts to rehabilitate Antonescu using any means, including Holocaust denial, to achieve their goal.

SLOVAKIAN HOLOCAUST DENIAL

A similar political process has been taken in Slovakia by Slovakian nationalists. Their goal is to rehabilitate Josef Tiso and his regime. To do so these

right-wing nationalists have to deny Tiso's role in cooperating with the
Nazis in the deportation of Slovak Jews to Nazi concentration camps. The
leader of this movement is Stanislav Pánis, an economist and the then head
of the Slovak National Unity Party, and his arguments resemble closely
those of Holocaust deniers in Western Europe and the United States.[55]
He stated in 1992 that "it would have been 'technically impossible' for the
Nazis to exterminate six million Jews in camps."[56] Panis continued that
Auschwitz was an "invention of the Jews to extort compensation from
Germany."[57] Despite the fact that it has never been the contention by histor-
ians that more than 4 million Jews had been killed in concentration camps,
Pánis's remarks did little to hinder his political career as later he served as
Deputy Culture Minister. Another prominent Slovak Holocaust denier is
Frantisek Vnuk, a historian and a leader of the Slovak Christian Democratic
Party.[58]

CONCLUSION

European Holocaust denial has expanded across Europe. In the beginning
French Holocaust deniers took the lead, and they remain the most active.
Robert Faurisson has developed a French school of Holocaust deniers.
It has been more difficult for German Holocaust deniers because of more
intense legal pressure, but a growing number of them have challenged
German laws. German authorities have also taken steps to stem the flow of
Holocaust denial and neo-Nazi materials arriving in Germany from abroad.
Swiss Holocaust deniers have become active in the last decade. Individuals
have popped up from a variety of countries: Irving in Great Britain,
Mattogno in Italy, Rami in Sweden, Varela in Spain, and Verbeke in Belgian.
The area of most potential for Holocaust denial expansion is in Eastern
Europe and Russia. Holocaust denial is a recent arrival there, but there is a
lengthy history of antisemitism that will allow it to grow.

PART III

American Holocaust Denial

8

Early American Holocaust Denial

INTRODUCTION

The Holocaust Denial movement came out of Europe, but it soon reached a receptive audience in the United States. It merged with two distinctive American intellectual strains—native antisemitism and the negative eugenics movement. Antisemitism had never been as virulent in the United States as in Europe, but it still exists in the American extreme Right. During the Great Depression and on the eve of World War II, antisemitism grew at an alarming rate. In a 1941 report on American antisemitism, the point was made that only 5 hate groups had been in existence in 1927 as opposed to 121 appearing between 1933 and 1940.[1] One explanation was the dislocation caused by the Depression, but there were other reasons. Two factors spread the antisemitic message in the United States—Henry Ford's *The International Jew: The World's Foremost Problem* and the radio talk show of Father Charles Coughlin in the late 1930s. Ford had achieved fame and success as a builder of automobiles, but his acceptance of the authenticity of the forged *The Protocols of the Learned Elders of Zion* and his publication of this work in *The International Jew* helped spread the message. Frank P. Mintz placed Ford's acceptance in perspective by stating, "the *Protocols* were a fraudulent concoction, but they satisfied the needs of ideologists who expounded a plot theory of history that pointed to collusion between high finance and the forces of rebellion and subversion."[2]

World War II discredited both Nazism and Fascism among most Americans. A tiny fringe maintained their antisemitic views, but, in general, these individuals kept a low profile. After the war, antisemites reappeared and they were as active promoting their agenda much as they had before the war. Numerous groups appeared eager to spread their antisemitic views.

Those supporters of Hitler and Nazism had the same dilemma as their European compatriots. Only by discrediting the Holocaust could a viable national socialist movement have any chance of success. American antisemitic and neo-Nazi extremists started looking to Europe and the growth of the Holocaust denial movement. They were willing to give credence to the ideas coming from Europe because these ideas conformed to antisemitism already present in the United States.

HARRY ELMER BARNES AND THE SPREAD OF HOLOCAUST DENIAL TO THE UNITED STATES

Holocaust denial had no difficulty in winning American adherents. Most receptive was Harry Elmer Barnes, a professor of history at Smith College and a famous revisionist critic of World War I and the Versailles peace settlement.[3] This was an abrupt change of opinion from his prowar stance during World War I. In the interwar period, Barnes became a champion of Germany, showing an early approval of Hitler. He was also active in the American isolationist movement. Barnes had an aggressive personality, and he was convinced that "his beliefs constituted objective truth; consequently anyone who took a different view was neither objective nor honest."[4] His "acerbic attacks on other scholars" in the field led to his losing credibility among historians.[5]

After World War II, he published a 1947 pamphlet, *The Struggle against the Historical Blackout,* which extended his argument that the Allies were responsible for World War II, absolving the Germans of any responsibility. He blamed the British and Franklin Delano Roosevelt for the war. He also made the charge that the German refugees from Poland and the Sudetenland had suffered more than the Jews did during World War II.[6] Over the years he became increasing attracted to Holocaust denial by his exposure to the writing of the French Holocaust denier Paul Rassinier and by his inclination to favor the Germans.[7] Rassinier's works confirmed to Barnes that the Allies rather than the Germans were the villains in World War II. In a 1966 essay in *The American Mercury* entitled "Zionist Fraud," Barnes showed his total adoption of Rassinier's ideas on the Holocaust.

> The courageous author [Rassinier] lays the chief blame for misrepresentation on those whom we must call the swindlers of the crematoria, the Israeli politicians who derive billions of marks from nonexistent, mythical and imaginary cadavers, whose numbers have reckoned in an unusually distorted and dishonest manner.[8]

Barnes also mentored David Hoggan and helped him publish his pro-Hitler and anti-Allies book *The Forced War (Der Erzwungene Krieg)*.[9] The 1966 article "The Public State in Revisionism" published in *Rampart Journal* clarified Barnes's attitude toward the Holocaust.

> The number of civilians exterminated by the Allies, before, during, and after the second world war, equaled, if it did not far exceed those liquidated by the Germans, and the Allies liquidation program was often carried out by methods which were far more brutal and painful than whatever extermination actually took place in German gas ovens.[10]

He remained an ally of the Holocaust denial movement until his death in August 1968. His legacy as a historian resides on his historical revisionism of World War I and the peace settlement, but his revisionism of World War II is generally ignored. Where Barnes is still considered an important historian is by the Holocaust deniers and libertarians.[11]

FRANCIS PARKER YOCKEY AND HOLOCAUST DENIAL

One of the most cynical of the early American Holocaust deniers was Francis Parker Yockey. He had been an unabashed admirer of Hitler and the Nazis. His book *Imperium* ranks with Adolf Hitler's *Mein Kampf* and William Pierce's *The Turner Diaries* (1978) for influence among American neo-Nazis. He was born on September 18, 1917, in Chicago, Illinois, into an upper-middle-class Catholic family. His father had training in the law, but he worked as a stockbroker. With an IQ approaching the 170 range, Yockey was always an outstanding student, and he displayed early talent as a classical pianist. He attended the University of Michigan before transferring to Georgetown University, and to the University of Arizona where he finally received a B.A. degree. Later, Yockey entered law school at Northwestern University and then DePaul University Law School before finally obtaining a law degree from University of Notre Dame Law School.

In the mid-1930s, Yockey began to display an attraction for Adolf Hitler and Nazism. Despite his pro-Nazi feelings, he enlisted in the U.S. Army, serving in an intelligence unit station in Georgia. In July 1943, Yockey received an honorable discharge from the army after suffering an alleged nervous breakdown.[12] It was about this time that his name appeared on a government list of Americans suspected of pro-Nazi leanings.

After the war, Yockey turned his attention toward Germany and rehabilitating Nazism. After a brief stint as an assistant prosecuting attorney for Wayne County, Michigan, Yockey found a job as a civilian member of the American prosecution team prosecuting Nazi war criminals in Wiesbaden, Germany. Yockey had always had trouble with relationships because of his outspokenness and dictatorial manners, and combining these personal characteristics with his neo-Nazi views made him a difficult person to be around, even by those in sympathy with his views.[13] His blatant efforts to help Nazi prisoners, his antagonistic attitude toward his fellow prosecutors, and his absenteeism became so obvious that he was fired. He relocated in the Republic of Ireland in 1947, abandoning his estranged wife and two young daughters in Germany. While in exile in Brittas Bay, Republic of Ireland, Yockey decided to write a book that would reflect his pro-Nazi worldview. After finishing the manuscript, Yockey had to find financial backing to have it published. After approaching several European sources, Yockey finally found financial support from the mysterious Baroness Alice von Pflugl.[14]

Yockey published *Imperium* in two volumes in 1949 under the name Ulick Varange. In his book, Yockey glorified Nazi Germany, and he charged that the Jews were to blame for the woes of the twentieth century and World War II. Yockey also realized that the Holocaust was an impediment to the growth of an international Nazi movement. Therefore, he denied the existence of the Holocaust by claiming that the Holocaust was merely Allied propaganda.[15]

> This propaganda announced that 6,000,000 members of the Jewish Culture-Nation-State-Church-People-Race had been killed in European camps, as well as an indeterminate number of other people. The propaganda was on a world-wide scale, and was of a mendacity that was perhaps adapted to a uniformized mass, but was simply disgusting to discriminating Europeans. The propaganda was technically quite complete. "Photographs" were supplied in millions of copies. Thousands of people who had been killed published accounts of their experiences in these camps. Hundreds of thousands more made fortunes in post-war black-markets. "Gas-chambers" that did not exist were photographed, and a "gasmobile" was invented to titillate the mechanically-minded.[16]

His cynical approach would not have been so influential except that it was adopted in toto by his fervent admirer Willis A. Carto.

Both American and European neo-Nazis and neo-Fascists welcomed Yockey's book with open arms. Yockey made certain that *Imperium* received maximum exposure by sending copies of it to prominent figures in the American and European extremist Right with special attention to British, French, German, and Italian leaders.[17] James Hartung Madole, the leader of the neo-Nazi American Renaissance Party, welcomed the book, and he classified it as the second greatest work on "racial nationalism since Hitler's *Mein Kampf*."[18] Among other Europeans praising the book were Maurice Bardèche, the French Fascist politician, and Julius Evola, the Italian Fascist philosopher.[19] Two British enthusiasts for his book were Major-General J. F. C. Fuller and Captain Basil Liddell Hart.[20]

Other extremists found *Imperium* full of faults, but they found it difficult to reject. This was the position of veteran American extremist Revilo P. Oliver. In a letter to right-wing activist Colonel Curtis B. Dall, the former son-in-law of Franklin Delano Roosevelt, on December 17, 1970, Oliver stated this.

> As I stated in print years ago, I am aware that *Imperium*, which was to be the basic doctrine of the N. Y. A. (National Youth Alliance), was not a perfect work because (1) it contained errors of historical fact that made it vulnerable to criticism, although the errors were merely incidental and did not affect its major thesis; (2) contained serious biological errors because Yockey relied on Spengler, who, in turn, relied partly on forged data so concocted by our enemies as to appear scientific, and partly on obsolete theories; (3) was written from a European, rather than an American, point of view; and (4) contained frequent references to, and projections from, a situation that was contemporary when Yockey wrote but was already more than two decades in the past. But despite these defects, *Imperium* was by far the best doctrine that was available. It was basically sound, and some of the shortcomings had been corrected in the preface that Carto wrote on the basis of my critique and suggestions. It was not perfect, but rational men use the weapons that are available now.[21]

Much of Yockey's efforts in 1948–1949 were spent in attacking the Nuremberg Trials. Kevin Coogan claims that some of Yockey's anti-Nuremberg Trial materials ended up in the hands of the French right-wing extremist Maurice Bardèche for his books attacking the Nuremberg Trials.[22] Bardèche later acknowledged his debt to Yockey for providing materials for his second Nuremberg book, *Nuremberg II or the Counterfeiters (Nuremberg II ou Les Faux Monnayeurs)*, in his memoirs.[23]

Yockey gathered a small group of European dissident Fascists and formed the European Liberation Front (ELF) in late 1949. The goal of the European Liberation Front was to expel Jews from Europe and promote a neutralist Europe. Yockey was the leading force of the ELF, and it was his ideas that appeared in its monthly bulletin *Frontfighter*. During his tenure as head of the ELF, Yockey traveled around Europe meeting with leading figures in the neo-Nazi and neo-Fascist movements. Bardèche described in a letter Yockey's meeting with the French right-wing extremist René Binet.

> Varange (Yockey) allowed absolutely no criticism of his ideas. He was the repository of an absolute, undebatable truth, and that the methods that he thought to be able to use allowed no discussion. I had absolutely abstained from taking a position and in fact the discussion, often passionate and violent, took place only between Varange and René Binet. I even refused to arbitrate between two adversaries whose personalities were equally opposed and intolerant and impermissible to all arbitration.[24]

It was this lack of flexibility and intolerance of other ideas that soon persuaded the British members to leave the ELF, so it withered away.

Yockey's anti-Americanism led him to consider the Soviet Union as a potential leader of a unified antisemitic Europe. He witnessed the growing antisemitism of the Soviet government in the 1952 Prague Purge Trials that convicted 14 Czech leaders of treason. Eleven of the 14 were Jews. This trial convinced Yockey that the Soviet Union was a prime candidate to become the leader of a unified antisemitic Europe.

Yockey wrote and then had published in 1953 a new pro-Europe and anti-American book for German consumption entitled *The Enemy of Europe* (*Der Feind Europas*). The printer made only 200 copies; it had to be distributed underground to avoid German laws against its subject matter.[25] He had to solicit funds from varying right-wing sources to get it published. Yockey made certain that the book reached German nationalists and prominent neo-Nazis.

Throughout the rest of his life Yockey advanced his pro-Nazi and Holocaust denial views. He traveled around Europe and the Middle East advancing his anti-American and antisemitic ideas. Yockey often made trips to the United States to consult with friends and collaborators. On one such trip to Oakland, California, his luggage was lost at the Dallas, Texas, airport. After an examination of the luggage, authorities found six passports issued to various persons. Yockey was arrested after he tried to pick up his luggage in Oakland. His only visitor while he was in jail was Willis A. Carto, the then head of the Liberty Lobby and future founder of the Institute for Historical Review. After Carto became a convert to his ideas, Yockey's ideas ended up having the most influence in the United States. Yockey committed suicide by swallowing a cyanide capsule on June 17, 1960, while in an Oakland jail. Because of the efforts of Carto, Yockey is more popular after his death than he ever was while he was alive.

GERALD K. SMITH AND HOLOCAUST DENIAL

Gerald K. Smith was one of the leaders of the American antisemitic movement from the 1930s to the 1970s, and he incorporated Holocaust denial as part of his antisemitic agenda. He was born on February 27, 1898, in Pardeeville, Wisconsin. His father was a combination small farmer and minister in the local First Christian Church. Smith attended Valparaiso University earning a degree in oratory in 1918. During college, he worked as a minister to earn money for his schooling. Smith held a number of ministries in Indiana before moving to Shreveport, Louisiana, becoming a minister at the King's Highway Christian Church. His involvement with the Louisiana populist politician Huey Long led to his resigning his ministry in August 1934 and joining Long's political machine. Smith worked for Long's Share Our Wealth clubs as an administrator until Long's death. Long's family fired him and told him to leave the state.

The rest of Smith's career was in extremist politics. After a flirtation with William Dudley Pelley's Fascist Silver Shirts, he attempted to defeat President Franklin Delano Roosevelt in the 1936 election by joining with the antisemitic

Father Charles Coughlin and Dr. Francis Townsend in the Union Party. After this attempt failed, Smith started the Committee of One Million in 1937 to oppose the policies of Roosevelt's New Deal. Smith began to flirt with the "isms" of the day: anticommunism, racism, antisemitism, and anti-Catholicism. He worked briefly with Gerald Winrod, the so-called Jayhawk Nazi minister, before moving to Detroit, Michigan, in 1939. While in Michigan, he became attracted to the antisemitism of Henry Ford and Adolf Hitler's National Socialism.[26] Smith also participated in the Isolationism movement.

During World War II, Smith continued to agitate against the policies of the U.S. government. He ran for and lost the nomination for the U.S. Senate seat in Michigan as an anti-Roosevelt candidate in 1943. More importantly, in 1942 Smith started the magazine *The Cross and the Flag* to provide a public forum for his increasing extremist views. He also founded the America First Party, which ran him as an unsuccessful candidate for the presidency in 1944.

Smith continued in American extremist politics in the postwar world. Immediately after the war, Smith moved to the Los Angeles, California, area where he launched the successor to the America First Party in the Christian National Crusade in 1947. The platform of the Christian National Crusade was for the deportation of all Zionists, removal of blacks to Africa, and the dissolution of the United Nations. Smith ran again for the presidency of the United States in 1948, but he garnered little support. By this time Smith's views had become even more extreme. He believed that communists and Jews had formed an international conspiracy against Christian America. Part of the conspiracy was the Holocaust. Smith published an article in *The Cross and the Flag* in 1959 entitled "Into the Valley of Death Rode the Six Million, Or Did They?" in which he maintained that all of the missing Jews in Germany and Eastern Europe had immigrated to the United States and had voted for Roosevelt.[27] His opposition to the United Nations was based on his belief that it was part of the international Jewish conspiracy.

Smith continued his extremist politics into the 1960s and 1970s. He never apologized for his hatred of Jews and minorities. One of Smith's disciples in Los Angeles was Wesley Swift, who later founded the modern Christian Identity movement. Smith was another extremist who lived off the contributions of his supporters. In the late 1960s, he moved to Eureka Springs, Arkansas, where he became the elder statesman of the antisemitic and white supremacist movements. On April 15, 1976, Smith died in Glendale, California. He was never a leader in the Holocaust denial movement, but he helped spread its ideas among other American extremists.[28]

JAMES HARTUNG MADOLE AND THE NATIONAL RENAISSANCE PARTY

James Hartung Madole was the head of the National Renaissance Party (NRP), and he was an early convert to Holocaust denial. A key member of the NRP was the German-American Frederick Charles Weiss. Weiss had extensive contacts in the postwar neo-Nazi German circles. He received materials from West Germany in a pamphlet entitled *The Jewish War against the German People* in 1954 that questioned the existence of the Holocaust.[29] Weiss obviously passed on the information to Madole, because in a meeting in New York City on June 3, 1955, Madole made the following statement:

> All reports about the fate of the six million Jews in Europe are false, . . . , because the whole obnoxious lot of them can be seen any day in the garment center in New York City.[30]

Madole retained control of the American Renaissance Party until his death in 1960. It had always been a small-time operation with Madole running it out of a New York City apartment. His major problem was fending off rivals. Members came through the American Renaissance Party before joining other extremist groups. Madole also made the mistake of opting for the pro-Soviet orientation of Yockey in the middle the Cold War. His chief rival George Lincoln Rockwell used the communist label with some success against Madole and his group. After Madole's death, the American Renaissance Party folded. It had never been as big a player in Holocaust denial as in neo-Nazism.

GEORGE LINCOLN ROCKWELL AND HOLOCAUST DENIAL

Another early convert to Holocaust denial was George Lincoln Rockwell, who became the head of the American Nazi Party. He was born March 9, 1918, in Bloomington, Illinois. His father, George (Doc) Lovejoy Rockwell, was a famous vaudeville comedian, and his mother was a dancer. After his parents divorced, Rockwell lived in a variety of places. After graduating from Hebron Academy in Lewiston, Maine, he attended Brown University until he joined the U.S. Navy on December 8, 1941. Rockwell served in the Naval Air Wing in World War II and as a pilot in Korea. He had always been fascinated with Hitler and Nazism, and this led him to form the American Nazi Party in 1959. To rehabilitate both Hitler and Nazism, Rockwell adopted Holocaust denial as a propaganda tool after his German mentor Bruno Armin Ludtke introduced him to the issues in the early 1960s.[31] Rockwell believed that this rehabilitation of Nazism was a necessary precondition for the American Nazi Party to achieve political success as a mass party in the United States. He helped popularize Holocaust denial with his April 1966 interview in *Playboy* during which he enumerated the arguments of the Holocaust deniers. Furthermore, he added the charge that the Jewish-controlled press in the United States promoted the Holocaust fraud.[32] Rockwell carried his views on Holocaust denial to his involvement with the World Union of National Socialists (WUNS). The WUNS was an attempt to unify neo-Nazi parties and groups from around the world under his leadership. As early as 1959, Rockwell had floated the idea for such an organization. Rockwell envisaged the WUNS to serve as a "revolutionary cadre for propaganda, agitation, and recruitment.[33] Rockwell turned to the British neo-Nazi Colin Jordan for help. They soon became fast friends. Jordan had connections with other prominent European neo-Nazi intellectuals such as French Fascist Savitri Devi and German neo-Nazi Bruno Armin Ludtke. Both Devi and Ludtke were easily converted to the idea of an international organization of National Socialists.

A world conference of National Socialists took place in July 1962 at a site in the Cotswold Hills of Gloucestershire in Great Britain. Delegates from seven European countries and the United States attended. At the end of the six-day conference the members had drafted the Cotswold Agreement, setting up the World Union of National Socialists. In this agreement the participants acknowledged a plan to recognize the spiritual leadership of Adolf Hitler, a pledge to destroy Zionism and Israel, and the creation of a plan for a National Socialist world revolution. His alliance with Jordan, Ludtke, and Devi allowed Rockwell to assume leadership of the WUNS. Jordan formally announced the existence of the WUNS on August 15, 1962, shortly after the British government had deported Rockwell on August 9.

By 1965, the World Union of National Socialists was a going concern with operating chapters in 20 countries. Rockwell remained the leader of the WUNS, but Jordan was number two in the hierarchy and its administrative head. Despite its apparent success, organizational problems developed in the leadership of various European chapters. Government pressure in Germany and Great Britain hindered the progress of the WUNS, making recruitment of members difficult. The assassination of Rockwell in 1967 was a blow from which the WUNS never fully recovered. A number of American and European neo-Nazi leaders headed the WUNS over the years, but by the mid-1990s it had all but disappeared. Holocaust denial played a role in the WUNS, but Rockwell and his successors played it down to make National Socialism more respectable.

AUSTIN J. APP AND HOLOCAUST DENIAL

The next important American Holocaust denial proponent was Austin J. App. Much as Barnes, App was pro-German and he had been active in various German-American groups. He was born on May 24, 1902, in Milwaukee, Wisconsin, to German immigrant parents. His parents were farmers. Always a good student, App obtained a liberal arts education from St. Francis Seminary near Milwaukee, graduating in 1923. After attending Catholic University in Washington, D.C., where he obtained a M.A. and Ph.D. in English literature, he found a teaching position at the University of Scranton starting in 1934. He remained at the University of Scranton until

1942. After a short tour in the U.S. Army Corps of Engineers in 1942, he moved to various colleges before ending up at LaSalle College in 1948 where he taught medieval English literature.

App was an active defender of Germany before, during, and after World War II. Before the war, he defended the policies of Nazi Germany in numerous publications. Even during the war, App was busy proclaiming Nazi Germany's innocence in starting the war in letters to magazines and newspapers. He continued this line of defense after the war, charging that the war was the fault of Jews and Bolsheviks.[34] Two of his postwar writings were *Ravishing the Women of Conquered Europe* (1946) and *History's Most Terrifying Peace* (1947). Later, he authored a defense of Nazi Germany in the short book *A Straight Look at the Third Reich* (1974) and an attack on the Jews for the crucifixion of Jesus Christ in *The Curse of Anti-Anti-Semitism* (1976).

App built his support for Germany and his antisemitic views into Holocaust denial. He became the president of the Federation of American Citizens of German Descent in 1945, and he remained its president for several years.[35] His major activity was in defending Germany from atrocity charges. App defended the German massacre of Lidice, Czechoslovakia, after the assassination of the SS commander Reinhard Heydrich, and then he extended the defense to German concentration camps.[36] He also wrote articles in the 1950s for Conde McGinley's anti-Semitic newspaper *Common Sense*.[37] App was a prodigious writer writing hundreds of books, pamphlets, articles, and reviews during his career. He began questioning the Holocaust by challenging the number killed and the existence of the gas chambers. In 1973, App wrote a pamphlet *The Six Million Swindle: Blackmailing the German People for Hard Marks with Fabricated Corpses* in which he tried to demonstrate that it was impossible for the Germans to have killed 6 million Jews.[38] Furthermore, he blamed Jewish leaders for what he called a massive deception.[39] He then transferred the responsibility for the deception to the Zionists and Israel. App crafted the so-called eight "incontrovertible assertions" around which Holocaust denial is built.

> First, the Third Reich wanted to get Jews to emigrate, not to liquidate them physically. Had they intended to extermination, 500,000 concentration camp survivors would not now be in Israel to collect fancy indemnities from West Germany.
>
> Second, absolutely no Jews were "gassed" in any concentration camps. There were crematoria for cremating corpses who had died from whatever cause, including especially also the victims of the genocidic Anglo–American air raids.
>
> Third, the majority of Jews who died in pograms and those who disappeared and are still unaccounted for fell afoul in territories controlled by the Soviet Russians, not in territories while under German control.
>
> Fourth, most of the Jews alleged to have met their death at the hands of Germans were subversives, partisans, spies, and criminals, and also often

victims of unfortunate but internationally legal reprisals. One reason for my denouncing the Nuremberg prosecutors as lynchers is that they hanged Germans for actions they themselves adopted!

Fifth, if there existed the slightest likelihood that the Nazis had in fact executed six million Jews, World Jewry would scream for subsidies with which to do research on the question, and Israel would throw its archives and files open to historians. They have not done so. On the contrary they have per-secuted anyone who tries to investigate impartially and even call him an anti-Semite. This is really devastating evidence that the figure is a swindle.

Sixth, the Jews and the media who exploit this figure have never offered a a shred of evidence of valid evidence for its truth. At most they misquote Hoettle, Höss, and Eichmann who spoke only casually of what they were in no position to know or to speak on reliably. Nor do the Jews themselves credit these wit-nesses as reliable even when they comment on what they could know, e.g., that the concentration camps were essentially work camps, not death camps!

Seventh, the burden of proof for the six million figure rests on the accusers, not the accused. This is a principle of all civilized law. Proving true guilt is easier than proving true innocence. It is hardly possible for a man accused of cheating on his wife to prove he did not cheat on her. Therefore the accuser must prove his charge. This responsibility the Zionists and Bolsheviks have not accepted, and the browbeaten Germans have rather paid billions than to dare to demand proof!

Eighth, obvious evidence that the figure of six million has no scientific foun-dation is that Jewish scholars themselves present ridiculous discrepancies in their calculations. And honest ones, whom we recognize by the fact that their co-racialists smear—terrorize them, and even beat them up, invariably lower the six million estimate.[40]

These so-called "inconvertible assertions" do not stand up under scrutiny. Assertions 1, 3, 4, 5, 6, 7, and 8 were then or have been proven since to be false. Scholars have agreed for a long time that no Jews were gassed in con-centration camps in Germany because the death camps were all situated in Poland.

App spent the last years of his life active in the Institute for Historical Review. From its inception in 1980, App served as a member of the Editorial Advisory Committee of the *Journal of Historical Review*. He remained on the board until his death. App died on May 4, 1984, and the editors of the *Journal of Historical Review* praised him for his contributions to Holocaust denial.

REVILO P. OLIVER AND HIS VERSION OF HOLOCAUST DENIAL

Revilo Pendleton Oliver was a dedicated white supremacist and neo-Nazi academic who also espoused Holocaust denial views. He was born on July 7, 1908, near Corpus Christi, Texas. Much of his early education was in schools in Lousiana and California. After his family moved to Illinois, he attended high school for two years there. Later, he moved to California, where he entered Pomona College in Claremont, California, at age 16. Oliver displayed talent in the classics after studying Sanskrit. His scholastic abilities enabled him to attend graduate school at the University of Illinois at Urbana-Champaign where he studied under the famous classics scholar William Abbot Oldfather. His studies earned him a master's degree and then a Ph.D. in 1940. Oliver's thesis was entitled "Niccolò Perotti's Translations of the Enchiridon." Still at the University of Illinois at Urbana-Champaign, Oliver taught graduate courses in both the Department of Classics and the Department of Spanish and Italian. During World War II, he served in the U.S. Army Signal Corps in cryptanalysis for the Army Security Agency at Arlington Hall in Virginia from 1942 to 1945. By the end of the war, Oliver was Director of Research at the Arlington Hall Signal Corps installation. He returned to the University of Illinois at Urbana-Champaign to resume his academic career as an assistant professor. In 1947, Oliver became an associate professor and then a professor in 1953. Despite his notoriety as a political figure, he was able to retain his position at the university as a tenured professor until his retirement as an Emeritus Professor in 1977.

By the 1950s Oliver had become deeply enmeshed in American conservative politics. His friendship with conservative Yale University professor Willmoore Kendall led to Oliver writing for the new conservative journal *National Review* beginning in 1955. Then in 1958, Oliver was one of the founding members of the John Birch Society. From 1958 until 1966, he was a member of the John Birch Society's national council. He also started writing for the Birch Society magazine *American Opinion.* Two of his articles, "Marxmanship in Dallas" and "Marxmanship in Dallas II," caused a major controversy when he blamed the JFK assassination on a "Communist Conspiracy." His political views hardened over the years, and he broke with the John Birch Society and its leader Robert Welch over his open advocacy of racism.[41] Oliver's antisemitism offended both John Birch Society leaders and its Jewish members.[42] Oliver then embraced a neo-Nazi agenda, and he worked with the neo-Nazi William Pierce to establish the National Alliance.[43]

Oliver became active in the Institute for Historical Review. He served on the *Journal of Historical Review*'s Editorial Advisory Committee from 1980 to 1994. During this time, Oliver published in 1982 a collection of his political writing under the title *America's Decline: The Education of a Conservative.* Although Oliver was eclectic in his hatred of anything that threatened white America, he shared the Holocaust denial views of the Institute for Historical Review. In November 1984, Oliver wrote a short opinion piece that he named "The 'Holohoax.'" In this piece, he attacked the idea of gas chambers.

> I really do not know why the Jews decided to discard that tale and substitute the wild fiction about the famous "gas chamber" when they had their American serfs perpetrate the foul murders at Nuremberg to teach the world what

happens to the lower animals that disobey the masters Yahweh set over them. It can't be that they thought to make the preposterous story more plausible by replacing electrical impossibilities with chemical impossibilities. Their contempt for the Aryan curs is so great that they never take the trouble to make their hoaxes even superficially plausible.[44]

Oliver continued with an attack on the diary of Anne Frank.

> Take, for example, the slop called "Anne Frank's Diary," which is said to make some feeble-minded Aryans snivel at its pathos. It is simply full of the most glaring inconsistencies. In that tale we are told that a band of poor, persecuted Jews had to hide from the terrible Gestapo in a whole series of rooms that formed a secret [!] part of the house, to which the entrance was through a secret door concealed behind a hinged bookcase. And we are expected to believe that those diabolical Germans couldn't guess how many rooms there were in a house of quite moderate size, and did not become curious when the postman on his rounds brought mail for the Jews in hiding, including lessons from a university in which some of them had enrolled for correspondence courses![45]

All of Oliver's speculation about Anne Frank was proven by a future Dutch government inquiry to be false, but facts like these never caused Oliver to back down. Oliver continued his attacks on the Jews and the Holocaust throughout the rest of his life. He died on August 10, 1994, in Urbana, Illinois. His colleagues in the Institute for Historical Review eulogized him, and one of them wrote that "his work and inspiration will live on."[46]

DAVID HOGGAN AND ACADEMIC HOLOCAUST DENIAL

David Hoggan was an American revisionist historian whose academic works have been accepted by Holocaust deniers. He was born on March 23, 1923, in Portland, Oregon. After studying at Reed College in Portland, Oregon, Hoggan entered the graduate program at Harvard University. He obtained a Ph.D. in history with a dissertation on German-Polish relations in 1938–1939. After graduation, Hoggan taught and studied history at the Amerika Institut of the University of Munich from 1949 to 1952. Returning to the United States, he found teaching positions at the Massachusetts Institute of Technology (MIT), University of California–Berkeley, San Francisco State College, and Carthage Lutheran College in Illinois. Hoggan left San Francisco State College after having a nervous breakdown.[47]

Hoggan's association with Harry Elmer Barnes led him to revise his dissertation to include the charge that Hitler was forced into war by the Allies. Unable to find an American publisher, Hoggan published it in German in West Germany under the title *The Forced War (Der Erzwungene Krieg)* in 1961. This work has been criticized by the German historian Hermann Graml for "citing a lot of that material and literature which have just one big problem: most of it is either a fake or a misinterpretation of authentic documents."[48] Most of his other books were also published in West Germany: *France's Resistance against the Second World War* (*Frankreichs Widerstand gegen den Zweiten Weltkrieg*) in 1963, *The Unnecessary War* (*Der Unnötige Krieg*) in 1976, *The Blind Century* (*Das blinde Jahrhundert*) in two volumes in 1979 and 1984, and *My Thoughts on Germany: The Anglo-American Crusade Mentality in the 20th Century* (*Meine Anmerkungen zu Deutschland: Der Anglo-amerikanische Kreuzzugsgedanke im 20. Jahrhundert*) in 1990. His revised dissertation was finally published by Noontide Press under the title *The Forced War: Why Peaceful Revisionism Failed* in 1989.[49]

Over the years Hoggan became converted to Holocaust denial. He wrote the book *The Myth of the Six Million* in 1969 under the pen name E. L. Anderson. In 1985, he attended and presented a paper at the Institute of Historical Review's Sixth Conference. Hoggan died of a heart attack in Menlo Park, California, on August 7, 1988.

ARTHUR R. BUTZ AND *THE HOAX OF THE TWENTIETH CENTURY*

App's and Hoggan's works were soon followed by Arthur R. Butz's *The Hoax of the Twentieth Century*. Few American Holocaust denial writers have produced a book that has had as much an impact in both Europe and the United States as Butz's book. Butz was born sometime in the mid-1940s and raised in New York City.[50] After graduating from MIT with a degree in electrical engineering, Butz received his Ph.D. in 1965 from the University of Minnesota in Control Sciences. His first teaching job began at Northwestern University in 1965, and he received tenure in 1974.

Almost out of blue Butz entered the ranks of the Holocaust deniers with the publication of his Holocaust denial book. He claimed that he had spent much of the period between 1972 and 1974 researching and writing the book. His book appeared in 1976, and its publisher was Willis A. Carto's Noontide Press. After proclaiming his belief that the Holocaust was a Jewish hoax, he continued by repudiating the sloppy research of earlier works, including the one by British Holocaust denier Richard Harwood and his *Did Six Million Really Die? The Truth at Last.*[51] By criticizing the works of early Holocaust deniers, Butz helped promote the idea that his work was more objective and viable, even if it was not.[52] Then, Butz advanced the thesis that the Holocaust was a propaganda hoax perpetrated by Jews with the assistance of the American, British, Soviet, and Israeli governments. Butz explained in a 1980 article in the *Journal of Historical Review* his reasons for selecting the title "hoax."

Let me assure you that the choice of "Hoax" was calculated, and that today I am even more convinced that it was a felicitous choice, for the reason that the thing really is trivial. The term "Hoax" suggests something cheap and crude, and that is precisely what I wish to suggest. A term such as "myth" although correct and sometimes used by me, does not convey this important description of the nature of the evidence supporting the extermination claim.[53]

According to him, there was a massive forgery of documents by Allied governments after World War II to blame the Germans.[54] He borrowed the charge of French Holocaust denier Paul Rassinier that the French Centre de Documentation Juive Contemporaine (Center of Contemporary Jewish Documentation) was the world center for the "falsification and fabrication of historical documents."[55] Deborah Lipstadt's telling counterpoint to this thesis of mass forgery of documents is in the absence of Hitler's written order.

> Why if the "propagandists" responsible for the hoax were so successful at producing such a vast array of documents, did they not produce the one piece of paper deniers claim would convince them there had been a Final Solution—that is, an order from Hitler authorizing the destruction of the Jews?[56]

The explanation is, of course, that was not Hitler's style to issue a written order but instead to make his wishes known to his subordinates. A Hitler wish had the same role in the Nazi regime as a written order. After all, Hitler was not oblivious to German public opinion, especially after he issued a written order for the euthanasia program. Butz also summarily dismissed the testimony of witnesses, including German participants. In Butz's eyes German participants confessed only because they were tortured or they hoped to strike advantageous deals with the Allies.[57] He even dismissed Nazi documents from participants written down at the time of the Final Solution, claiming that they were forgeries. Jewish eyewitnesses simply lied as part of an international Jewish conspiracy. Finally, Butz charged that the death toll was highly exaggerated and most of the victims died of typhus outbreaks or in the chaotic last days.[58] Yes, there are documents and eyewitness reports of typhus breaking out at the various concentration camps, but many of these same documents and accounts prove that the Germans were engaged in a massive killing of Jews and others. John C. Zimmerman quotes a reviewer of Butz's book:

> By the time one has subtracted all the material that Butz wants rejected, little remains of World War II documentation except for a few Nazi records and the apologia of SS men.[59]

Since the publication of this book, Butz has made a second career as a speaker at Institute for Historical Review (IHR) functions and by serving as a member of the Editorial Advisory Committee of the *Journal for*

Historical Review. His article on the state of Holocaust denial in 1980 was in the first issue of the *Journal of Historical Review*. He has also been a controversial figure at Northwestern University. Since Butz had already received tenure, efforts to have him fired have come to naught mainly because the faculty defended his tenure rights. Responding to threats from contributors and Jewish alumni, Northwestern University's administration supported a lecture series by the History Department on the Holocaust to counter Butz's views.[60] Butz weathered this and other controversies while steadfastly writing articles and giving speeches denying the Holocaust. In the spring of 1996, Butz placed his Holocaust views on a university Web site, sparking another controversy at Northwestern University.[61] In response, a part-time engineering instructor, Sheldon L. Epstein, a lawyer and engineer, responded in 1997 by incorporating anti-Holocaust denial materials in a course on engineering design and entrepreneurship. The Northwestern administration fired Epstein after officials warned him about bringing the Holocaust into the classroom.[62]

Butz is an international star in Holocaust denial circles. Butz's book has had wide distribution in Europe, Australia, and the Middle East. It has been translated into German and Spanish.[63] German Holocaust denier Wilhelm Stäglich showed his familiarity with Butz's book by writing a favorable review of it in the journal *Deutschland in Geschichte und Gegenwart* (*Germany Past and Present*).[64] Then, Gerhard Frey, head of the German right-wing Deutsche Volksunion (German People's Union) had Butz's book serialized in his newspaper *Nationale Zeitung* (*National Newspaper*). This book is a difficult read, much as one would expect from an engineer writing on a historical subject. While most of the sensational charges and research methodology have been debunked by historians in the field, the book remains such a staple in the Holocaust denial field that it has been characterized as the 'bible of the movement.'"[65]

Butz has remained active in the Holocaust denial movement since 1976. He was a frequent contributor to the Institute for Historical Review's *Journal of Historical Review* until its demise in 2002. Butz also has attended IHR's conferences, speaking at many of them. Holocaust deniers from Australia and Europe have funded his trips to speak at their gatherings. Butz also runs a Web site from Evanston, Illinois. His most recent controversy was his favorable comments on February 6, 2006, about Iranian President Mahmoud Ahmadinejad's statement calling the Holocaust a myth.[66]

WALTER N. SANNING AND THE 6 MILLION CONTROVERSY

The mystery man of the Holocaust denial movement is Walter N. Sanning. Sanning is a pen name; the Institute for Historical Review has given out some personal information, but how accurate this information is, is a subject of dispute. Supposedly Sanning was born in 1936 in an area that was a part of the former Soviet Union. Because his family was ethnic Germans, he spent his youth in Nazi Germany. He then moved to the United States sometime in the 1950s where he married an American. He attended a Pacific Northwest university where he earned a bachelor's degree in business. After graduation, he entered an Ivy League university where he studied international business, finance, and economics. His first job out of the university was teaching business at a West Coast university. Attracted to the private sector, Sanning moved his family to Germany in 1970, working for a financial institution. Returning to the United States, he taught again at a West Coast university. In the 1970s Sanning then turned to the private sector where he has remained. All of this information from the Institute for Historical Review is in vague terms so that it is impossible to identify him or verify the information.

Sanning's claim to fame in the Holocaust denial movement is his book challenging the number of Jews killed in the Holocaust. His book *The Dissolution of Eastern European Jewry* was published by the Institute for Historical Review in 1983. A German publisher, Grabert-Verlag, also published it in Germany. He used census figures compiled from as early as 1923 in Lithuania and during the 1930s for the rest. Sanning then projected the birthrate and combined it with a decreasing population caused by an imbalance between birth and deaths. He then postulated that it had been impossible for 6 million to have been killed because too many Jews escaped the Nazis. It is these assumptions that have caused scholars to reject his analysis. At the Wannsee Conference on January 20, 1942, the Germans estimated that there were more than 11 million Jews in the area that they had or projected to have control over for the Final Solution. Their figures for Russian and Ukrainian Jews were on the high side, and Germans never gained control of some of the areas that they assumed they would, but by January 1942 Jews were being killed at an increasing rate. It was the testimony of Dr. Wilhelm Hoettel, a Nazi physician with ties to the Schutzstaffel (SS), at the Nuremberg Trial that the figure of 6 million Jews had been either killed by action squads of the security police (2 million) or in the various concentration camps (4 million).[67] Collaborating evidence was the Korherr Report to Heinrich Himmler in 1944 using SS documents that concluded that 4 million Jews have been eliminated by December 31, 1942, which confirms that the total number of Jews killed by all means is in the 6 million range.

Influence of the Institute
of Historical Review
on Holocaust Denial

IMPORTANCE OF WILLIS A. CARTO IN THE HOLOCAUST DENIAL MOVEMENT

The leading proponent of Holocaust denial in the United States is Willis A. Carto. Carto was born on July 17, 1926, in Fort Wayne, Indiana, the oldest of two sons. His father was a salesman selling paper to printers. Together with the rest of the family, Carto listened to the radio broadcasts of Father Charles Coughlin.[1] He attended Harrison Hill Grade School and South Side High School. After graduating from high school in 1944, he was drafted into the U.S. Army the same year. Carto served with Company F, 132nd Infantry Regiment, 23rd Division (Americal Division) in the Philippines. While in the Philippines, a Japanese sniper wounded him in the arm.[2] Carto attended Denison University in Granville, Ohio, where he studied prelaw curriculum, but he left college after only two years. Then he took a few courses at the University of Cincinnati College of Law, but he again left without a degree. Carto held a job with Procter & Gamble in Cincinnati, Ohio, and in San Francisco, California. After losing his job, Carto worked first at the Anglo Bank and then as a bill collector for Household Finance Corporation in San Francisco.

By the early 1950s, Carto had become convinced that the radical right wing had the solution to political and social problems in the United States.

He began to sample various right-wing political groups sometime around 1954.[3] At first he joined Liberty and Property, an organization that combined free enterprise, libertarianism, and anticommunism. Around this time, Carto had published the first *National Directory of Rightist Groups, Publications, and Some Individuals in the United States.* Despite sharing most of its views, Carto soon found that this organization was not the right fit for him.

Carto had the ambition to become a national leader of the American right wing. He launched a right-wing magazine, *Right: The National Journal of Forward-Looking Americanism,* in 1955 to promote his right-wing views. By this time Carto was already expressing antisemitic views as can be seen by this private memorandum in the mid-1950s.

> Who is using who? Who is calling the shots? History supplies the answer to this. History tells us plainly who our Enemy is. Our Enemy today is the same Enemy of 50 years ago and before—and that was before Communism. The Communists are "using" the Jews we are told . . . who was "using" the Jews fifty years ago—one hundred or one thousand years ago. History supplies the answer. The Jews came first and remain Public Enemy No. 1.[4]

Then in 1957, he founded the Liberty Lobby and made its headquarters in Washington, D.C.[5] To make the Liberty Lobby more respectable, Carto made Colonel Curtis B. Dall, a former son-in-law of President Franklin Delano Roosevelt and an arch right-winger, nominal head of the Liberty Lobby. A new newsletter, *Liberty Letter,* replaced the older newsletter *Right* in January 1961.

He also briefly joined the John Birch Society in 1958, but his growing antisemitic views soon led to a disagreement with Robert Welch, the head of the John Birch Society.[6] Since Carto wanted to be a leader rather than a follower, it was inevitable that he would break with Welch.

Carto became enamored with the political views of Francis Parker Yockey. Yockey's book *Imperium* had been published in 1949, and it was a glorification of Hitler and the Nazis. Carto first learned about Yockey and his book in 1955 from John J. Hamilton, a veteran right-wing extremist with connections to Gerald K. Smith.[7] He immediately began praising Yockey in his publications. Carto was impressed enough with Yockey that he visited Yockey in a San Francisco jail only days before Yockey committed suicide in 1960.[8] Since then Carto had used his publications and his writings to advance Yockey's ideas, and later he had his Noontide Press publish a new printing of *Imperium.* Carto wrote a lengthy laudatory introduction to this edition.

Carto's activities in the 1960s continued his drive to become a force in the American radical right wing. Carto was a supporter of the presidential candidacy of Senator Barry Goldwater in 1964, but he used Goldwater's defeat to gain control of the Republican Party's lists of contributors and support-ers.[9] He used these lists to solicit funds for the Liberty Lobby. Then Carto gained control of the journal *The American Mercury* in 1966, and he turned this quarterly journal into an organ of antisemitic propaganda.[10] He also acquired the Noontide Press in 1966 to publish antisemitic and neo-Nazi publications. The newsletter *Liberty Letter* ceased publication in 1975, and Carto replaced it by the weekly newspaper *The Spotlight.*

Despite his obvious antisemitism, Carto attempted to downplay it by a series of defamation lawsuits against individuals and publications that had characterized him as an antisemite. His suit against the American journalist Jack Anderson for calling Carto a "Hitler fan" and the "leading anti-Semite in the country" was dismissed when the U.S. Supreme Court affirmed a lower court's dismissal of the suit in 1986.[11] A similar suit against the *Wall Street Journal* for calling the Liberty Lobby the "far right anti-Semitic Liberty Lobby" also ended up being dismissed in 1988 with U.S. Court of Appeals Judge Robert Bork's footnote of interest.

> Since its inception, Liberty Lobby has been an outspoken, often vicious critic of Jewish group and leaders, and of the United States domestic and foreign policy in regard to Jewish issues. In a letter to subscribers to *The Spotlight,* Liberty characterized "political Zionism" as the "most ruthless, wealthy, powerful and evil political force in the history of the Western world." *The Spotlight* has given extensive publicity to the fantastic claim that the Holocaust, the extermi-nation of 6,000,000 Jews by Nazi Germany, never occurred.[12]

Carto had already begun questioning the existence of the Holocaust soon after his contact with Francis Parker Yockey, and he started specializing in the publication of Holocaust denial materials. In 1978, Carto and William David McCalden (aka Lewis Brandon), a former member of the British National Party and later the British National Front, founded the Institute for Historical Review (IHR) with its headquarters in Southern California. McCalden was the first director of the IHR until he was fired in 1981 after personal conflicts with Carto.[13] Tom Marcellus succeeded McCalden and lasted until 1995 when Mark Weber became head of the IHR. The *Journal of Historical Review* to promote Holocaust denial literature first appeared in 1979, and it lasted until 2002. Carto formed a shadow company, the Legion for the Survival of Freedom, Inc., in 1980 to serve as an umbrella organization to protect his other holdings.

During his short tenure with the Institute for Historical Review, McCalden was the instigator of the ill-fated Mermelstein suit. One of his initiatives in 1979 had been to offer $50,000 to anyone who could prove the existence of the Holocaust. It was a publicity stunt to attract attention for the new Institute for Historical Review. By having the claim ruled on by a handpicked team of Holocaust deniers, the IHR never expected to have to pay off any claim.[14] A Holocaust survivor, Mel Mermelstein, claimed the prize in January 1981, and the IHR denied his proof. Mermelstein sued for the $50,000 and in a court trial won a judgment against the IHR in July 1985. By that time McCalden was long gone.

The Institute for Historical Review sought attention for its Holocaust denial views, but sometimes it received unexpected notoriety. One such occasion was the July 4, 1984, firebombing that destroyed the IHR office in Orange County, Southern California. This fire destroyed most of the IHR's inventory of books and tapes. Since then, the members of the IHR have been cautious about revealing their location to outsiders, and elaborate precautions have been taken to admit people to its offices. The institute also has a warehouse where it stores its merchandise from back issues of the *Journal of Historical Review* to promotional materials.

Carto was instrumental in the launching of the American Populist Movement in the early 1980s. In 1980, he began to experiment with Populism. Carto followed this by helping in 1984 to launch the Populist Party. He placed Bob Weems, a former Mississippi state chaplain for the Invisible Empire Knights of the Ku Klux Klan, as chairperson of the party before having to replace him due to the controversy over his appointment.[15] Carto wanted this party to combine economic and political nationalism, free enterprise capitalism, a conspiracist view of history, and racism. His antisemitism, devotion to Holocaust denial, and his authoritarian personality soon led to difficulties with other populist movement leaders. In 1985, these leaders combined to kick him out of the populist movement. Carto retaliated by forming a rival Populist Party with David Duke, the former Ku Klux Klan and white supremacist leader, as the presidential candidate in the 1988 presidential race. This attempt to subvert the American political process was no more successful than his earlier efforts.

The Institute for Historical Review has served as the forum for the international Holocaust denial movement since its foundation in 1978 by sponsoring Holocaust denial activities at conferences, and from 1979 to 2002 it provided a place for Holocaust denial authors to publish articles in the *Journal of Historical Review*. The institute also provided a safe haven for Holocaust deniers when they ran afoul of authorities in their countries. Because of the permissive legal environment in the United States, it was easy for Holocaust deniers to speak freely. Holocaust deniers also found it a lucrative place to raise funds or sell Nazi memorabilia and books. David Irving was able to survive financially in the late 1990s and early 2000s by milking the speaker's circuit in the United States. During its heyday, the Institute for Historical Review had a multitude of Holocaust deniers active in it—David Irving, Robert Faurisson, Carlo Mattogno, Jürgen Graf, Ahmed Rami, and Fred A. Leuchter among others.

Carto remained the head of the Institute for Historical Review until September 1993. He had always considered the institute as his personal fiefdom, but he had always left the day-to-day operations in the hands of others. At its peak the Institute for Historical Review employed a staff of six, and it had a budget of $500,000.[16] Senior staff members of the IHR led by Greg Raven and Mark Weber had become concerned over Carto's financial dealings. In particular, they were disturbed by his appropriation of a large inheritance to the tune of $7.5 million from the estate of Jean Farrell, the grandniece of the famous inventor Thomas Alva Edison.[17] Carto had placed the funds into a Swiss corporation, Vibet, and when he needed the funds he withdrew the money from a bank account at the Banque Centrade Lausanne in Switzerland.[18] By utilizing Swiss bank accounts, Carto was able to maintain complete control of the money. This inability to have access to the funds infuriated the staff at the Institute for Historical Review. They fired Carto for financial improprieties and sued him for wrongful use of the $7.5 million in funds. Carto countered by charging Weber as "part of a plot instigated by the Anti-Defamation League of the B'nai B'rith."[19] In a lengthy lawsuit in San Diego County Superior Court, Carto was convicted of illegally diverting millions of dollars from IHR and other corporations. The judge characterized Carto's attitude during the trial as "one of arrogance, deceit, evasiveness and convenient memory."[20] Then the court ordered him to pay IHR $6.43 million of which Liberty Lobby was to receive $2.5 million of this sum. In May 1998, Carto declared bankruptcy to avoid paying the settlement.

Despite losing control of the Institute for Historical Review, Carto has retained a power base in the extremist world. He launched a new Holocaust denial publication, *The Barnes Review*. Carto has engaged in a lengthy war of polemics against his former colleagues in the neo-Nazi and white supremacist movements, and, in particular, against the Institute for Historical Review. He charged that the Institute for Historical Review had been taken over by the "Zionist Anti-Defamation League."[21] These attacks, however, resulted in his newsletter, *The Spotlight,* losing readership.[22] Finally in July 2001, financial losses caused Carto to close the Liberty Lobby and shut down his newsletter *The Spotlight.*[23] Despite controversies and financial reverses, Carto remains an influential figure in the international Holocaust denial movement with contact with all the major actors.

ANALYSIS OF THE *JOURNAL OF HISTORICAL REVIEW*

An analysis of the subject matter and contributors to the *Journal of Historical Review* throughout its 21-year history showed that it was cleverly intertwined between Holocaust denial and what might be considered as historical revisionism. The journal first appeared in the spring of 1980 under the editorship of the British right-wing extremist William David McCalden. He remained its editor until his bitter political breakup with Willis A. Carto in 1981. Tom Marcellus succeeded him as editor, and he remained in this position until 1983 when Keith Stimely replaced him. Stimely remained editor another two years with Mark Weber replacing him in 1985. Weber survived as editor until the demise of the journal in the May/August 2002 issues because of financial reasons. Throughout this period the journal consistently attracted authors who wrote articles promoting Holocaust denial and a form of historical revisionism. Sometimes to fill up space, selected articles were republished from long dead authors, such as Mark Twain and Dwight David Eisenhower. Deborah E. Lipstadt is undoubtedly correct that the Institute for Historical Review was founded and has concentrated on Holocaust denial, but to fill a journal of only Holocaust denial articles would have been nearly impossible.[24]

In its history of publication the *Journal of Historical Review* attracted authors from a variety of countries. Of the 200 authors who produced articles of some substance, 124 were Americans, 59 Europeans, and 17 others from a variety of other countries. Among the Europeans the Germans contributed the most with 20, followed by the British with 7, Australians with 5, French with 5, Polish with 4, and Canadians and Russians with 3 each. The remaining 12 European authors were evenly divided among other nationalities.

The general subject orientation of the journal leaned heavily toward European issues. Out of the 511 articles, 285 (55.8 percent) were on exclusively European topics. In contrast, American topics attracted 108 articles (21.2 percent). The remaining 80 articles (15.6 percent) were on international subjects, and another 38 articles (7.4 percent) were on esoteric subjects ranging from the Dead Sea Scrolls to philosophic topics that intrigued only the editors of the journal.

On more specific subjects the editorial emphasis was on Holocaust denial and its related historical revisionism. Out of the 511 articles, 176 (34.4 percent) could be interpreted as exclusively on Holocaust denial topics. European historical revisionism with undertones of Holocaust denial ranked second with 106 (20.7 percent). American historical revisionism followed with 66 (13.0 percent). Other unrelated topics had 66 (13.0 percent) of the articles. The last significant total was the 40 (7.8 percent) articles that dealt with general revisionism. If one converts all types of revisionism together, the articles on revisionism numbered 212 (41.5 percent) outnumber those produced with definite Holocaust denial orientation. This total, however, is deceptive because much of the historical revisionism either directly or indirectly dealt with topics that had a Holocaust denial intent by the authors.

A question remains whether American or European authors were more prone to writing articles on Holocaust denial or on historical revisionism. American authors produced 338 articles and of these 97 (28.7 percent) articles were on exclusively Holocaust denial subjects. The emphasis was more on historical revisionism with the 80 (23.7 percent) articles on European revisionism and another 56 (16.6 percent) on American revisionism. They were also active in historical revisionism on international topics.

Combining the articles on all types of revisionism the number of revisionist articles by American authors outnumbers those on Holocaust denial 164 to 97. In contrast, European authors focused mostly on the Holocaust denial subject with a total of 73 (55.2 percent) of the total of 132 articles. This output was heavily influenced by the large number of Holocaust denial articles by Robert Faurisson. His 40 articles distorted the final totals. European revisionism remained a distant second with 38 (28.8 percent). It is safe to say that after studying the contents of the articles that American authors tended toward generalized articles on Holocaust denial topics and on revisionism while European authors specialized on narrow aspects of Holocaust denial such as on gas chambers and body disposal at the concentration camps.

WILLIAM DAVID MCCALDEN'S CAREER IN HOLOCAUST DENIAL

William David McCalden was the co-founder of the Institute for Historical Review, but he had a short history with it. He was born in 1951 in Belfast, Northern Ireland, into a working-class family. After obtaining an education in Belfast, he attended the University of London's Goldschmidt's College where he received a teaching certificate in sociology in 1974. An early convert to British right-wing extremism, McCalden became active in the National Front. His job was to edit antisemitic and racist publications. After reading Richard Verrall's *Did Six Million Really Die?*, he converted to Holocaust denial.[25] In 1978, McCalden moved to Southern California, and he starting working on Willis A. Carto's *The American Mercury*. In the same year, Verrall's book *Nuremberg and Other War Crimes Trials* appeared in print under the pen name Richard Harwood. After helping start the Institute of Historical Review and its *Journal of Historical Review*, he remained active in both until the spring of 1981 when his growing disagreements with Carto led to his leaving the IHR.

McCalden remained active in Holocaust denial circles and engaged in a lengthy vitriolic public fight with Carto. He founded the new organization Truth Missions in Manhattan Beach, California. Two of his publications issued from the new group were *Holocaust News* and *David McCalden's Revisionist Newsletter*. In 1985, McCalden engaged in a dispute with the California Library Association (CLA) over displaying his Holocaust denial materials at its conference. After his request was turned down, McCalden sued the CLA for damages. He was arrested on charges of assault with a deadly weapon, property destruction, and civil rights violations in 1989 after he attacked a man in the Congregation Mogen David Synagogue in West Los Angeles. This case was still unresolved when McCalden died in 1991 of AIDS-related pneumonia in 1991. His widow, Virginia McCalden, continued the lawsuit against the CLA for contract interference after her husband's death.

MARK WEBER AND POST-CARTO INSTITUTE FOR HISTORICAL REVIEW

Mark Weber has been in charge of the Institute for Historical Review since the lawsuit between Carto and the staff of the IHR was settled. He was born in October 1951 in Portland, Oregon. After graduating from Jesuit High School in 1969, he studied history at the University of Illinois at Chicago. He also attended the University of Munich in West Germany before transferring to Portland State University. After graduation from Portland State University with a degree in history, he entered Indiana University at Bloomington, Indiana, where he obtained a master's degree in European history in 1977.[26] Weber traveled extensively in Europe and Africa before settling in Washington, D.C., in 1978. Weber joined the Institute for Historical Review in 1980 after a brief stay as a member of William Pierce's National Alliance. This move was after the IHR published his pamphlet *The Holocaust: Let's Hear Both Sides* established his reputation as a Holocaust denier. While at the National Alliance, he served as the news editor of its publication *National Vanguard*.[27] He has never renounced his neo-Nazi past. His colleague at the time, David Cole, stated that

> Weber doesn't really see any problems with a society that is not only disciplined by fear and violence, but also where a government feeds its people lies in order to keep them well-ordered.[28]

Weber wrote a number of antisemitic and Holocaust denial articles throughout the 1980s. Weber wrote in the May 1989 *IHR Newsletter*:

> The Holocaust hoax is a religion. Its underpinnings in the realm of historical fact are nonexistent—no Hitler order, no plan, no budget, no gas chambers, no autopsies of gassed victims, no bones, no ashes, no skulls, no nothing.[29]

In early 1991, Weber moved to Southern California to work at the Institute for Historical Review. His involvement as emcee for IHR conventions and writing led to his promotion to editorship of the *Journal of Historical Review* in 1992.[30] Weber also appeared on the *Montel Williams Show,* a TV talk show, on April 30, 1992, where he stated that "the total number of Jews in Europe who died under German control or Axis control during the Second World War is probably in the neighborhood of a million, a million and a half."[31]

Weber played a leading role in the IHR lawsuit against Carto, and he had to weather the full fury of Carto. After the staff of the IHR won the lawsuit, the prestige and the financial base of the IHR fell on hard times. Carto has never delivered any of the funds ordered by the court. Leaders of the IHR sent out a mass mailing in 1994 to raise funds because the cut-off funding from Carto had placed the institute in danger of bankruptcy. Since 1994, the IHR has been less aggressive in promoting Holocaust denial as it had earlier, but it still attempts to play an active role. Its suspension of the *Journal of Historical Review* in 2002 was a blow both to the prestige of the IHR and the future viability of the institute.

BRADLEY SMITH AND CODOH

Bradley Smith initiated an outreach program for Holocaust denial by attempting to recruit college students under the name Committee for Open Debate on the Holocaust (CODOH). Smith founded CODOH with Mark Weber as his co-founder in 1987. The strategy of this campaign was to challenge the existence of the Holocaust by placing ads in student newspapers at major universities promoting debate over the Holocaust. William Curry, a Nebraska businessman, had been active in the antisemitc movement in the United States, and he financed the activities of the CODOH until his death in 1988.[32] Smith's first ads appeared in college newspapers in April 1991.[33] The ads had the title "The Holocaust Story: How Much Is False? The Case for Open Debate."

Smith had been a longtime Holocaust denier before engaging the CODOH campaign. He was born on February 18, 1930, in Los Angeles, California. After a standard education in California schools, he spent a tour of duty in the U.S. Army with the 7th Cavalry in Korea. He was wounded twice in combat. Smith lived for a while in New York City before returning to California. Among his other jobs, he was a merchant seaman, playwright, construction worker, and a deputy sheriff in Los Angeles County. From the early 1960s until the 1980s, Smith lived in Hollywood, California, where he ran a bookstore. Smith had a brief fling with notoriety when he was arrested and jailed in the early 1960s for selling Henry Miller's *Tropic of Cancer*. In 1989, Smith moved to Visalia, California. Then in 1997, he moved to Rosarito, Mexico, with his Mexican-born wife and two daughters.

Smith converted to Holocaust denial in 1979 after reading an article in *Le Monde* by French Holocaust denier Robert Faurisson. Faurisson's thesis was that the gas chambers had never existed, and this made sense to Smith.[34] In the mid-1980s, he founded the newsletter *Prima Facie* that specialized in publishing Holocaust denial materials.[35] He also began an affiliation with the Institute of Historical Review. Although Smith has never been an active member of the IHR staff, his association with that organization has been close with him earning a living from the IHR as a writer beginning in 1985.

Now I'm writing for publication and for money too. My publisher is the most despised and vilified in America and perhaps in the Western World—the

Institute for Historical Review. I'm writing on the great taboo subject of the late 20th century—the alleged genocide of the Jews by Adolf Hitler and his Nazis. I have no scholarly or academic credential, and no professional ones. As I intend to go straight ahead with what I am doing, and as I'm aware of the implications of doing it, I understand that I may be heading for my last fall as a writer.[36]

Throughout the early 1990s Smith had mixed success in placing ads in student newspapers, but he did garner considerable publicity for the anti-Holocaust activities of the Institute for Historical Review. These ads caused great controversy on campuses with Jewish groups at odds with the editors of student newspapers.[37] A majority of the campus newspapers turned down the ads, but the difference between the turndowns and acceptance was close. Some universities took the opportunity to start offering courses on the Holocaust to counter the Holocaust deniers. By the mid-1990s, most of the controversy and the drive of the CODOH had begun to diminish because the heads of it became caught in the middle of a dispute between the Institute for Historical Review and Carto.

After Smith moved to Mexico, he became less enthused about CODOH and began looking for other avenues for his energies. Much of his energy was devoted to a new Holocaust denial journal, *The Revisionist: Journal for Critical Historical Inquiry,* in 1999. After four issues, Smith converted it to an online magazine in late 2000 because of financial problems. Then in early 2003, Smith found a publisher in Germar Rudolf's Castle Hill Publishers, and since then the magazine has been printed in paper. Smith also founded a new organization, The Campaign to Decriminalize World War II History, to challenge the traditional view of World War II. Smith followed this by writing his memoirs, *Break His Bones: The Private Life of a Holocaust Revisionist,* that appeared in 2002. This book continues his justification for Holocaust denial by arguing that attempts to suppress it are an attack on intellectual freedom.

MICHAEL COLLINS PIPER AS SUPPORTER OF CARTO

Michael Collins Piper has been a longtime backer of Willis A. Carto. Piper lives in Washington, D.C., and he has been a regular contributor to the Carto-backed *American Free Press*. For over 20 years, Piper wrote for the Holocaust denier publication *The Spotlight*. He classifies himself as a political writer and talk radio host. He is also known as a prominent conspiracy theorist.

Piper has spent his career as a writer for Far Right publications. His older brother served in the Vietnam War, and he claims that his interest in politics came from his brother's comments in the press. It is probable that he was born around 1960. He attended college where he majored in history. He graduated from college in 1982. Already as a student, he had begun working part time for the Liberty Lobby.[38] He entered law school, but dropped out after a year to work full time for the Liberty Lobby.

Over the years Piper has established a reputation as a conspiracy theorist. In his book *Final Judgment: The Missing Link in the JFK Assassination Conspiracy* (1994), he charged that the assassination of President John F. Kennedy was a joint operation of the CIA and the Israeli intelligence service Mossad.[39] They combined because of efforts by Kennedy to end the Vietnam War and in the process cut the CIA's connection with the illegal Asian drug trade and because of Kennedy's opposition to Israel's atomic bomb program.

Piper has also alleged a Jewish conspiracy concerning the September 11, 2001, attacks. He claims that the official story of the 9/11 attacks is false. The Mossad "knew of the attacks in advance but they allowed it to take place because it served their interest" in the Arab-Israel conflict.[40] It is his contention that the collapse of the World Trade Center buildings was caused by controlled demolition explosions. Piper discounts photo evidence and testimony from witnesses.

Piper has made open public attacks on the Anti-Defamation League (ADL). These attacks have come in response to the ADL's charges that Piper has promoted antisemitic conspiracy theories. His response was a 2006 book, *The Judas Goats: The Shocking Story of the Infiltration and Subversion of the American Nationalist Movement,* in which he accused the ADL of employing unethical infiltration and information-gathering techniques.

Piper has been outspoken in his criticism of Israel and the American Jewish lobby. In 2004, Piper published the book *The New Jerusalem: Zionist Power in America* in which he attacked the American Jewish lobby and its political power in Washington, D.C. He has also on occasion claimed that the War on Terror is a calculated campaign to discredit Islam.

Besides his long affiliation with Carto's *American Free Press,* Piper has expanded into the radio talk show format. He started a radio show, *The Piper Report,* in 2006 that appeared on the Republic Broadcasting Network. He has interviewed a variety of individuals holding extremist viewpoints.

Piper has been careful about a public advocacy of Holocaust denial. His attendance at Holocaust denial conferences, such as the Tehran Conference in 2006, belies his public stance. Iranian President Mahmoud Ahmadinejad made him a personal guest during his time in Iran.[41] Moreover, he has remained loyal to his mentor Carto through all of Carto's misadventures.[42] In fact, Piper has never repudiated any of Carto's ideas

KEITH STIMELY'S CAREER AS A HOLOCAUST DENIER

Keith Stimely had a short career as a Holocaust denier. He was born on April 9, 1957, in Connecticut, but at an early age his family moved to Oregon. After completing high school in Oregon, Stimely attended San Jose State University. Later, he transferred to the University of Oregon. Stimely graduated from there in 1980 with a bachelor's degree in history. After finishing his schooling, he joined the U.S. Army as a reserve officer.

Stimely was an early convert to Holocaust denial. He joined the Institute for Historical Review and presented a paper on "The Elements of Revisionism: A Historiographic Survey" at the second Institute for Historical Review Conference at Pomona College, California, in 1980. In 1981, Stimely published the *Revisionist Bibliography: A Select Bibliography of Revisionist Books Dealing with the Two World Wars and Their Aftermaths*. His participation and Holocaust denial activities led the leaders of the Institute for Historical Review to offer him a position on the editorial staff of *Journal of Historical Review* in June 1982. Then, Stimely was offered the post of chief editor of the *Journal of Historical Review* in February 1983. He held this position until he resigned in February 1985. His two major academic interests were Oswald Spengler and Francis Parker Yockey.

Stimely retained his interest in the Institute for Historical Review, but his health began to deteriorate. This was an era when AIDS was a serious health concern, and Stimely was gay. He came down with AIDS and died on December 19, 1992, in Portland, Oregon. His essay "Oswald Spengler: An Introduction to His Life and Ideas" was published by the *Journal of Historical Review* in 1998.

ROBERT COUNTESS AS A HOLOCAUST DENIER

Robert Countess was a longtime Holocaust denier and supporter of the Institute for Historical Review. He was born in August 1937 in Memphis, Tennessee. He attended Bob Jones University where he obtained both master's and doctoral degrees. Countess also studied at Georgetown University where he earned a Master of Liberal Studies in Philosophy of History in 1978. During the course of his academic career, Countess taught at various institutions—Covenant College, Tennessee State University, and the University of Alabama at Huntsville—in subjects including foreign languages, history, and philosophy. Along the way, he published the book *The Jehovah's Witnesses' New Testament*. Besides his college teaching, Countess was an ordained minister serving as a U.S. Army chaplain from 1976 to 1984. After the end of his academic career, Countess retired to a farm outside of Huntsville.

Countess was also a prominent Holocaust denier. He claimed that it was his reading of Arthur R. Butz's *The Hoax of the Twentieth Century* that converted him.[43] His conversion led him to order multiple copies for his survey course at the University of Alabama at Huntsville. At the Institute of Historical Review's 2001 Conference, he confided his views to *Esquire* writer John Stack.

He (Countess) believes that Hitler wanted the Jews out of Europe but that he didn't order their extermination, that the Germans had no homicidal gas chambers at any of their concentration camps, and that the number of Jews who died from all causes in World War II wasn't six million but somewhere between several hundred thousand and one and a half million.[44]

These views led the Institute for Historical Review to appoint him to its Board of Directors. This position landed him in the middle of the dispute between Willis A. Carto and the staff of the Institute for Historical Review. Attacked from both sides, Countess resigned from the board, but he remained a loyal follower of the IHR's Holocaust denial campaign. In early 2005, Countess learned that he had a brain tumor. He died on March 18, 2005. Countess was never a star in the Holocaust denial movement, but his prestige as a history professor helped make it more respectable.

CARLOS WHITLOCK PORTER AND MAVERICK HOLOCAUST DENIAL

Carlos Whitlock Porter has been a Holocaust denier since the mid-1970s. He was born in 1947 in California. His father was a graduate of Harvard Law School and was a lieutenant in the U.S. Navy during World War II. At least some of his formal education was in Europe. His ability with languages enabled him to have a career as a professional translator. His specialty was translating German, French, Italian, Spanish, and Portuguese works into English. Because of his hostility toward the United States, Porter renounced his American citizenship on November 8, 1984. Since then, Porter and his family have lived in Belgium.

Porter became a Holocaust denier sometime between 1976 and 1987. He claims that his conversion was because of discrepancies over chemical reactions described in Holocaust literature.[45] These discrepancies led him to publish the 1978 short book *The Chemistry of the Hoaxoco$t*, which he admitted has a mistake in it on Zyklon B and that it has been superceded by later research.[46] His next book was *Made in Russia, the Holocaust* in 1988 in which he claimed that it proved lies about the Holocaust, but he was surprised by "almost no reaction to this book."[47] Later in 1988, he had *Not Guilty at Nuremberg* published to correct the errors in William David McCalden's (appeared under the name of Richard Harwood) *Nuremberg and Other War Crimes Trials* (1978). A few years later, he wrote another book on the Nuremberg Trials using the French version of the Nuremberg transcript with Vincent Reynouard—*Delire à Nuremberg*. Porter also became engaged in revisionism on Japanese guilt and atrocities in World War II. He wrote *Japs Ate My Gall Bladder* in 1992. His interest in comparing the injustices of the Nuremberg Trials and those of the Japanese has continued to this day.

Porter's publications led to judicial proceedings against him. His first brush with the law was in a German court in Munich in April 1998 for incitement to racial hatred. Porter refused to attend the trial, and although he was convicted in absentia, his fine was miniscule. Then in September 1998, the Belgian social security system took him to court. A financial assessment led to his bankruptcy, and he deserted his family. Despite the abandonment of his American citizenship, Porter has retained his ties with the Institute of Historical Review.

DAVID COLE'S ROLE IN HOLOCAUST DENIAL

David Cole's role in Holocaust denial is unique because he is Jewish. He was born in 1972 and raised in West Los Angeles, California. His biological father was a research scientist at the University of Southern California and had a private medical practice before having legal problems over drugs. After his parents divorced, his mother remarried. His biological father died when Cole was 14 years of age. He attended Hamilton High School in West Los Angeles, but he left before graduation. Cole had a fight with the drama and music teacher during his senior year, and the teacher flunked him in three classes, so he left school.[48] His youth ambition was to be a screenwriter or a writer. After joining various organizations from the Revolutionary Communist Party to the John Birch Society, Cole began reading Holocaust denial materials. He had previously joined the Jewish Defense League (JDL). Then, he met William David McCalden, the British co-founder of the Institute for Historical Review, at an atheist group in 1988. Cole worked for McCalden, infiltrating the JDL and becoming acquainted with its leader Irv Rubin.[49] He finally joined the Institute for Historical Review in 1991. Cole gives his reason why people become Holocaust deniers:

> Every person has his unique motivation. Every person comes to this spot from their own personal journey. Statistically the greatest percentage of people in revisionism now are there because they're either German nationalists, or want something that knocks Jews in some way. They are anti-Semites.[50]

He also states that Holocaust denial can become profitable:

> What people don't realize about Willis Carto and Ernst Zundel, these people are businessmen, they live off ideology, they don't have day jobs. They don't have a wife who works outside. Carto has built a financial empire. He is a very wealthy man. Carto does not believe a lot of what he tells his supporters.[51]

Cole's claim to fame was his September 1992 interview at Auschwitz. Bradley Smith raised funds ($15,000 to $20,000) for him to travel to Poland and conduct interviews.[52] He interviewed Dr. Franciszek Piper, Senior Curator of the Polish government's Auschwitz State Museum about gas chambers at Auschwitz. Disguising his political affiliation by wearing a yarmulke,

Cole videotaped his interview with Piper and others at Auschwitz.[53] Dr. Piper admitted that the gas chambers had been reconstructed after World War II. Armed with this information, Cole returned to the United States and made his videotape available for distribution. American and European Holocaust deniers had a field day with the videotape.

Cole's next contribution to the Holocaust denial movement was his appearances on national television shows. He appeared with Bradley Smith, the head of the CODOH, on *The Phil Donohue Show* on March 14, 1994, to debate Michael Shermer, publisher of the journal *Skeptic,* and an Auschwitz survivor, Edith Gleick.

Since his Auschwitz videotape and TV fame, Cole has left the Holocaust denial movement under mysterious circumstances. Once it was known that Cole was a Holocaust denier, the Jewish Defense League targeted him for abuse. In 1992, JDL's Rubin attacked him, physically beating him badly. A member of the JDL, Robert J. Newman, posted to the December 30, 1997, JDL Web site an attack on Cole entitled "David Cole: Monstrous Traitor." Newman all but called for his death in the following words:

> What is a David Cole? Is it a sickness? Is it a mental disease? Is Cole merely a human parasite who clings to his ardent Nazi supporters and friends who back his ideas whole-heartedly? After all, this Cole mania that the media have played on, don't you think it's time that we flush this rotten, sick individual down the toilet, where the rest of the waste lies? One less David Cole in the world will certainly not end Jew-hatred, but it will have removed a dangerous parasitic, disease-ridden bacteria from infecting society.[54]

Soon after this message appeared, David Cole repudiated Holocaust denial and everything that it stands for with the words that he had been "wracked with self-hate and loathing" and that he had been "seduced by pseudo-historical nonsense and clever-sounding but empty ideas and catch-phrases."[55]

MICHAEL A. HOFFMAN II AND HIS BRAND OF HOLOCAUST DENIAL

Michael A. Hoffman II is yet another Holocaust denier with ties to the Institute for Historical Review. He was born in 1954 in New York. His education was at the State University of New York at Oswego. Hoffman pursued a career in journalism with a position as a former reporter for the New York Bureau of the Associated Press. Since leaving this position, Hoffman has been a free-lance journalist specializing in Holocaust denial subjects. He also moved from New York to Idaho.

Hoffman has been active in writing and publishing books that reflect his viewpoints. He is the author of six books. These are *The Great Holocaust*

Trial (1985), *A Candidate for the Order* (1987), *They Were White and They Were Slaves: The Untold History of the Enslavement of Whites in Early America* (1991), *Secret Societies and Psychological Warfare* (1995; revised 2001), *Judaism's Strange Gods* (2000), and *The Israeli Holocaust against the Palestinians* (2002). For a while Hoffman was an assistant director of the Institute for Historical Review, and he has kept his contacts with it. Presently, Hoffman is the managing editor of the Holocaust denial newsletter *Revisionist History*.

By combining antisemitism with Holocaust denial, Hoffman has made a number of sensational assertions. Hoffman has charged those who believe in the Holocaust as belonging to the Holocaust cult. He has advanced that the real Holocaust of World War II was the deaths caused by the Allies.

> The overwhelming holocaust of the modern era, for which there is all the forensic proof the Jewish "Holocaust" is supposed to contain and from which it is also intended to distract, is the merciless Allied firebombing holocaust against Hamburg, Berlin, Dresden, Tokyo, Hiroshima, Nagasaki and dozens of other major civilian centers.[56]

Hoffman followed by denying the existence of the gas chambers.

> Just as there was no material, scientific proof for the existence of the devil, there is no material scientific proof for the existence of Nazi homicidal gas chambers. There are no autopsies available from any source showing that even one Jew died as a result of Zyklon B (hydrocyanic acid) poisoning, among the millions who are alleged to have been killed in this manner, an esoteric but revolutionary fact clumsily admitted by the prestigious Exterminationist genie, Dr. Raul Hilberg.[57]

Many of Hoffman's other writings have been attacks on Israel and the Catholic Church's accommodation with Jews. He even charges that contemporary Judaism is a fraud.

> Contemporary Judaism is a fraud which tends to discredit the Old Testament in the eyes of those who cannot detect the cheat. For example, persons reading the following report of the inquisition perpetrated by the Pharisees and their allies, may falsely ascribe to the Bible the attitude of the rabbi-cop. Hence the Bible, the supreme standard of Law and Ethics, is discredited in the eyes of many, because of the perverted actions of the Khazar impostors who pretend to represent it.[58]

Hoffman is another in a line of Holocaust deniers who makes a living off of contributions from the Holocaust denial constituency.

FRIEDRICH PAUL BERG AND DIESEL GAS

Yet another contributor to Holocaust denial is Friedrich Paul Berg. He was born on November 11, 1943, in New York City. His parents were

German immigrants. Berg graduated from Columbia University with a degree in Mining Engineering. Since graduation, he has worked as an environmental engineer. Berg also shares Austin J. App's belief in the "inherent goodness and decency of the German people."[59]

Berg has used his technical expertise as an environmental engineer in the service of Holocaust denial. His first public activity was his participation in a protest of the TV miniseries *Holocaust* in April 1978. He petitioned the National Broadcasting Company for equal airtime to respond to the television program.[60] Since then Berg has been most active in writing Holocaust denial articles. His specialty has been attacking the scientific details of the use of diesel gas at German concentration camps. Most of his articles have appeared in the *Journal of Historical Review*. His most famous article was "The Diesel Gas Chambers: Myth within a Myth."[61] In another article in 2005, Berg maintained that "the Holocaust story is a hoax because no one was murdered by the 'Nazis' in gas chambers or gas vans, and because the total number of Jews who could have possibly died in German-occupied territory is minuscule compared to what is alleged."[62]

HANS SCHMIDT AND HOLOCAUST DENIAL

Hans Schmidt is another leading American Holocaust denier with an affiliation to the Institute for Historical Review. He was born in 1927 in Germany. Like most German boys of that era, he belonged to the Hitler Youth. Schmidt claims to have been a member of the Waffen-SS in the later stages of World War II.[63] If so, he would have been in his late teens. After leaving West Germany, Schmidt arrived in the United States in 1949. He moved around the United States before ending up in Pensacola, Florida. Schmidt became a naturalized citizen in 1955. He has been able to support himself by running a business.

Schmidt has never relinquished his ideological ties to Germany and Hitler. While living for a time in Santa Monica, California, he founded the German-American National Public Affairs Committee (GANPAC) in 1983. Through this organization and its publication *GANPAC Brief,* Schmidt has defended the actions of the Nazi Party in Germany and denied the existence of the Holocaust. Schmidt warned Jewish leaders that if they "persist in retaining a religious aura for the 'Holocaust' then we may well see the explosive growth of attempts by non-Jewish Europeans and Americans to elevate Hitler as the messiah of the Nordics."[64] Much of his energies in the 1980s was devoted to opposing the building of the United States Holocaust Memorial Museum in Washington, D.C. To publicize further his antisemitic and Holocaust denial viewpoints, Schmidt started the German-American Information and Education Association (GIEA).[65] Schmidt also had close contacts with William Pierce and the National Alliance. Although Schmidt has kept his independence from the Institute for

Historical Review, he attended several of its conferences in the late 1980s and early 1990s.

Schmidt has been able to escape legal troubles over his writings and presentations in the United States, but he has been less successful in Germany. German authorities arrested Schmidt on August 9, 1995, for the distribution of his publication *U.S.A. Bericht* on the grounds that it incited racial hatred and denied the Holocaust.[66] His trial began on January 4, 1996, but his lawyers persuaded the judge to release him from jail on his personal recognizance. Schmidt seized the opportunity to flee back to the United States. Since then, Schmidt has devoted his energies to Holocaust denial in the United States from his headquarters in Pensacola.

FRED A. LEUCHTER AND *THE LEUCHTER REPORT*

The Leuchter Report is considered by Holocaust deniers as the scientific evidence that proves the Nazis did not use gas chambers to exterminate the Jews. Fred A. Leuchter was the researcher and the author of *The Leuchter Report*. He was born in 1943 in Maiden, Massachusetts. His father worked for the Massachusetts prison system and would take young Fred around the prison, including the death-house area.[67] After earning a degree in history from Boston University in 1964, he started working as a self-educated engineer specializing in building execution equipment. Then he formed a company, Fred A. Leuchter Associates, to design, build, and maintain execution equipment. His company had contracts with several states on providing execution equipment specializing in electric chairs.

Leuchter had little contact with Holocaust denial until he received a commission from Ernst Zündel. Zündel commissioned him in January 1988 to travel with associates to Poland's concentration camps to discredit the claims of Nazi use of gas chambers. He authorized a payment of $30,000 to pay Leuchter and cover expenses.[68] Faurisson had already convinced him at a two-day meeting in Boston, Massachusetts, on February 3 and 4, 1988, that no gas chambers were possible.[69] Leuchter, his wife, and three associates visited the concentration camps of Auschwitz, Birkenau, and Majdanek between February 25 and March 3, 1988, and collected 32 samples of brick and cement materials over that period. They never had permission from any of the authorities at Auschwitz, Birkenau, and Majdanek to gather samples. Several times members of the team made illegal entries to gain access to materials, and they had to rush to avoid officials and guided tours. These samples were then sent to an American chemist at the Alpha Analytical Laboratories in Ashland, Massachusetts, for chemical analysis with the explanation that it was for a "workman's compensation case."[70] This chemist was never told what to look for, but he determined that there was little trace of cyanide in the materials. Leuchter then concluded that without significant presence of cyanide residue in these materials that gas chambers never existed.[71] This was the conclusion of his report: *The Leuchter Report: The End of a Myth: A Report on the Alleged Execution Gas Chambers at Auschwitz, Birkenau and Majdanek, Poland.*

The judge in the 1988 Zündel trial refused to allow most of Leuchter's testimony after questioning his scientific credentials. His report was not allowed to be presented as evidence. The judge was clearly "appalled by Leuchter's lack of training as an engineer as well as his (Leuchter's) deprecation of the need for such training."[72] Moreover, the judge also had questions about his historical knowledge since "Leuchter was unaware of a host of documents pertaining to the installation and construction of the gas chambers and crematoria."[73] He was, however, allowed to testify on the use of gas in American prison's gas chambers. Furthermore, the judge permitted Leuchter to give his opinion on the nature of the structures in the concentration camps that he had studied.

Since the publication of this report, Holocaust denial supporters have cited it as proof conclusive that the Holocaust never took place. Leuchter became a featured speaker at conferences of the Institute for Historical Review. Both Leuchter's scientific evidence and his conclusions produced a firestorm of criticism. Scientists disputed Leuchter's findings and his scientific credentials. Authorities in several states questioned Leuchter about his so-called expertise, and an Alabama official accused him of running a "death-row shakedown scheme."[74] After investigations, Leuchter lost his credentials as an engineer in several states, and a consulting job in Illinois. He had to sign a Massachusetts consent agreement on June 12, 1991, that he had misrepresented himself as an engineer.[75] The more Leuchter and his report were attacked, the more intense was the defensive response from the Holocaust denial movement. Leuchter responded to the criticism of his credentials by blaming the Jews.

> This witch hunt must and will stop. I give fair warning to all those who are part of this international cabal, to all those who have unjustly attacked me and violated my rights—to the Klarsfelds, Shapiros, and Kahns of the world. Fred Leuchter is coming for you! You will be brought to answer to those same courts and before the same judicial system you have sought to destroy.[76]

Leuchter has had to defend himself in other venues. In 1999, Errol Morris produced a documentary film entitled *Mr. Death: The Rise and Fall of Fred A. Leuchter, Jr.* In this film the chemist who had performed the original chemical analysis produced evidence contrary to Leuchter's conclusions. A subsequent French study by Jean-Claude Pressac did find evidence of cyanide on the surface of the gas chambers at German concentration camps. Pressac also added that Leuchter had been manipulated into a false report.

> Faurisson's intellectual dishonesty and historical deficiencies are manifest in his "writings". It was foreseeable that Leuchter's report, manipulated by Faurisson, would be subject to these same defects. Indeed, this proved to be the case. The work's lamentable level of professionalism confirms to the customary standards of nihilist publications. Based on misinformation, which leads to false reasoning and misinterpretation of data, "The Leuchter Report" is unacceptable. It was researched illegally, ignoring the most straightforward of historical data, and flounders in gross errors of measurement and calculation.[77]

While Leuchter's famous report has been discredited for both its faulty science and its erroneous conclusions, it is still cited by Holocaust deniers as proof certain that the Holocaust never happened.

GARY LAUCK AND HOLOCAUST DENIAL

Another American who has had an influence on the Holocaust denial movement is Gary Lauck. He is the head of the National Socialist German Workers' Party—Overseas Organization (NSDAP-AO), and the leading producer of Holocaust denial and neo-Nazi propaganda for distribution in Europe. He is second only to Ernst Zündel in providing these materials to Germany.

Lauck is another German-American who has been attracted to Holocaust denial. He was born on May 12, 1953, in Milwaukee, Wisconsin, into a German-American family. The family moved to Lincoln, Nebraska, in 1965. His father was an engineering professor at the University of Nebraska. Lauck grew up in Lincoln, and at an early age he became fascinated by all things Nazi. After high school, he moved to Chicago and joined Frank Collin's National Socialist Party of America. After Collin was discredited because of child pornography charges, Lauck formed the NSDAP-AO. This organization was strictly a one-person show, and Lauck used it to print and distribute Nazi memorabilia and works that idealized Adolf Hitler. At this time Lauck also became a Holocaust denier, and he once made the statement that "Hitler's only mistake was that he was too humane."[78] Holocaust denial materials appeared frequently in his bimonthly newspaper *The New Order*.[79]

Lauck earned an international reputation for his distribution of Holocaust denial and neo-Nazi materials around the world, but it also landed him into legal difficulties. He was a frequent visitor to Germany, meeting with prominent neo-Nazis. Among the materials that Lauck distributed in Germany was Adolf Hitler's speeches. German authorities seized these materials and prepared a case against Lauck. After a brief trial, Lauck served a four-month jail sentence in 1976. This time in jail did not deter Lauck from sending Nazi materials to Germany in the intervening years. Lauck also started publishing a neo-Nazi newspaper *National Socialist Battle Cry* (*NS-Kampfruf*). German authorities frequently complained to the American government about his activities, but American officials were reluctant to intervene.[80]

Avoiding Germany's strict laws on distribution of Nazi materials, Lauck operated out of Denmark until Danish officials arrested him on March 20, 1995, at a neo-Nazi convention in Denmark on an international warrant from Germany. Lauck appealed all the way to the Danish Supreme Court contesting his arrest, but in the end he lost. In August 1995, Danish authorities extradited him to Hamburg, Germany, where he was charged with 38 counts of the German federal penal code for the dissemination of Nazi materials.[81] In a trial that lasted from May to August 1996, Lauck was convicted and received a prison sentence of four years. Lauck served most of his sentence, leaving prison in March 1999. He returned to the United States and settled in Chicago still an unrepentant Holocaust denier and neo-Nazi. Most of his recent activities have been distributing Holocaust denial and neo-Nazi materials through a Web site. He uses his Web site to send this type of material throughout the world:

> They say you should six million vermin THESE questions: Are six million vermin perverts obsessed with women during that time of the month? Are six million vermin child molesters who approve sexual molestation of three year Christian girls? Are six million vermin hate mongers who says Jesus Christ should be boiled in manure? Are six million vermin dealers in stolen Christian icons? Are six million vermin pornographers? Are six million vermin "hole-in-the-sheet" sex fetish fans? Are six million vermin subverters of Christianity and Christian morals? Are six million vermin hypocrites who promote race-mixing for non-Jews and at the same time condemning if for Jews? Are six million vermin communist apologists who deny the communist holocaust against Christians? Are six million vermin ingrates who do not appreciate the special resort camps like Auschwitz? Are six million vermin swindler who use the big lie of the six million to extort money? Are six million vermin traitors who keep the extorted money for themselves instead of passing it on to the so-called victims? Are six million vermin "Jew-Nazis" aka "Zionist" collaborators?[82]

It is this type of antisemitic invective that places Gary Lauck in the ranks of current Holocaust deniers.

DAVID DUKE AS HOLOCAUST DENIER

David Duke is a white supremacist politician, who has adopted Holocaust denial as part of his political agenda. He was born on July 1, 1950, in Tulsa, Oklahoma. His father was an engineer for Royal Dutch Shell Oil Company with strong conservative leanings. After a brief stay in the Netherlands, the Duke family moved to New Orleans, Louisiana. His parents sent him to a private military school, Riverside Military Academy in Gainesville, Georgia, for his junior year. Duke returned to New Orleans for his senior year, graduating from John F. Kennedy High School. Before Duke became active in the Ku Klux Klan, he had been attracted to Nazism. While a student at Louisiana State University, Duke posed in a Nazi uniform after forming the National Socialist Liberation Front in November 1969. Only later did Duke downplay his early infatuation with Nazism because he realized that Nazism was too inflammatory to appeal to the general public.

Duke also was an early reader of Holocaust denial literature. One of his favorites was William Grimstad's *The Six Million Reconsidered* (1977), and he later had Grimstad write a column for his Klan newspaper the *Crusader*.[83] Duke attended the first Institute for Historical Review conference in 1979. At this conference, Duke became converted to Holocaust denial as evidenced in the *Crusader,* where Duke in print denied the existence of gas chambers.[84] Duke also attended the 1983 and 1986 IHR annual conferences where he expressed a high opinion of Willis A. Carto.[85] In an interview with Evelyn Rich on March 18, 1985, in Metairie, Louisiana, Duke insisted that "the Holocaust was a hoax trumped up by Jews to win support for creating the state of Israel following World War II."[86] He also rejected the testimony of camp survivors by alluding to the "fact that they survived themselves is a tremendous argument for the fact that extermination didn't take place."[87] Duke admitted that he did not talk much about the Holocaust because he found it a "non-productive thing for me."[88] Finally, he concluded that his ideal country was Nazi Germany, but he appreciated more civil liberties than that regime allowed.[89] There have been other statements by Duke since then that could be interpreted an antisemitic. In his 1991 candidacy for Louisiana governor, Duke sold Hitler's *Mein Kampf* and Holocaust denial materials to raise funds.[90] Duke also became acquainted with David Irving, and Irving wrote the Holocaust segments of Duke's book *My Awakening* (1998).[91] Duke loaned Irving money and gave him access to a list of names of prominent donors for Irving to solicit funds from in the future in return for editorial help and writing parts of the book.[92]

In recent years, Duke's writings and remarks have become increasingly antisemitic. Before going to jail at a facility in Big Spring, Texas, for mail fraud in 2002, Duke founded the European-American Unity and Rights Organization. Following 15 months in prison, Duke published a new antisemitic book, *Jewish Supremacism: My Awakening on the Jewish Question,* which appeared in 2004. He then became affiliated with the notoriously antisemitic Ukrainian Interregional Academy of Personnel Management (MAUP) in the mid-2000s. His association led to him receiving in September 2005 a Ph.D. in History from MAUP, writing a thesis entitled "Zionism as a Form of Ethnic Supremacism." Duke's views on Holocaust denial remain the same, and it is an active component of his antisemitism.

ROBERT L. BROCK AND HOLOCAUST DENIAL

Robert L. Brock is an Afro-American black nationalist, antisemite, and Holocaust denier. He was born in 1926 in Louisiana and raised in the Watts area of Los Angeles, California. His father was a longshoreman, and his mother worked in a hospital. After completing high school, Brock served in the U.S. Army. Leaving the military, Brock worked as a merchant seaman. He also attended Southwestern Law School in Los Angeles, but he never graduated with a law degree. This lack of a degree has not prevented him from posing as a lawyer.[93] He also ran a restaurant in Los Angeles. Brock's entry into politics was during the 1965 Watts riots. He became known in the black community as a black nationalist, but he had little impact on the national level.

Brock became active in the extremist movement in the 1980s. He fell under the influence of Daniel Johnson, a right-wing extremist and a Los Angeles attorney, and his advocacy of the Pace Amendment. The Pace Amendment was the controversial plan to restrict the rights of permanent U.S. citizenship to white people of Northern European descent, and to deport within a year those who did not meet this criterion. Of course, this amendment never had a chance of success, but it led to Brock joining Willis A. Carto's Liberty Lobby and then the Populist Party. Brock became active in writing in the Liberty Lobby's weekly newspaper *The Spotlight* where he espoused racial separation.

Brock became nationally prominent in the Black Reparations Movement. In the 1960s, he formed The Self Determination Committee to lobby the federal government to provide reparation payments to descendants of slaves. Feelings in the black community ran deep that the federal government had reneged on its Civil War promise to give them "40 acres and a mule." When the reparation movement gained steam in the 1990s, Brock was in the middle of it. Brock has received criticism for taking $50 for a reparations claim when there has been no reparations settlement, or legislation proposing it.[94] He has also attacked the federal income tax. Brock made the statement in 1995 that since in his opinion the Fourteenth Amendment to the Constitution was ratified illegally, African-Americans were entitled to avoid payment of the federal income tax.[95] Twice Brock filed suits against having to pay income taxes, but both times his suits were thrown out of court.

Brock's views on racial separation and on the Holocaust made allies for him in the Holocaust denial movement. Several Christian Identity and neo-Nazi groups have invited him to speak at their events. After founding a group called United for Holocaust Fairness, Brock sponsored a conference in Los Angeles in 1992 that tried to unite the black nationalist movement with the Holocaust denial movement.[96] This conference proved to be a bust as there were only three speakers and an audience of 13.[97] Brock responded in 1995 by publishing with the collaboration of a German newspaper a book of essays by non-German historians, *Not Guilty for Germany!* (*Freispruch für Deutschland!*), that attacked anti-German history and the facts of the Holocaust. Then the same year, Brock wrote the book *Holocaust Dogma of Judaism: Keystone of the New World Order* under the pseudonym of Ben Weintraub in which he denied the number of Jews killed in the Holocaust by calling it a rabbinical hoax derived from occult readings of the Hebrew letters in the text of the Torah. The Anti-Defamation League has described the central argument of this book:

> The book itself, one of the most outlandish, anti-Jewish tracts to appear recently, argues that Jews have used gematria, a Kabbalistic numerological technique of Biblical exegesis, to generate the figure of 6 million Jews murdered in the Holocaust, The subsequent history of the Nazi genocide, according to the book, was fabricated to substantiate the "prophesied" death count.[98]

He also attacked government funding of the United States Holocaust Memorial Museum.

Brock has continued his claims on reparation and attacks on the Holocaust, but his lack of success in winning government support for reparations has hurt his credence in the black community. Before Khalid Abdul Mohammad's death, Brock had made some inroads among the black separatists in the New Black Panther Party. What his relationship with Mohammad's successor will be is uncertain. Brock remains the only black nationalist leader with close ties to the white supremacist and Holocaust denial movements.

BLACK HOLOCAUST DENIAL

Black antisemitism made its appearance beginning in the 1970s. Earlier Elijah Muhammad, the head of the Nation of Islam (NOI), had expressed "an admiration for Jews' 'psychology' and business acumen, and the NOI had sympathized with them after being 'roasted like peanuts' during the Holocaust."[99] It was in 1984 that Louis Farrakhan's feud with Jews flared up almost out of control. Farrakhan's feud had tones of antisemitism tinged with admiration for Jews. Farrakhan helped the feud along by making pro-Hitler remarks, but it was his followers who amplified his remarks.

> Followers of Farrakhan have used the Holocaust as a way to vent their anti-Semitism. Not only is the Holocaust diminished as an historical event in order to claim greater victimization for slavery and the slave trade; slavery is blamed on Jews and the history of the Holocaust twisted beyond recognition.[100]

Black antisemitism has led to interaction between leaders of the Nation of Islam and Holocaust deniers. Arthur R. Butz addressed the Nation of Islam at its Saviour's Day celebration in 1985.[101]

The most notable of the Nation of Islam's Holocaust deniers was Khalid Abdul Muhammad. In April 1994, Muhammad held a press conference on April 18, 1994, after a visit to the United States Holocaust Memorial Museum, during which he questioned the magnitude of the Jewish losses during the Holocaust in comparison to the genocide against black people.[102] In a speech at Howard University on April 19, 1994, he stated that the black genocide was still in progress.[103] Among Khalid's remarks were those that belittled the Holocaust by indicating that "reports on the six million Jews murdered by the Nazis were bloated, exaggerated, probably fabricated."[104] Muhammad became such a controversial figure that Farrakhan expelled him from the Nation of Islam. After a spell without an affiliation, Muhammad became the head of the New Black Panther Party where he continued his antisemitic agitation until his untimely death in February 2001.

FELLOW TRAVELERS OF HOLOCAUST DENIAL

There are American extremist political figures who have displayed Holocaust denial as part of their political agendas. Most of them are antisemites with Holocaust denial only one aspect of their hatred of Jews. These fellow travelers make Holocaust denial statements on occasion, but their concern is to attack Israel, or what they consider the international Jewish conspiracy. Among those who could be classified as fellow travelers are Edward Fields, Eustace Mullins, Lawrence T. Patterson, and E. Stanley Rittenhouse.

Edward "Ed" Fields, a nonpracticing chiropractor, has been more noted for his leadership in the white supremacist movement than Holocaust denial, but in recent years he has added Holocaust denial rhetoric to his antisemitism. He was born in 1932 and raised in Marietta, Georgia. His claim to fame was as the long head of the National State's Rights Party (NSRP) until his ouster in 1983. Fields and his longtime associate J. B. Stoner were staunch white supremacists with ties to the Ku Klux Klan movement. After losing control of the NSRP, Fields started another organization, the America First Party. Fields continued his association with the members of the Council for Conservative Citizens and various Ku Klux Klan groups, but he extended his agenda to include Holocaust denial as part of his antisemitic campaign. In a 1992 pamphlet Fields expressed the following views:

> Beginning at December 5, 1992, The National Campaign to Expose the Holocaust will be launched by concerned American taxpayers all across the land! The goal is to reveal to the American people what many of us have long suspected. This is the fact that during World War II there was never any deliberate extermination of the Jews.[105]

Fields followed this with open attacks on the 1993 opening the United States Holocaust Memorial Museum in Washington, D.C. While Holocaust denial is only a part of Fields's agenda for his campaign for white supremacy, it has become an important weapon to him.

Eustace Mullins is another active antisemite who has incorporated Holocaust denial as part of his attacks against Jews. He was born in 1923 and raised in Virginia. After serving in the U.S. Air Force in World War II, he attended several universities in the United States and one in Mexico. He worked for awhile at the Library of Congress in Washington, D.C. Mullins also became a champion of the Fascist poet Ezra Pound, and he wrote a book on Pound, *This Difficult Individual Ezra Pound* (1940). He also worked for Senator Joe McCarthy and his anticommunist crusade in the 1950s. Mullins has written 12 books with the most notorious being *The Biological Jew* (1968) and *The Secrets of the Federal Reserve* (1952). Holocaust denial is a part of his virulent antisemitism, but it is not a major concern. In a 2004 interview with James Dyer, Mullins placed Holocaust denial among his political objectives.

> It wasn't really an issue until the late '50s. All of the sudden, they (Jews) remembered that six million Jews died in WWII. I've often said that after six million Jews died, most of them went on to own apartments in Manhattan and Tel Aviv. It's not really a topic that interests me much beyond how it's used as propaganda and mind control.[106]

Despite this minimal interest in Holocaust denial except for exploiting, Mullins has long had ties to Willis A. Carto and the Liberty Lobby.

Lawrence T. Patterson is another prominent antisemite with strong ties to the Holocaust denial movement. He was born in 1935 and raised in Cincinnati, Ohio. Patterson attended Miami University (Ohio) where he received a bachelor of science degree, and the University of Michigan where he obtained a master's degree in Business Administration. After completing his education, he found employment in sales and marketing. After he married a Swiss national, Patterson has kept a dual residency in Switzerland and the United States. Patterson started his publishing career in 1975 with *The L. T. Patterson Strategy Letter,* but he renamed it later *A Monthly Lesson in Criminal Politics;* since 1989 its title has been *Criminal Politics.* He was a confidant of Willis A. Carto and his newsletter *The Spotlight,* but this changed when Patterson sided with the Institute of Historical Review's staff in the 1993 breakup with Carto.[107] Patterson has been a strong supporter of the conspiracy school of history, and he has often written about the Jewish international conspiracy. He has charged that all American presidents have either been agents of the international Zionist conspiracy or stooges.[108] Several times Patterson has written in *Criminal Politics* Holocaust denying statements asserting that the death toll of the Holocaust is a "horrendously hard-to-believe claim," questioning why is "America so preoccupied with the ill-treatment of Jews by Nazi Germany," and charging that Holocaustamania is designed "to justify the pro-Israel content and direction of U.S. foreign policy."[109]

E. Stanley Rittenhouse is a Holocaust denier with a close association with Hans Schmidt and the German-American National Political Action Committee. He was born in 1935. Rittenhouse lives in Burke, Virginia, where he is an ordained Baptist minister and a former stockbroker. He is also an adherent of Christian Identity and is violently antisemitic. Among the many extremist publications Rittenhouse has written for are Willis A. Carto's *The Spotlight,* James K. Warner's *CDL Report,* and Sons of Liberty's *World Intelligence Review.* Several times he has run for public office for extremist groups but without success. His blatant antisemitism has led him to Holocaust denial. In a 1979 article he claimed that "it would be physically impossible to kill that many people systematically with the equipment and time available."[110] He has also attacked the TV movie about Anne Frank while maintaining that "there were no 'gas chambers' at Auschwitz (or anywhere else)."[111] Rittenhouse is another Holocaust denier who was a violent critic of the opening of the United States Holocaust Memorial Museum in Washington, D.C.

Jack Wikoff is another in a line of Holocaust denial's fellow travelers. He was born in 1959. Wikoff now lives in Aurora, New York. Most of his activities have been in publishing his antisemitic periodical *Remarks* that he began in August 1990 and in writing reviews for the *Journal of Historical Review* and other extremist journals. The major editorial emphasis of his periodical is Holocaust denial.[112] His most notable review in the *Journal of Historical Review* was that of Jean-Claude Pressac's *Auschwitz: Technique and Operation of the Gas Chambers* (1989) in which he tries to demolish Pressac's arguments. Wikoff and other Holocaust deniers have pursued Pressac with a vengeance because he had formerly shared their views about the Holocaust.

Another type of fellow traveler is the leadership of the modern neo-Nazi movement. The neo-Nazi movement has accepted Holocaust denial as an article of faith. The primary spokesperson for this point of view is the veteran neo-Nazi leader Harold Covington. He is cynical about his conversion to Holocaust denial. He explained his Holocaust denial views in a July 24, 2008, issue of his Internet Web site *NSNet Bulletin #5.*

> Take away the Holocaust and what do you have left? Without their precious Holocaust, what are the Jews? Just a grubby little bunch of international bandits and assassins and squatters who have perpetrated the most massive, cynical fraud in human history ... I recall seeing a television program on revisionism a few years ago which closed with Deborah Lipstadt making some statement to the effect that the real purpose of Holocaust revisionism is to make National Socialism an acceptable political alternative again. I normally don't agree with anything a Jew says, but I recall exclaiming, "Bingo! Got it in one! Give that lady a cigar!"[113]

This quotation aptly sums up the position of the neo-Nazi movement and its derivates.

INGRID RIMLAND AND THE ZUNDELSITE

Ingrid Rimland's close association with the Canadian-German Holocaust denier Ernst Zündel brought her into the ranks of the Holocaust deniers. She was born in 1936 in the Ukraine, Soviet Union, into a German Mennonite family. In 1943, her family fled the Soviet Union with the German troops fearing reprisals. The family settled briefly in Germany before moving to Paraguay shortly after World War II. Rimland grew up, married, and had children in Paraguay. In 1960, Rimland decided to move to Canada. Then, in 1967, Rimland relocated again. This time the move was to the United States. She became a U.S. citizen sometime in the early 1970s. Soon after her arrival in the United States, Rimland started her education. Eventually, she earned an Ed.D. in special education from the University of the Pacific.

Rimland has always been a Nazi sympathizer. She was grateful that the German army rescued her and her family in World War II. In her eyes Hitler was a great man, and he has been denied the respect due to him for his accomplishments. This pro-Nazi viewpoint comes out in her trilogy *Lebensraum* that tells the story of the German Mennonites in the Soviet Union and their rescue by the Germany army. Rimland was receptive to Holocaust denial because it was a way to restore the reputation of Hitler and his regime.

Rimland's political orientation was firmly established when she met Ernst Zündel in 1994. They were at a Holocaust denial conference in Los Angeles, California. At the time Rimland, then a free-lance writer, lived in California and Zündel in Canada. They found their pro-Nazi and Holocaust denial views compatible. Zündel gave her $850 to study online publishing, and she used this money to start up the Zundelsite on the Internet.[114] Their business relationship soon turned to romance, and they married in 2001. Rimland was Zündel's third wife. The couple bought a house in a small town in Tennessee's Smoky Mountains where they remained until American authorities arrested him on February 19, 2003. Since his arrest and deportation first to Canada and then to Germany, Rimland has continued to support him. Rimland moved to Carlsbad, California, where she uses the Web site to drum up support for Zündel and his views on Holocaust denial.

LARRY DARBY AND HOLOCAUST DENIAL

A new entry into the Holocaust denial debate is Alabama politician Larry Darby. He was born in 1957 in Conecuh County, Alabama, into a longtime Alabama family. Darby attended the University of Alabama earning a bachelor of science degree. After obtaining a master of business administration at

Auburn University, he entered law school at Faulkner University's Thomas Goode Jones School of Law. After earning his doctor of jurisprudence degree, Darby became a practicing lawyer. On September 11, 2002, Darby was a co-founder of the Atheist Law Center with Carol Moore of Columbiana, Alabama. The goal of the center was to be an advocate for the constitutional principle of separation of religion and government and personal liberties. He became its president and its legal counselor. As its president Darby was active in the controversy over Chief Justice Roy Moore and the Ten Commandments monument. Darby opposed the Ten Commandments because it represented to him Jewish law.[115]

During his tenure as president of the Atheist Law Center, Darby became an active Holocaust denial spokesperson. He invited David Irving to speak before the Atheist Law Center on July 6, 2005. Darby defended his invitation by stating that

> Mr. Irving is a genuine historian in that his works are based on original research of documents and interviews with persons who actually knew and worked for Adolf Hitler or the German government or otherwise had first-hand knowledge of the subject matter, as opposed to the recycling of oft-unverifiable assertions put forth as history and recycled by conformist historians that serve the preeminence of Jewry in the United States and elsewhere.[116]

Soon afterward Darby resigned as president of the Atheist Law Center in the fall of 2005. Then on July 6, 2006, he legally dissolved the Atheist Law Center.

By the time that he dissolved the Atheist Law Center, Darby decided to enter Alabama politics as a white supremacist and Holocaust denier. At the same time he renounced atheism and announced that he was a Christian. His first run for public office was as a candidate for Alabama Attorney-General in the 2006 Democratic Party Primary. Although Darby suffered a defeat, he garnered 43 percent of the vote. During his campaign Darby made it plain that he had made the conversion to Holocaust denier. He denied that there were millions of deaths during the Holocaust, and his estimate was that only around 140,000 Jews had died mostly of typhus. Darby also attended a meeting of the New Jersey unit of the neo-Nazi National Vanguard in May 2006. His commitment to Holocaust denial has made the Alabama Democratic Party denounce him and reject him as a member of the Democratic Party. Despite rejection, Darby is dedicated to having a political career.

Canadian Holocaust Deniers

INTRODUCTION

Holocaust denial has had a lively history in Canada. Much as the United States, Canada has a tradition of allowing free speech with certain exceptions. Canada has also had an open immigration policy that has created a diverse citizenry. These factors have made Canada an open society that has allowed extremist opinions to flourish. Much as in any other country, Canada has had an antisemitic movement that prepared the groundwork for Holocaust denial. Whereas the total number of Canadian antisemites and Holocaust deniers has been relatively few, they have been vocal at times.

Efforts to curtail Holocaust denial have had a mixed history because the Canadian courts have been reluctant to restrict free speech. What has happened has been an open war of words between Holocaust survivors and Holocaust deniers. This war of words has led to several spectacular trials of Canadian Holocaust deniers. Worldwide attention has been directed to the trial of Ernst Zündel and James Keegstra, and Holocaust deniers flocked to Canada to testify in their behalf and give them moral support. The fact that the Holocaust deniers have lost most of their court cases has turned them into martyrs to Holocaust deniers the world over.

ERNST ZÜNDEL AS HOLOCAUST DENIER

Ernst Zündel is Canada's leading Holocaust denier. He was born on April 24, 1939, in the village of Calmback in the Black Forest area of

Germany. Zündel was one of three children. His father was a woodcutter by profession and a veteran of the German army in World War II, and his mother was a housewife. Neither parent played a role in postwar German politics. Zündel grew up in postwar West Germany where he attended a trade school beginning in 1953 earning a degree in photo retouching. He worked as a photo retoucher for several years in north Germany before immigrating to Canada in 1958. There are rumors that he immigrated to avoid service in the German army because at the time he was "a self-described pacifist."[1] Soon after his arrival in Canada, he attended Sir George Williams University (now Concordia University) in Montreal where he studied history and political science. Zündel left school without a degree with the justification that "he had only wanted to prove to himself that he was capable of doing university-level studies."[2] He also began to complain about anti-German feelings in Canada. In Montreal Zündel became acquainted with the Quebec Fascist leader Adrien Arcand. Arcand opened his home and his library of 4,000 books, including many German books from the Nazi period, to Zündel.[3] Zündel became the protégé of Arcand and through him met the leading neo-Nazis in Canada.[4] In the mid-1960s, Zündel moved his wife and children to Toronto where he established a successful advertising agency and a commercial studio. His specialty was photo retouching, which gave him a good business with Canadian magazines. He also won several awards for the quality of his work.

Zündel became attracted to Canadian politics. Soon after his arrival in Toronto, Zündel established relations with the leaders of the neo-Nazi movement in that city. He began associating with David Stanley and John Beattie and their political groups.[5] In 1968, Zündel was persuaded by Canada's leading Fascist, John Ross Taylor, to run for a leadership post in the Liberal Party. In a controversial campaign Zündel charged that Pierre Trudeau, a leading Canadian Liberal Party politician, was a communist. This mistake and other miscalculations led Zündel to suffer a humiliating defeat that he was slow to recover from.[6] His nomination received nary a single vote.

Zündel started a publishing business, Samisdat Publishing Company, in 1976, specializing in publishing and republishing Holocaust denial materials. He was extremely aggressive in marketing tactics going so far as to send Holocaust denial materials to members of the Canadian Parliament.[7] Zündel also sent these types of materials to Canadian libraries and schools, eliciting protests from school authorities.[8] His distribution of Holocaust denial and neo-Nazi literature reached all over the world, including the Arab world. His publishing activities were lucrative, earning him in the range of $60,000 to $100,000 annually.[9] But his special target was West Germany.[10]

Among the materials sent to West Germany were those that challenged the legitimacy of the West German government. He charged that the West German government was illegitimate because it was an occupation government.[11] He also wanted to overturn the verdicts of the Nuremberg Trials.[12] German authorities collected enough of his materials on raids of German neo-Nazis that the "German Ministry of Interior identified Zündel as one of the country's most important suppliers of radical right and neo-Nazi propaganda materials."[13]

In 1978, Zündel published a eulogy to Adolf Hitler entitled *The Hitler We Loved and Why*. The main reasons that Zündel loved Hitler were because he was first a white man, he wrestled the creation of money away from the Jews, he sterilized those with genetic defects, he replaced the penal system with productive labor and punishment with redemption, and he was a deeply spiritual man who did not allow the Jews to confuse Christian teachings. Zündel also wrote *UFO's: Nazi Secret Weapons?* in 1974. He created the German-Jewish Historical Commission and Concerned Parents of German Descent to advance his Holocaust denial views.

Except for his brief excursion into Canadian politics in 1968, Zündel kept a low profile preferring to operate behind the scenes until 1978. In April 1978 Zündel used his Concerned Parents of German Descent to organize public demonstrations against the television miniseries *Holocaust*.[14] He followed these demonstrations with another public protest against the movie *The Boys from Brazil* in October 1978. Then in January 1979, Zündel and his followers demonstrated before the Israeli and West German consulates to show their opposition to the screening of the *Holocaust* miniseries in West Germany. In a 1979 flyer Zündel stated his views on the Holocaust in the following language.

> The Holocaust is a gigantic hoax which cynically and diabolically aims at blackmailing the German people all over the world . . . . There were no "six million holocaust victims". There was no Nazi genocide programme. There were no gas chambers of "exterminating" Jews or anybody else. The Second World War caused tremendous suffering on all sides—German Jew, Axis and Allied. None were the victors; all were the victims. But I repeat THERE WAS NO JEWISH HOLOCAUST.[15]

Zündel worked with fellow Holocaust denier Ernst Nielsen in an attack on teaching the Holocaust at the University of Toronto. Nielsen had served in the German air force as an air-sea rescue pilot during World War II before his capture in July 1940. After serving as a prisoner of war in England and then Canada, he immigrated to Canada in the early 1950s. Nielsen became a follower of Zündel, and they decided to challenge the teaching of the Holocaust by two Jewish professors at the University of Toronto. During the academic years 1979–1980 and 1980–1981, Nielson audited the course. His constant harassment of the professors and fellow students led to his being asked to leave the class both years.[16] Nielson appealed his removal from class on the second occasion in a letter to a university administrator charging the professors with bias.[17] Zündel used this incident to publicize his Holocaust denial views by defending Nielson.

Zündel's open advocacy of Holocaust denial and his published works supporting it soon earned him legal troubles from Canadian authorities. In May 1981, the Canadian Holocaust Remembrance Association tried to have his postal rights revoked, but this effort failed after a postal board review. His distribution of Richard Verrall's pamphlet *Did Six Million Really Die?* was the official reason for judicial proceedings. A member of the Canadian Holocaust Remembrance Association and a Holocaust survivor, Sabrina Citron, brought charges against Zündel, citing a law against making "false news."[18] Zündel hired a prominent right-wing lawyer, Doug Christie, to defend him. Holocaust deniers Robert Faurisson from France, Ditlieb Felderer from Sweden, and William Lindsey and Mark Weber from the United States appeared at the 1985 trial as defense witnesses.

The trial assumed more importance when it became apparent that the Holocaust was also on trial. Because the judge, Huck Locke, refused to take judicial notice of the Holocaust as a fact, this meant that the prosecution had to prove that the information in the pamphlet *Did Six Million Really Die?* was false.[19] This ruling brought the Holocaust into question, and Zündel's lawyer seized the opportunity. Stanley R. Barrett stated, "To a great extent it seemed that the Jewish people and the Holocaust—not Zündel—were on trial."[20] Christie's tactics were to engage in "brutal cross-examinations of survivor witnesses, seeking to undermine their testimony, cast doubt on their suffering and deprive their experiences of any real significance."[21] He also flooded the court with hundreds of maps, photographs, articles, and books. Defense witnesses mocked the Holocaust, leading an observer to remark as follows:

> Among the 20 other defense witnesses were buffoons who joked about the Olympic-sized swimming pools and dance halls at Auschwitz, and that the genocidal death camp was actually a "happy" place where they got plumper as they worked.[22]

As Zündel testified at his trial and under cross-examination, it became clear that he was "a firm believer in Aryan superiority and a die-hard anti-Semite."[23] After receiving an acquittal on the first charge of publishing *The West, War and Islam* in 1980 but a guilty verdict on the second charge of publishing the tract *Did Six Million Really Die?*, Christie appealed the conviction. An Ontario Court five-judge panel upheld the constitutionality of the verdict, but they sent the case back because of errors committed by the judge.[24]

Before the 1988 trial, Zündel decided to challenge the historical authenticity of the gas chambers. He commissioned an amateur engineer, Fred A. Leuchter, to travel to the Polish concentration camps and study the gas chambers to disprove their existence. His report was finished before the trial, but at the trial the judge refused to allow it to be introduced as evidence, questioning Leuchter's engineering credentials. The judge did allow Leuchter to testify on his experiences with execution chambers. This time the presiding judge took judicial notice of the Holocaust, ending the type of exchanges between Zündel's lawyer Christie and Holocaust survivors.[25] This ruling did not prevent those testifying for Zündel, Robert Faurisson, David Irving, Udo Walendy, and Mark Weber, from bringing up their Holocaust denial views. Weber, a Holocaust denier affiliated with the Institute for Historical Review, defended Zündel's assertion in a pamphlet that "no living authentic eyewitness to the gassing at extermination camps has ever been published and validated."[26] This argument is sophistry because no active participant in a gassing would survive and be able to describe it in detail.

Zündel used these trials to pose as a champion of free speech and to increase his public exposure on the international Holocaust denial scene. Each day of the 1988 trial Zündel showed up in court in a bulletproof vest and a blue hard hat sporting the words "Freedom of speech."[27] His entourage of supporters wore yellow helmets. This time the Canadian Supreme Court overturned this last verdict by declaring the "false news" law unconstitutional. Zündel used both verdicts as vindication of his Holocaust denial views.

Zündel's next target was the Academy Award–winning movie *Schindler's List* (1993). He considered this movie to be anti-German hate propaganda, and he attacked it as such. Even with his increased popularity among Holocaust deniers, Zündel was unable to prevent the showings of the movie.

Zündel wanted to become a Canadian citizen. He had been a resident of Canada since 1958, and he had married a Canadian citizen. As long as he remained a citizen of Germany, it was possible that he could be deported to Germany. Zündel wanted to avoid this at all costs. Twice his attempts to gain Canadian citizenship were rejected. His efforts to become a citizen were blocked by the Canadian Security Intelligence Service because this agency considered him a right-wing threat to the security of Canada.[28] In the meantime, Zündel ran afoul of German law in 1991 in Munich, Germany. A German court found him guilty of inciting racial hatred and fined him $10,000 before kicking him out of the country.

Next Zündel turned his attention to the potential of the Internet. In the summer of 1995, he established the Internet Zundelsite to spread his views. Ingrid Rimland, a Ukrainian/Paraguayan German Mennonite and Zündel's new wife, ran the site for Zündel. Shortly after its appearance, the Canadian government moved against the Zündelsite, citing laws against hate propaganda, defamation, and obscenity on the Internet. In a Canadian Human Rights Tribunal court in Toronto in December 1998, Zündel was charged with violating Section 13(1) of the Canadian Human Rights Act for communicating any matter that is likely to expose a person or persons to hatred or contempt by reason of the fact that person or those persons are identifiable on the basis of a prohibited ground for discrimination (that is, by race, ethnicity, religion, and so forth).[29] In this hearing Mark Weber attested to Zündel's role in the international Holocaust denial movement:

> We [revisionists] regard him [Zündel] as a facilitator, a publicist if you will or, to use his word, an impresario. That is not an apology for Ernst Zündel ... He is not a scholar. He doesn't play the same role in the revisionist community or movement, or whatever you care to call it, that a Robert Faurisson does, or that I do, or that others do. His motives are different.[30]

Under further Canadian government threats to prosecute, Zündel moved the Zundelsite to eastern Tennessee.

Zündel found asylum in the lax American legal system until once again he ran into legal difficulties. He remained in Sevierville, Tennessee, for several years until American authorities arrested him for overstaying his visa. In February 2003 American authorities deported him to Canada where he claimed political asylum to prevent the Canadian government from deporting him to Germany.[31] At a May 2003 hearing Zündel asserted his love for Hitler.

> I am entitled to admire a man who brought Germany work, bread, peace, and honour and a place in the sun. There is more to Adolf Hitler and his government than Jews, Auschwitz and violence. The violent acts were committed as wartime measures. My mother told me in 1968 or '69, "Ernst, you would not have been born if it weren't for Adolf Hitler." He said his father had no hope in Germany before Hitler took power and then, afterward, his father got a job and his parents could afford to have another child; that child was Mr. Zündel, who was born in 1939. I owe that man my life.[32]

By blocking deportation Zündel hoped to avoid a lengthy prison sentence in Germany. He even briefly considered claiming his mother was Jewish to enable him to immigrate to Israel.[33] On March 1, 2005, the Canadian government deported Zündel to Germany where he was immediately arrested to await trial on charges of denying the Holocaust and inciting hatred. Zündel announced in November 2005 that he was going to sue the Canadian government for $10 million, claiming that his imprisonment and deportation had been illegal.[34] On February 15, 2007, a Mannheim court sentenced Zündel to five years in prison based on a conviction for 14 counts of inciting racial hatred and Holocaust denial. Since then, he has been serving his prison term.

JAMES KEEGSTRA AND HOLOCAUST DENIAL

James Keegstra is another famous Canadian antisemite and Holocaust denier. His case produced a firestorm of publicity for Keegstra and the community of Eckville in central Alberta. Keegstra was born in 1934 in Vulcan, Alberta, Canada. He was the youngest of seven children. Both of his parents were Dutch immigrants who lived on a farm in rural Alberta near the hamlet of Kirkcaldy before moving to another farm near Alhambra, Alberta. The family belonged to the strongly Calvinist Dutch Reformed Church. After graduation from Rocky Mountain House High School in 1954, Keegsta worked as an auto mechanic before attending Premier Aberhart's Prophetic Bible Institute in Calgary in 1957. His family had been converts to the right-wing antisemitic Social Credit Party of C. H. Douglas. Keegstra joined the Social Credit Party at an early age, and he accepted its twin principles of conservative economic and strong religious orientation. Still working as an automobile mechanic, he entered the University of Alberta at Calgary (now the University of Calgary) in 1959 where he majored in industrial arts. While in school Keegstra taught at schools in Cremona, Red Deer, and at the fundamentalist Hillcrest Christian College in Medicine Hat. After graduation in 1967, Keegstra found employment in 1968 as a high school teacher in Eckville, Alberta. His teaching subjects were industrial arts and social studies. Keegstra was one of seven full-time teachers.

Keegsta and his family soon adjusted to the Eckville community. Eckville was an oil and farming community of only 872 people. He joined the Diamond Valley Full Gospel Church where he became a deacon and a Sunday School teacher. Keegstra also served for some time as the mayor of Eckville.[35] As Alan Davies put it, "his rigid moralistic views, however, did not make the non-smoking, non-drinking, anti-dancing, anti-card playing, Bible-believing Christian a favorite with everyone in town."[36] He had also remained a member of the antisemitic extremist party, the Social Credit Party, running three times in 1972, 1974, and 1983 for federal and in 1971 for provincial office.[37] In none of these elections was Keegstra successful, and he became bitter over the results, particularly over the 1971 provincial election.[38] Keegstra's interest in political extremism continued with him establishing contacts with the Canadian Ku Klux Klan beginning in 1972.[39]

Keegstra developed his antisemitic and Holocaust denial views from extensive reading of antisemitic works. One of his early readings was from the notorious Russian antisemite Rev. Justinus Bonaventura Pranaitis, and his 1892 book *The Talmud Unmasked: The Secret Rabbinal Teachings Concerning Christians.*[40] Pranaitis had taken mistranslated and out-of-context excerpts of the Talmudic texts that showed anti-Christian attitudes.[41] Keegstra based much of his anti-Jewish attitude from material out of this book.[42] He also found the neo-Nazi Elizabeth Dilling's 1964 book *The Plot against Christianity* (later reissued as *The Jewish Religion: Its Influence Today*) and its thesis that Judaism is anti-Christian convincing.[43] Another source was Nesta Webster's 1921 book *World Revolution or the Plot against Civilization* in which she blamed the Jews for an international conspiracy to promote revolutions.[44]

Keegstra was an obscure teacher until he began to alienate parents with his anti-Catholic and antisemitic pronouncements in classes to his students. Although there had been complaints about inappropriate remarks as early as 1973, an Alberta school official warned Keegstra about his anti-Catholic remarks in his classes beginning in 1978.[45] For years Keegstra had taught his students that the Jews were the children of the devil and that there was an international Jewish conspiracy bent on world domination. His reasoning followed along these lines:

> The Bible declares Jews are the children of the devil, and that the devil is the father of lies (John 8:44); consequently, no other opinion is acceptable. One is either for Christ or against him, and, since the Jews are obviously against him, they must be for the devil, which means that they favour the destruction of the Christian church and Christian society—in short, the destruction of everything that Keegstra deemed precious and good. Judaism, it follows, is an evil religion, premised on a hatred of Christ and Christianity, so that Jews who take Judaism seriously must also be evil.[46]

Among his arguments was that the Jews were not descendents of the original Twelve Tribes of Israel and they were instead descendents of the Khazars from the Russian steppes.[47] Finally, he considered the Holocaust to be a fraud and Israel a menace to civilization. Stanley R. Barrett interviewed him extensively and this is Barrett's conclusion about Keegstra's views on the Holocaust:

> Keegstra contended that the Holocaust as popularly perceived never took place. He defined "holocaust" as massive death by fire. A holocaust in that sense, he said, did occur in Germany during the Second World War, but it consisted of the Allied bombing of Dresden. According to Keegstra, it is now official that no gas chambers in Germany were used for human beings. He also believed personally that nowhere did gas chambers, in the hands of Germans, exist for the purpose of killing human beings, nor was there an official German policy to kill Jews; the "final solution," instead, consisted of deportation and emigration. The camps in Poland were inaccessible behind the Soviet Iron Curtain for ten years following the war, he pointed out, and thus any kind of fabrication would have been possible. Like others I interviewed Keegstra claimed that Jews were far safer in concentration camps than outside them, where partisans and undisciplined soldiers could attack them.[48]

When Barrett asked Keegstra about what kind of evidence would change his mind about Holocaust denial, "he admitted that virtually nothing would do the trick, repeating his observation that even what might look like proof for the gas chambers could easily have been constructed after the war itself."[49] Moreover, Keegstra believed it was his duty to inform his students about the dangers of the "conventional interpretations of the Jewish-intimidated historians who were afraid to tell the real truth about past and current events."[50] Keegstra was dogmatic about what he considered to be the truth.

> This is his (Keegstra's) idea that a single explanation can be given to all important events experienced by society for at least the last two centuries—that of a Jewish conspiracy to take over the world, destroy Christianity and establish "one world" government.[51]

School officials were reluctant to fire Keegstra even after the complaints continued to appear. A serious complaint came to the school administrators about his linking of the Irish Republican Army with communism.[52] Then, a complaint came from a parent over Keegstra's anti-Catholic remarks in class, so Keegstra toned down his anti-Catholic teaching and replaced it with more anti-Jewish material.[53] Another parent compiled her son's class notes about Keegstra's antisemitic remarks. Then one of his former students was quoted saying, "If you didn't agree with him, you didn't pass."[54] This was particularly true on tests about the French Revolution of 1789. If the student did not regurgitate his thesis about Adam Weishaupt, the Illuminati, and the Jews, then the student was in danger of not passing.[55] Another student recounted that she had used library materials for an essay on Catholicism, but Keegstra had refused to grade it.[56]

These complaints from parents led school officials to conduct a meeting where Keegstra could defend himself. At the Lacombe School Board meeting on February 9, 1982, Keegstra stated "his belief in the Jewish conspiracy, of which the Holocaust hoax was a part, and arguing that his perspective merely offset the socialist line of other, uninformed teachers, and thus enhanced the students' overall educational development."[57] Even this statement did not persuade the school board to fire Keegstra until another complaint by the mother of one of his students in October 1982.[58] Following up on these parents' complaints, school board officials fired him with reluctance at a December 7, 1982, meeting with the dismissal actually taking place on January 8, 1983.

The Canadian government then tried Keegstra for teaching hatred against Jews in a 1985 trial in Red Deer, Alberta. He hired the right-wing lawyer Doug Christie to represent him. The trial began on April 9, 1985, and it lasted 71 days. In this first trial he was convicted of the charges of violating Section 319, subsection 2 of the Criminal Code and fined $5,000, but an Alberta Court of Appeals overturned the verdict in 1988 on the grounds that the sentence violated the freedom-of-speech guarantees in the new Canadian Charter of Rights.[59] The Supreme Court of Canada subsequently overturned the lower court's ruling and sent the case back to the Alberta Appeals Court. In a second trial in 1992 Keegstra was again found guilty and received a two-year jail sentence and was fined $3,000. In 1994 the Alberta Court of Appeals rejected the second conviction. Finally, the Canadian Supreme Court upheld the second conviction in a February 1996 decision.[60]

The Holocaust denial community turned the various Keegstra trials into a test case for its viewpoint. During the intervals between the trials, Keegstra worked as an auto mechanic. His cause attracted Canada's leading right-wing lawyer, Doug Christie, to represent him at both of his trials. Keegstra's conviction only reinforced the belief among his supporters that a Jewish conspiracy was still at work. Besides Holocaust deniers, Keegstra attracted supporters from "old-fashioned Douglasite diehards or from European immigrants in rural Alberta already predisposed to a certain measure of anti-Jewish prejudice."[61] Since the loss of his teaching position, Keegstra has been working as a full-time mechanic in Eckville.

MALCOLM ROSS AND HOLOCAUST DENIAL

Another prominent Holocaust denier in Canada is Malcolm Ross. He was born in May 1946 in Winnipeg, Canada. His father was a Presbyterian minister. At an early age his family moved to the Miramichi region of New Brunswick near Newcastle. It was there that Ross received his elementary and high school education. His most apparent personal characteristic as a youth was his strong religious views. He attended the University of New Brunswick majoring in education. After graduating in 1968, Ross spent the next decade as a teacher in a variety of small schools.

During most of this decade, Ross studied antisemitic and Holocaust denial materials. It was in 1978 that Ross finally entered the ranks of Holocaust denial by the publication of his book *Web of Deceit*. In this work Ross attacked the authenticity of the diary of Anne Frank, and he declared the Holocaust a hoax.[62] He also proclaimed that there was an international conspiracy of "international Communists, international financiers, and international Zionists" united to destroy Christianity.[63]

Publication of this book produced a firestorm of controversy in Canada. Most of the criticism revolved around his role as a teacher of impressionable youth. Ross made it plain that he had not been indoctrinating students, but that his viewpoint had been advanced outside of school hours. Nevertheless, David Attis, a local Jewish community leader, led a movement to restrict the sale of the book at bookstores, but, despite his efforts, the book sold out. Despite calls to have him fired, Ross was able to retain his teaching position.

His next book was on abortion, and it made Ross even more controversial. This short book appeared in 1983 under the title *The Real Holocaust: The Attack on Unborn Children and Life Itself*. Ross combined an attack on abortion with antisemitism and Holocaust denial. Warren Kinsella tied both together:

> Calling the Holocaust an "imaginary mass slaughter" that "has been used to create a false sense of guilt in Christian nations." Ross suggests the Nazis' final solution with the prevalence of abortion in Canada.[64]

Again this book caused a public outcry. Dr. Julius Israel, a retired chemist living in Miramichi, complained to the New Brunswick attorney-general about both books. He launched a series of investigations of Ross for possible infringement of Canadian laws. After four investigations that lasted nearly three years, the attorney-general decided not to press charges.

Ross responded to the public criticism of the previous books by writing yet a third book. This book received the title *Spectre of Power* and it appeared in 1988. In it Ross recounted his experiences with critics of his other works and justified the ideas in them. Again this book sparked a controversy. This time the accumulated negative publicity threatened Ross's teaching position as School Board District 15 began sending letters of warning about his political activities.

When it became apparent that Ross's job as a teacher might be in danger, a Ross network of supporters formed. An alliance of Canadian antisemites, neo-Nazis, and white supremacists mobilized to back Ross. A massive letter-writing campaign inundated the desk of the New Brunswick government of Frank McKenna.[65] His response was to launch a formal investigation of Ross and his political activities. He appointed a one-person commission—New Brunswick law professor Brian Bruce. Justification for the commission was a complaint lodged by David Attis. Ross's works were critiqued by James A. Beverley, a professor of theology and ethics from Mount Allison University, in June 1990, and he documented hundreds of factual errors in Ross's writings.[66] After weeks of testimony at two separate sessions, Bruce ordered the school board in late August 1991 to place Ross on a leave of absence without pay for 18 months, and he told the board to find a nonteaching job for him or else fire him.[67] Bruce also ruled that Ross could be fired if he continued to advance his antisemitism in a public forum. In December 20, 1995, the New Brunswick Court of Appeals overturned Bruce's rulings, citing that since Ross had never taken his antisemitic views in the classroom he could resume teaching.

DOUG COLLINS AND HIS CONTRIBUTIONS TO HOLOCAUST DENIAL

An influential Canadian Holocaust denier was Doug Collins. His importance was as a journalist for a local Vancouver newspaper where he had a ready forum to advance his views on antisemitism and Holocaust denial by posing as a champion of free speech. He was born on September 8, 1920, in England. Of military age when World War II broke out, Collins served in the British army. He had obtained the rank of sergeant in the infantry before the Germans captured him at Dunkirk. From 1940 until 1944 Collins was a German prisoner of war despite 10 escape attempts. His escape attempts are chronicled in his book *POW: A Soldier's Story of His Ten*

Escapes from Nazi Prisons in 1968. Ultimately, Collins won his freedom in 1944 when Romania capitulated. He returned to the British army and served out the rest of the war in an infantry unit.

Unhappy with his career prospects in postwar Great Britain, Collins immigrated to Canada in 1952. He pursued a career in journalism working for a variety of Canadian newspapers, including the *Calgary Herald,* the *Vancouver Sun,* and the *Vancouver Province.* For a time Collins worked for Canada's CBC television network. After moving to Vancouver, he also was a radio talk show host. In 1984, Collins moved to the *North Shore News* where he wrote a column until his retirement in 1997.

Collins became a supporter of Holocaust denial and deniers. In both his speeches and writings he made provocative statements backing Holocaust denial and ridiculing its critics. Collins was a frequent contributor to the Institute for Historical Review's (IHR) *Journal of Historical Review,* and he spoke at the IHR's 1990 conference. In his newspaper columns Collins frequently advanced Holocaust denial themes. At one time or another he called the 6 million Holocaust toll figure nonsense, and in 1994 he attacked the movie *Schindler's List* by characterizing it as Swindler's List.

Collins's attacks on the Holocaust and on Canada's Jewish groups led to legal complaints against him. The Canadian Jewish Congress responded to his charge that *Schindler's List* had been "hate literature in the form of films" by charging Collins with violation of British Columbia's Human Rights Act.[68] The British Columbia Human Rights Tribunal turned down the first charge in November 1997, but it later upheld a second charge. This judgment was under appeal when he died on September 29, 2001.

PAUL FROMM AND HOLOCAUST DENIAL

Another influential Canadian Holocaust denier is Frederick Paul Fromm. He was born on January 3, 1949, in Canada. He attended the University of Toronto's St. Michael's College. As a student in February 1967, he was a co-founder with Don Andrews, Al Overfield, Leigh Smith, and Wolfgang Droege of the Edmund Burke Society.[69] This society was a right-wing anti-communist group that later became the white supremacist Western Guard Party. Once this transition had been completed Fromm left it in 1972. Fromm graduated with an education degree, and he found a job as a high school teacher in 1974 with the Peel Region Board of Education. Later, he obtained a M.A. in English literature and linguistics from the University of Toronto.

During his years as a school teacher, Fromm was also active in Canadian right-wing politics. In 1979, he founded Citizens for Foreign Aid Reform (C-FAR) to oppose foreign aid to third-world countries. Fromm followed in 1980 by starting the Canadian Association for Free Expression (CAFE) to counter the activities of the Canadian Human Rights Commission. His next venture was the Canada First Immigration Reform Committee with the goal of reducing immigration and opposing immigration by nonwhites. Of the three organizations, Fromm has spent the most time and energy with CAFE. He has been an ardent defender of Holocaust deniers Ernst Zündel, James Keegstra, and Wolfgang Droege.

Fromm's political activities caused him to encounter legal problems. In the early 1990s there were complaints made to the Peel Board of Education and to the Ontario Ministry of Education about his suitability to be a high school teacher. Issues at point were Fromm's participation in a neo-Nazi Heritage Front rally in December 1990 and in an April 1991 meeting to celebrate Adolf Hitler's birthday. An inquiry led by a lawyer, J. G. Cowan, recommended his discharge as a high school teacher and a reassignment to teach adult education.[70] The Peel Region Board of Education gave him a warning against continuing his activities with white supremacists in 1993.[71] Fromm's continued association with Holocaust deniers and neo-Nazis led to his dismissal from the Peel Board of Education in 1997. A March 2002 ruling of Ontario's Labour Relations Board upheld his 1997 firing.[72]

Since his firing, Fromm has been even more active in Holocaust denial and neo-Nazi causes. His C-FAR has published books supporting apartheid, Holocaust deniers, and eugenics. Fromm was a leader in protesting Ernst Zündel's fight to avoid deportation to Germany in 2005, and he has been active in rebuilding the Canadian neo-Nazi and Holocaust denial movements.[73] In a December 2005 interview with the Iranian news service, Fromm stated that he agreed with Iranian President Mahmoud Ahmadinejad's views on the Holocaust.

As the Iranian president said, Europe you can deny the existence of God. However, if you question the slightest aspect of the self-serving story of Jewish sufferings in World War II, called "the holocaust", you can end up in prison in Europe. Historians like Irving, now imprisoned in Austria and publishers Ernst Zundel and Germar Rudolf, now imprisoned in Germany, are good examples of this phenomenon. "The Holocaust" has become a religion. It's a religion created by the Jews for non-Jews. Like many religions, it's a means of controlling the believers. As a religion, the holocaust demands faith and belief. Its supporters shun rational discussion and debate. You must believe. To question is to be a heretic and heretics must be punished.[74]

JOHN CLIVE BALL AND AERIAL PHOTOGRAPHY

Another form of Holocaust denial has been introduced by John Clive Ball. Little is known about his early life except that he attended and graduated from the University of British Columbia, Vancouver, with a bachelor of science degree in geology in 1981. He has also claimed that he studied air photo interpretation while at the university. Since graduation, he has been a consulting geologist in British Columbia who specializes in interpreting aerial photos used in mineral exploration. Ernst Zündel recruited him in November 1987 to study aerial photographs to support him in his 1988 trial.[75] Ball obtained wartime aerial photographs from the National Archives in Washington, D.C., and he interpreted them. Zündel's lawyer called him as an expert witness, but the judge interrogated him and determined that "Ball was not sufficiently qualified as an expert to do the job," disqualifying him.[76]

He has expanded his expertise to become a critic of the Holocaust by charging that Allied aerial reconnaissance photographs taken in 1944 and 1945 prove that mass executions using poison gas did not take place at Auschwitz. Furthermore, he has claimed that the aerial photographs had been altered before a study by Dino A. Brugioni and Robert G. Poirier, *The Holocaust Revisited: A Retrospective Analysis of the Auschwitz-Birkenau Extermination Complex,* appeared in 1979. Ball published his charges in a book *Air Photo Evidence* published by Zündel's Samisdat Publishers, Ltd. in 1992. Ball continued to make these charges and others at the 12th IHR Conference in September 1994. At one time both Irving and Zündel considered Ball's book almost as important as the one by Leuchter, but it ended up not having much of an impact.[77]

Ball's charges have produced a variety of counterclaims. He triggered much of this attention by offering on his Web site in March/April 1997 a $100,000 reward to have three air photo experts agree that the 3-D maps are not accurate copies of the air photos, and marks were not drawn on August 25, 1944, Auschwitz air photos showing evidence of air photo tampering. To win, the experts must meet the approval of Ball, making it impossible for him to lose. When John Morris of the Nizkor Project attempted to contact Ball in 1997 to take him up on his challenge, Ball had disappeared. Several attempts to contact him failed, and his $100,000 reward was quietly removed from the Ball Web site. Further complicating Ball's life was another study that contradicted his analysis of the Auschwitz-Birkenau photos. In his study Brian Harmon concluded that Ball was either incompetent or a fraud.

> Ball's defenders are left with a nasty situation: either Ball missed the pits and smoke unintentionally, or he deliberately lied about them by omission. In the former case, Ball's integrity remains but his credentials as an "Air Photo Expert" are left in tatters. In the latter case, he is nothing more than a charlatan and a fraud.[78]

Ball no longer has a high profile in the Holocaust denial movement, but his work is still cited by Holocaust deniers as proving that gas chambers were never in operation at Auschwitz-Birkenau.

CONCLUSION

Holocaust denial in both the United States and Canada continues to pick up adherents, but at a much slower rate. Several factors have retarded the rate of growth. Most important has been the schism in Holocaust denial between Willis A. Carto and the staff of the Institute of Historical Review. Mark Weber's IHR is only a shadow of its former status in the movement. It suffers from a lack of funding and the hostility of Carto. Carto's starting of *The Barnes Review* and his constant attacks against others in the Holocaust denial movement have weakened it because deniers have had to choose between the competing groups. Most of the prominent international Holocaust deniers have stayed with the Institute for Historical Review, but even this loyalty was unable to prevent the shutting down of the *Journal of Historical Review*.

Notwithstanding the trials and tribulations in the American Holocaust denial movement show no signs of going away. New adherents have been taking the place of those dying off. American Holocaust deniers still have *The Barnes Review* and Bradley R. Smith's *The Revisionist: Journal for Critical Historical Inquiry* to publish their articles in.

PART IV

Third-World Holocaust Denials

Holocaust Denial
in the Muslim World

INTRODUCTION

Holocaust denial reached the Muslim world soon after its first appearance in Europe. It met with a resounding acceptance because many in the Arab world had been pro-Nazi during World War II. Foremost among the supporters of Nazism then and after the war was Haj Amin al-Husseini, the Mufti of Jerusalem. He had spent much of the war in Berlin supporting the Nazi war effort against the Allies. Even the defeat of Nazi Germany did not prevent Arab sympathizers from adhering to Nazi ideals, including hatred of the Jews. The advent of the state of Israel in 1948 and the struggle over the lands of Palestine in a series of wars have not lessened Arab suspicions about Jews or the state of Israel. Gamal Abdel Nasser, the president of Egypt, established the Institute for the Study of Zionism in 1959, and it employed several ex-Nazis as propaganda experts.

Arab antisemitism and Holocaust denial also has a religious element. It goes back to the times of the prophet Mohammed and his difficulties with the Jews in establishing Islam. In traditional accounts, a Jewish woman poisoned the prophet Mohammed.[1] Then the founder of the Shi'ite sect, Abdullah Ibn Saba, was a Yemenite Jew, and his rebellion caused a schism in the Muslim world.[2] Treatments of both incidents have served as archetypes in the Arab world as described by Ronald L. Nettler.

These ancient archetypes persisted during the long history of Islam's subjugation of the Jews, as a routine part of doctrine and historiography. Devoid of hatred, the archetypes were prosaically recounted as part of Islam's portrayal of the "proper" world order where the malevolent, conspiratorial Jews were finally humbled under Muslim rule. The archetypes represent an Islamic victory pageant as well as a reminder of the evil nature of the Jews: they are, in essence, a morality tale in which good conquers evil. But the catastrophic humbling of Muslims themselves in the modern world and the liberation of the Jews, symbolized by their building a successful state, have revivified the archetypes in a most dramatic manner. The twentieth century has yet to include any tales of Muslim success in curbing "evil" Jewish proclivities. This has engendered the need to adapt and update ancient archetypes in modern costume.[3]

Holocaust denial has thus gained a place among the Arab archetypes.

Even before modern times there existed tensions between the Muslim and Jewish worlds that sometimes broke out into violence. In the Moroccan city of Fez more than 6,000 Jews were killed in 1033 for religious reasons. There were also massacres of Jews in Muslim areas of southern Spain in the years 1010 to 1013 and again in 1066. Robert S. Wistrich has described it best.

Indeed, in the Islamic world from Spain to the Arabian peninsula the looting and killing of Jews, along with punitive taxation, confinement to ghettos, the enforced wearing of distinguishing marks on clothes (an innovation in which Islam preceded medieval Christiandom) and other humiliations, were rife.[4]

Even in periods of prosperity, resentment against Jews for worldly success has been widespread. Attacks against the Jews particularly in North Africa continued well into the nineteenth century.

The development of the Zionist movement and the influx of Jews into the Holy Land beginning in the late nineteenth century but expanding in the early twentieth century intensified the tension between Jews and the Muslim world. Jewish immigration into Palestine led to several Muslim pogroms against Jews, but these outbreaks were unable to prevent the expansion of the Jewish population in Palestine. The establishment of the Jewish state was especially traumatic to the Arab world. Now antisemitism and anti-Zionism became intertwined with opposition to Israel. Because the state of Israel came into existence after the Holocaust and partly as a response to it, the existence of the Holocaust became a topic of dispute among Arab political leaders and intellectuals. In this environment of distrust and resentment, Holocaust denial has found a permanent home.

ARAB ATTACKS ON ZIONISM

Holocaust denial has become an important weapon in the Arab arsenal of arguments against Zionism and Israel. Among early Holocaust deniers was

Egypt President Gamal Abdel Nasser.[5] Walter Laqueur reported Nasser saying, "[N]o person, not even the most simple one takes seriously the lie of the
six million Jews who were killed."[6] Ernst Zündel, the Canadian-German
Holocaust denier, attempted to stimulate Holocaust denial support among
Muslims when he published a pamphlet entitled *The West, War, and Islam*
and sent it to Muslim heads of state in the late 1970s.[7] Kenneth R. Timmerman reported that in his interviews with Arabs in the early 1990s, they
believed in the Jewish plot to rule the world and destroy Islam as outlined
in *The Protocols of the Learned Elders of Zion*.[8] Robert Fisk, a British journalist, reported in 1996 that he has heard from Arabs from all over the
Middle East that "Hitler's destruction of Europe's Jews was a 'myth'
invented by the Israelis to justify their seizure of Palestinian Arab land."[9]

Arab leaders have adopted Holocaust denial as a means to help the Palestinian cause by undermining Israeli legitimacy. Bernard Lewis has characterized the Muslim response to the Holocaust as denying, or minimizing it,
excusing, extenuating, or even justifying what happened.[10] Goetz Nordbruch expressed the attitude in the following words:

> Since many Arab authors believe that the Holocaust is used by Zionists as [the]
> primary argument for the legitimacy of the Jewish state, their writings therefore
> seek to explain the historical origins of anti-Jewish aggression in European
> societies, and go on to blame the Jews themselves for their being rejected and
> excluded from these societies.[11]

Funds from Arab sources have been used to finance Holocaust denial
since the 1960s. This support has also reached outside of the Middle East.
Saudi sources helped finance Willis A. Carto's Institute for Historical
Review.[12]

Arab critics have come to equate Zionism and Nazism. Numerous works
have appeared making this connection.[13] Among the most prominent
converts to Holocaust denial have been Mahmoud Abbas, president of
the Palestinian Authority and veteran al-Fatah leader, and Ahmed Rami, a
former Moroccan army officer, operating out of Sweden.

MAHMOUD ABBAS AND HOLOCAUST DENIAL IN THE PALESTINE LIBERATION ORGANIZATION

Mahmoud Abbas was one of the early Holocaust deniers. Abbas is now
the president of the Palestinian Authority and a longtime leader in
al-Fatah. As a student, he attended the Moscow Oriental College in the
Soviet Union in the late 1970s. There Abbas wrote his doctoral dissertation
on Nazi-Zionist collaboration. In 1983, Abbas's book denying the Holocaust appeared under the title *The Other Side: The Secret Relations between
Nazism and the Leadership of the Zionist Movement*. He concluded that the

Zionist movement inflated the death figures during the Holocaust for post-war political reasons.[14] He misquoted figures from historian Raul Hilberg to ascertain that fewer than 1 million Jews were killed by the Germans during World War II.[15] Furthermore, Abbas concluded that Robert Faurisson had proven that the Germans never used gas chambers to kill Jews.[16] In the last few years, Abbas has moderated his Holocaust denying views by admitting that the Holocaust was a horrible event. But he has not repudiated his earlier views.

SAUDI HOLOCAUST DENIAL

The Saudi regime has long been a financial supporter for the Holocaust denial movement. Antisemitism has a long history in Saudi Arabia, and the Saudi kingdom allows no Jews to reside within its boundaries. In March 1976 the Saudi Arabian representative to the United Nations made Holocaust denial as part of a speech to the United Nations Security Council, claiming that gas chambers were an invention of the Zionist press and the diary of Anne Frank was a forgery. Criticism for these remarks fell on deaf years in Saudi Arabia.

Besides charges of Holocaust denial, Saudi authorities found other outlets to express their position. They sponsored the production of William Grimstad's *The Six Million Reconsidered*.[17] This work and another Holocaust denial publication by William Grimstad, *Anti-Zion*, were mailed to all members of the U.S. Senate and British Parliament by the World Muslim Congress in 1981 and 1982.[18] Rumors have been circulating for years that Saudi funds helped set up and subsidized for years the American Institute for Historical Review.

ABDULLAH MOHAMMAD SINDI AND HOLOCAUST DENIAL

Abdullah Mohammad Sindi is one of the most active Muslim Holocaust deniers, but he does it from the United States instead of from the Middle East. He was born in 1944 in Mecca, Saudi Arabia. Always a brilliant student, he graduated seventh among all graduates from high school in Saudi Arabia in 1963. Receiving full scholarships from the Saudi government to study abroad, he studied at two French universities, University of Grenoble and University of Poitiers, in the academic year of 1963–1964. He then moved to the United States where he attended Indiana University in 1965–1966. Transferring again, Sindi received his B.A. in 1970 and his M.A. in 1971 in International Relations from California State University in Sacramento. Later, he obtained a Ph.D. in International Relations from the University of Southern California in 1978.

Sindi spent his academic career divided between institutions in Saudi Arabia and in the United States. Between the years 1978 and 1987, he taught at the King Abdul Aziz University in Jeddah and at the Institute for Diplomatic Studies in Jeddah. Since then, he has held positions at a variety of American institutions, including University of California at Irvine, California State University in Pomona, and two community colleges. He blames ethnic-based hostility, from both Jews and Christians, for his lack of promotion at these institutions.[19] Sindi has since retired from academia, but he lives in Placentia, California, with his American wife.

Most of Sindi's early research was on Middle Eastern international relations topics, but beginning in the late 1990s his research interests turned to Holocaust denial. Early in his academic career, he clashed with Saudi Arabian authorities because of his Nasserite pro-Arab nationalism and opposition to the Saudi's Wahhabism. His dislike for Wahhabism comes out strongly in his 2004 article on Britain and the rise of Wahhabism and the House of Saud.[20] But it is his 1999 article on Ahmed Rami's Radio Islam entitled "Holocaust Is a Typical Zionism Myth" that announced his full conversion to Holocaust denial. In that article he denied that "Nazi Germany committed a 'holocaust' by 'gassing and/or incinerating six million Jews' during World War II."[21] To him the reason for the Holocaust myth was as follows:

> To acquire world-wide support, compassion, and sympathy for their (Jews) plan to colonize Arab Palestine, Zionist leaders in and out of the US suddenly began to circulate terribly horrifying stories that the Nazis had "incinerated" or "gassed" six million Jews in various "gas chambers", "ovens," and "crematoria" in and out of Germany between the end of 1942 and November 1944 (five months prior to Adolph Hitler's suicide in April 1945) . . . . The first person in the world to mention this dreadful information about the so-called "holocaust" and the "extermination of six million Jews" was the Zionist Rabbi Israel Goldstein.[22]

He follows these contentions by citing Holocaust denier researchers, including Austin J. App, Arthur R. Butz, Roger Garaudy, and Richard Verrall, to prove his points.

Sindi reinforced his Holocaust denial credentials by his comments following Iranian President Mahmoud Ahmadinejad's anti-Holocaust remarks. In a December 18, 2005, interview with the Iranian Mehr News Agency, Sindi made several controversial remarks.

> I agree wholeheartedly with President Ahmadinejad. There was no such thing as the "holocaust". The so-called "Holocaust" is nothing but Jewish-Zionist propaganda. There is no proof whatsoever that any living Jew was ever gassed or burned in Nazi Germany or in any of the territories that Nazi Germany occupied during World War Two. The holocaust propaganda started by the Zionist Jews in order to acquire world-wide sympathy for the creation of Israel After World War Two.[23]

IBRAHIM ALLOUSH AND JORDANIAN HOLOCAUST DENIAL

The leading Holocaust denier in Jordan is Ibrahim Alloush. He is a Palestinian-Jordanian who spent 13 years in the United States studying at Ohio University and Oklahoma State University. He earned a Ph.D. in economics from Oklahoma State University. Since returning to Jordan, he became a journalist. Alloush is now a journalist with the Jordanian weekly *Assabeel,* and he is editor of the Free Arab Voice Web site. He has also long been active in the Jordanian Writers Association.

At a May 13, 2001, meeting of the Jordanians Writers Association in Amman, Jordan, Alloush expressed his Holocaust denial views. After quoting extensively from a statement by the French Holocaust denier Robert Faurisson, Alloush remarked that Zionists have used the Holocaust as a "free license from the West to act with impunity against anyone any time."[24] Then, Alloush made further remarks.

> Revisionists do not deny that Jews died in the Second World War. On the contrary, revisionists affirm that "hundreds of thousands of Jews, died, along with forty-five million who perished in that war." Revisionist scholars apply science to prove that gas chambers were not used to exterminate Jews systematically. Crematories, on the other hand, were used to "dispose of the corpses of people of different nationalities to circumvent plagues."[25]

MAHMOUD AHMADINEJAD'S CHARGE OF HOLOCAUST DENIAL

A new stage in Muslim Holocaust denial emerged with the statements of Iranian President Mahmoud Ahmadinejad. In a December 14, 2005, mass rally in the city of Zahedan, Ahmadinejad called the Holocaust a myth.[26] He stated that "They (Jews) have created a myth that Jews were massacred and place this above God, religions and the prophets."[27] Earlier in October Ahmadinejad had called for the Jewish state to be "wiped off the map." He then modified his position slightly by calling for Israel to be moved to Europe. These moves have been interpreted in a variety of ways. Perhaps the most impressive theory is that Ahmadinejad wants Iran to resume the revolutionary role of the Ayatollah Ruhollah Khomeini by assuming the leadership position in the Muslim world.[28] One interpretation is that Ahmadinejad is seeking "to prevent a rapprochement between Israel and conservative Arab states that have a security interest in containing an ascendant Iran."[29] Another theory is that Ahmadinejad attacked Israel as part of an agenda to make Iran an international pariah, like North Korea, enabling it to develop its nuclear program without outside interference.[30] Regardless of the reason, the reaction in the Muslim world indicates that Holocaust denial is widely accepted.

Although other Middle East figures have dismissed the Nazi Holocaust, Ahmadinejad has changed the discourse with his stridency. His gambit may serve him well amid the increasing polarization between Islamic countries and the United States. His confrontation has elevated him to a central player on the international scene. By championing Holocaust revisionism, Ahmadinejad has demonstrated his bona tides to the Islamic world and tapped into the reservoir of resentment against Israel that transcends sectarian differences. By radicalizing the Middle East, Ahmadinejad seeks to prevent a rapprochement between Israel and conservative Arab states that have a security interest in containing an ascendant Iran. In doing so, Ahmadinejad could conceivably draw support from Sunni radicals that have been traditionally hostile to the Shi'a.[31]

Ahmadinejad has also become a hero to the international extreme Right. Even before Ahmadinejad's outburst in December 2005, prominent Holocaust deniers had been made welcome in Iran. In November 2000 the Swiss Holocaust denier Jürgen Graf found sanctuary from Swiss law in Iran.[32] Earlier in May 2000 Graf's supporter, Wolfgang Fröhlich, had also gained sanctuary in Iran. Other Holocaust deniers have been made welcome in Iran, including the Australian-German Frederick Töben. He has made two talks in Iran in 2003 and 2006 about Holocaust denial.

A columnist in the Iranian government newspaper *Tehran Times,* Hossein Amiri, followed up Ahmadinejad's assertions with an essay denying the Holocaust. Amiri wrote that those Jews who died in Nazi camps "died of hunger, illness, and other causes."[33] Moreover, he insisted that "the revisionist historians have proven in two decades of study that if Hitler had carried out a systematic program to eradicate the Jews, it would have taken more time than the six years that the war lasted."[34] Finally, he closed with the assertion that the revisionists have proven that "such an act of ethnic cleansing through the use of the poison gas Zyklon-B, as the Zionists claim, was not possible at the time."[35]

To continue their Holocaust denial campaign, Iranian authorities launched an international, Web-based cartoon competition. The goal of this competition was to debunk the Holocaust and question the existence of its victims.[36] Judges awarded a series of prizes based on cartoons that satirized Israel and the Holocaust.

HOLOCAUST DENIAL IN EGYPT'S *AL AHRAM AL-MASSAI*

The Egyptian government daily *Al-Ahram al-Massai* has produced a number of Holocaust denier articles. Editor in chief Mursi Atallah has made various charges, including that Israel and world Jewry have lied about "the number of Jews exterminated by Nazi Germany," and he maintained that Jews had been "secretly deported to Palestine with the assistance of Nazi Germany."[37] Then, columnist Hisham Abd al-Rauf wrote an article on December 12, 2005, with the title "The Execution Chambers Were No

More Than Rooms for Disinfecting Clothing."[38] In this article al-Rauf wrote the following:

> We've had enough of the lies and the falsification of the facts with which the [Israeli] textbooks are replete. The most serious lie is the Jews' Holocaust, which they have exploited in order to extort global solidarity. When Iranian President Mahmoud Ahmadinejad refutes this lie, the entire world is up in arms, and the Iranian president is inundated with accusations of madness, fanaticism, and falsification. [Ahmadinejad] was inundated with these accusations even though he did nothing more than state the truth, which a number of honest researchers have [also] reached. What this truth means is that these massacres, which Israel alleges that the Nazis perpetrated against the Jews, never happened. The famous execution chambers [i.e., the gas chambers] were no more than rooms for disinfecting clothing.[39]

Another Egyptian voice reinforcing Ahmadinejad's statements was the Holocaust denial claims by Mohammed Mahdi Akef, the head of Egypt's Muslim Brotherhood. In an article that appeared on the Muslim Brotherhoods' official Web site on December 21, 2005, he described that World War II's Holocaust of European Jews was a myth.[40] Akef made this charge in context of an attack on "the United States and other Western powers for what he described as a campaign against Islam."[41]

ZAYED CENTER FOR COORDINATION AND FOLLOW-UP AND HOLOCAUST DENIAL

The Zayed Center for Coordination and Follow-Up was a think tank of the League of Arab States that in its brief life flirted with antisemitism and Holocaust denial. This think tank was founded in 1999 by H. H. Sheikh Sultan Bin Zayed Al Nahyan. His father was Sheikh Zayed Bin Sultan Al Nahyan, the president of the United Arab Emirates (UAE). Most of the funding for this institute came from the president. It was based in Abu Dhabi, UAE. Sponsorship for the center came from the association of 22 Arab states.

At first the think tank earned a reputation for being a place where Western heads of state and diplomats could give lectures. Over the years, the roster of speakers included many making wild charges against Jews and Israel. Soon Jewish groups and individuals began to complain about the Zayed Center's antisemitism, but spokesmen from the center denied the antisemitism charge.[42] At a symposium on "Semitism" held on August 28, 2002, the Holocaust was called a "false fable," leading to the following reaction from Abraham H. Foxman of the Anti-Defamation League.

> It is outrageous that an official think-tank of the Arab League has convened a symposium that labels the Holocaust a "false fable" perpetuated by Israel.

The growing use of Holocaust denial has become increasingly common in the Arab world as a weapon to attack Israel and the Jewish people.[43]

In a 2001 report issued by the center, *The Zionist Movement and Its Animosity to Jews*, it was claimed that "Zionists—not Nazis—killed the Jews in Europe."[44] Another report appeared in the same year, giving support for Holocaust deniers Roger Garoudy and David Irving.

The government of the UAE closed down the Zayed Center in August 2003. Western officials had been decrying the increasing anti-American tone of the lectures and publications of the center. This and the increasing criticism over the center's involvement in antisemitism and Holocaust denial led to the decision by the UAE government.

OUTSIDERS' INFLUENCE ON ARAB HOLOCAUST DENIAL

The Garaudy Affair in France has attracted the most attention among Arabs in the Middle East. Roger Garaudy has been a constant champion of the Palestinian cause in the Middle East since his conversion to Islam in 1982. His conversion coincided with his marriage to a Palestinian woman. Expressions of support for Garaudy in his 1998 trial for advancing Holocaust denial in his writing came from all over the Muslim world.[45] The most notable expression of support came in the form of $50,000 donated to his defense from the wife of the president of the United Arab Emirates—Sheikh Zayed Sultan Al Nahayn. In a 1998 visit to Cairo, Egypt, for the Cairo International Book Fair by the invitation of Farouk Hosni, the Egyptian Minister for Culture, Garaudy was received with great pomp, ceremony, and appreciation.[46] Garaudy and his publications remain popular in the Arab world.

Another significant outsider influencing Arab Holocaust denial is David Duke. He made tours of the Arab world in 2002 and again in 2005. Both times he presented lectures and talked on network talk shows promoting his book *Jewish Supremacism: My Awakening to the Jewish Question*. A Syrian journalist gave a copy of Duke's book to Ahmadinejad.[47]

CONCLUSION

Holocaust denial is growing in the Muslim world, but it not without its critics. Many Muslim intellectuals may oppose Israel and its policies toward the Palestinians without resorting to the type of reasoning by the Holocaust deniers. Hussein Ibish, communications director of the American-Arab Anti-Discrimination Committee, has denounced the Holocaust deniers.

In the end, the overwhelming majority of educated Arabs who have any kind of grasp of history, who are educated in history, I don't think they are going to listen to this. I think the overwhelming majority of Arabs, and Palestinians, understand that we have no stake whatever in humoring this ridiculous idea. The historical record is absolutely clear. And one can quibble about details, but the fact that a massive genocide took place during the last few years of the Second World War in Europe, involving an all-out attempt to exterminate Jewish Europeans, gypsies, and eventually Slavs and others, is just beyond question, and I think most Arabs know it.[48]

Holocaust Denial Elsewhere in the World

INTRODUCTION

Holocaust denial in Australia and lesser so in New Zealand is a growth industry. Three individuals have spearheaded Holocaust denial in this area of the world: Eric Butler, John Tuson Bennett, and Fredrick Töben. Although each has come out of a different political tradition, they are united in denying the Holocaust. Despite their advocacy, a 1994 survey found that 93 percent of Australians believe the Holocaust took place.[1] Nevertheless, these individuals continue to seek publicity to make their case. It is illustrative that each of them has made a living off their supporters with Holocaust denial as their cash cow. These Holocaust deniers continue to follow the same path as other Holocaust deniers in that they "engage in inventing information and presenting it as fact; quoting information again and again until it is no longer checked and in fact; and focusing on single claims to disprove the whole."[2]

ERIC DUDLEY BUTLER AND THE AUSTRALIAN LEAGUE OF RIGHTS

The oldest Holocaust denial organization in Australia is the Australian League of Rights (ALR). Erick Dudley Butler founded the Australian League of Rights in 1946. Butler had been an early convert to the Social Credit Party of the British economist C. H. Douglas.[3] Social credit adherents blamed the Great Depression on Jewish financiers "bent on world domination."[4] Butler was active in the Social Credit Movement in the 1930s organizing the movement in Australia. He was also a contributor to its journal *New Times*. Before the war he was pro-Nazi, and he continued advancing its agenda during World War II. After the war, he became an early advocate of Holocaust denial because he believed the Nazis were innocent of atrocities and because he considered Judaism to be a threat to Christianity.[5]

Butler remained the head of the Australian League of Rights until his retirement in 1991. His championing of Holocaust denial and antisemitism made him controversial. In 1946, Butler published *The Protocols of the Learned Elders of Zion* in Melbourne in a new form under the title *The International Jew*. He acknowledged that although *The Protocols* may be a forgery, it contains the truth of an international Jewish conspiracy.[6] He also wrote several books during World War II and afterward associated Jews with communism. Among these were *The War behind the War* (1940), *The Red Pattern of World Conquest* (1961), and *Censored History* (1978). Butler also achieved considerable attention in the Australian press because of his attacks on the Anne Frank Museum in Amsterdam and on the Simon Wiesenthal Centre in America.

Butler developed a close working relationship with David Irving. During Irving's first visit to Australia in March 1986, they became fast friends.[7] They also collaborated in Winnipeg, Canada, in 1987. Butler's Australian League of Rights sponsored Irving's 1987 tour of Australia. Butler and his successors have championed Irving during his various legal difficulties in gaining an Australian visa in 1993.

Butler remained the head of the Australian League of Rights until his retirement in 1991. After Butler's retirement, David Thompson became head of the ALR. He continued the advocacy of Holocaust denial. The current head of the ALR is Betty Luks, who replaced Thompson in 1999. She also shares Butler and Thompson's views on denying the Holocaust.

JOHN TUSON BENNETT AND THE AUSTRALIAN CIVIL LIBERTIES UNION

The Australian Civil Liberties Union (ACLU) is Australia's leading Holocaust denial and neo-Nazi group. John Tuson Bennett founded the ACLU in 1980 to promote his neo-Nazi agenda. He was born on June 2, 1944, in Melbourne, Australia. His background is vague. What is known is that he graduated from the University of Melbourne, and he obtained a law degree. Bennett served as secretary of the Victorian Council for Civil Liberties from 1966 to 1980.

Bennett is one of Australia's leading Holocaust deniers. He claimed that it was his reading in 1979 of Arthur R. Butz's *The Hoax of the Twentieth Century* that converted him to Holocaust denial. His advocacy of Holocaust denial led to his expulsion from the Victorian Council for Civil Liberties in 1980.[8] This conversion led him to send 200 copies of Butz's book and thousands of copies of Robert Faurrison's articles to public figures around Australia.[9] Shortly afterward, he founded the Australian Civil Liberties Union (ACLU). He has remained the president and main spokesperson for the ACLU since its founding. His goal has been to rehabilitate Adolf Hitler and Nazi Germany by denying the Holocaust. The ACLU has always remained a small organization with no more than 250 members. Its headquarters is in Bennett's home. Most of its recruits have come from the Australian working classes, which have been suffering from bad economic times. Bennett has also published the citizens' rights handbook *Your Rights* since 1974. This booklet is intended to give civil rights advice, but Bennett also exposes its readers to Holocaust denial claims.[10]

Soon after he founded ACLU, Bennett established close ties with the American Institute for History Review (IHR), and he has served on its Editorial Advisory Committee for the *Journal of Historical Review*. As an important member of IHR, Bennett has periodically invited Holocaust denial speakers to Australia, including the British popular military historian David Irving. Bennett was one of the co-sponsors of Irving's frequent trips to Australia in the mid-1980s. He also established strong working relationships with Fredrick Töbin's neo-Nazi Adelaide Institute and Pauline Hanson's One Nation Party. Bennett also owns a bookstore in Melbourne that sells and distributes neo-Nazi and antisemitic literature. He also contributes legal advice to Holocaust deniers who are in legal trouble in Australia.

Bennett has made anti-Americanism part of the Australian Civil Liberties Union's campaign of hate. He blamed the United States for the introduction in Australia of a series of antiterrorist laws.[11] His opposition helped water down these laws. Bennett also opposed the American-British assault on Iraq in 2003 as unnecessary and to the benefit of Israel. Bennett has been careful not to endorse the idea of an international Jewish conspiracy, but the ACLU's vice-president, Jonathan Graham, has openly endorsed the idea.[12]

DR. FREDRICK TÖBEN AND THE ADELAIDE INSTITUTE

Another prominent Australian Holocaust denier is Dr. Fredrick Töben. His Adelaide Institute sponsors Holocaust denial activities in Australia. He was born on June 2, 1944, in northern Germany, but his family moved to Australia when Töben was one year of age. After obtaining undergraduate degrees at Melbourne University and Wellington University in New Zealand, he studied at various German universities, including Heidelberg, Tübingen, and Stuttgart. Töben earned a doctorate in philosophy from the

University of Stuttgart with a dissertation on Karl Popper and C. S. Peirce. Along the way Töben also picked up a master's degree in education, enabling him to work as a schoolteacher in Victoria, Australia. Töben worked at the Victoria Department of Education and Training in Melbourne until he was dismissed in 1985 allegedly "on the grounds of incompetence and disobedience."[13] After that he drove a school bus before going on relief.

Töben founded the Adelaide Institute in 1994 to serve as a forum for Holocaust denial in Australia. Part of its mission has been to distribute Holocaust denial materials but also to hold Holocaust denial conferences. The headquarters of the institute is in his home in Melbourne. The membership of the Adelaide Institute is in the neighborhood of 250, and the members are all dedicated Holocaust deniers.[14] Töben had no trouble sending Holocaust denial materials abroad until some of his materials ended up in Germany. In April 1999 Töben visited Germany and German authorities arrested him on April 8, 1999, in Mannheim on charges of "incitement to racial hatred."[15] After a seven-month stay in a Mannheim prison, a German court convicted him of the charge but let him off with a fine of $3,500 and for time served. Töben returned to Australia where he continues to work with John Tuson Bennett's Australian Civil Liberties Union in distributing Holocaust denial materials. He also wrote down his experiences in a book entitled *Fight or Flight: The Personal Face of Revisionism* (2003). Töben makes a living off the activities of the Adelaide Institute.

Töben has been restrained in his endorsement of the international Jewish conspiracy as outlined in *The Protocols of the Learned Elders of Zion,* but this restraint has not been shared by some of his followers. David Brockschmidt, who was born in Berlin and spent two years in Israel before moving to Australia, has been adamant that an international Jewish conspiracy exists in the financial and media world.[16] Others sharing similar views have been Adelaide Institute officers Olga Scully and Geoff Muirden.

Töben and the Adelaide Institute's most effective method of transmitting its message has been with its electronic version of its newsletter *Adelaide Institute Online.* It is a jazzed up version of its newsletter *Adelaide Institute.* This online version has been successful although it has attracted the attention of Australian legal entities. Töben was forced in 2003 to remove Holocaust denial material from the Web site after a legal finding against him.[17]

Töben has developed extensive contacts with other prominent Holocaust deniers. His frequent trips to Europe have allowed him to confer with Holocaust deniers such as the German Germar Rudolf, the Pole Tomo Gabis, the Austrian Emil Lachout, and the French Robert Faurisson. He also sponsored an Australian Holocaust denial conference in August 1998 and frequent tours where Holocaust deniers such as Arthur R. Butz and David Irving have appeared. His contacts with the American Institute for Historical Review have also proven fruitful in garnering contacts.

Töben was a participant at the Iranian Holocaust Denial Conference in December 2006. At this conference Töben continued his assault on the Holocaust by claiming that the Nazi gas chambers hoax was "the products of a feverish pathological mind filled with pure hatred, mostly directed against Germans and anything German."[18] He returned to Australia to face a charge that he be imprisoned for contempt of orders for antisemitic comments on the Adelaide Institute Web site.

RICHARD KREGE AND TREBLINKA

An emerging figure in the Adelaide Institute and a possible successor to Töben in the Adelaide Institute and the Australian Holocaust denial movement is Richard Krege. He was born in 1970 in Australia, but little is known about his background except that he earned a degree in electrical engineering. His engineering credentials allowed him to find a position in the Australian government agency Airservices Australia in Canberra. This agency services air traffic control facilities around Australia.

Krege became active in the Adelaide Institute in the 1990s. In the fall of 1999 Krege took a leave of absence from his job to lead a team of Adelaide Institute members to Poland to investigate Holocaust sites at Treblinka and Belzec. Over a six-day period members of the team examined the soil around Treblinka and later Belzec with ground-penetrating radar (GPR). GPR sends out vertical radar signals that are visible on a computer monitor. Krege concluded after examining the computer data that there had never been any mass graves at either Treblinka or Belzec.[19] He announced his findings to his fellow Holocaust deniers to great acclaim. Mark Weber in the *Journal of Historical Review* expressed his delight.

> The team carefully examined the entire Treblinka II site, especially the alleged "mass graves" portion, and carried out control examinations of the surrounding area. They found no soil disturbance consistent with the burial of hundreds of thousands of bodies, or even evidence that the ground had ever been disturbed. In addition, Krege and his team found no evidence of individual graves, bone remains, human ashes, or wood ashes.[20]

Krege has since been invited to lecture in Holocaust denial circles, and he attended the Holocaust Denial Conference in Tehran, Iran, in December 2006.

The problem with Krege's research is that it contradicts a postwar Polish government investigation of Treblinka in 1945. In November 1945, the Polish government sent Polish judge Zdzislaw Lukaszkiewicz to Treblinka with a group of workers to examine the grounds and undertake excavations. In his final report on November 11, 1945, Lukaszkiewicz attested that there was evidence of the mass killings.

The largest of the craters produced by explosions (numerous fragments attest to the fact that these explosions were set off by bombs), which is at maximum 6 meters deep and has a diameter of about 25 meters—its walls give recognizable evidence of the presence of a large quantity of ashes as well as human remains—was further excavated in order to discover the depth of the pit in this part of the camp. Numerous human remains were found by these excavations, partially still in a state of decomposition. The soil consists of ashes interspersed with sand, is of a dark gray color and granulous in form. During the excavations, the soil gave off an intense odor of burning and decay.[21]

Despite this evidence, testimony of escaped inmates, and Nazi guards, Krege still maintains his stance. Other Holocaust deniers maintain Treblinka was a transit camp. The most charitable critics of Krege allege that he did not investigate correctly or picked the wrong parts of the camp for his investigation. Less charitable critics charge that Krege was lying when he claimed that he found no evidence of soil disturbance.

MICHÈLE RENOUF AND DAVID IRVING

Michèle Renouf is an Australian-born, British-based follower of David Irving and his brand of Holocaust denial. She was born in 1946 at The Entrance on the Central Coast of Australia under the name Mainwaring. Her father was a truck driver and amateur photographer. He used her as a model as she studied dancing at an early age. Her first public exposure was when she danced jazz ballet on television as a 15-year-old. Renouf attended Hunter Girls High School and later the Newcastle art and teachers' colleges. Her goal was to be a teacher. Landing a teaching job at Swansea High School, Ranouf stayed there for a time before moving to the Queensland University of Technology. She also dabbled in Brisbane television both as a commentator and in commercials. In 1968, Renouf won the beauty title Miss Newcastle and Hunter Valley. Deciding that she wanted more opportunity, Ranouf moved to England to study at the Royal Academy of Dancing in Knightsbridge. She brought with her a boyfriend, Daniel Griaznoff. He claimed Russian aristocracy in his background, and, after their marriage, she began marketing herself as Countess Griaznoff. She used this title to crash London society. Her marriage to Griaznoff lasted 20 years, and they had two daughters. After her divorce from Griaznoff, she married New Zealand multimillion dollar financier Sir Francis "Frank the Bank" Renouf. He was 28 years older and under the impression that she was from the Russian nobility. After Sir Francis Renouf found out that she had misrepresented herself, he divorced her. This marriage allowed her to remarket herself as Lady Renouf. She started studying for an advance degree in psychology at London University.

Renouf had a reputation in London's social circles as a socialite, but her entry into the Holocaust denier world came at the Irving-Lipstadt trial in

London in 2000. She showed up and was a vocal supporter of Irving. How she described it comes from this interview:

> I went down to the Royal Courts of Justice to hear him speak. And I ended up attending every day for 2½ months. I had lunch with him in the court canteen quite often, and one day, he asked me how I thought he had done the day before. I explained to him that I had arrived late and couldn't get a seat in the Court. He said that he had room on the bench next to him. So I sat right next to him for the rest of the trial.[22]

Even before the Irving-Lipstadt trial, Renouf had been a critic of Israel and had questioned aspects of the Holocaust. This position was because of her antisemitic views. In an interview in 2003, Renouf stated,

> You have to go back and look at the Jews's religious texts. You see, the Torah and the Talmud state quite clearly that only Jews have a soul. The rest of us are merely cattle. That is the reason why they treat people the way they do— and why they are so despised throughout history. People act as though Judaism is just another religion like Christianity or Islam. It's not. It's a creed of domination and racial superiority.[23]

Since the Irving-Lipstadt trial, Renouf has been busy trying to arrange financing for Irving so he can continue Holocaust denial activities. She thought that she had managed to accomplish this task by introducing Irving to Prince Fahd bin Salman, the eldest nephew of then King Fahd of Saudi Arabia.[24] Unfortunately for Irving, Salman died in 2001 before turning any money over to him.

Renouf has continued her activities in the Holocaust denial movement. Soon after Irving's arrest in Austria, Renouf sprang to his defense. She attended his trial and proclaimed it to be unfair to Irving. Along the way she has suggested that "so-called Holocaust victims should be exhumed to see what they died from, typhoid or gas."[25] The problem with this approach is that the Germans burned the bodies of Holocaust victims in both Germany and Poland. What body remains there are could not be examined forensically. Besides, more than 60 years have passed, and whatever remains would be degraded.

CHRISTIAN IDENTITY MINISTRIES AND HOLOCAUST DENIAL

The Australian Christian Identity Ministries (CIM) is an offshoot of the American Christian Identity movement, and it has embraced Holocaust denial. This organization is based in North Queensland. Following the two-seed theory of Christian Identity, Jews are considered the spawn of Satan. Because members of Christian Identity believe Jesus was an Aryan and the lost tribes of Israel settled in Northern Europe and then to the United

States, it is easy to dehumanize the Jews. Consequently, it is easy for members of Christian Identity to adopt Holocaust denial. It has become a core belief of the CIM that the Holocaust never happened and there were no gas chambers at Auschwitz.[26] Several prominent members of the CIM have made statements to this effect.[27] They have also been strong supporters of David Irving's tours of Australia. Both Olga Scully and Geoff Muirden have written material that indicates that they subscribe to a Christian Identity viewpoint.[28]

SKINHEAD HOLOCAUST DENIAL

The leading skinhead group in Australia, the National Alliance, has openly advocated Holocaust denial. Two incidents—one in 1988 and another in 1994—showed that the leaders and membership espoused Holocaust denial. Once the group left Holocaust denial material at a progressive church, and the other was at a protest of the showing of the movie *Schindler's List*. The leader of National Action is Michael Brander, and he lost a court case against a newspaper because of the racism implied by Holocaust denial and the idealization of Nazi Germany.[29]

HOLOCAUST DENIAL IN NEW ZEALAND

Holocaust denial has even reached New Zealand in the case of Joel Hayward. He was born in 1965 in New Zealand. Hayward was a history graduate student at Canterbury University who wrote a master's thesis entitled "The Fate of Jews in German Hands" in 1993 on the historical evidence produced by Holocaust deniers. In this thesis Hayward accepted many of the conclusions of the Holocaust deniers and challenged some of the contentions of other scholars. Hayward received the degree of master of arts (with first class honors). After the thesis was kept secret for six years, it attracted the attention of the New Zealand Jewish Council (NZJC), which demanded action against Hayward to revoke his degree.

Then the council commissioned Dr. Richard J. Evans, a professor of modern history at Cambridge University and a member of the team that had challenged David Irving's credentials at the Lipstadt libel trial in 2000, to examine the thesis and give his opinion on the academic merits of the case. His final report was that Hayward's thesis "was not a bona fide work of scholarship, and that the degree of MA should be withdrawn."[30]

The "Holocaust denial" literature Hayward was considering was well known to specialists and others as anti-Semitic, racist, and frequently neo-Fascist propaganda masquerading as scholarship. Yet Hayward not only treated it on an equal footing with genuine historical research but consistently denigrated the many historians in many countries who had carried out bona fide research into the Holocaust, claiming, for instance, that they were mainly Jewish (not true) and therefore produced tendentious and unscholarly work (which did not follow, and was also untrue). He presented Holocaust deniers as objective scholars searching for truth, and concluded that in many cases deniers' claims were justified. Hayward's dissertation was systematically tendentious and dishonest in its appraisal of the literature. I found evidence that he had suppressed material he claimed to have read if it counted against the deniers.[31]

Canterbury University formed a three-person committee to study the Hayward thesis in light of the request of the NZJC and the Evans report. This committee found fault with Hayward's thesis in that his attempt to "assess the merits of Holocaust Revisionism to be neither impartial nor dispassionate" contrary to his claims.[32] The final conclusion was that "the Working Party finds the thesis seriously flawed in the manner described earlier, it cannot find the subjective element necessary to establish dishonesty."[33] It did, however, criticize him for depending on "the assistance of a number of Holocaust Revisionists and their critics" and that he had sent copies of his thesis to "at least two informants," raising ethical issues.[34] In July 2003, Dr. Thomas Fudge, a history lecturer at Canterbury University, charged in a newspaper letter that the prosecution of Hayward was a "witch-hunt" and that Evans had misrepresented Hayward's thesis.[35] By that time, Hayward had resigned as a senior lecturer in history at Massey University. After the publication of his letter and the refusal of Canterbury University to allow his article on the case in *History Now* to be published, Fudge resigned his university position.[36] Evans responded to Fudge's criticisms that his treatment of Hayward had been fair and impartial.[37]

COSTAS ZAVERDINOS AND HOLOCAUST DENIAL IN SOUTH AFRICA

Costas Zaverdinos is the leading Holocaust denier in South Africa. He was born in 1938 in Johannesburg, South Africa. Zaverdinos attended Rhodes University where he received a bachelor of science degree. Next, Zaverdinos moved to the University of Witwatersrand (Johannesburg) where he received a bachelor of science (honors) degree in applied mathematics. Finally, he studied and received a masters of science degree in 1965 from the University of Natal (Durban). After teaching at the Athens Technical University for three years, Zaverdinos obtained a position at the University of Natal (Pietermaritzburg) in 1970. Since then, Zaverdinos earned a Ph.D. in mathematics in 1984, and he is presently an honorary senior lecturer in the University's School of Mathematics, Statistics and Computer Technology. Reflecting a long-held interest in Greek antiquity, Zaverdinos achieved a Bachelor of Arts (Honors) in ancient Greek studies in 1989.

He became a Holocaust denier beginning in 1986. His area of specialty is the history of World War II. After writing several Holocaust denial articles, the Institute for Historical Review added him in 1997 to the *Journal of Historical Review*'s Editorial Advisory Committee. He has been a frequent contributor to *Journal of Historical Review* and its conferences.

HOLOCAUST DENIAL IN JAPAN

Antisemitism had never played much of a political role in Japan until it made its appearance in Japanese wartime propaganda in World War II. Japanese translations of *The Protocols of the Learned Elders of Zion* and Hitler's *Mein Kampf* had already appeared before the war, but the war witnessed an outburst of anti-Jewish feeling in Japan. Japanese media with the encouragement of the government produced a variety of antisemitic articles. Since World War II, antisemitism never caught on as a viable movement in Japan until the 1980s. Two factors that helped the Japanese understand the Holocaust were the publication in 1952 of Anne Frank's *The Diary of a Young Girl* and the trial of Adolf Eichmann in the early 1960s.[38]

What happened in Japan that contributed to the renewal of antisemitism was the development of a moral equivalency movement equating the Holocaust with the Hiroshima and Nagasaki bombings. Some Japanese writers even suggested that it was worse for the survivors of the atomic bomb attacks because of having to live with invisible radioactivity inside their bodies.[39] Then, the Japanese have engaged in a denial movement of their own involving the wartime massacre of Chinese civilians in Nanjing, China, during World War II. Together these two movements have prepared the grounds for the development of a Japanese Holocaust denial movement that finally appeared in the 1980s.

Masami Uno is Japan's leading Holocaust denier. He was born in 1942 and raised in Osaka, Japan. His education was in economics at Osaka Metropolitan University. After teaching in a public high school as a geography and history teacher for 11 years, Uno founded The Middle-East Problem Research Institute in Osaka in 1975. Since then Uno has started another research institute, a publishing company, and a merchandise cataloging service. He also became a Christian fundamentalist preacher. In two books that appeared in 1986, *If You Understand the Jews, You Will Understand the World* and *Understand the Jews You Will Understand Japan,* Uno launched an attack on Jews. Both books became best sellers in Japan.[40] In 1986 alone his books sold a combined total of 1.1 million copies.[41] Two other antisemitic books appeared, *The Invisible Empire: The Zionist Jews Will Control the World in 1993* (1991) and *The Jewish Economic Strategy for 1992* (1992).

In his writings Uno charges that the Zionists have exploited the Holocaust to win worldwide sympathy for the establishment of the state of Israel.

Uno also believes that the Jews control the U.S. government. He also claims that the Jews took their revenge against Germany by dividing West Germany and Berlin and then began supplying a labor-short West Germany with Turkish immigrant workers and refugees.[42] Uno is another Holocaust denier to attack the authenticity of the diary of Anne Frank. Uno charged that "the diary was a fiction written by an American Jew who received $50,000 from Anne's father.[43] His body of work attracted the attention of the American Institute for Historical Review, and he has formed a strong working relationship with the IHR. In his latest book, *Revealing the Evils of Modern Globalism* (1997), Uno continues his attacks on what he perceives as Jewish control of the world's economy.

Holocaust denial appeared dramatically to the Japanese public in the Marco Polo Affair. In February 1995, Masanori Nishioka, a physician from Kanagawa Prefecture, submitted an article entitled "The Greatest Taboo of Postwar World History: There Were No Nazi Gas Chambers" to the monthly magazine *Marco Polo*. This magazine had a circulation of about 200,000, and its audience was "young, affluent, and educated male readers."[44] Nishioka had earlier tried to get the article published in other magazines without success.[45] That editor explained that Nishioka had been upset about recent German legislation making Holocaust denial a crime.[46] After reading Thies Christophersen's book *The Auschwitz Lie* (*Die Auschwitz-Lüge*), he had been converted to Holocaust denial.[47]

Nishioka's article produced a political backlash in Japan. Foreign Jewish groups, the American Anti-Defamation League and the Simon Wiesenthal Center, and the Israeli government protested the publication of the article and demanded a public retraction. The magazine *Marco Polo* was owned by Bungei Shunju, one of Japan's largest publishers. At first the company defended the article. Responding to both foreign and domestic pressure, Kengo Tenaka, president of Bungei Shunju, fired the editor of *Marco Polo* and closed down the magazine. This shutdown was a major financial decision because the magazine had a circulation of 250,000.[48] This affair received massive media coverage in Japan. It also attracted the attention of the Institute of Historical Review. Several articles appeared in the *Journal of Historical Review*, publicizing Nishioka's article.

A follow-up Holocaust denial book appeared by the free-lance journalist Aiji Kimura. Kimura was born in 1937, and he worked in the research section of NTV television in Tokyo. He had written several books on Japanese and American roles in the Gulf War and other subjects. In 1995, Kimura produced a book entitled *Controversial Points about Auschwitz* that attacked the Holocaust and the Nazi operations at Auschwitz. Earlier in November 1994, Kimura had visited the Institute for Historical Review in Los Angeles, and he had talks with Mark Weber about the Holocaust. Shortly after the appearance of the book, an Austrian citizen of Japanese origins living in Japan, Martin Kaneko, and Taichiro Kajimura, a Berlin-based free-lance journalist, criticized the book in a popular weekly magazine, *Shukan Kinyobi*.[49] These criticisms enraged Kimura enough that he sued his critics and the magazine publisher for libel.

The results of the trial proved to be unsatisfactory for Kimura. Kimura expected a quick trial, but the judge on the Tokyo District Court stalled. What the judge finally did was to focus only on the issue of whether the suit would count as a libel case. This decision came down on September 7, 1997. Then, on February 16, 1999, the court dismissed Kimura's libel suit and ruled that Nazi Germany had murdered in its concentration camps many Jews by poison gas following the precedent of the international tribunal for war crimes at Nuremberg.[50]

Conclusion

Holocaust denial has become a dangerous international movement. Each European country has at least one prominent Holocaust denier active on the scene. It has advocates in Australia, Canada, Europe, most Middle Eastern states, New Zealand, and the United States. Contributing factors to the spread of Holocaust denial have been the low cost of Internet publishing plus the growing computer expertise of its editors.[1]

Various political forces have joined together to promote its spread, because it fits their political agendas. Antisemites, anti-Zionists, neo-Nazis, and white supremacists have combined to provide a willing pool of adherents. In the past, most of the Holocaust denial and antisemitic writings and agitation came almost exclusively from extremists of the extreme Right, but increasing leftists are making significant contributions. Part of the reason for the conversion of the left-wingers is the growing disenchantment with the political stance of the Israeli government vis-à-vis the Palestinians. As is pointed out by Alain Finkielkraut,

> Formerly, Israel was untouchable because of the proximity of the genocide. Today the genocide is subject to dispute due to alleged behavior by Israel. Two distinct sorts of resentment come together and join forces in the negation of the gas chambers: acrimony over an atypical fact, and irritation caused by the prestige and impunity.[2]

Even in the United States there have been serious inroads by Holocaust deniers. The Anti-Defamation League closely monitors antisemitic and Holocaust denial in the United States. In 1993, its leadership concluded a favorable report with reservations.

> Thus, although current American attitudes toward the significance of the Holocaust seem generally sympathetic and well informed, there is no guarantee

that they will remain so. As Holocaust "revisionists" become increasingly sophisticated in their tactics, the relatively small segment of the population indifferent to or ignorant of the Holocaust is increasingly vulnerable to their falsehoods. Becoming informed of the contentions and tactics of the "revisionists" is therefore vital to limiting and countering their impact.[3]

Holocaust denial also continues to appear in strange places. The father of popular actor Mel Gibson, Hutton Gibson, took the occasion of his son's movie *The Passion of The Christ* to launch into an attack on the Jews and the Holocaust during a February 16, 2004, radio telephone interview.[4] Hutton Gibson is a traditionalist Catholic, and he had long been a hostile critic of the Pope and the Papacy to the point that he included the Vatican as part of a Jewish plot.[5] In a March 9, 2003, interview with the *New York Times*, Hutton Gibson and his wife, Joye Gibson, indicated that they considered the Holocaust to be a hoax and that it had been "fabricated to hide a secret deal between Hitler and 'financiers to move Jews from Germany to the Middle East to fight the Arabs.' "[6]

Another public figure who made Holocaust denial statements was Bobby Fischer. Fischer, a former world chess champion, made Holocaust denial assertions on his Web site. Among his statements was the charge that the "so-called 'Holocaust' of the Jews during World War II is a complete hoax!"[7] Fischer had been in legal difficulties since the United States pulled his passport for his violation of American sanctions against Yugoslavia in 1992. At the time of his death in January 2008, Fischer had never repudiated his Holocaust denial views.

Efforts to outlaw Holocaust denial have been sporadic. Most of the major European countries have passed laws banning Holocaust denial—Austria, Belgium, France, Germany, and Spain. Denmark, Great Britain, and Sweden have such strong traditions of free speech that such legislation has not even been seriously considered. Such a prohibition against free speech is also strong in the United States. The European Union passed legislation on April 19, 2007, that would make denying the Holocaust punishable by jail sentences of up to three years, but it allowed its member states the option of not enforcing the law if those countries did not have an anti-Holocaust denial legislation.[8] It took six years of negotiations to come up with this legislation before the law passed.

Holocaust denial continues to grow as the events of the Holocaust recede into history. As witnesses and participants die off in increasingly rapid numbers, it is much easier to dismiss their testimonies. Each inconsistency in testimony or documentation is seized upon by the Holocaust deniers as evidence of a conspiracy. The Holocaust has also been caught up in the controversies about the state of Israel and its policies. Holocaust deniers follow the line of Joseph Goebbels, Hitler's propaganda chief, that if a "Big Lie" is repeated often enough, it will be believed. Michael Shermer, however, points out the fallacy of Holocaust denial.

> Within all of these fallacies of thinking about both evolution and the Holocaust, there is an assumption by the creationists and the revisionists that if they can just find one tiny crack in the structure the entire edifice will come tumbling down. This is the fundamental flaw in their reasoning. The Holocaust was 10,000 events in 10,000 places, and is proved by 10,000 bits of data that converge on one conclusion. Neither evolution nor the Holocaust can be disproved by minor errors or inconsistencies here and there, for the simple reason that they were never proved by these lone bits of data in the first place.[9]

What ensures that the Holocaust denial debate will continue and perhaps intensify is the fact that the Holocaust deniers are heavily engaged and are possibly winning the Internet wars. Upon examination of the various subjects that involve Holocaust denial, such as *The Leuchter Report,* on Google, it becomes apparent that a majority of the sites have been set up by Holocaust deniers. They have used Web sites, blogs, hyperlinks, e-mail, discussion boards, and chat rooms to spread their message.[10]

> The Internet has emerged then as a propaganda weapon par excellence for emboldening haters while demoralizing their targets—innocent and decent people everywhere. In addition to being cheap, the Internet is difficult to monitor and it's virtually impossible permanently to block a message. In some visually attractive web sites, racist groups aim at women's hearts and minds—and if possible, their money. Others are targeting Muslims, whites, children, or frustrated young Algerians in France. Messages can be tailored specifically to the market one is trying to reach.[11]

Students or interested adults are bombarded with Holocaust denial materials, some disguised as serious academic work. Robert Angove reminisces about his experiences with Holocaust denial in the classroom at the University of Saskatchewan, and he concludes,

> To expect of young students the ability to discern between denial literature and history proper—or at least the ability to decide which is the more legitimate claim—is to suggest that they have been appropriately educated about the Holocaust and, moreover, that they have the analytical skills to understand denial for what it is in spite of deniers' ability to mimic style of professional historians. Only then could they be expected to reject Holocaust denial out of hand.[12]

In British schools a growing problem is that teachers are dropping courses covering the Holocaust because of fears that Muslim students might express antisemitic and anti-Israel sentiments in class.[13] Winning the academic war but losing the information war will make certain that Holocaust denial will continue to attract new adherents from around the world. The best summation of the threat of Holocaust denial is by the journalist Johann Hari in an article for the British *Independent on Sunday* (London) on the 2003 conference of the Institute for Historical Review at the Irvine Marriott Hotel in Orange County, California.

> The IHR (Institute for Historical Review), frankly, aren't capable of organizing an egg-and spoon race, never mind another genocide. They are ridiculous. But, in a drip-drip manner, they are making it seem as though the Holocaust has a question mark hanging over it. In fact, it is as preposterous to deny the existence of the Holocaust as it is to deny the existence of Australia—yet the deniers' arguments are, worryingly, seeping into the public consciousness. History professors across Europe and the US are increasingly confronted by students who ask, "Did the Holocaust really happen?" A poll in the 1990s found that an extraordinary 20 per cent of the US public thought it was possible that the Holocaust did not happen. The Holocaust Denial website run by Bradley Smith, who spoke at the IHR conference, has received over 20 million hits, and the internet is making denial literature more available than ever before. The next Hitler will probably not rise from among the ranks of freaks and losers who make up the IHR. But the next anti-semitic leader does offer his siren call, his path will have been made easier by the IHR and the lies they are keeping alive.[14]

The saving grace is that so much of Holocaust denial material transcends reason. Robert Jan van Pelt found out much the same in his research on Holocaust denial works.

> In an endnote, I commented that the hours spent reading those negationism writings "were among the worst I have had in my professional work." Characterizing this literature as an insult to the intellect, I observed that "their evidence is doctored and in their attempts to reveal a great conspiracy to blot the reputation of Germany, these scholars . . . ignore half of the evidence and that part of the evidence they attempt to discredit they butcher and mutilate beyond recognition."[15]

The main target for Holocaust deniers remains Auschwitz-Birkenau. By attacking the symbol of the Holocaust, they hope to discredit Holocaust. Auschwitz-Birkenau, however, is a two-edged sword. Jean-Claude Pressac, a former Holocaust denier turned into a believer of the Holocaust, wants to turn Auschwitz-Birkenau into a living memorial.

> I want people to experience exactly what it meant to enter a gas chamber at Auschwitz-Birkenau. I want them to walk down the stairs into the chamber, to stand before the ovens and see that this was insane and criminal. I want it to be a slap in the face. You can't create memory, but you can create an experience that is as powerful as memory.[16]

Notes

INTRODUCTION

1. Kenneth S. Stern, "Lying about the Holocaust; National Borders Don't Mean Much in the International Holocaust Denial Business, but America Is Playing a Special Role," *Southern Poverty Law Center's Intelligence Report* 103 (Fall 2001), p. 50.

2. Robert Fulford in Eberhard Jäckel, *David Irving's Hitler: A Faulty History Dissected* (Port Angeles, WA: Ben-Simon Publications, 1993), p. 2.

3. Eberhard Jäckel, *Hitler in History* (Hanover, CT: University Press of New England, 1984), pp. 44–45.

4. Kenneth S. Stern, *Holocaust Denial* (New York: American-Jewish Committee, 1993), p. 2.

5. Eric Zorn, "NU Is Wrestling Slippery Problem," *Chicago Tribune* (May 7, 1991), p. 1.

6. Robert Jay Lifton, *The Nazi Doctors: Medical Killing and the Psychology of Genocide* (New York: Basic Books, 2000), p. 4.

7. Lifton, *The Nazi Doctors,* p. 13.

8. John Weiss, *Ideology of Death: Why the Holocaust Happened in Germany* (Chicago: Elephant Paperbacks, 1996), p. x.

CHAPTER 1

1. The table for these figures was provided by Michael Shermer and Alex Grobman, *Denying History: Who Says the Holocaust Never Happened and Why Do They Say It?* (Berkeley: University of California Press, 2000), p. 177.

2. Ibid., p. 175.

3. Jocelyn Hellig, *The Holocaust and Antisemitism: A Short History* (Oxford, UK: Oneworld Publications, 2003), p. 16.

4. Joseph Kessel, *The Man with the Miraculous Hands: The Fantastic Story of Felix Kersten, Himmler's Private Doctor* (Short Hills, NJ: Burford Books, 1960), p. 130.

5. Enzo Traverso, *The Jews & Germany: From the 'Judeo-German Symbiosis' to the Memory of Auschwitz* (Lincoln: University of Nebraska Press, 1995), p. 110.

6. Léon Poliakov, *The History of Anti-Semitism: From Voltaire to Wagner* (Philadelphia: University of Pennsylvania Press, 1975), pp. 311–318.

7. Robert S. Wistrich, *Antisemitism: The Longest Hatred* (New York: Schocken Books, 1991), p. 47.

8. Poliakov, *The History of Anti-Semitism: From Voltaire to Wagner,* pp. 317–318.

9. Ibid., p. 319.

10. Joseph L. Graves, Jr., maintained that Charles Darwin "recognized that all of the human races were really members of the same species as opposed to being separate species of humans, but this concept was too radical for that period of history." Joseph L. Graves, *The Race Myth: Why We Pretend Race Exists in America* (New York: Dutton, 2004), pp. 4–5.

11. Neil MacMaster, *Racism in Europe, 1870–2000* (Houndsmill, UK: Palgrave, 2001), p. 34.

12. Joachim C. Fest, *Hitler* (New York: Harcourt Brace Jovanovich, 1974), p. 56.

13. Robert N. Proctor, *Racial Hygiene: Medicine under the Nazis* (Cambridge, MA: Harvard University Press, 1988), p. 15.

14. Edwin Black, *War against the Weak: Eugenics and America's Campaign to Create a Master Race* (New York: Four Walls Eight Windows, 2003), pp. 12–13.

15. Hellig, *The Holocaust and Antisemitism,* pp. 70–72. Marr blamed Jews for his professional failure as a journalist. Lucy S. Dawidowicz, *The War against the Jews, 1933–1945* (New York: Bantam Books, 1986), p. 34.

16. Hermann Graml, *Anti-Semitism in the Third Reich* (Oxford, UK: Blackwell, 1992), p. 58.

17. MacMaster, *Racism in Europe,* p. 8.

18. Ibid., p. 88.

19. Proctor, *Racial Hygiene,* p. 12.

20. Léon Poliakov, *The History of Anti-Semitism: Suicidal Europe, 1870–1933* (Philadelphia: University of Pennsylvania Press, 1985), pp. 39–42. Drumont made the Jewish France representative of all that he disapproved of in modern France, and, in particular, its modernness, republicanism, and secularism. Norman Cohn charged that Drumont had appropriated sections of his book from Roger Gougenot des Mousseaux and his 1869 book *The Jew, Judaism and the Judaization of the Christian Peoples* (*Le Juif, le judaism et la judaisation des peuples chrétiens*).

21. Wistrich, *Antisemitism,* p. 127.

22. Henry H. Weinberg, "The Image of the Jew in Late Nineteenth Century French Literature," *Jewish Social Studies* 95 (Summer–Fall, 1983), pp. 241–250.

23. Bernard Lewis, *Semites and Anti-Semites: An Inquiry into Conflict and Prejudice* (New York: Norton, 1999), p. 70.

24. Graml, *Anti-Semitism in the Third Reich,* p. 65.

25. Robert S. Wistrich, *Hitler and the Holocaust* (New York: Modern Language, 2003), p. 20.

26. Wistrich, *Antisemitism,* p. 171.

27. MacMaster argues against this thesis because the Russian government feared mass movement regardless of the cause. MacMaster, *Racism in Europe,* p. 106.

28. Norman Cohn, *Warrant for Genocide: The Myth of the Jewish World Conspiracy and the Protocols of the Elders of Zion* (London: Serif, 1996), p. 120.

29. Stephen Eric Bronner, *A Rumor about the Jews: Reflections on Antisemitism and the Protocols of the Learned Elders of Zion* (New York: St. Martin's Press, 2000), p. 60.

30. Binjamin W. Segel, *A Lie and a Libel: The History of the Protocols of the Elders of Zion* (Lincoln: University of Nebraska Press, 1995), pp. 65–67. Segel attributes the discovery of Goedsche's contribution to Dr. J. Stanjek in May 1920, and the identification of Joly's contribution to Philip Graves, the *Times* (London) correspondent in Istanbul in August 1921. Norman Cohn published Graves's letter of August 1921 explaining how he learned of the plagiarism of Joly's book. Cohn, *Warrant for Genocide,* pp. 78–79.

31. Cohn, *Warrant for Genocide,* pp. 85–90.

32. Bronner, *A Rumor about the Jews,* p. 76.

33. Sergei Alexandrovich Nilus's statement to Alexandre du Chayla in January 1901 at the monastery of Optina Pustyn, quoted in Cohn, *Warrant for Genocide,* p. 102.

34. Bronner, *A Rumor about the Jews,* p. 2.

35. Ibid., p. 108.

36. MacMaster, *Racism in Europe,* pp. 98–99.

37. Ibid., p. 99.

38. Traverso, *The Jews & Germany,* p. xx.

39. Ibid., p. 16.

40. Karl Dietrich Bracher, *The German Dictatorship: The Origins, Structure, and Effects of National Socialism* (New York: Praeger, 1970), p. 36.

41. Wistrich, *Antisemitism,* p. 56. Wagner held these views despite his close association with Jewish performers and conductors. Klaus P. Fischer, *The History of an Obsession: German Judeophobia and the Holocaust* (New York: Continuum, 1998), p. 106.

42. Marvin Perry and Frederick M. Schweitzer, *Antisemitism: Myth and Hate from Antiquity to the Present* (New York: Palgrave, 2002), p. 93.

43. Fischer, *The History of an Obsession,* p. 49.

44. Fest, *Hitler,* p. 58.

45. Fritz Stern, *The Politics of Cultural Despair: A Study in the Rise of the Germanic Ideology* (Garden City, NY: Anchor Books, 1965), p. 92.

46. Ibid., pp. 92–93.

47. Ibid., p. 93.

48. Ibid., p. 97.

49. Graml, *Anti-Semitism in the Third Reich,* p. 47.

50. Ibid., p. 47.

51. Ibid., p. 47.

52. Weiss, Ibid., p. 86.

53. Fischer, *The History of an Obsession,* p. 107.

54. Weiss, *Ideology of Death,* pp. 43–44.

55. MacMaster, *Racism in Germany,* p. 102.

56. Fischer, *The History of an Obsession,* p. 112.

57. Adolf Hitler was one of Lueger's biggest fans. MacMaster, *Racism in Germany,* p. 100.

58. Wistrich, *Antisemitism,* p. 59.

59. Graml, *Anti-Semitism in the Third Reich,* p. 37.

60. Traverso, *The Jews & Germany*, p. 20.

61. Graml, *Anti-Semitism in the Third Reich*, p. 55.

62. Christopher Browning, *The Origins of the Final Solution: The Evolution of Nazi Jewish Policy, September 1939–March 1942* (London: William Heinemann, 2004), p. 6.

63. Michael Burleigh and Wolfgang Wippermann, *The Racial State: Germany 1933–1945* (Cambridge, UK: Cambridge University Press, 2005), p. 36.

64. Graml, *Anti-Semitism in the Third Reich*, p. 75.

65. Proctor, *Racial Hygiene*, p. 145.

66. Burleigh and Wippermann, *The Racial State*, p. 37.

67. Norman Cohn charges that Prince Dr. Otto zu Salm-Horstmar raised funds for it and members of the Hohenzollern family contributed to the fund. Cohn, *Warrant for Genocide*, p. 147.

68. Cohn, *Warrant for Genocide*, p. 151.

69. Wistrich, *Hitler and the Holocaust*, p. 7.

70. Ibid.

71. Poliakov, *The History of Anti-Semitism: Suicidal Europe, 1870–1933*, p. 212.

72. Henry Ford had already had antisemitic views that were reinforced by *Protocols*. A Russian émigré, Boris Brasol, introduced this work to Ernest Gustave Liebold, Ford's chief advisor in 1919. Neil Baldwin, *Henry Ford and the Jews: The Mass Production of Hate* (New York: Public Affairs, 2003), p. 85.

73. Frank P. Mintz, *The Liberty Lobby and the American Right: Race, Conspiracy, and Culture* (Westport, CT: Greenwood Press, 1985), pp. 13–17. Some of the antisemitic materials in Ford's book were supplied by former members of the U.S. Justice Department. Leo P. Ribuffo, *The Old Christian Right: The Protestant Far Right from the Depression to the Cold War* (Philadelphia: Temple University Press, 1983), p. 10.

74. Ribuffo, *The Old Christian Right*, p. 12.

75. Max Wallace, *The American Axis: Henry Ford, Charles Lindbergh, and the Rise of the Third Reich* (New York: St. Martin's Press, 2003), p. 128.

76. This verdict was overturned by a Swiss appeals court over the technical definition of smut and pornography. Bronner, *A Rumor about the Jews*, p. 121.

77. Mintz, *The Liberty Lobby and the American Right*, p. 13.

78. Ribuffo, *The Old Christian Right*, p. 10.

79. Francis Galton, *Inquiries into Human Faculty and Its Development*, 2nd ed. (London: Dent, 1907), p. 17.

80. Ibid., p. 17.

81. Fischer, *The History of an Obsession*, p. 48.

82. Black, *War against the Weak*, p. 18.

83. MacMaster, *Racism in Europe*, pp. 37–38.

84. Among the many notables was Winston Churchill. He was one of the vice-presidents of the First Congress and a strong advocate of eugenics. MacMaster, *Racism in Europe*, pp. 51–52.

85. New York Times Staff, "Would Check Birth of All Defectives," *New York Times*, September 21, 1912, p. 7.

86. Elof Axel Carlson, *The Unfit: A History of a Bad Idea* (Cold Spring Harbor, NY: Cold Spring Harbor Laboratory, 2001), p. 12.

87. MacMaster, *Racism in Europe*, p. 43.

88. The United States took the international lead in forced sterilizations after the 1927 U.S. Supreme Court decision. Between 1927 and 1944 there were an estimated 40,000 cases of forced sterilizations in the United States. Wallace, *American Axis,* pp. 95–96.

89. Nancy Ordover, *American Eugenics: Race, Queer Anatomy, and the Science of Nationalism* (Minneapolis: University of Minnesota Press, 2003), p. 9.

90. Black, *War against the Weak,* p. 261.

91. Burleigh and Wippermann, *The Racial State,* p. 30.

92. MacMaster, *Racism in Europe,* pp. 39–40.

93. Werner Maser, *Hitler: Legend, Myth and Reality* (New York: Harper and Row, 1973), p. 168.

94. Mattias Gardell, *Gods of the Blood: The Pagan Revival and White Separatism* (Durham, NC: Duke University Press, 2003), p. 22.

95. Burleigh and Wippermann, *The Racial State,* p. 35.

96. Gardell, *Gods of the Blood,* p. 22.

97. Gardell, *Gods of the Blood,* p. 22.

98. Dawidowicz, *The War against the Jews, 1933–1945,* p. 9.

99. This quote was taken from *Ostara* in 1908, no. 29, and it appears in Maser, *Hitler,* p. 167.

100. Gardell, *Gods of the Blood,* p. 23.

101. Fest, *Hitler,* p. 37.

102. Dawidowicz, *The War against the Jews, 1933–1945,* p. 9.

103. Bracher, *The German Dictatorship,* p. 62. John Lukacs indicates that there is disagreement among Hitler scholars about whether or not Hitler associated with Lanz von Liebenfels. John Lukacs, *The Hitler of History* (New York: Vintage Books, 1997), p. 62.

104. Proctor, *Racial Hygiene,* p. 18.

105. Ibid., pp. 24–25.

106. Ibid., p. 28.

107. Opposition from the faculty came as some of them classified Günther "more of a party hack and a dilettante than a serious scholar." Alan E. Steinweis, *Studying the Jew: Scholarly Antisemitism in Nazi German* (Cambridge, MA: Harvard University Press, 2006), p. 26.

108. George L. Mosse, *Nazi Culture: Intellectual, Cultural and Social Life in the Third Reich* (New York: Grosset and Dunlap, 1966), p. 57.

109. Gill Seidel, *The Holocaust Denial: Antisemitism, Racism and the New Right* (Leed, UK: Beyond the Pale, 1986), p. 19.

110. This quote from Günther's works is reproduced in Mosse, *Nazi Culture,* p. 62.

111. This statement comes from Mosse, *Nazi Culture,* p. 63.

112. Benno Müller-Hill, *Murderous Science: Elimination by Scientific Selection of Jews, Gypsies, and Others, Germany 1933–1945* (Oxford, UK: Oxford University Press, 1988), p. 22.

CHAPTER 2

1. August Kubizek, *The Young Hitler I Knew* (London: Greenhill Books, 2006), p. 49.

2. Fest, *Hitler,* p. 57.

3. Kubizek, *The Young Hitler I Knew,* p. 94. Other historians maintain that it was in Vienna that Hitler became an antisemite, basing their conclusions on what Hitler wrote in *Mein Kampf.* Lukacs makes the case that his antisemitism crystallized in Munich in 1919. Lukacs, *The Hitler of History,* pp. 185–186.

4. Gerald Fleming, *Hitler and the Final Solution* (Berkeley: University of California Press, 1984), p. 7.

5. Fest, *Hitler,* p. 28.

6. Wistrich, *Antisemitism,* p. 65.

7. Fischer, *The History of an Obsession,* p. 146.

8. Helmut Krausnick and Martin Broszat, *Anatomy of the SS State* (London: Granada, 1982), p. 36.

9. Letter quoted in Fest, *Hitler,* p. 121.

10. Graml, *Anti-Semitism in the Third Reich,* p. 76.

11. Philippe Burrin, *Nazi Anti-Semitism: From Prejudice to the Holocaust* (New York: New Press, 2005), p. 41.

12. Maser, *Hitler,* p. 170.

13. Ibid., p. 171.

14. Fischer, *The History of an Obsession,* p. 150.

15. Ibid., p. 20.

16. Quoted from a document in Gerald Fleming, *Hitler and the Final Solution* (Berkeley: University of California Press, 1984), p. 17.

17. Baldwin, *Henry Ford and the Jews,* pp. 172–173. Later, Hitler bestowed on Ford the Grand Cross of the German Eagle on July 30, 1938.

18. Hellig, *The Holocaust and Antisemitism,* p. 25.

19. Hermann Rauschning, *The Voice of Destruction: Conversations With Hitler 1940* (New York: Putnam's, 1940), p. 238. Rauschning was a conservative landowner and former president of the Danzig Senate and in the beginning was an early member of the Nazi Party. By 1935 Rauschning had become disillusioned by Hitler and the Nazi regime and fled Germany.

20. Hellig, *The Holocaust and Antisemitism,* p. 25.

21. Black, *War against the Weak,* p. 259.

22. Ibid.

23. Ibid.

24. Madison Grant, *The Passing of the Great Race* (New York: Charles Scribner's Sons, 1936), p. 49. This book had come out in a German translation under the title *Der Untergang der grossen Rasse: Die Rassen als Grundlage der Geschichte Europas* in 1925.

25. Black, *War against the Weak,* p. 270.

26. Ibid., p. 283.

27. Fest, *Hitler,* p. 216.

28. Wistrich, *Antisemitism,* pp. 67–68.

29. Ibid., p. 68.

30. Lukacs, *The Hitler of History,* p. 43. Lukacs also claims that Hitler was a voracious reader with a phenomenal retention capacity. Lukacs, *The Hitler of History,* p. 49.

31. Wistrich, *Hitler and the Jews,* pp. 39–40.

32. Ibid., pp. 40–41.

33. Dawidowicz, *The War against the Jews, 1933–1945*, p. 20.

34. Fest, *Hitler*, p. 106.

35. Wistrich points out that it is impossible to have two chosen peoples. Wistrich, *Hitler and the Jews*, p. 8.

36. Rauschning, *The Voice of Destruction*, p. 241.

37. Kühl quotes this from the unpublished autobiography of Leon F. Whitney. Stefan Kühl, *The Nazi Connection: Eugenics, American Racism, and German National Socialism* (New York: Oxford University Press, 1994), p. 85.

38. Fest, *Hitler*, p. 222.

39. Rauschning, *The Voice of Destruction*, pp. 241–242.

40. Ibid., p. 235.

41. Ibid., p. 236.

42. Fest, *Hitler*, p. 555.

43. Ibid.

44. Graml, *Anti-Semitism in the Third Reich*, p. 77.

45. Wistrich, *Hitler and the Holocaust*, p. 135.

46. Ibid.

47. Fischer, *The History of an Obsession*, p. 148.

48. Ibid.

49. Ibid., p. 202.

50. Ibid.

51. Ibid., p. 223.

52. The language comes from the *Declaration of the Boycott by the Nazi Party Leaders* on March 28, 1933. Michael Berenbaum, *Witness to the Holocaust: An Illustrated Documentary History of the Holocaust in the Words of Its Victims, Perpetrators and Bystanders* (New York: HarperCollins, 1997), p. 3.

53. Fest, *Hitler*, p. 438.

54. This provision is taken from the Law for the Restoration of the Professional Civil Service of April 7, 1933. Berenbaum, *Witness to the Holocaust*, p. 11.

55. Krausnick and Broszat, *Anatomy of the SS State*, p. 44.

56. Even after it was legal for Jews to serve in the civil service and the military in 1870, conservatives had used informal means to keep Jews out of them. Weiss, *Ideology of Death*, p. 82.

57. Proctor, *Racial Hygiene*, p. 147.

58. Dawidowicz, *The War against the Jews, 1933–1945*, p. 66.

59. The text of the Law for the Protection of German Blood and German Honor of September 15, 1935, is in Berenbaum, *Witness to the Holocaust*, p. 27.

60. Wistrich, *Hitler and the Holocaust*, p. 53. The irony of this law was that Hitler would have had difficulty proving the identity of one of his grandfathers. Fest, *Hitler*, pp. 15–16.

61. Graml, *Anti-Semitism in the Third Reich*, p. 123.

62. Mosse, *Nazi Culture*, p. 332.

63. Steinweis, *Studying the Jew*, p. 44.

64. Krausnick and Broszat, *Anatomy of the SS State*, p. 47.

65. Graml, *Anti-Semitism in the Third Reich*, p. 130.

66. Dawidowicz, *The War against the Jews, 1933–1945*, p. 82.

67. Graml, *Anti-Semitism in the Third Reich*, pp. 5–7.

68. Ibid., p. 12.

69. Wistrich, *Hitler and the Jews,* pp. 61–63.

70. Richard Breitman, *The Architect of Genocide: Himmler and the Final Solution* (Hanover, NH: Brandeis University Press, 1991), p. 53. Both Himmler and Göring objected to the anti-Jewish riots on both tactical and economic grounds. Graml, *Anti-Semitism in the Third Reich,* p. 13.

71. Graml, *Anti-Semitism in the Third Reich,* p. 16. The SS actually arrested nearly 30,000 Jews in the roundups. Graml, *Anti-Semitism in the Third Reich,* p. 25.

72. Wistrich, *Hitler and the Jews,* p. 63.

73. Ibid., p. 65.

74. Wistrich, *Antisemitism,* p. 74.

75. Rauschning, *The Voice of Destruction,* pp. 88–89.

76. Graml, *Anti-Semitism in the Third Reich,* p. 147.

77. Wallace, *American Axis,* pp. 96–97.

78. This passage is quoted in Mosse, *Nazi Culture,* p. 39.

79. Burrin, *Nazi Anti-Semitism,* p. 55.

80. Lifton, *The Nazi Doctors,* p. 42.

81. Ibid., p. 15.

82. Nazis accused the Gypsies of "hereditary racial inferiority, economic parasitism and/or sexual immorality." Wistrich, *Hitler and the Holocaust,* pp. 4–5.

83. Lifton, *The Nazi Doctors,* pp. 23–24.

84. Proctor, *Racial Hygiene,* p. 60.

85. Lifton, *The Nazi Doctors,* p. 24.

86. Proctor, *Racial Hygiene,* pp. 39–42.

87. Ibid., p. 102.

88. Lifton, *The Nazi Doctors,* p. 25.

89. Müller-Hill, *Murderous Science,* p. 29.

90. Proctor, *Racial Hygiene,* p. 102.

91. Lifton, *The Nazi Doctors,* p. 27.

92. Lifton, *The Nazi Doctors,* p. 27. Benno Müller-Hill estimated 350,000–400,000 sterilizations between 1934 and 1939. Müller-Hill, *Murderous Science,* p. 32.

93. Proctor, *Racial Hygiene,* p. 107.

94. Hitler sent the author a letter of appreciation. Kühl, *The Nazi Connection,* p. 85.

95. Proctor claimed that around 500 so-called Rhineland bastards were sterilized. Proctor, *Racial Hygiene,* p. 114. Müller-Hill cited another study and listed the total at 385. Müller-Hill, *Murderous Science,* p. 30.

96. Müller-Hill, *Murderous Science,* p. 32.

97. Guenter Lewy, *The Catholic Church and Nazi Germany* (New York: McGraw-Hill, 1964), pp. 258–263.

98. Lifton, *The Nazi Doctors,* p. 46.

99. Ibid.

100. Ibid., p. 47.

101. Ibid.

102. Alexis Carrel, *Man the Unknown* (New York: Harper, 1935), p. 319.

103. Wallace, *American Axis,* p. 98.

104. Fest, *Hitler,* p. 555.

105. Jochen von Lang, *The Secretary: Martin Bormann: The Man Who Manipulated Hitler* (New York: Random House, 1979), p. 142.

106. Proctor, *Racial Hygiene*, p. 181.

107. Lifton, *The Nazi Doctors*, p. 50.

108. Browning, *The Origins of the Final Solution*, p. 186.

109. Proctor, *Racial Hygiene*, p. 186.

110. Ibid., pp. 186–187.

111. Ibid., p. 187.

112. This figure is quoted in Proctor, *Racial Hygiene*, p. 188.

113. Von Lang, *The Secretary*, p. 142.

114. Alexander Mitscherlich and Fred Mielke, *Doctors of Infamy: The Story of the Nazi Medical Crimes* (New York: Schuman, 1949), p. 92.

115. This code name Aktion T4 came from the address of the Nonprofit Patient Transport Corporation at Tiergartenstrasse 4 in Berlin. Proctor, *Racial Hygiene*, p. 189.

116. Shermer and Grobman, *Denying History*, p. 125.

117. Lifton, *Nazi Doctors*, p. 71.

118. Proctor, *Racial Hygiene*, p. 189.

119. Ibid., pp. 189–190.

120. Henry Friedlander, *Origins of the Nazi Genocide: From Euthanasia to the Final Solution* (Chapel Hill: University of North Carolina Press, 1995), p. 97.

121. Proctor, *Racial Hygiene* p. 191. A side effect of the euthanasia program was the loss of esteem for the psychiatry profession because of the killing off of its patients. Müller-Hill, *Murderous Science*, p. 42.

122. Eugen Kogon, Hermann Langbein, and Adalbert Rückerl (eds.), *Nazi Mass Murder: A Documentary History of the Use of Poison Gas* (New Haven, CT: Yale University Press, 1993), p. 32.

123. Proctor, *Racial Hygiene*, p. 191.

124. Shermer and Grobman, *Denying History*, p. 175.

125. Lewy, *The Catholic Church and Nazi Germany*, p. 264.

126. Top Nazis even considered hanging Bishop Count von Galen for treason, but it was decided that this action would be too controversial. Lewy, *The Catholic Church and Nazi Germany*, pp. 265–266. Evidently Hitler gave a direct order not to take reprisals against von Galen. Lukacs, *The History of Hitler*, p. 90.

127. Mitscherlich and Mielke, *Doctors of Infamy*, p. 114.

128. Lifton, *Nazi Doctors*, p. 96.

129. Jäckel, *Hitler in History*, p. 32.

130. Lifton, *Nazi Doctors*, p. 77.

131. Proctor, *Racial Hygiene*, p. 205.

132. Ibid., p. 289.

133. Browning, *The Origins of the Final Solution*, pp. 187–188.

134. Ibid.

135. Ibid., p. 188.

136. Ibid., p. 189.

137. Volker Riesse, *Die Anfänge der Vernichtung "lebensunwerten Lebens" in den Reichgauen Danzig-Westpressen und Wartheland 1939/40* (Frankfurt, Germany: Peter Lang, 1995), p. 355.

138. Most of the following analysis comes from Hellig, Hellig, *The Holocaust and Antisemitism*, pp. 44–48.

139. Traverso, *The Jews & Germany*, p. 113.

140. Ibid., p. 114.

141. Jäckel, *Hitler in History*, p. 30.

142. Ibid., p. 46.

143. Gerald Reitlinger, *The Final Solution: The Attempt to Exterminate the Jews of Europe, 1939–1945* (New York: Perpetua Book, 1961), p. 81. Dr. Felix Kersten, however, claims to have witnessed a document signed by Hitler stating that "Hitler took complete responsibility for all orders relating to the torture and extermination of the Jews and other prisoners of the camps," absolving Heinrich Himmler and the SS for all responsibility. Joseph Kessel, *The Man with the Miraculous Hands: The Fantastic Story of Felix Kersten, Himmler's Private Doctor* (Short Hills, NJ: Burford Books, 1960), p. 132.

144. Brietman, *The Architect of Genocide*, p. 44.

145. Max Domarus (ed.), *Hitler: Reden und Proklamationen, 1932–1945* (Wiesbaden, Germany: R. Löwit, 1973), Vol. 4, p. 1713.

146. Traverso, *The Jews & Germany*, p. 117.

147. Heinz Höhne, *The Order of the Death's Head: The Story of Hitler's SS* (New York: Penguin Books, 2000), p. 9.

148. Herman Goring said it best: "In the last analysis, it is the Führer alone who decides." Wistrich, *Hitler and the Jews*, p. 70.

149. Albert Speer, *Infiltration: How Heinrich Himmler Schemed to Build an SS Industrial Empire* (New York: Macmillan, 1981), p. 22.

150. Quoted in Raul Hilberg, *The Destruction of the European Jews* (New York: Holmes and Meier, 1967), p. 257. This is also the contention of Mark Roseman in his study of the Wannsee Conference. Mark Roseman, *The Wannsee Conference and the Final Solution: A Reconsideration* (New York: Metropolitan Books, 2002), p. 5.

151. Burrin, *Nazi Anti-Semitism*, p. 73.

152. This comment by Goebbels must be placed in the context that Goebbels was at least as much if not even more antisemitic than Hitler. Joseph Goebbels, *The Goebbels Diaries, 1942–1943* (Garden City, NY: Doubleday, 1948), pp. 243–244.

153. Roseman, *The Wannsee Conference and the Final Solution*, p. 12.

154. Fleming, *Hitler and the Final Solution*, p. 19.

155. Ibid.

156. Browning, *The Origins of the Final Solution*, pp. 10–11.

157. Bracher, *The German Dictatorship*, p. 350.

158. Fest, *Hitler*, p. 435.

159. Ibid., pp. 435–436.

160. Rauschning, *The Voice of Destruction*, p. 137. Hermann Rauschning's conversations with Hitler and this quote have been challenged by Holocaust deniers. Mark Weber sites a Swiss Holocaust denier historian, Wolfgang Haenel, in claiming that Rauschning had invented or lifted from others the conversations in his book. Mark Weber, "Rauschning's Phony 'Conversations with Hitler': An Update," *Journal of Historical Review* 6 (Winter 1985–86), no. 4, p. 499. The problem is that other respected historians have accepted that Rauschning's interviews are legitimate.

161. Breitman, *The Architect of Genocide*, p. 63.

162. Ibid., pp. 61–62.

163. Krausnick and Broszat, *Anatomy of the SS State*, p. 73.

164. This scheme had been championed by Adolf Eichmann, the SS officer in charge of the transportation of Jews, and he described its history in his interrogations

in 1960. Jochen von Lang, *Eichmann Interrogated: Transcripts from the Archives of the Israeli Police* (New York: Da Capo Press, 1999), pp. 65–69.

165. Fest, *Hitler*, p. 708.

166. Mitscherlich and Mielke, *Doctors of Infamy*, p. 135.

167. Jäckel, *Hitler in History*, p. 57.

168. Helmut Krausnick et al., "Denkschrift Himmlers über die Behandlung der Fremdvölkischen im Osten," *Vierteljahrshefte für Zeitgeschicte* (April 1957), p. 196.

169. Heinz Höhne, *The Order of the Death's Head: The Story of Hitler's SS* (New York: Penguin Books, 2000), p. 293. The Nazis had already shown their severity during the Polish campaign. Special SS troops in Task Forces (Einsatzgruppen) had undertaken the task to liquidate Polish elites—businessmen, doctors, landowners, officials, priest, and teachers. Höhne, *The Order of the Death's Head*, pp. 297–299.

170. Höhne, *The Order of the Death's Head*, p. 295.

171. Von Lang, *Eichmann Interrogated*, p. 124.

172. Wistrich, *Hitler and the Holocaust*, p. 135.

173. Hitler had already authorized murder as a method of social control against possible Polish opposition and against the unfit. Roseman, *The Wannsee Conference and the Final Solution*, pp. 34–35.

174. Burleigh and Wippermann, *The Racial State*, p. 64.

175. Walter Laqueur and Richard Breitman, *Breaking the Silence: The German Who Exposed the Final Solution* (Hanover, NH: University Press of New England, 1994), pp. 265–266.

176. Lewis, *Semites and Anti-Semites*, p. 26.

177. This statement is quoted in Fast, *Hitler*, p. 223.

178. Goebbels, *The Goebbels Diaries*, p. 86.

179. Ibid., pp. 147–148.

180. Herma Briffault and Ernest Morwitz (eds.), *The Memoirs of Doctor Felix Kersten* (Garden City, NY: Doubleday, 1947), p. 124.

181. Von Lang, *Eichmann Interrogated*, p. 98.

182. Ibid.

183. This incident was reported by SS-Captain Kurt Gerstein, and it is cited in Müller-Hill, *Murderous Science*, p. 55.

184. Van Lang gives the history of this report. Von Lang, *The Secretary*, pp. 198–199. Bormann was also notorious for his hatred of Jews.

185. Berenbaum, *Witness to the Holocaust*, p. 165.

CHAPTER 3

1. Browning, *The Origins of the Final Solution*, p. 32.

2. Ibid., p. 35.

3. Ibid., p. 35.

4. Graml, *Anti-Semitism in the Third Reich*, p. 165.

5. Lucy S. Dawidowicz, *The Holocaust and the Historians* (Cambridge, MA: Harvard University Press, 1981), p. 6.

6. Krausnick and Broszat, *Anatomy of the SS-State*, p. 80.

7. Wistrich, *Hitler and the Jews*, p. 92.

8. Sonderkommando 4a in collaboration with Einsatzgruppe HQ and two Kommandos of police regiment South of Einsatzgruppe C conducted the massacre. Ytizhad Arad, Shmuel Krakowski, and Shmuel Spector (eds.), *The Einsatzgruppen Reports: Selections from the Dispatches of the Nazi Death Squads' Campaign against the Jews, July 1941–January 1943* (New York: Holocaust Library, 1989), p. 173.

9. Graml, *Anti-Semitism in the Third Reich*, p. 172.

10. Wistrich, *Hitler and the Jews*, p. 99.

11. The men had the greatest difficulty concerning shooting women and children, especially children. Lifton, *The Nazi Doctors*, p. 15.

12. Graml, *Anti-Semitism in the Third Reich*, pp. 173–174.

13. Krausnick and Broszat, *Anatomy of the SS-State*, p. 87.

14. Wistrich, *Hitler and the Jews*, p. xiii.

15. Müller-Hill, *Murderous Science*, p. 47.

16. This letter is cited in Müller-Hill, *Murderous Science*, p. 48.

17. Breitman, *The Architect of Genocide*, p. 38.

18. Briffault, *The Memoirs of Doctor Felix Kersten*, p. 41.

19. Breitman, *The Architect of Genocide*, p. 38.

20. Bracher, *The German Dictatorship*, p. 283.

21. Höhne, *The Order of the Death's Head*, p. 11. This observation came from Felix Kersten, Himmler's doctor, and it is further elaborated on by Albert Speer. Speer, *Infiltration*, p. 28.

22. Speer, *Infiltration*, p. 27.

23. Breitman, *The Architect of Genocide*, pp. 44–45.

24. Ibid., p. 45.

25. Graml, *Anti-Semitism in the Third Reich*, p. 159.

26. Browning, *The Origins of the Final Solution*, p. 79.

27. Von Lang, *Eichmann Interrogated*, p. 59.

28. Fleming learned of this statement from Dr. Otto Bradfisch in interviews with Bradfisch in the late 1950s. Fleming, *Hitler and the Final Solution*, pp. 50–51.

29. Speer, *Infiltration*, p. 6.

30. Ibid., pp. 5–6.

31. Ibid., p. 45.

32. Breitman, *The Architect of Genocide*, p. 19.

33. Höhne, *The Order of the Death's Head*, p. 174.

34. This statement is quoted by Wolfgang Sofsky in his book on concentration camps. Wolfgang Sofsky, *The Order of Terror: The Concentration Camp* (Princeton, NY: Princeton University Press, 1997), pp. 3–4.

35. Peter Padfield, *Himmler: Reichsführer—SS* (London: Cassell, 2000), p. 128.

36. Eicke had been a former watchman, who had a checkered past with arrests and a brief tenure in a mental institution. Michael Thad Allen, *The Business of Genocide: The SS, Slave Labor, and the Concentration Camps* (Chapel Hill: University of North Carolina Press, 2002), p. 39. His stay in a medical institution was at the Würzburg University Psychiatric Clinic where he was the patient of Dr. Werner Heyde. Heyde was a fanatic Nazi and one of the leaders of the Nazi euthanasia program. Lifton, *Nazi Doctors*, p. 153.

37. Padfield, *Himmler*, p. 129.

38. Ibid., p. 130.

39. Ibid., pp. 132–133.

40. Rauschning, *The Voice of Destruction,* p. 83.

41. Ibid.

42. Padfield, *Himmler,* pp. 194–195.

43. Ibid., p. 195.

44. Rudolf Höss, *Death Dealer: The Memoirs of the SS Kommandant at Auschwitz* (New York: Da Capo Press, 1996), p. 27.

45. Ibid., p. 28.

46. In private talks with his wife, however, Heydrich displayed little respect for Himmler. Höhne, *The Order of the Death's Head,* p. 165.

47. Christopher R. Browning, *Fateful Months: Essay on the Emergence of the Final Solution* (New York: Holmes and Meier, 1991), p. xv. Adolf Eichmann described his tactics. Von Lang, *Eichmann Interrogated,* pp. 49–57.

48. Von Lang, *Eichmann Interrogated,* p. 75.

49. Much as the other leading Nazis, Pohl was also busy enriching himself. Briffault, *The Memoirs of Doctor Felix Kersten,* pp. 46–49.

50. Allen, *Business of Genocide,* p. 1.

51. Ibid., p. 32.

52. Ibid., p. 41.

53. Ibid., p. 20.

54. Fischer, *The History of an Obsession,* p. 230.

55. Gudren Schwarz, *Die Nationalsozialistischen Lager* (Frankfurt, Germany: Campus, 1990), pp. 221–222.

56. David A. Hackett, *The Buchenwald Report* (Boulder, CO: Westview Press, 1995), p. 29.

57. Burleigh and Wippermann, *The Racist State,* p. 62.

58. Johannes Neuhaüsler was a Catholic priest who spent several years in the Dachau concentration camp. Johannes Neuhaüsler, *What Was It Like in the Concentration Camp at Dachau? An Attempt to Come Closer to the Truth:* Trustees for the Monument of Atonement in the Concentration Camp at Dachau, 1998) 27th ed., p. 17.

59. Neuhaüsler, *What Was It Like in the Concentration Camp at Dachau?,* pp. 17–18.

60. Ibid., p. 24.

61. Ibid., pp. 28–29.

62. Ibid., p 41.

63. Ibid., pp. 66–67.

64. Hackett, *The Buchenwald Report,* p. 29.

65. Allen, *Business of Genocide,* p. 46.

66. Wistrich, *Hitler and the Holocaust,* p. 108.

67. Ytizhak Arad, *Belzec, Sobibor, Treblinka: The Operation Reinhard Death Camps* (Bloomington: Indiana University Press, 1987), p. 15. Odilo Globocnik had strong personal ties to Himmler and was slavishly devoted to carrying out his orders. Himmler had rehabilitated him after Globocnik had been dismissed from the SS over his illegal speculation in foreign currency. Arad, *Belzec, Sobibor, Treblinka,* p. 14.

68. French L. MacLean, *The Camp Men: The SS Officers Who Ran the Nazi Concentration Camp System* (Atglen, PA: Schiffer Military History, 1999), p. 282.

69. Yitzhak Arad, et al. (eds.), *Documents on the Holocaust: Selected Sources on the Destruction of the Jews of Germany and Austria, Poland, and the Soviet Union* (Lincoln: University of Nebraska Press, 1999) 8th ed., p. 249.

70. Jürgen Matthäus, "Controlled Escalation: Himmler's Men in the Summer of 1941 and the Holocaust in the Occupied Soviet Territories," *Holocaust and Genocide Studies* 21 (Fall 2007) no. 2: p. 219.

71. Ibid.

72. Ernst Klee, Willi Dressen, and Volker Riess (eds.), *"The Good Old Days": The Holocaust as Seen by Its Perpetrators and Bystanders* (Old Saybrook, CT: Konecky & Konecky, 1991), p. 24.

73. Arad, Krakowski, and Spector, *The Einsatzgruppen Reports,* p. 174.

74. Klee, *"The Good Old Days,"* p. 60. August Becker, chemist and gas-van inspector, claimed that "a number of members of these death squads had to be committed to mental asylums. Klee, *"The Good Old Days,"* p. 69.

75. Matthäus, "Controlled Escalation," p. 234.

76. This report is quoted in Burleigh and Wippermann, *The Racial State,* p. 101.

77. Arad, Krakowski, and Spector, *The Einsatzgruppen Reports,* p. 211.

78. Arad, *Belzec, Sobibor, Treblinka: The Operation Reinhard Death Camps,* p. 8.

79. Ibid., p. 10.

80. Kogan, Langbein, and Rückerl, *Nazi Mass Murder,* p. 71.

81. Klee, *"The Good Old Days,"* p. 70.

82. Ibid., pp. 196–207.

83. Ibid., pp. 201–202.

84. Arad, *Belzec, Sobibor, Treblinka,* p. 8.

85. Proctor, *Racial Hygiene,* p. 207.

86. Lifton, *Nazi Doctors,* pp. 134–135.

87. Ibid., p. 135.

88. Ibid., p. 137.

89. Ibid., p. 138.

90. Ibid., p. 142.

91. Ibid., p. 143.

92. Leon Goldensohn, *Nuremberg Interviews* (New York: Knopf, 2005), p. 299.

93. Ibid.

94. Robert Jan van Pelt, *The Case for Auschwitz: Evidence from the Irving Trial* (Bloomington: Indiana University Press, 2002), p. 72.

95. Goldensohn, *Nuremberg Interviews,* p. 299.

96. Pery Broad, "Reminiscences of Pery Broad," in *KL Auschwitz Seen by the SS* (Oświęcim, Poland: Auschwitz-Birkenau State Museum, 1994), p. 106. Broad describes the fate of the Soviet prisoners of war.

97. Wieslaw Kielar was a Polish political prisoner at Auschwitz who worked in a body disposal unit. Wieslaw Kelar, *Anus Mundi: 1,500 Days in Auschwitz/Birkenau* (New York: Times Books, 1980), p. 54.

98. Kielar, *Anus Mundi,* p. 54.

99. Kielar learned of these deaths by rumor, the return of their camp clothing, and the removal of their names from the list of the living. Kielar, *Anus Mundi,* pp. 60–61.

100. Proctor, *Racial Hygiene,* p. 208.

101. Goldensohn, *Nuremberg Interviews,* p. 300.

102. Höss, *Death Dealer*, pp. 27–28.

103. Ibid., p. 28.

104. Ibid.

105. Ibid., pp. 29–30.

106. Goldensohn, *Nuremberg Interviews*, p. 296. Later in the interview Höss confessed that the 2.5 million figure was too high, but he had no proof. Goldensohn, *Nuremberg Interviews*, p. 305.

107. Robert Jan van Pelt discussed the number of those gassed at Auschwitz-Birkenau and basically agrees with the figures provided by Franciszek Piper, scholar at the Auschwitz Museum, who concluded that there were 1,082,000 gassed. Van Pelt, *The Case for Auschwitz*, pp. 106–119.

108. State of Israel, Ministry of Justice, *The Trial of Adolf Eichmann: Record of Proceeding in the District Court of Jerusalem* (Jerusalem: The Trust for the Publication of the Eichmann Trial, 1992), vol. 3, pp. 1005–1006.

109. Goldensohn, *Nuremberg Interviews*, p. 296.

110. Ibid., p. 298.

111. Broad, "Reminiscences of Pery Broad," p. 106.

112. Miklos Nyiszli, *Auschwitz: A Doctor's Eyewitness Account* (New York: Arcade Publishing, 1993), p. 27.

113. Broad, "Reminiscences of Pery Broad," p. 106.

114. Up until March 9, 1943, doctors were used to make the selections, but it was not required. After that date, it was required that a license to practice medicine was required for those making the selections. Müller-Hill, *Murderous Science*, p. 55.

115. Nyiszli, *Auschwitz*, p. 17. Dr. Mendele met Nyiszli's train and selected him as an assistant. He also told him that every day hundreds of prisoners were transported to the crematoria after the selection process was completed. Nyiszli, *Auschwitz*, pp. 24–25.

116. Zyklon B had been developed by German scientists during World War I as a chemical weapon, but its best use after the war had been as a pest-control agent. It was supplied to Auschwitz by the company Degesch (Deutsche Gesellschaft für Schädlingsbekämpfung, or German Company for Pest Control). Müller-Hill, *Murderous Science*, p. 70.

117. Johan Paul Kremer, "Diary of Johann Paul Kremer," in *KL Auschwitz Seen by the SS* (Oświęcim, Poland: Auschwitz-Birkenau State Museum, 1994), p. 163.

118. Philippe Burrin, *Nazi Anti-Semitism: From Prejudice to the Holocaust* (New York: New Press, 2005), p. 132.

119. Lifton, *Nazi Doctors*, p. 149.

120. Nyiszli, *Auschwitz*, p. 40.

121. Ibid., p. 38.

122. Ibid.

123. Ibid., pp. 50–51.

124. Kielar, *Anus Mundi*, p. 178.

125. Report of from the U.S. War Refugee Board in 1994 and quoted in Kogon, Langbein, and Rückerl, *Nazi Mass Murder*, pp. 164–165.

126. Court testimony by Szlama Dragon to a Craco court on May 10, 1945, and quoted in Kogon, Langbein and Rückerl, *Nazi Mass Murder*, p. 167.

127. Nyiszli, *Auschwitz*, p. 53.

128. Kielar, *Anus Mund*, p. 81.

129. Nyiszli, *Auschwitz*, p. 53.

130. Nyiszli described the planning and the battle. Nyiszli, *Auschwitz*, pp. 153–167. Kielar confirms the battle. Wieslaw Kielar, *Anus Mundi*, pp. 261–262.

131. Nyiszli, *Auschwitz*, p. 167.

132. Ibid.

133. Black, *War against the Weak*, pp. 344–345.

134. Ibid., p. 354.

135. Lifton, *Nazi Doctors*, p. 355.

136. Olga Lengyel, *Five Chimneys: A Woman Survivor's True Story of Auschwitz* (Chicago: Academy Chicago Publishers, 1995, c.1947), p. 13.

137. Sylvia Rothchild, *Voices from the Holocaust* (New York: New American Library, 1981), p. 121.

138. Ibid., p. 163.

139. Höss claimed that Eichmann told him this. Goldensohn, *Nuremberg Interviews*, p. 307.

140. Nyiszli, *Auschwitz*, p. 180.

141. Van Pelt, *The Case for Auschwitz*, p. 12.

142. Arad, *Belzec, Sobibor, Treblinka*, p. 16.

143. Estimate of German concentration camp guard at Belzec and Treblinka, Kurt Franz, based on his experience. Klee, *"The Good Old Days,"* p. 247.

144. Arad, *Belzec, Sobibor, Treblinka*, p. 17.

145. Evidence from SS-Untersturmführer Josef Oberhauser about the early days at Belzec. Klee, *"The Good Old Days,"* p. 228.

146. Wirth and his staff simply disappeared from Belzec in March 1942 without his superior Odilo Globocnik knowing about it. This action caused operations to slow down at Belzec for about six weeks. Wirth reappeared in the middle of May 1942, and the gassings continued at an accelerated rate. Klee, *"The Good Old Days,"* pp. 229–230.

147. Testimony taken from SS-Untersturmführer Josef Oberhauser from his experiences at Belzec. Burleigh and Wippermann, *The Racial State*, pp. 104–105.

148. This estimate may be on the low side. SS-Oberscharführer Erich Bauer was at Sobibor, and he estimated the number of Jews gassed at Sobibor at 350,000. He overheard some of the German guards stating that Sobibor had come in last among the Operation Reinhard death camps. Klee, *"The Good Old Days,"* p. 232.

149. Klee, *"The Good Old Days,"* p. 240.

150. Kogon, Langbein, and Rückerl, *Nazi Mass Murder*, p. 127.

151. Lifton, *Nazi Doctors*, p. 124.

152. Kogon, Langbein, and Rückerl, *Nazi Mass Murder*, p. 137. After the war these escaped prisoners were able to testify how Treblinka had operated.

153. Klee, *"The Good Old Days,"* p. 247.

154. Burleigh and Wippermann, *The Racist State*, p. 102.

155. Ibid.

156. Von Lang, *Eichmann Interrogated*, pp. 77–78.

157. Evidently one of the special vehicles blew up, supposedly caused by a technical failure. Müller-Hill, *Murderous Science*, p. 48.

158. Müller-Hill, *Murderous Science*, p. 48.

159. Ibid.

160. Kogon, Langbein, and Rückerl, *Nazi Mass Murder*, p. 101.

161. Barbara Distel, "29 April 1945: The Liberation of the Concentration Camp at Dachau," *Dachau Review* 1 (1988), p. 4.

162. Sarah Rembiszewski, *The Final Lie: Holocaust Denial in Germany a Second-Generation Denier as a Test Case* (Tel Aviv, Israel: Tel Aviv University, 1996), p. 5.

163. Charlotte Wardi, *Le genocide dans la fiction Romanesque* (Paris: Press Universitaires de France, 1988), p. 22.

164. Neuhäuser, *What Was It Like in the Concentration Camp at Dachau?*, p. 6.

165. Primo Levi, *The Drowned and the Saved* (New York: Summit Books, 1988), pp. 11–12. Levi committed suicide in 1987, never fully recovering from his experiences in the concentration camps.

166. Breitman, *The Architect of Genocide*, p. 7.

167. Van Pelt, *The Case for Auschwitz*, pp. 102–103.

168. Traverso, *The Jews & Germany*, p. 135.

169. Pierre Vidal-Naquet goes into more depth in this analysis. Pierre Vidal-Naquet, *Assassins of Memory: Essays on the Denial of the Holocaust* (New York: Columbia University Press, 1992), pp. 21–24.

PART II

1. Bonner, *A Rumor About the Jews*, p. 134.

2. Deborah E. Lipstadt, *Denying the Holocaust: The Growing Assault on Truth and Memory* (New York: Free Press, 1993), p. 23.

3. Karl Jaspers and Rudolf Augstein, "The Criminal State and German Responsibility: A Dialogue," *Commentary* 41 (February 1966), p. 35.

4. Hellig, *The Holocaust and Antisemitism*, p. 33.

5. Richard J. Green and Jamie McCarthy, "Chemistry Is Not the Science: Rudolf, Rhetoric & Reduction," *The Holocaust History Project*, p. 1, http://holocaust-history.org/auschwitz/chemistry/not-the-science/.

6. This is the title of a book by Pierre Vidal-Naquet, *Assassins of Memory: Essays on the Denial of the Holocaust* (New York: Columbia University Press, 1992). Vidal-Naquet claims that he borrowed the phrase from Yosef Hayim Yerushalmi. Pierre Vidal-Naquet, *Holocaust Denial in France: Analysis of a Unique Phenomenon* (Tel Aviv, Israel: Tel Aviv University, 1994), p. 1. Vidal-Naquet's mother was a victim of the Holocaust.

7. Alain Finkielkraut, *The Future of a Negation: Reflections on the Question of Genocide* (Lincoln: University of Nebraska Press, 1998), p. 60.

8. Walter Reich, "Erasing the Holocaust," *New York Times* (July 11, 1993), p. 34.

9. Vidal-Naquet, *Assassins of Memory*, pp. 18–19.

10. Raul Hilberg communicated these thoughts to D. D. Guttenplan in an interview. D. D. Guttenplan, *The Holocaust on Trial* (New York: Norton, 2001), p. 303.

CHAPTER 4

1. David Weinberg, "France," in David S. Wyman (ed.), *The World Reacts to the Holocaust* (Baltimore, MD: Johns Hopkins University Press, 1996), p. 11.

2. Weinberg, "France," pp. 11–12.

3. Valérie Igounet, *Histoire du negationism en France* (Paris: Éditions du Seuil, 2000), p. 116.

4. Richard C. Vinen, "The End of an Ideology" Right-Wing Antisemitism in France, 1944–1970," *Historical Journal* 37 (June 1984), p. 371.

5. This statement by Louis Darquier de Pellepoix, who had been the director of the General Commissariat on the Jewish Question in Vichy France and had played a prominent part in sending French Jews to Auschwitz, was political dynamite. Weinberg, "France," p. 23.

6. Henry Rousso, "The Political and Cultural Roots of Negationism in France," *South Central Review* 23 (Spring 2006) 1:67.

7. Rousso, "The Political and Cultural Roots of Negationism in France," p. 67.

8. Vidal-Naquet, *Holocaust Denial in France*, p. 6.

9. Rousso, "The Political and Cultural Roots of Negationism in France," 1:74.

10. This estimate appeared in a book published after his death entitled *Debunking the Genocide Myth: A Study of the Nazi Concentration Camps and the Alleged Extermination of European Jewry*. Shermer and Grobman, *Denying History*, p. 41.

11. His publishers were extreme right-wing firms. Vidal-Naquet, *Assassins of Memory*, p. 33.

12. Lipstadt, *Denying the Holocaust*, p. 54.

13. Finkielkraut, *The Future of a Negation*, p. 83.

14. Vidal-Naquet, *Assassins of Memory*, p. 13.

15. Alain Finkielkraut explains how the anarcho-Marxist editor Pierre Guillaume could justify support for Holocaust denial. Finkielkraut, *The Future of a Negation*, pp. 26–27.

16. Igounet, *Histoire du négationnisme en France*, p. 65.

17. Ibid., p. 71.

18. Lipstadt,*Denying the Holocaust*, p. 55.

19. Ibid., p. 56.

20. Ibid., pp. 58–60.

21. Igounet, *Histoire du négationnisme en France*, p. 73.

22. Seidel, *Denying the Holocaust*, p. 67.

23. Lipstadt, *Denying the Holocaust*, p. 51.

24. Weinberg, "France," p. 27.

25. Nicholas Fraser, *The Voice of Modern Hatred* (Woodstock, NY: Overlook Press, 2000), p. 36.

26. Michael Hoffman, "Céline, Smasher of Every Known Taboo," *Instauration* (October 1996), p. 1.

27. Fraser, *The Voice of Modern Hatred*, p. 37.

28. Ibid., p. 38.

29. Igounet, *Histoire du négationnisme en France*, p. 37.

30. Despite his support, Holocaust deniers have never embraced him because of his Fascist credentials. Lipstadt, *Denying the Holocaust*, p. 50.

31. Igounet, *Histoire du négationnisme en France*, pp. 44–45.

32. Vidal-Naquet, *Holocaust Denial in France*, p. 28. René Coty, the president of the Fourth Republic, granted him amnesty.

33. Lipstadt, *Denying the Holocaust*, p. 50.

34. Igounet, *Histoire du négationnisme en France*, p. 129.

35. Ibid., p. 164.

36. Nicolas Lebourg, "L'Invention d'une doxa Néo-Fascists: le Rôle de l'Avant-Garde Nationaliste-Révolutionnnaire: Idéologie Négationniste, Propagandes Anti-Américaine, Anti-Immigration, Anti-Juive," *Domitia* (October 2001), no. 1, p. 19.

37. Igounet, *Histoire du négationnisme en France,* p. 167.

38. Harvey G. Simmons, *French National Front: The Extremist Challenge to Democracy* (Boulder, CO: Westview Press, 1996), pp. 264–265.

39. Gollnisch is still serving a five-year expulsion from Lyon III for antisemitic remarks. Rousso, "The Political and Cultural Roots of Negationism in France," p. 69.

40. Rousso, "The Political and Cultural Roots of Negationism in France," p. 70.

41. Igounet, *Histoire du negationism en France,* p. 143.

42. Faurisson has described his method as the Ajax method because "it scours as it cleans as it shines." Seidel, *Denying the Holocaust,* p. 100.

43. Van Pelt, *The Case for Auschwitz,* p. 24.

44. Vidal-Naquet, *Holocaust Denial in France,* p. 49.

45. Fraser, *The Voice of Modern Hatred,* p. 120.

46. Vidal-Naquet, *Holocaust Denial in France,* p. 50.

47. This passage is quoted by Jeffrey Mehlman in his introduction to Pierre Vidal-Naquet's book. Vidal-Naquet, *Assassins of Memory,* p. xiii.

48. Three assailants accosted him and beat him near his home in Vichy. Suzanne Lowry, "Rewriters of Holocaust Face Wrath of Zionists," *Sunday Telegraph* (London) (September 24, 1989), p. 14.

49. Van Pelt, *The Case for Auschwitz,* pp. 24–25.

50. Vidal-Naquet, *Holocaust Denial in France,* p. 54.

51. Claude Adams, "Through the Finger," *Canadian Lawyer* (April 1985), p. 18.

52. Nicholas Fraser asserts that Faurisson had traveled to Auschwitz with Fred A. Leuchter and David Irving to investigate the gas chamber issue, but there is no evidence to substantiate this contention. Fraser, *The Voices of Modern Hatred,* p. 94.

53. Michel Zlorowski, "Furor at Holocaust Denier's Trial," *Jerusalem Post* (March 24, 1991), p. 1.

54. During the trial fistfights broke out between Holocaust survivors and their supporters and those of Faurisson's. Michel Zlotowoski, "Furor at Holocaust Denier's Trial, "*Jerusalem Post* (March 24, 1991), p. 1.

55. Rousso, "The Political and Cultural Roots of Negationism in France," p. 84.

56. Igounet, *Histoire du négationnisme en France,* p. 185.

57. Finkielkraut, *The Future of a Negation,* p. 28.

58. Ibid., p. 31.

59. Rousso, "The Political and Cultural Roots of Negationism in France," pp. 79–80.

60. Robert S. Wistrich, "Left-Wing Anti-Zionism in Western Societies," in Robert S. Wistrich (ed), *Anti-Zionism and Antisemitism in the Contemporary World* (Washington Square: New York University Press, 1990), p. 48.

61. Serge Thion, *Vérité historique ou vérité politique?* (Paris: La Vieille Taupe, 1980), pp. 33–34.

62. Igounet, *Histoire du négationnisme en France,* p. 142.

63. Didier Daeninckx, *Quand le négationnisme s'invite à l'université: Chapitre: L'Aaffaire du jury Henri Roques, le Lyonnais débarquent à Nantes,* Chap. 9, p. 2, http://www.amnistia.net.

64. Anti-Defamation League, *Hitler's Apologists: The Anti-Semitic Propaganda of Holocaust "Revisionism"* (New York: Anti-Defamation League, 1993), p. 43.

65. Rousso, "The Political and Cultural Roots of Negationism," p. 67.

66. Andrew Diamond, "Taking on France's 'Fascist University,' " *Jerusalem Post* (August 3, 2001), 5B.

67. Robert Faurisson, "The Notin Affair," *Journal of Historical Review* 10 (Fall 1990) 3:367.

68. Michèle Mazel, "The Scandals at Lyon III," *Jewish Political Studies Review* 18 (Spring 2006) 1–2:1.

69. Diamond, "Taking on France's 'Fascist University,' " p. 5B.

70. Other members of this commission were the historian Annette Becker, professor of Contemporary History at the University of Paris X–Nanterre; the historian Philippe Burrin, director of the Geneva University Institute of Advanced International Studies; and the historian Florent Brayard, researcher at the Institute of Contemporary History (CNRS). Rousso, "The Political and Cultural Roots of Negationism in France," p. 67.

71. Rousso, "The Political and Cultural Roots of Negationism in France," pp. 68–69.

72. New York Times Staff, "French Red Quits Two Party Posts: Action Discloses a Dispute—Another Reprimanded," *New York Times* (October 22, 1968), p. 11.

73. Henry Giniger, "French Communists Out Dissenter from Party Posts," *New York Times* (February 9, 1970), p. 3.

74. Richard J. Golsan, *Vichy's Afterlife: History and Counterhistory in Postwar France* Lincoln: University of Nebraska Press, 2000), p. 125.

75. Fraser, *The Voice of Modern Hatred,* p. 115.

76. François Bonnet and Nicolas Weill, "Pierre Vidal-Naquet: Analyse des relais dont disposent les négationnistes," *Le Monde* (May 4, 1996), p. 1.

77. The Institute for Historical Review's version of the Garaudy Affair is in Theodore J. O'Keefe's "Origin and Enduring Impact of the 'Garaudy Affair,' " *Journal of Historical Review* (July/August 1999) 18:4: p. 31.

78. Agence France Press, "European Rights Courts Refuses Case of Holocaust Denier," *Agence France Presse* (July 7, 2003), p. 1.

79. Golsan, *Vichy's Afterlife,* p. 127.

80. Alan Riding, "French Icon Falls from Grace, in Debate on Holocaust," *New York Times* (May 1, 1996), p. A10.

81. Philo Bregstein, "The Garaudy-Abbe Pierre Affair," *Antisemitism Research* (March 1997) 1:1: p. 1.

82. Dina Porat and Ester Webman (eds.), *Antisemitism Worldwide 2007: General Analysis* (Tel Aviv, Israel: Tel Aviv University, 2008), p. 6.

CHAPTER 5

1. Brigitte Bailer-Galanda, " 'Revisionism' in Germany and Austria: The Evolution of a Doctrine," in Hermann Kurthen, Werner Bergmann, and Rainer Erb (eds.), *Antisemitism and Xenophobia in Germany after Unification* (New York: Oxford University Press, 1997), p. 175.

2. Fraser, *The Voice of Modern Hatred,* p. 109.

3. Coogan, *Dreamer of the Day,* p. 371. Lucy S. Dawidowicz described Dr. Walter Frank and his Reich Institute for the History of the New Germany during the Nazi regime. Dawidowicz, *The Holocaust and the Historians,* pp. 49–55.

4. Arnold Forster and Benjamin R. Epstein, *Cross-Currents* (New York: Doubleday, 1956), p. 222.

5. Ibid., pp. 243–244.

6. Baler-Galanda, " 'Revisionism' in Germany and Austria," p. 176.

7. Ibid., pp. 176–177.

8. Ibid., p. 177.

9. Fabian Virchow, "German Revisionism Ain't Dead, But Living in Exile," in Kate Taylor (ed.), *Holocaust Denial: The David Irving Trial and International Revisionism* (London: Searchlight Educational Trust, 2000), p. 70.

10. Jeffrey Kaplan and Leonard Weinberg, *The Emergence of a Euro-American Radical Right* (New Brunswick, NJ: Rutgers University Press, 1998), p. 57.

11. Michael Schmidt, *The New Reich: Violent Extremism in Unified Germany and Beyond* (New York: Pantheon Books, 1993), p. 186.

12. Schmidt, *The New Reich,* p. 186.

13. Martin A. Lee, *The Beast Reawakens* (Boston: Little, Brown, 1997), p. 229.

14. Ibid., p. 260.

15. Bailer-Galanda, " 'Revisionism' in Germany and Austria," p. 183.

16. Rembiszewski, *The Final Lie,* p. 57.

17. Mark Weber, "Thies Christophersen," *Journal of Historical Review* 16 (May/June 1997) no. 3, p. 32.

18. Thies Christophersen, "Reflections on Auschwitz and West German Justice," *Journal of Historical Review* 6 (Spring 1985), no. 1, p. 67.

19. This videotape was shown first in Sweden in September 1991, and then it made the rounds of most European countries. Perry and Schweitzer, *Antisemitism,* p. 211.

20. Wilhelm Stäglich, *The Holocaust Myth: A Judge Looks at the Evidence* (Torrance, CA: Institute for Historical Review, 1986), pp. 28–29.

21. Stäglich, *The Holocaust Myth,* p. 53.

22. Mark Weber, "Dissident German Historian Published for Revisionist Writings," *The Journal of Historical Review* 17 (July/August 1998), no. 4, p. 15.

23. Bailer-Galanda, " 'Revisionism' in Germany and Austria," p. 182.

24. Brigitte Bailer-Galand, et al., "The Lachout 'Document' Anatomy of a Forgery," *The Nizkor Project,* pp. 1–2. http://nizkor.org./ftp.cgi/orgs/austrian/austrian-resistance-archives/lachout-document/.

25. Anthony Long, "Forgetting the Führer: the Recent History of the Holocaust Denial Movement in Germany," *Australian Journal of Politics and History* 48 (2002), no. 1, pp. 73–74.

26. Ibid., p. 74.

27. Quoted in Lee, *The Beast Reawakens,* p. 258.

28. Long, "Forgetting the Führer," p. 74.

29. Ibid., p. 75.

30. Ibid.

31. Ibid., p. 77.

32. Ibid.

33. Ibid.
34. Ibid., p. 78.
35. Ibid.
36. Rembisqewski, *The Final Lie,* p. 29.
37. Long, "Forgetting the Führer," p. 79.
38. Ibid.
39. Ibid.
40. Ibid., p. 78.
41. Rembiszewski, *The Final Lie,* pp. 30–32.
42. Long, "Forgetting the Führer," p. 78.
43. Ibid.
44. Catherine E. Smith, "Refuge for Hate? After His Conviction in Germany for Holocaust Denial Activities, A Revisionist Requests Political Asylum in the United States," *Southern Poverty Law Center's Intelligence Report* (Fall 2004) 115: p. 45.
45. Rembiszewski, *The Final Lie,* p. 39.
46. Long, "Forgetting the Führer," p. 80.
47. Rembiszewski, *The Final Lie,* pp. 29–30.
48. Sarah Rembiszewski, *The "Rudolf-Report": A "Scientific Landslide?"* (Tel Aviv, Israel: Tel Aviv University, 1994), p. 2.
49. Ibid., p. 10.
50. Rembiszewski, *The Final Lie,* p. 54.
51. Long, "Forgetting the Führer," p. 80.
52. Jessica Berry and Chris Hastings, "German Neo-Nazi Fugitive Is Found Hiding in Britain," *Sunday Telegraph* (London) (October 17, 1999), p. 7.
53. Long, "Forgetting the Führer," p. 90.
54. Rembiszewski, *The Final Lie,* p. 34.
55. Long, "Forgetting the Führer," p. 81.
56. Mark Weber, "German Rudolf Joins Journal Advisory Committee," *Journal of Historical Review* 19 (September/October 2000), no. 5, p. 24.
57. Rafael Medoff and Alex Grobman, *Holocaust Denial: A Global Survey—2005* (Melrose Park: PA: David S. Wyman Institute for Holocaust Studies, 2006), p. 7.
58. Rembiszewski, *The Final Lie,* p. 19.
59. Seidel, *Denying the Holocaust,* p. 55.
60. Long, "Forgetting the Führer," p. 73.
61. David Binder, "Suspects' Lawyer Denies Danger to Humphrey," *New York Times* (April 7, 1967), p. 11.
62. Desmond Butler, "Marxist to Rightist, and Back to Court," *New York Times* (January 25, 2003), p. A6.
63. William Grim, "The Strange Case of Horst Mahler," *Jewish Press on the Web* (May 13, 2004).

CHAPTER 6

1. Shermer and Grobman, *Denying History,* p. 41; and Colin Holmes, "David Irving and Holocaust Denial: An Introduction," in Kate Taylor (ed.) *Holocaust*

Denial: The David Irving Trial and International Revisionism (London: Searchlight Educational Trust, 2000), p. 6.

2. Michael Whine, "Holocaust Denial in the United Kingdom," in Jan Brinks, Stella Rock, and Edward Timms (eds.), *Nationalist Myths and Modern Media: Contested Identities in the Age of Globalization* (London: Tauris, 2005), p. 70.

3. Lipstadt, *Denying the Holocaust,* pp. 111–112.

4. Willis A. Carto owned the Noontide Press and published Hoggan's *Myth of the Six Million.* Lipstadt, *Denying the Holocaust,* p. 105.

5. Seidel, *Denying the Holocaust,* p. 113.

6. Ibid., p. 118.

7. Ibid., p. 119.

8. Deborah E. Lipstadt, *History on Trial: My Day in Court with David Irving* (New York: HarperCollins, 2005), p. 18.

9. Guttenplan, *The Holocaust on Trial,* p. 41.

10. Fraser, *The Voice of Modern Hatred,* p. 101.

11. Kate Taylor, "Irving in Denial: The Trial," in Kate Taylor (ed.), *Holocaust Denial: The David Irving Trial and International Revisionism* (London: Searchlight Educational Trust, 2000), pp. 11–12.

12. Irving evidently wrote to Thyssen steel works requesting a job. Guttenplan, *The Holocaust on Trial,* p. 42.

13. Ian Buruma, "Blood Libel: Hitler and History in the Dock," *New Yorker* (April 16, 2001), p. 83. Whether this is the same professor who failed him in math or another professor is unknown.

14. Guttenplan, *The Holocaust on Trial,* p. 43.

15. Ibid.

16. Taylor, "Irving in Denial," p. 12.

17. In 1977, a German journalist, Gitta Sereny, researched Irving's quote from a diary note of Joachim von Ribbentrop in *Hitler's War* that seemed to indicate that von Ribbentrop, the former foreign minister in Nazi Germany, doubted that Hitler could have ordered the destruction of the Jews. She found that Irving had left off the second part of the quote that indicated that Hitler must have known about the destruction of the Jews if he did not also order it. Tim Adams, "Memoirs Are Made of This," *Observer* (London) (February 24, 2002), pp. 1–2.

18. Material for this small book appeared in Peter Märtesheimer and Ivo Frevel (eds.), *Der Fernsehfilm "Holocaust"—Eine Nation ist Betroffen* (Frankfurt, West Germany: Fischer Taschenbuch Verlag, 1979), p. 6.

19. Lipstadt, *History on Trial,* p. 23.

20. Dawidowicz, *The War against the Jews, 1933–1945,* p. 39.

21. Dawidowicz, *The Holocaust and the Historians,* pp. 37–38.

22. Ibid., p. 38.

23. Lipstadt, *History on Trial,* p. 19.

24. Ibid., p. 20.

25. Seidel, *Denying the Holocaust,* p. 55.

26. Schmidt, *The New Reich,* p. 200.

27. Ibid., p. 201.

28. Guttenplan, *Holocaust on Trial,* p. 98.

29. Taylor, "Irving in Denial," p. 14.

30. Quoted in van Pelt, *The Case for Auschwitz*, p. 43, and it was taken from the transcript of Errol Morris's documentary *Mr. Death: The Rise and Fall of Fred A. Leuchter, Jr.*

31. Nicholas Fraser maintains that Irving accompanied Fred Leuchter and Robert Faurisson to Auschwitz to disprove the use of gas chamber there. Fraser, *The Voices of Modern Hatred*, p. 94 Other evidence indicates that Irving did not make the trip. He said as much in the libel trial against Deborah Lipstadt. Guttenplan, *Holocaust on Trial*, p. 158.

32. Guttenplan, *Holocaust on Trial*, p. 54.

33. Kate Taylor described this club's membership as "hardline Nazis drawn from the upper echelons of the elite nazi group, the League of St. George, and other far-right groups." Taylor, "Irving in Denial," p. 13.

34. Lipstadt, *History on Trial*, p. 84.

35. Shermer and Grobman, *Denying History*, p. 50.

36. The *Sunday Times* of London had commissioned him to translate this diary. This commission was lost due to Jewish protests against the use of Irving. Kenneth S. Stern, *Holocaust Denial* (New York: American Jewish Committee, 1993), p. 2.

37. Lipstadt, *Denying the Holocaust*, p. 181.

38. Guttenplan, *Holocaust on Trial*, p. 26.

39. Gill Glauber, "Britain's Most Disliked Historian; Irving," *Baltimore (MD) Sun* (June 17, 1996), p. 2A.

40. Jacob Heilbrunn, "Meet the Real David Irving," *New Republic* (October 21, 1996), p. 1.

41. Paul Gray, "Revisiting a Revisionist," *Time* 147 (April 15, 1996), no. 16, p. 35.

42. Heilbrunn, "Meet the Real David Irving," p. 3.

43. Lukacs, *The Hitler of History*, p. 132.

44. Taylor, "Irving in Denial," p. 9.

45. Van Pelt, *The Case for Auschwitz*, p. 2.

46. Buruma, "Blood Libel," p. 82.

47. Adams, "Memories Are Made of This," p. 1.

48. Kenneth S. Stern, "Lying About the Holocaust: National Borders Don't Mean Much in the International Holocaust Denial Business, but America Is Playing a Special Role," *Southern Poverty Law Center's Intelligence Report* 103 (Fall 2001), p. 50.

49. D. D. Guttenplan and Martin Bright, "The Model, the Saudi Prince and the U-Boat Commander: David Irving's Secret Backers," *Observer* (London) (March 3, 2002), p. 8.

50. Ibid., p. 8.

51. Ibid.

52. Ruth Elkins, "Irving Gets Three Years' Jail in Austria for Holocaust Denial," *Independent* (London) (February 21, 2006), p. 4.

53. Ibid.

54. Andrew Anthony, "Flying the Flag: He's the Cambridge Law Graduate and Father of Four Who Is Transforming the British Far Right," *Observer* (London) (September 1, 2002), p. 26.

55. Nick Ryan, "Demagogues in Denial: The Holocaust 'Revisionist' Industry Is Running a Brisk Trade," *New Internationalist* 372 (October 2004), p. 26.

56. Ibid.

57. Anthony, "Flying the Flag," pp. 23–24.

58. Daily Telegraph Staff, "Obituary of John Tyndall National Front Leader Who Set Up the British National Party," *Daily Telegraph* (London) (July 20, 2005), p. 31.

59. Zoe Nauman and Grant Hodgson, "Peddlers of Poison: Exposed: Vile Truth Behind BNP's Votes Drive," *Sunday Mirror* (London) (May 23, 2004), pp. 6–7.

60. UNCOVERED, "BNP and Antisemitism," http://www.stopthebnp.org.uk /uncovered/pg08.htm/.

CHAPTER 7

1. John C. Zimmerman, "My Response to Carlo Mattogno," http://www. holocaust-history.org/auschwitz/response-to-mattogno/.

2. John F. Burns, "Canada Puts Neo-Nazi's Ideas on Trial, Again," *New York Times* (March 30, 1988), p. A12.

3. New York Times Staff, "Holocaust Survivor Wins Suit," *New York Times* (January 18, 1986), p. 10.

4. Stern, *Denying the Holocaust,* p. 51.

5. Igal Avidan, "Legal Steps Taken to Defend Anne Frank's Diary," *Jerusalem Post* (January 11, 1994), p. 5.

6. Ibid.

7. Ronny Naftaniel, "The Legal Fight Against Anti-Semitism in the Netherlands," *Justice* (Winter 1998), p. 1.

8. José L. Rodriguez Jimenez, *Antisemitism and the Extreme Right in Spain (1962–1977)* (Jerusalem, Israel: SICSA, 1999), p. 3.

9. Ibid., p. 4.

10. Ibid., p. 10.

11. Ibid., p. 11.

12. Ibid., p. 16.

13. Mark Weber, "Spanish Court Sentences 'Thought Criminal,' " *Journal of Historical Review* 17 (Nov./Dec., 1998), no. 6, p. 21. This order to burn the books was placed on hold until Varela's sentence was finalized.

14. Mark Weber, "Free Speech Victory in 'Holocaust Denial' Case, *Journal of Historical Review* (March/April 1999), vol. 18, no. 2, p. 29.

15. Mark Weber, "Switzerland: Prison Term for 'Holocaust Denial,' " *Journal of Historical Review* (March/April 2000), vol. 19, no. 2, p. 58.

16. Kevin Coogan, "The Mysterious Achmed Huber: Friend to Hitler, Allah and Ibn Ladin?" *Hitlist Magazine* (April/May 2002), p. 1.

17. Jürgen Graf, *Holocaust Revisionism and Its Political Consequences* (Glen Rock, NJ: National Journal, 2001), p. 2.

18. Ibid., p. 4.

19. Porat and Webman, *Antisemitism Worldwide 2007,* p. 11.

20. Ibid.

21. Matthew Vella, "Norman Lowell Unveils Grandiose March on Brussels Tomorrow," *Malta Today* (February 8, 2004), p. 1.

22. Ibid.

23. Matthew Vella, "My Democracy or His?" *Malta Today* (July 3, 2005), p. 1.

24. Dan Bilefsky, "Malta Fears Sinking under Migrants," *International Herald Tribune* (June 7, 2006), p. 1.

25. Michael Shafir, *Between Denial and 'Comparative Trivialization': Holocaust Negationism in Post-Communist East Central Europe* (Jerusalem, Israel: SICSA, 2002), p. 2.

26. Randolph L. Braham, "Anti-Semitism and the Holocaust in the Politics of East Central Europe," in Randolph L. Braham (ed.), *Anti-Semitism and the Treatment of the Holocaust in Postcommunist Eastern Europe* (New York: Rosenthal Institute for Holocaust Studies, 1994), p. 14.

27. Leon Volovici, *Antisemitism in Post-Communist Eastern Europe: A Marginal or Central Issue?* (Jerusalem: SICSA, 1994), p. 8.

28. Stella Rock, "Russian Revisionism: Holocaust Denial and the New Nationalist Historiography," *Patterns of Prejudice* 35 (2001), no. 4, p. 67.

29. Ibid.

30. Wistrich, *Antisemitism*, p. 188.

31. Rock, "Russian Revisionism," p. 66.

32. Ibid., p. 71.

33. Mark Weber, "A Major Revisionist Breakthrough in Russia," *Journal of Historical Review* 16 (July/August 1997), no. 4, pp. 36–37.

34. Rock, "Russian Revisionism," p. 75.

35. Shafir, *Between Denial and 'Comparative Trivialization,'* p. 9.

36. Rafal Pankowski, "From the Lunatic Fringe to Academic: Holocaust Denial in Poland," in Kate Taylor (ed.), *Holocaust Denial: Holocaust Denial: The David Irving Trial and International Revisionism* (London: Searchlight Educational Trust, 2000), p. 75.

37. Pankowski, "From the Lunatic Fringe to Academia," pp. 75–76.

38. Ibid., p. 77.

39. Ibid., p. 78.

40. Mark Weber, "Polish Professor Fired for Dissident History Book,"*Journal of Historical Review* 19 (May/June 2000), no. 3, p. 25.

41. Ibid.

42. Pankowski, "From the Lunatic Fringe to Academia," p. 78.

43. Ibid.

44. Efraim Zuroff, "Eastern Europe: Anti-Semitism in the Wake of Holocaust-Related Issues," *Jewish Political Studies Review* 17 (Spring 2005), no. 1–2, p. 9.

45. Ibid.

46. Braham, "Anti-Semitism and the Holocaust," p. 15.

47. Franjo Tudjman, *Wastelands—Historical Truth* (Zagreb: 1989), 2nd ed., p. 156.

48. Ibid., p. 160.

49. Radu Ioanid, "Anti-Semitism and the Treatment of the Holocaust in Postcommunist Romania," in Randolph L. Braham (ed.), *Anti-Semitism and the Treatment of the Holocaust in Postcommunist Eastern Europe* (New York: Rosenthal Institute for Holocaust Studies, 1994), pp. 170–171.

50. Ibid., pp. 171–172.

51. Radu Ioanid, "Romania," in David S. Wyman (ed.), *The World Reacts to the Holocaust* (Baltimore, MD: Johns Hopkins University Press, 1996), p. 246.

52. Ibid., p. 247.

53. Volovici, *Antisemitism in Post-Communist Eastern Europe,* p. 3.

54. Shafir, *Between Denial and 'Comparative Trivialization,'* p. 8.

55. Raphael Vago, "Anti-Semitism and the Treatment of the Holocaust in Post-communist Slovakia," in Randolph L. Braham (ed.), *Anti-Semitism and the Treatment of the Holocaust in Postcommunist Eastern Europe* (New York: Rosenthal Institute for Holocaust Studies, 1994), p. 199.

56. Shafir, *Between Denial and 'Comparative Trivialization,'* p. 8.

57. Zuroff, "Eastern Europe," p. 9.

58. Vago, "Anti-Semitism and the Treatment of the Holocaust in Postcommunist Slovakia," pp. 199–200.

CHAPTER 8

1. Donald Strong, *Organized Anti-Semitism in America* (Westport, CT: Greenwood Press, 1941), pp. 15–16.

2. Frank P. Mintz, *The Liberty Lobby and the American Right: Race, Conspiracy, and Culture* (Westport, CT: Greenwood Press, 1985), p. 13.

3. Barnes had been pro-Allies during World War I, but after the war he became a violent revisionist blaming the Allies for the outbreak of World War I and for the failure of the postwar settlement. Lipstadt, *Denying the Holocaust,* p. 67.

4. Lipstadt, *Denying the Holocaust,* p. 67.

5. Brian Levin, "History as a Weapon: How Extremists Deny the Holocaust in North America," *The American Behavioral Scientist* 44 (February 2001), issue 6, p. 1006.

6. Stern, *Holocaust Denial,* p. 6.

7. Lipstadt, *Denying the Holocaust,* pp. 74–79.

8. Harry Elmer Barnes, "Zionist Fraud," in David Hoggan, *The Myth of the Six Million* (Newport Beach, CA: Noontide Press, 1969), p. 117.

9. This book was an expansion of Hoggan's Harvard University dissertation. At the time of publication Hoggan was a professor at the University of California–Berkeley. Lipstadt, *Denying the Holocaust,* pp. 71–73.

10. This article was reprinted in *Journal of Historical Review.* Harry Elmer Barnes, "The Public Stake in Revisionism," *Journal of Historical Review* (Fall, 1980), vol. 1, no. 1, p. 219.

11. Lipstadt, *Denying the Holocaust,* pp. 82–83.

12. Marvin A. Lee, *The Beast Reawakens* (Boston: Little, Brown, 1997), p. 93.

13. A FBI profile of Yockey characterized his personality as "nervous, high-strung, erratic, unpredictable, and dictatorial." Lee, *The Beast Reawakens,* p. 92.

14. Kevin Coogan reported that her title and money came from Austria. She was also Yockey's lover in 1948, but they broke up after the printing of *Imperium.* Kevin Coogan, *The Dreamer of the Day: Francis Parker Yockey and the Postwar Fascist International* (Brooklyn, NY: Autonomedia, 1999), p. 172.

15. Marvin A. Lee reported that in private conversations Yockey had praised the German extermination campaign to rid Europe of Jews in World War II. Lee, *The Beast Reawakens,* p. 96.

16. Francis Parker Yockey, *Imperium: The Philosophy of History and Politics* (Newport Beach, CA: Noontide Press, 2000), p. 533.

17. Coogan, *Dreamer of the Day*, p. 168.

18. Lee, *The Beast Reawakens*, p. 100.

19. Ibid.

20. Coogan, *Dreamer of the Day*, p. 164.

21. Letter from Revilo P. Oliver to Colonel Dall on December 17, 1970. This letter is held in the Special Collections section of the Knight Library at the University of Oregon.

22. Coogan, *Dreamer of the Day*, p. 162.

23. Maurice Bardèche, *Souvenirs* (Paris: Buchet/Chastel, 1993), p. 252.

24. Coogan, *Dreamer of the Day*, p. 214.

25. Ibid., p. 399.

26. Smith met Henry Ford in early 1937, and Ford provided financial backing for Smith's radio broadcasting career in the late 1930s. Baldwin, *Henry Ford and the Jews*, p. 306.

27. Levin, "History as a Weapon," p. 1007.

28. Ibid., pp. 1007–1008.

29. Forster and Epstein, *Cross-Currents*, pp. 243–244.

30. Ibid., p. 362.

31. Frederick J. Simonelli, *American Fuehrer: George Lincoln Rockwell and the American Nazi Party* (Urbana: University of Illinois Press, 1999), p. 107.

32. Simonelli, *American Fuehrer*, p. 113.

33. Frederick J. Simonelli, "The World Union of National Socialists and Postwar Transatlantic Nazi Revival," in Jeffrey Kaplan and Tore Bjørgo (eds.), *Nation and Race: The Developing Euro-American Racist Subculture* (Boston: Northeastern University Press, 1998), p. 35.

34. Lipstadt, *Denying the Holocaust*, p. 86.

35. Ibid., p. 85.

36. Ibid., pp. 88–89.

37. Forster and Epstein, *Cross-Currents*, p. 53.

38. This pamphlet was published by Boniface Press in Takoma Park, Maryland. Seidel, *Denying the Holocaust*, p. 71.

39. Lipstadt, *Denying the Holocaust*, p. 92.

40. Austin App, "The 'Holocaust' Put in Perspective," *Journal for Historical Review* (Spring 1980), vol. 1, no. 1, p. 48. An earlier version with minor discrepancies from the 1980 version appeared in Austin App, *The Six Million Swindle: Blackmailing the German People for Hard Marks with Fabricated Corpses* (Tacoma Park, MA: Boniface Press, 1973), pp. 18–19.

41. Dennis Roddy, "Birch Society Won't Tolerate Being Called a Hate Group," *Pittsburgh Post-Gazette* (June 21, 2003), p. D1.

42. Michael, *Willis Carto and the American Far Right*, p. 97.

43. Mark Weber, "Revilo P. Oliver: 1910–1994," *Journal of Historical Review* 14 (September/October 1994), no. 5, p. 19.

44. Revilo P. Oliver, "The 'Holohoax,' " p. 1. http://karws.gso.uri.edu/JFK/the_-critics/oliver/The_holohoax.html.

45. Ibid.

46. Weber, "Revilo P. Oliver," p. 20.

47. Bruce Cole, "A Conversation with Vartan Gregorian," *Humanities* 24 (September/October 2003), no. 5, p. 2.

48. Hermann Graml, *Europas Weg in den Krieg: Hitler and die Mächte 1939* (Berlin, Germany: R. Oldenbourg, 1990), p. 70.

49. Back in 1969, Hoggan had sued Noontide Press for publishing his book *The Forced War*. George Michael, *Willis Carto and the American Far Right* (Gainesville: University Press of Florida, 2008), p. 126.

50. Lipstadt, *Denying the Holocaust,* p. 123.

51. Arthur R. Butz, *The Hoax of the Twentieth Century: The Case Against the Presumed Extermination of European Jewry* (Newport Beach, CA: Institute of Historical Review, 1992), pp. 10–12.

52. Robert Angove, *Holocaust Denial and Professional History-Writing* (Saskatoon, Canada: M.A. thesis, Department of History, University of Saskatchewan, 2005), p. 24.

53. Arthur R. Butz, "The International 'Holocaust' Controversy," *Journal of Historical Review* (Spring 1980), vol. 1, no. 1, p. 8.

54. Butz, *The Hoax of the Twentieth Century,* p. 158.

55. Butz, *The Hoax of the Twentieth Century,* p. 242. Pierre Vidal-Naquet makes the connection between them. Vidal-Naquet, *Assassins of Memory,* p. 35.

56. Lipstadt, *Denying the Holocaust,* pp. 127–128.

57. Butz, *The Hoax of the Twentieth Century,* pp. 158–160.

58. Ibid., p. 30.

59. John C. Zimmerman, *Holocaust Denial: Demographics, Testimonies and Ideologies* (Lanham, MD: University Press of America, 2000), p. xii.

60. Stern, *Holocaust Denial,* p. 11.

61. Pamela Mendels, "Professor Puts Holocaust Theories Online, Prompting Accusations at Northwestern," *New York Times* (January 10, 1997), p. 1.

62. Ibid.

63. Udo Walendy, a German Holocaust denier, had Butz's book translated into German. Seidel, *Denying the Holocaust,* p. 71. Pedro Varela had an abridged edition translated into Spanish. Jimenez, *Antisemitism and the Extreme Right in Spain,* p. 10.

64. Seidel, *Denying the Holocaust,* p. 53.

65. Shermer and Grobman, *Denying History,* p. 40.

66. Jodi S. Cohen, "NU Rips Holocaust Denial: President Calls Prof an Embarrassment But Plans No Penalty," *Chicago Tribune* (February 7, 2006), p. 1.

67. Shermer and Grobman, *Denying History,* p. 175.

CHAPTER 9

1. Michael, *Willis Carto and the American Far Right,* p. 20.

2. Ibid., p. 21.

3. Mintz, *The Liberty Lobby and the American Right,* p. 79. C. H. Simonds states that it was after 1954 that Carto devoted himself to full-time political activity. C. H. Simonds, "The Strange Story of Willis Carto—His Fronts, His Friends, His Philosophy, His 'Lobby for Patriotism,' " *National Review* (September 10, 1971), p. 979.

4. Simonds, "The Strange Story of Willis Carto," p. 979.

5. Michael claims that the actual date for the founding of the Liberty Lobby is unclear ranging from 1955 to its formal incorporation in 1962, but it was formally announced in the August 1957 issue of *Right*. Michael, *Willis Carto and the American Far Right*, p. 63.

6. C. H. Simonds mentions that Carto had a dispute of an unknown nature with Robert Welch. Simonds, "The Strange Story of Willis Carto," p. 979. Martin A. Lee maintains that the falling out was over Welch's refusal to make the John Birch Society adhere to the antisemitic position that Carto advocated. Lee, *The Beast Reawakens*, p. 157. Michaels adds that Carto wanted to have Welsh include the Liberty Lobby in his network of organizations and Welch refused to do so. Michael, *Willis Carto and the American Far Right*, p. 48.

7. Coogan, *Dreamer of the Day*, p. 468.

8. Mintz, *The Liberty Lobby and the American Right*, p. 22.

9. Lee, *The Beast Reawakens*, p. 159.

10. Anti-Defamation League, *Danger: Extremism: The Major Vehicles and Voices of America's Far-Right Fringe* (New York: Anti-Defamation League, 1996), p. 21.

11. Levin, "History as a Weapon," p. 1009.

12. This quote is from Liberty Lobby, Inc. v. Dow Jones & Co., 1988, Note 7. Levin, "History as a Weapon," p. 1009.

13. Shermer and Grobman, *Denying History,* p. 43.

14. The proposed IHR team was to be Robert Faurisson, Arthur R. Butz, and Ditlieb Felderer. Lipstadt, *Denying the Holocaust*, p. 140.

15. Leonard Zeskind, "Cartography: Willis Carto Has History of Splits," *Southern Poverty Law Center's Intelligence Report* (Summer 1997), 87: p. 12.

16. Leonard Zeskind, "The Institute for Historical Review: US Revisionism," in Kate Taylor (ed.), *Holocaust Denial: The David Irving Trial and International Revisionism* (London: Searchlight Educational Trust, 2000), p. 88.

17. Michael Granberry, "Revisionists' Founder Sued for $7.5 Million," *Los Angeles Times* (October 28, 1996), p. B1. Farrell left in 1985 an estate worth $16 million in bonds, real estate, jewels, and precious metals. In a settlement with the heirs Carto's Legion for the Survival of Freedom received $7.5 million, which Carto then diverted to a Swiss bank account. Leonard Zeskind, "Money Matters: Holocaust Denial Leaders Battle Over Millions," *Southern Poverty Law Center's Intelligence Report* (Summer 1997) 87: pp. 10–11.

18. Zeskind, "The Institute for Historical Review," p. 91.

19. Zeskind, "Money Matters," p. 10.

20. Ibid., p. 11.

21. Shermer, "Proving the Holocaust," p. 38.

22. Todd Blodgett, former marketing consultant for *The Spotlight,* explained the reason that it was not able to expand its readership in an interview with the Southern Poverty Law Center. Southern Poverty Law Center Staff, " 'Paying the Price': After Four Years as a Player on the Radical Right, a Washington, D.C. consultant Says He Wants to Come Clean," *Southern Poverty Law Center's Intelligence Report* (Winger, 2000) 97: p. 55.

23. Andrea Billups, "Liberty Lobby Goes Under, Ends Spotlight," *Washington Times* (July 10, 2001), p. 1.

24. Lipstadt, *History on Trial,* p. 17.

25. Lipstadt, *Denying the Holocaust*, p. 138.

26. This master's degree has given Weber credibility in Holocaust denial circles that has eluded others. Anti-Defamation League, *Danger: Extremism,* pp. 163–164.

27. Michael Shermer, "Proving the Holocaust: The Refutation of Revisionism & the Restoration of History," *Skeptic* (1994) vol. 2, no. 4, p. 35.

28. Shermer, "Proving the Holocaust," p. 35.

29. Anti-Defamation League, *Danger: Extremism,* p. 164.

30. Anti-Defamation League, *Hitler's Apologists,* p. 11.

31. The transcript of the TV show appears in Stern, *Holocaust Denial,* p. 122.

32. Anti-Defamation League, *Hitler's Apologists,* p. 13. Curry was active in contacting newspapers to carry Holocaust denial material as early as 1986. Smith denies that Curry had anything to do with the initial funding of the CODOH because he printed 50 copies at an Iranian-Jewish copy shop on Highland Boulevard in Hollywood that cost around $2.50.

33. Anti-Defamation League, *Danger: Extremism,* p. 144.

34. Bradley R. Smith, *Confessions of a Holocaust Revisionist, Part 1* (Los Angeles, CA: Prima Facie, 1988), pp. 14–24.

35. The IHR gave financial backing for this publication. Anti-Defamation League, *Hitler's Apologists,* p. 12.

36. Smith, *Confessions of a Holocaust Revisionist,* p. 78.

37. At the University of Miami (Florida), a Jewish philanthropist withdrew a gift of $2 million after a Holocaust denial ad appeared in the University of Miami's student newspaper. Anti-Defamation League, *Danger: Extremism,* p. 145.

38. Michael, *Willis Carto and the American Far Right,* p. 108.

39. Jihad al-Khazen, "Good Morning: The Jewish Connection," *Moneyclips* (May 9, 1994), p. 1.

40. Eddie Chua, "American Writer: Mossad Knew of 9–11' Attack Plan," *Malay Mail* (August 25, 2004), p. 1.

41. Michael, *Willis Carto and the American Far Right,* p. 139.

42. Ibid., p. 109.

43. John Sack, "Inside the Bunker," *Esquire* (February 2001), p. 3.

44. Ibid., p. 4.

45. Carlos Whitlock Porter, "The Website of Carlos Whitlock Porter," p. 2. http://www.cwporter.com.

46. Ibid., p. 3.

47. Ibid.

48. David Cole, "Interview," (May 6, 1995) *The Nizkor Project,* p. 1.

49. Ibid., p. 3.

50. Ibid., p. 4.

51. Ibid., p. 5.

52. Michael Shermer, "Proving the Holocaust: The Refutation of Revisionism & the Restoration of History," *Skeptic* (1994), vol. 2, no. 4, p. 37.

53. Dr. Piper released a letter charging that Cole had come under false pretenses. Cole, "Interview," p. 6.

54. This inflammatory text was removed from the JDL Web site soon after David Cole left the Institute for Historical Review and Holocaust denial. It now shows up on Web sites of the Institute of Historical Review as an example of the type of extremist rhetoric used against Holocaust deniers.

55. Michael Shermer, "Holocaust Revisionism Update," *Skeptic* (July 1998), p. 1.

56. Michael A. Hoffman II, "The Psychology and Epistemology of 'Holocaust' Newspeak," *Journal of Historical Review* 6 (Winter 1985), no. 4, p. 470.

57. Hoffman, "The Psychology and Epistemology of 'Holocaust' Newspeak," p. 472.

58. Michael Hoffman II, "In His Words: The Mouth and Mind of Michael Hoffman II—November 1994," *The Nizkor Project*, p. 1. http://www.nizkor.org/hweb/people/h/hoffman-michael/in-his-words-9411.html/.

59. Friedrich Paul Berg, "Poison Gas Über Alles," *The Revisionist: Journal for Critical Historical Inquiry* (2005), no. 1, p. 1.

60. Levin, "History as a Weapon," p. 1011.

61. Friedrich Paul Berg, "The Diesel Gas Chambers: Myth within a Myth," *Journal of Historical Review* (Spring 1984) 5; no. 1, p. 15.

62. Berg, "Poison Gas Über Alles," p. 2.

63. Anti-Defamation League, *Danger: Extremism*, p. 135.

64. Anti-Defamation League, *Hitler's Apologists*, p. 31.

65. The GIEA lost its tax-exempt status in 1992 after the Anti-Defamation League complained about its political agenda to the Internal Revenue Service. Anti-Defamation League, *Danger: Extremism*, p. 136.

66. Anti-Defamation League, *Danger: Extremism*, p. 137.

67. Lipstadt, *History on Trial*, p. 34.

68. Shermer and Grobman, *Denying History*, p. 129. Lipstadt quotes the payment at $40,000. Lipstadt, *History on Trial*, p. 35. Whatever the final sum, it was a substantial sum of money.

69. Robert Faurisson, "The Zündel Trials (1985–1988)," *Journal of Historical Review* (Winter 1988), vol. 8, no. 4, p. 429.

70. Lipstadt, *Denying the Holocaust*, p. 162.

71. This analysis is weakened by the fact that the Germans blew up the gas chambers before the Soviet army arrived at Auschwitz. Lipstadt, *History on Trial*, p. 35.

72. Lipstadt, *Denying the Holocaust*, p. 164.

73. Ibid., p. 166.

74. Shelly Shapiro "An Investigation," in Shelly Shipiro (ed.), *Truth Prevails: Demolishing Holocaust Denial: The End of the Leuchter Report* (New York: Beate Klarsfeld Foundation, 1990), pp. 17 and 21.

75. Shapiro, *"An Investigation,"* p. 21.

76. Anti-Defamation League, *Hitler's Apologists*, p. 9.

77. Jean-Claude Pressac, "The Deficiencies and Inconsistencies of 'The Leuchter Report,' " in Shelly Shapiro (ed.), *Truth Prevails: Demolishing the Holocaust Denial: The End of "The Leuchter Report,"* (New York: Beate Klarsfeld Foundation, 1990), p. 36.

78. Elizabeth Neuffer, "German Court Convicts US Nazi Publisher," *Boston Globe* (August 23, 1996), p. A2.

79. Shermer and Grobman, *Denying History*, p. 86.

80. Marc Fisher and Steve Coll, "Farm-Belt Hitler Sows Seed of Hate," *Guardian* (London) (May 13, 1995), p. 11.

81. Rick Atkinson, "Germany Set to Try U.S. White Supremacist," *Washington Post* (May 9, 1996), p. A36.

82. Quoted from Gary Lauck's Web site, http://www.nazi-lauck-nsdapao.com/.

83. Tyler Bridges, *The Rise of David Duke* (Jackson: University Press of Mississippi, 1994), p. 112.

84. Stern, *Denying the Holocaust*, p. 8.

85. Bridges, *The Rise of David Duke*, p. 123.

86. Ibid., p. 114.

87. Ibid., p. 115.

88. Ibid., p. 116.

89. Ibid., p. 117.

90. Stern, *Denying the Holocaust*, p. 18.

91. Lipstadt, *History on Trial*, p. 181.

92. Kenneth S. Stern, "Lying About the Holocaust: National Borders Don't Mean Much in the International Holocaust Denial Business, But America Is Playing a Special Role," *Southern Poverty Law Center's Intelligence Reports* 103 (Fall 2001), p. 50.

93. Tatsah Robertson, "Reparations Pitch Draws Hope, Scorn," *Boston Globe* (October 17, 2000), p. A1.

94. Robertson, "Reparations Pitch Draws Hope, Scorn," p. A1.

95. Anti-Defamation League, *Danger: Extremism*, p. 14.

96. Anti-Defamation League, *Hitler's Apologists*, p. 52–53.

97. Ibid., p. 53.

98. Anti-Defamation League, *Danger: Extremism*, p. 16.

99. Arthur J. Magida, *Prophet of Rage: A Life of Louis Farrakhan and His Nation* (New York: Basic Books, 1996), p. 137.

100. Stern, *Denying the Holocaust*, p. 20.

101. Ibid.

102. Rene Sanchez, "Comparing the Suffering of Millions; Ex-Farrakhan Aide Minimizes Holocaust," *Washington Post* (April 19, 1994), p. B1.

103. Wendy Melillo and Hamil R. Harris, "Dissent Raised as Ex-Farrakhan Aide Returns to Howard U.," *Washington Post* (April 20, 1994), p. B1.

104. Perry and Schweitzer, *Antisemitism*, p. 235.

105. Anti-Defamation League, *Danger: Extremism*, p. 45.

106. James Dyer, "A Recent Visit with Eustace Mullins—May 8, 1004," p. 3, http://www.whale.to/b/mullins_i.html.

107. Anti-Defamation League, *Danger: Extremism*, p. 100.

108. Ibid.

109. Ibid., pp. 101–102.

110. Ibid., p. 121.

111. Ibid., p. 121.

112. Anti-Defamation League, *Hitler's Apologists*, p. 26.

113. Quoted from the home page of Covington in Economic expert.com, http://www.economicexpert.com/a/Holocaust:denial:examined.html.

114. Peter Cheney, "The Wives, the Marriages of Chameleon Ernst Zundel," *Globe and Mail* (Toronto) (March 8, 2003), p. A4.

115. Larry Darby, "History of the Atheist Law Center and Statement Disavowing Atheism," posted on July 7, 2006 from *Mathaba News Agency*. http://www.mathaba.net/, p. 2.

116. Ibid.

CHAPTER 10

1. Stanley R. Barrett, *Is God a Racist? The Right Wing in Canada* (Toronto, Canada: University of Toronto Press, 1987), p. 157.

2. Ibid.

3. Manuel Prutschi, "The Zundel Affair," in Alan Davies (ed.), *Antisemitism in Canada: History and Interpretation* (Waterloo, Canada: Wilfrid Laurier University Press, 2000), p. 254.

4. Vidal-Naquet, *Holocaust Denial in France*, p. 56.

5. Prutschi, "The Zundel Affair," p. 255.

6. Barrett, *Is God a Racist?* p. 158.

7. Lipstadt, *Denying the Holocaust*, p. 158.

8. Prutschi, "The Zundel Affair," p. 263.

9. Ibid., p. 264.

10. Zündel told a reporter of the *Toronto Star* in 1981 that he sent Holocaust denial and neo-Nazi materials to "45,000 people in forty-five countries and in fourteen languages." Barrett, *Is God a Racist?* p. 159.

11. Barrett, *Is God a Racist?* p. 158.

12. Ibid., p. 158.

13. Lipstadt, *Denying the Holocaust*, p. 158.

14. Prutschi, "The Zundel Affair," p. 257.

15. This quote is cited by Manuel Prutschi. Prutschi, "The Zundel Affair," p. 258.

16. Prutschi, "The Zundel Affair," pp. 265–266.

17. Ibid., p. 266.

18. Citron forced the case on Ontario Attorney General Roy McMurtry, after he had shown reluctance to charge Zündel. Prutschi, "The Zundel Affair," p. 250.

19. A. Marouf Hasian, Jr., "Canadian Civil Liberties, Holocaust Denial and the Zundel Trial," *Communication and the Law* 21 (September 1999), no. 3, p. 46.

20. Barrett, *Is God a Racist?* p. 161.

21. Prutschi, "The Zundel Affair," p. 252.

22. Hasian, "Canadian Civil Liberties, Holocaust Denial and the Zundel Trial," p. 48.

23. Barrett, *Is God a Racist?* p. 163.

24. Prutschi, "The Zundel Affair," p. 254.

25. Hasian, "Canadian Civil Liberties, Holocaust Denial and the Zundel Trial," p. 49.

26. Paul Bilodeau, "Zundel Trial Testimony of Survivors 'Unreliable', Court Told," *Toronto Star* (March 24, 1988), p. A2.

27. Kate Taylor, "Ernst Zündel," in Kate Taylor (ed.), *Holocaust Denial: The David Irving Trial and International Revisionism* (London: Searchlight Educational Trust, 2000), p. 92.

28. Ernst Zündel, "Zundel Condemns Secret Hearings," *Vancouver Sun* (June 11, 1996), p. A7.

29. Mark Weber, "The Importance of the Zündel Hearing in Toronto," *Journal of Historical Review* 19 (Sept./Oct. 2000), no. 5; p. 2.

30. Weber, "Importance of the Zündel Hearing in Toronto," p. 2.

31. Allan Thompson, "Zundel Haunts Us Still," *Toronto Star* (April 19, 2003), p. F1.

32. Adrian Humphreys, "Zundel Says He Owes His Life to Hitler," *National Post* (Don Mills, Ontario, Canada) (May 10, 2003), p. A4.

33. Mark Bonokoski, "The Jewish Card," *Toronto Star* (March 2, 2005), p. 10.

34. Medoff and Grobman, *Holocaust Denial,* p. 4.

35. Keegstra remained mayor even after he had been charged with a crime despite efforts to have him removed. Douglas Martin, "Hate-Mongering Teacher Tests Canada's Patience," *New York Times* (May 26, 1983), p. A2.

36. Alan Davies, "The Keegstra Affair," in Alan Davies (ed.), *Antisemitism in Canada: History and Interpretation* (Waterloo, Canada: Wilfrid Laurier University Press, 2000), p. 228.

37. Keegstra had been elected third vice-president of the Alberta Social Credit Party, but he was suspended from his post shortly after the beginning of the Eckville controversy. He was later reinstated and he ran for Parliament in the September 1984 national election without success. Martin, "Hate-Mongering Teacher Tests Canada's Patience," p. A2.

38. David Bercuson and Douglas Wertheimer, *A Trust Betrayed: The Keegstra Affair* (Toronto, Canada: Doubleday Canada, 1985), p. 30.

39. Warren Kinsella, *Web of Hate: Inside Canada's Far Right Network* (Toronto, Canada: HarperCollins, 1994), pp. 26–27.

40. Bercuson and Wertheimer, *A Trust Betrayed,* p. 11.

41. Ibid.

42. Ibid., pp. 11–12.

43. Ibid., p. 13.

44. Ibid., p. 33.

45. David Climenhaga, "Court Quashes Keegstra Conviction," *Ottawa Citizen* (September 8, 1994), p. A5.

46. Davies, "The Keegstra Affair," p. 229.

47. This theory had long been discredited by scholars in the field. Lewis, *Semites and Anti-Semites,* p. 48.

48. Barrett, *Is God a Racist?* p. 250.

49. Ibid., p. 251.

50. Davies, "The Keegstra Affair," p. 230.

51. Bercuson and Wertheimer, *A Trust Betrayed,* p. 48.

52. A Catholic parent, Margaret Andrew, brought charges against Keegstra. Martin, "Hate-Mongering Teacher Tests Canada's Patience," p. A2.

53. Bercuson and Wertheimer, *A Trust Betrayed,* p. 84.

54. Martin, "Hate-Mongering Teacher Tests Canada's Patience," p. A2.

55. Davies, "The Keegstra Affair," p. 232.

56. Bercuson and Wertheimer, *A Trust Betrayed,* p. 68.

57. Barrett, *Is God a Racist?* p. 219.

58. Ibid., p. 220.

59. Section 319 of the Criminal Code deals "with inciting or willfully promoting hatred, other than in a private conversation, against any of the same identifiable groups." Section 381 "prohibits the act of publicly advocating or promoting genocide of a group identified by colour, race relation or ethnic origin. Mirko Petricevic, "Preaching … or Spewing Hate?" *The Record* (Kitchener-Waterloo, Canada) (February 1, 2003), p. J8.

60. Leonard Stern, "Keegstra a Hate-Monger, Top Court Rules,"

61. Davies, "The Keegstra Affair," p. 244.

62. Kinsella, *Web of Hate,* p. 313.

63. Ibid.

64. Ibid., p. 316.

65. Ibid., pp. 321–327.

66. Ibid., p. 328.

67. Ibid., p. 330.

68. Ian Haysom, "Free Speech or Hatred: Journalist Faces Tribunal," *Gazette* (Montreal, Canada) (May 9, 1997), p. A1.

69. Kinsella, *Web of Hate* p. 207.

70. Donovan Vincent, "Teacher with Neo-Nazi Links Is Reassigned by Peel Board," *Toronto Star* (June 11, 1993), p. A7.

71. Paul Lungen, "Fromm Tries to Keep Teaching Licence," *Canadian Jewish News* 35 (February 3, 2005), no. 6, p. 14.

72. Ellie Tesher, "Fromm Ruling Raises Bar for Teachers," *Toronto Star* (April 9, 2002), p. A25.

73. Christopher Shulgan, "Will He Be the Next Zundel?; With Canada's Best-Known Supremacist Deported, Former Teacher Paul Fromm Is Working to Revive the Far-Right Movement," *Glob and Mail* (Toronto) (March 5, 2005), p. M2.

74. Paul Fromm, "Holocaust Supporters Shun Rational Discussion and Debate: Paul Fromm," *Mehr News Agency* (December 24, 2005), http://www.mehrnews.com/en/NewsDetail.aspx?NewsID=269706.

75. Jamie McCarthy, "John Ball: Air Photo Expert?" *Holocaust History Project,* p. 7, http://www.holocaust-history.org/auschwitz/john-ball/.

76. Ibid.

77. Van Pelt, *The Case for Auschwitz,* pp. 56–57.

78. Brian Harmon, "See No Evil: John Ball's Blundering Air Photo Analysis," *Holocaust History Project,* p. 3. http://www.holocaust-history.org/see-no-evil/.

CHAPTER 11

1. Ronald L. Nettler, "Islamic Archetypes of the Jews: Then and Now," in Robert S. Wistrich, *Anti-Zionism and Antisemitism in the Contemporary World* (Washington Square, NY: New York University Press, 1990), p. 65.

2. Nettler, "Islamic Archetypes of the Jews," p. 66.

3. Ibid., p. 67.

4. Wistrich, *Antisemitism,* p. 196.

5. Harold Brackman and Aaron Breitbart, *Holocaust Denial's Assault on Memory: Precursor to Twenty-First Century Genocide?* (Los Angeles, CA: Simon Wiesenthal Center, 2007, p. 10.

6. Walter Laqueur, *The Changing Face of Antisemitism: From Ancient Times to the Present Day* (New York: Oxford University Press, 2006), pp. 140–141.

7. Anti-Defamation League, "Holocaust Denial in the Middle East: The Latest Anti-Israel, Anti-Semitic Propaganda Theme," (New York: ADL, 2001) http://www.adl.org/.

8. Kenneth R. Timmerman, *Preachers of Hate: Islam and the War on America* (New York: Three Rivers Press, 2004), pp. 1–2.

9. Robert Fisk, "A Blind Eye to History," *Independent* (London) (August 30, 1996), p. 12.

10. Lewis, *Semites and Anti-Semites*, pp. 15–16.

11. Goetz Nordbruch, *The Socio-Historical Background of Holocaust Denial in Arab Countries: Arab Reactions to Roger Garaudy's The Founding Myths of Israeli Politics* (Jerusalem: SICSA, 2001), p. 3.

12. Brackman and Breitbart, *Holocaust Denial's Assault on Memory*, p. 11.

13. Nordbruch, *The Socio-Historical Background of Holocaust Denial in Arab Countries*, pp. 3–4.

14. Medoff and Grobman, *Holocaust Denial*, p. 16.

15. Brackman and Breitbart, *Holocaust Denial's Assault on Memory*, p. 11.

16. Medoff and Grobman, *Holocaust Denial*, p. 16.

17. Seidel, *Holocaust Denial*, pp. 82–83.

18. Wistrich, *Antisemitism*, p. 254.

19. Abdullah Mohammad Sindi, "How the Jewish-Zionist Grip on American Film and Television Promotes Bias against Arabs and Muslims," *Journal of Historical Review* (September/October 1998) vol. 17, no. 5, p. 12.

20. Abdullah Mohammad Sindi, "Britain and the Rise of Wahhabism and the House of Saud," *Kana'an Bulletin* 14 (January 16, 2004) issue 361, pp. 1–2.

21. Abdullah Mohammad Sindi, "Holocaust Is a Typical Zionist Myth," *Radio Islam*, p. 3, http://www.radioislam.net/sindi/typic.htm.

22. Ibid., p. 4.

23. Abdullah Mohammad Sindi, "Israel Has Created a Real Holocaust for Palestinians: Sindi," *Mehr News* (December 28, 2005), p. 11 http://www.mehrnews.ir/en/NewsDetail.aspx?NewsID=270634.

24. Mark Weber, "An Anti-Holocaust Intifada Grows Among the Arabs," *Journal of Historical Review* 20 (May/June 2001), no. 3, pp. 4–5.

25. Weber, "An Anti-Holocaust Intifada Grows Among the Arabs," p. 5.

26. Nahid Siamdoust, "Iranian President Calls the Holocaust a 'Myth,'" *Los Angeles Times* (December 15, 2005), p. A5.

27. Siamdoust, "Iranian President Calls the Holocaust a 'Myth,'" p. A5.

28. Nazila Fathi and Michael Slackman, "Iranian's Oratory Reflects Devotion to '79 Revolution," *New York Times* (December 20, 2005), p. A3.

29. Michael, "Desciphering Ahmadinejad's Holocaust Revisionism," p. 12.

30. Fathi and Slackman, "Iranian's Oratory Reflects Devotion to '79 Revolution," p. A3.

31. George Michael, "Deciphering Ahmadinejad's Holocaust Revisionism (Mahmoud Ahmadinejad)," *Middle East Quarterly* 14 (Summer 2007), no. 3, p. 15.

32. Abraham H. Foxman, *Never Again? The Threat of the New Anti-Semitism* (New York: HarperSan Francisco, 2003), p. 223. Graf has since relocated to Moscow, Russia, after marrying a Belarusian woman in 2001.

33. Medoff and Grobman, *Holocaust Denial*, pp. 13–14.

34. Ibid., p. 14.

35. Ibid.

36. Brackman and Breitbart, *Holocaust Denial's Assault on Memory*, p. 13.

37. Medoff and Grobman, *Holocaust Denial*, p. 13.

38. Ibid.

39. Ibid.

40. Salah Nasrawi, "Muslim Brotherhood Leader Says Holocaust Is a Myth, Lashes Out at U.S.," *Associated Press Worldstream* (December 22, 2005), p. 1.

41. Ibid.

42. Nadim Kawach, "Zayed Centre Rejects Anti-Semitism Charge," *Gulf News* (August 19, 2003), p. 1.

43. National Desk, "ADL: Arab League Think-Tank Labels Holocaust "A Fable,' " *U.S. Newswire* (August 28, 2002), p. 1.

44. Alan Cooperman, "For Harvard, Questions on Arab Leader's Gift; Graduate Crusades over Alleged Anti-Semitic Links," *Washington Post* (July 19, 2003), p. A3.

45. Douglas Davis, "Mideast Defenders of Garaudy," *Jerusalem Post* (March 2, 1998), p. 17.

46. Goetz Nordbruch, *The Socio-Historical Background of Holocaust Denial in Arab Countries,* p. 2.

47. Michael, "Deciphering Ahmadinejad's Holocaust Revisioniam (Mahmoud Ahmadinejad)," p. 12.

48. Elli Wohlgelernte, "In a State of Denial" *Jerusalem Post* (June 8, 2001), p. 4B.

CHAPTER 12

1. Danny Ben-Moshe, *Holocaust Denial in Australia* (Jerusalem, Israel: SICSA, 2005), p. 48.

2. Ben-Moshe, *Holocaust Denial in Australia,* p. 48.

3. Ibid., p. 3.

4. Ibid.

5. Ibid., pp. 3–4.

6. Ibid., p. 8.

7. Ibid., p. 27.

8. Ibid., p. 5.

9. Lucy Dawidowicz, "Lies About the Holocaust," *Commentary* (December 1980), p. 35.

10. Ben-Moshe, *Holocaust Denial in Australia,* p. 13.

11. AAP Information Services, "Liberties Union Says Anti-Terrorist Laws Over-Reaction," *AAP Newsfeed* (May 17, 2002), p. 1.

12. Ben-Moshe, *Holocaust Denial in Australia,* p. 9.

13. Ibid., p. 6.

14. Ibid., p. 7.

15. Anthony Long maintained that Töben wanted to be arrested for the publicity being a martyr would bring. His case attracted considerable publicity both in Germany and in Australia. Long, "Forgetting the Führer," p. 83.

16. Ben-Moshe, *Holocaust Denial in Australia,* pp. 9–10.

17. Ibid., p. 15.

18. Pia Akerman and Richard Sproull, "Holocaust Disputer Can't Find a Lawyer," *Australian* (Sydney, Australia) (January 17, 2007), p. 6.

19. Pia Akerman, and Richard Sproull, "Second Aussie in Holocaust Denial," *Australian* (Sydney, Australia) (December 14, 2006), p. 3.

20. Mark Weber, "Treblinka Ground Radar Examination Finds No Trace of Mass Graves," *Journal of Historical Review* 19 (May/June 2000), no. 3, p. 20.

21. Nick Terry, et al., "Polish Investigations of the Treblinka Killing Site Were a Complete Failure; What Concerns Evidence to the Mass Murder of Hundreds of Thousands of People, or so 'Revisionist' Guru Carlo Mattaogno Would Like His Readers to Believe," *Holocaust Controversies* (July 10, 2006), pp. 2–3.

22. Ian McPhedran, "The It Girl and the Pariah—How a Controversial Socialite Fell from Grace," *Daily Telegraph* (London) (February 25, 2006), p. 66.

23. Johann Hari, "A Life in Full; M'Lady's Not for Turning;" *Independent on Sunday* (London) (April 13, 2003), p. 18.

24. Guttenplan and Bright, "The Model, the Saudi Prince and the U-Boat Commander," p. 8.

25. Staff, "Australian Causes Stir at Irving Trial," *Sydney Morning Herald* (Australia) (February 21, 2006), p. 1.

26. Ben-Moshe, *Holocaust Denial in Australia*, p. 36.

27. Ibid.

28. Ibid., pp. 36–7.

29. Ibid., p. 34.

30. Richard J. Evans, "Thesis Full of Faults," *Press* (Christchurch, New Zealand) (September 3, 2003), p. 17.

31. Ibid.

32. Executive Summary, *Report by the Joel Hayward Working Party* (December 18, 2000), p. 3.

33. Ibid., p. 4.

34. Ibid.

35. Thomas A. Fudge, "Holocaust, History and Free Speech," *New Zealand Herald* (Christchurch) (July 23, 2003), p. 1.

36. Angela Gregory, "'Book-Burners' Feared Libel Suit," *New Zealand Herald* (Christchurch) (July 23, 2003), p. 1.

37. Evans, "Thesis Full of Faults," p. 17.

38. Kowner, "Tokyo Recognizes Auschwitz," pp. 259–260.

39. Ibid., p. 260.

40. Perry and Schweitzer, *Antisemitism*, p. 117.

41. Rotem Kowner, "Tokyo Recognizes Auschwitz: The Rise and Fall of Holocaust Denial in Japan, 1989–1999," *Journal of Genocide Research* 2 (2001), no. 2, p. 257.

42. William Wetherall, "The Anti-Semitic Book Boom: It Damages Japan's Reputation in the World," *Japan Times* (Minato) (September 9, 1987), p. 16.

43. Kowner, "Tokyo Recognizes Auschwitz," p. 261.

44. Ibid., p. 262.

45. Tatou Takahama, "Holocaust Denial in Japan: Marco Polo Demonstrates Insensitivity," *JPRI Critique* (March 1995) vol. 2, no. 3, p. 2.

46. Ibid.

47. Ibid.

48. Ibid.

49. Kowner, "Tokyo Recognizes Auschwitz," p. 265.

50. Ibid., p. 266.

CONCLUSION

1. Michael Marriott, "Rising Tide: Sites Born of Hate," *New York Times* (March 18, 1999), p. G1.

2. Finkielkraut, *The Future of a Negation,* p. 89.

3. Anti-Defamation League, *Hitler's Apologists,* p. 2.

4. Nat Hentoff, "Dad's Jabs at Jews Cry Out for Gibson Response," *Chicago Sun-Times* (March 7, 2004), p. 38.

5. Ibid.

6. Alex Grobman and Rafael Medoff, *Holocaust Denial: A Global Survey—2003* (Melrose Park, PA: David S. Wyman Institute for Holocaust Studies, 2004), p. 3.

7. Eric Talmadge, "Fischer's Holocaust Denial May Impact Deportation Fight," *Jerusalem Post* (August 5, 2004), p. 6.

8. Dan Bilefsky, "EU Adopts Prohibition on Holocaust Denial; But National Laws Can Take Precedence," *International Herald Tribune* (April 20, 2007), p. 3.

9. Shermer, "Proving the Holocaust," p. 41.

10. Brackman and Breitbart, *Holocaust Denial's Assault on Memory,* p. 14.

11. Ibid.

12. Angove, *Holocaust Denial and Professional History-Writing,* p. 121.

13. George Jonas, "Throwing the Holocaust Down a Memory Hole," *National Post* (Toronto) (April 7, 2007), p. A22.

14. Hari, "A Life in Full; M'Lady's Not for Turning," p. 23.

15. Van Pelt, *The Case for Auschwitz,* pp. 69–70.

16. Kalman Sultanik, "Auschwitz-Birkenaus: A Sacred Zone of Inviolability," *Midstream* (November/December 2003), p. 2.

Bibliography

GENERAL REFERENCE WORKS

Atkins, Stephen E. *Encyclopedia of Modern American Extremists and Extremist Groups*. Westport, CT: Greenwood Press, 2002.
———. *Encyclopedia of Modern Worldwide Extremists and Extremist Groups*. Westport, CT: Greenwood Press, 2004.
———. *Terrorism: A Reference Handbook*. Santa Barbara, CA: ABC-CLIO, 1992.
Baumel, Judith Taylor, and Walter Laqueur, eds. *The Holocaust Encyclopedia*. New Haven, CT: Yale University Press, 2001.
Charny, Israel W., ed. *Encyclopedia of Genocide*. Santa Barbara, CA: ABC-CLIO, 1999.
Edelheit, Abraham J. *History of the Holocaust: A Handbook and Dictionary*. Boulder, CO: Westview, 1994.
Edelheit, Hershel, and Abraham J. Edelheit. *A World in Turmoil: An Integrated Chronology of the Holocaust and World War II*. Westport, CT: Greenwood Press, 1991.
Gutman, Israel. *Encyclopedia of the Holocaust*. New York: Macmillan, 1990.
Kaplan, Jeffrey. *Encyclopedia of White Power: A Sourcebook on the Radical Racist Right*. Walnut Creek, CA: Altimira Press, 2000.
Rees, Phillip. *Biographical Dictionary of the Extreme Right Since 1890*. New York: Simon & Schuster, 1990.
Rozett, Robert, and Shmuel Spector, eds. *Encyclopedia of the Holocaust*. New York: Facts on File, 2000.
Snyder, Louis L. *Encyclopedia of the Third Reich*. New York: Marlowe, 1976.
Spector, Shmuel, ed. *The Encyclopedia of Jewish Life Before and During the Holocaust*. Washington Square: New York University Press, 2001.

SERIALS

Dachau Review: History of Nazi Concentration Camps—Studies, Reports, Documents. Dachau, Germany: Verlag Dachauer Hefte, 1988–1989.

BIBLIOGRAPHIES

Edelheit, Abraham J., and Hershel Edelheit. *Bibliography on Holocaust Literature.* Boulder, CO: Westview Press, 1986.

Edelheit, Abraham J., and Hershel Edelheit. *Bibliography on Holocaust Literature: Supplement.* Boulder, CO: Westview Press, 1993.

HANDBOOKS AND SURVEYS

Anti-Defamation League. *Antisemitism Worldwide 2000/1.* New York: Anti-Defamation League, 2002.

———. *Audit of Anti-Semitic Incidents.* New York: Anti-Defamation League, 2000.

———. *Danger: Extremism: The Major Vehicles and Voices on America's Far Right Fringe.* New York: Anti-Defamation League, 1996.

———. *Hitler's Apologists: The Anti-Semitic Propaganda of Holocaust "Revisionism."* New York: Anti-Defamation League, 1993.

———. *The Skinhead International: A Worldwide Survey of Neo-Nazi Skinheads.* New York: Anti-Defamation League, 1995.

———. *Young Nazi Killers: The Rising Skinhead Danger.* New York: Anti-Defamation League, 1993.

Grobman, Alex, and Rafael Medoff. *Holocaust Denial: A Global Survey—2003.* Melrose Park, PA: David S. Wyman Institute for Holocaust Studies, 2004.

Medoff, Rafael, and Alex Grobman, *Holocaust Denial: A Global Survey—2005.* Melrose Park, PA: David S. Wyman Institute for Holocaust Studies, 2006.

AUTOBIOGRAPHIES, DIARIES, AND MEMOIRS

Bardèche, Maurice. *Souvenirs.* Paris: Buchet/Chastel, 1993.

Briffault, Herma, ed. *The Memoirs of Doctor Felix Kersten.* Garden City, NY: Doubleday, 1947.

Caitung, Severin, and Marge Caitung. *The Darkest Years.* Northbrook, IL: Caitung, 1994.

Goebbels, Joseph. *The Goebbels Diaries, 1942–1943.* Garden City, Doubleday, 1948.

Greene, Joshua, and Shiva Kumar, eds. *Witness: Voices from the Holocaust.* New York: Free Press, 2000.

Hilberg, Raul. *The Politics of Memory: The Journey of a Holocaust Historian.* Chicago: Ivan R. Dee, 1996.

Höss, Rudolph. *Death Dealer: The Memoirs of the SS Kommandant at Auschwitz.* New York: Da Capo Press, 1996.

Kielar, Wieslaw. *Anus Mundi: 1,500 Days in Auschwitz/Birkenau.* New York: Times Book, 1980.

Kubizek, August. *The Young Hitler I Knew.* London: Greenhill Books, 2006.

Lengyel, Olga. *Five Chimneys: A Woman Survivor's True Story of Auschwitz.* Chicago: Academy Chicago Publishers, 1995.

Levi, Primo. *The Drowned and the Saved.* New York: Summit Books, 1988.

———. *If This Is a Man and The Truce.* London: Abacus, 1987.

Müller, Filip. *Eyewitness Auschwitz: Three Years in the Gas Chambers*. Chicago: Ivan R. Dee, 1979.

Nyiszli, Miklos. *Auschwitz: A Doctor's Eyewitness Account*. New York: Arcade, 1993.

Rauschning, Hermann. *The Voices of Destruction*. New York: Putnam's, 1940.

Sakowicz, Kazimierz. *Ponary Diary, 1941–1943: A Bystander's Account of a Mass Murder*. New Haven, CT: Yale University Press, 2005.

Speer, Albert. *Infiltration: How Heinrich Himmler Schemed to Build an SS Industrial Empire*. New York: Macmillan, 1981.

BIOGRAPHIES

Angier, Carole. *The Double Bond: Primo Levi: A Biography*. New York: Farrar, Straus and Giroux, 2002.

Anissomov, Myriam. *Primo Levi: Tragedy of an Optimist*. Woodstock, NY: The Overlook Press, 1999.

Bridges, Tyler. *The Rise of David Duke*. Jackson: University Press of Mississippi, 1994.

Cesarani, David. *Eichmann: His Life and Crimes*. London: Vintage, 2004.

Coogan, Kevin. *Dreamer of the Day: Francis Parker Yockey and the Postwar Fascist International*. Brooklyn, NY: Autonomedia, 1999.

Fest, Joachim C. *Hitler*. New York: Harcourt Brace Jovanovich, 1974.

Goodrick-Clark, Nicholas. *Hitler's Priestess: Savitri Devi, the Hindu-Aryan Myth, and Occult Neo-Nazism*. New York: New York University Press, 1998.

Kessel, Joseph. *The Man with the Miraculous Hands: The Fantastic Story of Felix Kersten, Himmler's Private Doctor*. Short Hills, NJ: Burford Books, 1960.

Lang, Jochen von. *The Secretary: Martin Bormann: The Man Who Manipulated Hitler*. New York: Random House, 1979.

———. *Top Nazi: SS General Karl Wolff: The Man Between Hitler and Himmler*. New York: Enigma Books, 2005.

Magida, Arthur J. *Prophet of Rage: A Life of Louis Farrakhan and His Nation*. New York: Basic Books, 1996.

Marcus, Sheldon. *Father Coughlin*. South Bend, IN: Notre Dame University Press, 1973.

Maser, Werner. *Hitler: Legend, Myth, and Reality*. New York: Harper and Row, 1973.

Padfield, Peter. *Himmler: Reich Führer-SS*. London: Cassell, 2001.

Rose, Douglas D., ed. *The Emergence of David Duke and the Politics of Race*. Chapel Hill: University of North Carolina Press, 1992.

Simonelli, Frederick J. *American Fuehrer: George Lincoln Rockwell and the American Nazi Party*. Urbana: University of Illinois Press, 1999.

Skidelsky, Robert. *Oswald Mosley*. London: Macmillan, 1981.

Warren, Donald. *Radio Priest: Charles Coughlin the Father of Hate Radio*. New York: Free Press, 1996.

Worth, Richard. *Heinrich Himmler: Murderous Architect of the Holocaust*. Berkeley Heights, NJ: Enslow Publishers, 2005.

MONOGRAPHS

Able, Deborah. *Hate Groups*. Springfield, IL: Enslow Publishers, 1995.

Allen, Michael Thad. *The Business of Genocide: The SS, Slave Labor, and the Concentration Camps*. Chapel Hill: University of North Carolina, Press, 2002.

Aly, Götz, and Susanne Heim. *Architects of Annihilation: Auschwitz and the Logic of Destruction*. London: Weidenfeld and Nicolson, 2002.

Aly, Götz, Peter Chroust, and Christian Pross. *Cleansing the Fatherland: Nazi Medicine and Racial Hygiene*. Baltimore, MD: Johns Hopkins University Press, 1994.

Angove, Robert. "Holocaust Denial and Professional History-Writing." M.A. thesis, History Department, University of Saskatchewan, Saskatoon, Canada, 2005.

Arad, Yitzhak. *Belzec, Sobibor, Treblinka: The Operation Reinhard Death Camps*. Bloomington: Indiana University Press, 1999.

Arad, Yitzhak, Shmuel Krakowski, and Shmuel Spector. *The Einsatzgruppen Reports: Selections from the Dispatches of the Nazi Death Squads' Campaign against the Jews in Occupied Territories of the Soviet Union July 1941–January 1943*. New York: Holocaust Library, 1989.

Arad, Yitzhak, et al., eds. *Documents on the Holocaust: Selected Sources on the Destruction of the Jews of Germany and Austria, Poland, and the Soviet Union*. 8th ed. Lincoln: University of Nebraska Press, 1999.

Baldwin, Neil. *Henry Ford and the Jews: The Mass Production of Hate*. New York: Public Affairs, 2003.

Barrett, Stanley. *Is God a Racist? The Right Wing in Canada*. Toronto, Canada: University of Toronto Press, 1987.

Ben-Moshe, Danny. *Holocaust Denial in Australia*. Jerusalem, Israel: SICSA, 2005.

Bercuson, David, and Douglas Wertheimer. *A Trust Betrayed: The Keegstra Affair*. Toronto: Doubleday Canada, 1985.

Berenbaum, Michael, ed. *Witness to the Holocaust*. New York: HarperCollins, 1997.

Black, Edwin. *War against the Weak: Eugenics and America's Campaign to Create a Master Race*. New York: Four Walls and Eight Windows, 2003.

Botwinick, Rita Steinhardt. *A History of the Holocaust: From Ideology to Annihilation*. 3rd ed. Upper Saddle River, NJ: Pearson Prentice Hall, 2004.

Bracher, Karl Dietrich. *The German Dictatorship: The Origins, Structure, and Effects of National Socialism*. New York: Praeger, 1970.

Brackman, Harold, and Aaron Breitbart. *Holocaust Denial's Assault on Memory: Precursor to Twenty-First Century Genocide?* Los Angeles: Simon Wiesenthal Center, 2007.

Braham, Randolph L. *Anti-Semitism and the Treatment of the Holocaust in Postcommunist Eastern Europe*. New York: Rosenthal Institute for Holocaust Studies, 1994.

Breitman, Richard. *The Architect of Genocide: Himmler and the Final Solution*. Hanover, CT: Brandeis University Press, 1991.

Brinks, Jan Herman, Stella Rock, and Edward Timms, eds. *Nationalist Myths and Modern Media: Contested Identities in the Age of Globalisation*. (London: Tauris, 2005.

Bronner, Stephen Eric *A Rumor About the Jews: Reflections on Antisemitism and the Protocols of the Learned Elders of Zion.* New York: St. Martin's Press, 2000.

Browning, Christopher R. *Fateful Months: Essays on the Emergence of the Final Solution.* New York: Holmes and Meier, 1991.

———. *Nazi Policy, Jewish Workers, German Killers.* Cambridge: Cambridge University Press, 2000.

———. *Ordinary Men: Reserve Police Battalion 101 and the Final Solution in Poland.* New York: Harper Perennial, 1998.

———. *The Origins of the Final Solution.* London: William Heinemann, 2004.

Burleigh, Michael, and Wolfgang Wippermann. *The Racial State: Germany 1933–1945.* Cambridge: Cambridge University Press, 2005.

Burrin, Philippe. *Nazi Anti-Semitism: From Prejudice to the Holocaust.* New York: New Press, 2005.

Carlson, Elof Axel. *The Unfit: A History of a Bad Idea.* Cold Spring Harbor, NY: Cold Spring Harbor Laboratory, 2001.

Cercle Marc Bloch, et al. *Pour la Memoire: Contre-Rapport: les Dix Affaires qui ébranlèrent le Monde Universitarie Lyonnais (1978–1999).* Lyon, France: Cercle Marc Bloch, 1999.

Clendinnen, Inga. *Reading the Holocaust.* Cambridge: Cambridge University Press, 1999.

Cohn, Norman. *Warrant for Genocide: The Myth of the Jewish World Conspiracy and the Protocols of the Elders of Zion.* London: Serif, 1996.

Davies, Alan, ed. *Antisemitism in Canada: History and Interpretation.* Waterloo, Canada: Wilfrid Laurier University Press, 1992.

Dawidowicz, Lucy S. *The Holocaust and the Historians.* Cambridge, MA: Harvard University Press, 1981.

———. *A Holocaust Reader.* West Orange, NJ: Behrman House, 1976.

———. *The War against the Jews, 1933–1945.* New York: Bantam, 1986.

Des Pres, Terrence. *The Survivor: An Anatomy of Life in the Death Camps.* New York: Oxford University Press, 1975.

Dinnerstein, Leonard. *Antisemitism in America.* New York: Oxford University Press, 1994.

Domarus, Max, ed. *Hitler: Reden und Proklamation, 1932–1945.* 4 vols. Wiesbaden: R. Löwit, 1973.

Dundes, Alan, ed. *The Blood Libel Legend: A Casebook in Anti-Semitic Folklore.* Madison: University of Wisconsin Press, 1991.

Dwork, Deborah, and Robert Jan van Pelt. *Holocaust: A History.* New York: Norton, 2002.

Dymerskaya-Tsigelman, Liudmila, and Leonid Finberg. *Antisemitism of the Ukrainian Radical Nationalists: Ideology and Policy.* Jerusalem: SICSA, 1999.

Eaglestone, Robert. *Postmodernism and Holocaust Denial.* Cambridge, UK: Icon Books, 2001.

Evans, Richard J. *The Coming of the Third Reich.* New York: Penguin Books, 2004.

———. *Lying about Hitler: History, Holocaust, and the David Irving Trial.* New York: Basic Books, 2001.

Ezekiel, Rafael S. *The Racist Mind: Portraits of American Neo-Nazis and Klansmen.* New York: Penguin Books, 1995.

Fenster, Mark. *Conspiracy Theories: Secrecy and Power in American Culture.* (Minneapolis: University of Minnesota Press, 1999.

Finkelstein, Norman G. *The Holocaust Industry: Reflections on the Exploitation of Jewish Suffering.* London: Verso, 2000.

Finkielkraut, Alain. *The Future of a Negation: Reflections on the Question of Genocide.* (Lincoln: University of Nebraska Press, 1998.

Fischer, Klaus P. *The History of an Obsession: German Judeophobia and the Holocaust.* New York: Continuum, 1998.

Fleming, Gerald. *Hitler and the Final Solution.* (Berkeley: University of California Press, 1984.

Forster, Arnold, and Benjamin R. Epstein. *Cross-Currents.* New York: Doubleday, 1956.
———. *The New Anti-Semitism.* New York: McGraw-Hill, 1974.

Foxman, Abraham H. *Never Again? The Threat of the New Anti-Semitism.* New York: HarperCollins, 2003.

Fraser, Nicholas. *The Voice of Modern Hatred: Tracing the Rise of Neo-Fascism in Europe.* Woodstock, NY: The Overlook Press, 2000.

Fresco, Nadine. *Fabrication d'un antisemite.* Paris: Édition du Seuil, 1999.

Friedlander, Henry. *Origins of the Nazi Genocide: From Euthanasia to the Final Solution.* Chapel Hill: University of North Carolina Press, 1995.

Friedländer, Saul. *Nazi Germany and the Jews.* Vol. 1. New York: HarperCollins, 1997.

Galton, Francis. *Inquiries into Human Faculty and Its Development.* 2nd ed. London: Dent, 1907.

Gardell, Mattias. *Gods of the Blood: The Pagan Revival and White Separatism.* Durham, NC: Duke University Press, 2003.

Goldensohn, Leon. *The Nuremberg Interviews.* New York: Knopf, 2005.

Goldhagen, Daniel Jonah. *Hitler's Willing Executioners: Ordinary Germans and the Holocaust.* New York: Knopf, 1996.

Golsan, Richard J., ed. *Fascism's Return: Scandal, Revision, and Ideology since 1980.* Lincoln: University of Nebraska Press, 1998.

Goodman, David G., and Masanori Miyazawa. *Jews in the Japanese Mind: The History and Uses of a Cultural Stereotype.* Expanded ed. Lanham, MD: Lexington Books, 2000.

Gottfried, Ted. *Deniers of the Holocaust: Who They Are, What They Do, Why They Do It.* Brookfield, CT Twenty-First Century Books, 2001.

Graml, Hermann. *Antisemitism in the Third Reich.* Oxford, UK: Blackwell, 1992.
———. *Europas Weg in den Krieg: Hitler und die Mächte 1939.* Berlin, Germany: R. Oldenbourg, 1990.

Graves, Joseph L. *The Race Myth: Why We Pretend Race Exists in America.* New York: Dutton, 2004.

Gray, Charles. *The Irving Judgement: David Irving v. Penguin Books and Professor Deborah Lipstadt.* Harmondworth, UK: Penguin Books, 2000.

Greif, Gideon. *We Wept without Tears: Testimonies of the Jewish Sonderkommando from Auschwitz.* New Haven, CT: Yale University Press, 2005.

Gurock, Jeffrey S., ed. *Anti-Semitism in America.* 2nd ed. New York: Routledge, 1998.

Gutman, Yisrael, and Michael Berenbaum, eds. *Anatomy of the Auschwitz Death Camp.* Bloomington: Indiana University Press, 1998.

Guttenplan, D. D. *The Holocaust on Trial.* New York: Norton, 2001.

Hackett, David A. *The Buchenwald Report.* Boulder, CO: Westview, 1995.

Hamann, Brigitte. *Hitler's Vienna: A Dictator's Apprenticeship.* New York: Oxford University Press, 1999.

Harris, Geoffrey. *The Dark Side of Europe: The Extreme Right Today.* Edinburgh, UK: Edinburgh University Press, 1994.

Hellig, Jocelyn. *The Holocaust and Antisemitism: A Short History.* Oxford, UK: Oneworld Publications, 2003.

Henry, Francis, and Carol Tator. *Holocaust Denial: Bigotry in the Guise of Scholarship.* Toronto: Canada: Simon Wiesenthal Center, 1994.

Herbert, Ulrich, ed. *National Socialist Extermination Policies: Contemporary German Perspectives and Controversies.* New York: Berghahn Books, 2000.

Hilberg, Raul. *The Destruction of the European Jews.* New York: Holmes and Meier, 1967.

———. *Perpetrators, Victims, Bystanders: The Jewish Catastrophe, 1933–1945.* New York: Harper Perennial, 1992.

Höhne, Heinz. *The Order of the Death's Head: The Story of Hitler's SS.* New York: Penguin Books, 2000.

Igounet, Valérie. *Histoire du négationnisme en France.* Paris: Seuil, 2000.

Jäckel, Eberhard. *David Irving's Hitler: A Faulty History Dissected.* Port Angeles, WA: Ben-Simon Publications, 1993.

———. *Hitler in History.* Hanover, CT: University Press of New England, 1984.

Jimenez, José L. Rodriguez. *Antisemitism and the Extreme Right in Spain (1962–1977).* Jerusalem, Israel: SICSA, 1999.

Johnson, Eric A. *Nazi Terror: The Gestapo, Jews, and Ordinary Germans.* New York: Basic Books, 2000.

Jones, Mitchell. *The Leuchter Report: A Dissection.* Cedar Park, TX: 21st Century Logic, 1995.

Kaplan, Jeffrey, and Tore Bjørgo, eds. *Nation and Race: The Developing Euro-American Racist Subculture.* Boston: Northeastern University Press, 1998.

Kaplan, Jeffrey, and Leonard Weinberg. *The Emergence of a Euro-American Radical Right.* New Brunswick, NJ: Rutgers University Press, 1998.

Kater, Michael H. *Doctors Under Hitler.* Chapel Hill: University of North Carolina Press, 1989.

KL Auschwitz Seen by the SS: Rudolf Höss, Pery Broad, Johann Paul Kremer. Oświęcim, Poland: Auschwitz-Birkenau State Museum, 1994.

Klee, Ernst, Willi Dressen, and Volker Riess. *"The Good Old Days" The Holocaust as Seen by Its Perpetrators and Bystanders.* Old Saybrook, CT: Konecky & Konecky, 1991.

Kinsella, Warren. *Web of Hate: Inside Canada's Far Right Network.* Toronto, Canada: HarperCollins, 1994.

Kleg, Milton. *Hate Prejudice and Racism.* Albany: State of New York Press, 1993.

Kogan, Eugen, Hermann Langbein, and Adalbert Rückerl, eds. *Nazi Mass Murder: A Documentary History of the Use of Poison Gas.* New Haven, CT: Yale University Press, 1993.

Kovács, András. *Antisemitic Prejudices in Contemporary Hungary.* Jerusalem, Israel: SICSA, 1999.

Krausnick, Helmut, and Martin Broszat. *Anatomy of the SS State.* London: Paladin, 1970.

Kühl, Stefan. *The Nazi Connection: Eugenics, American Racism, and German National Socialism.* New York: Oxford University Press, 1994.

Kurthen, Hermann, Werner Bergmann, and Rainer Erb, eds. *Antisemitism and Xenophobia in Germany after Unification.* New York: Oxford University Press, 1997.

Lagnado, Lucette Matalon, and Sheila Cohn Dekel. *Children of the Flames: Dr. Josef Mengele and the Untold Story of the Twins of Auschwitz.* New York: Penguin Books, 1991.

Landau, Ronnie S. *The Nazi Holocaust.* Chicago: Ivan R. Dee, 1994.

Langbein, Hermann. *Against All Hope: Resistance in the Nazi Concentration Camps, 1938–1945.* New York: Paragon House, 1994.

Langerbein, Helmut *Hitler's Death Squads: The Logic of Mass Murder.* College Station: Texas A&M Press, 2004.

Laqueur, Walter, and Richard Breitman. *Breaking the Silence: The German Who Exposed the Final Solution.* Hanover, NH: University Press of New England, 1994.

Lee, Marvin A. *The Beast Reawakens.* Boston: Little, Brown, 1997.

Lewis, Bernard. *Semites and Anti-Semites: An Inquiry into Conflict and Prejudice.* New York: Norton, 1999.

Lewy, Guenter. *The Catholic Church and Nazi Germany.* New York: McGraw-Hill, 1964.

Lifton, Robert Jay. *The Nazi Doctors: Medical Killing and the Psychology of Genocide.* New York: Basic Books, 2000.

Lipstadt, Deborah. *Denying the Holocaust: The Growing Assault on Truth and Memory.* New York: Plume, 1993.

Lehrer, Steven. *Wannsee House and the Holocaust.* Jefferson, NC: McFarland, 2000.

Lukacs, John. *The Hitler of History.* New York: Vintage Books, 1997.

MacLean, French L. *The Camp Men: The SS Officers Who Ran the Nazi Concentration Camp System.* Atglen, PA: Schiffer Military History, 1999.

Macmaster, Neil. *Racism in Europe, 1870–2000.* Houndsmill, UK: Palgrave, 2001.

Märtesheimer, Peter, and Ivo Frevel, eds. *Der Fernsehfilm "Holocaust"—Eine Nation ist Betroffen.* Frankfurt, West Germany: Fischer Taschenbuch Verlag, 1979.

Mayer, Arno J. *Why Did the Heavens Not Darken? The "Final Solution" in History.* New York: Pantheon, 1988.

McKale, Donald M. *Hitler's Shadow War: The Holocaust and World War II.* Lanham, MD: Taylor Trade Publishing, 2002.

Mintz, Frank P. *The Liberty Lobby and the American Right: Race, Conspiracy, and Culture.* (Westport, CT: Greenwood Press, 1985.

Mitscherlich, Alexander. *Doctors of Infamy: The Story of the Nazi Medical Crimes.* New York: Schuman, 1949.

Mosse, George L. *Nazi Culture: Intellectual, Cultural and Social Life in the Third Reich.* New York: Grosset and Dunlap, 1966.

Müller-Hill, Benno. *Murderous Science: Elimination by Scientific Selection of Jews, Gypsies, and Others, Germany 1933–1945*. Oxford, UK: Oxford University Press, 1988.
Neuhäusler, Johannes. *What Was It Like in the Concentration Camp at Dachau?* 27th ed. Dachau, Germany: Trustees for the Monument of Atonement in the Concentration Camp at Dachau, 1998.
Neville, Peter. *The Holocaust*. Cambridge: Cambridge University Press, 1999.
Nordbruch, Goetz. "The Socio-Historical Background of Holocaust Denial in Arab Countries: Arab Reactions to Roger Garaudy's *The Founding Myths of Israeli Politics*." Jerusalem, SICSA, 2001.
Novick, Peter. *The Holocaust in American Life*. Boston: Houghton Mifflin, 1999.
Ordover, Nancy. *American Eugenics: Race, Queer Anatomy, and the Science of Nationalism*. Minneapolis: University of Minnesota Press, 2003.
Paris, Erna. *Long Shadows: Truth, Lies and History*. New York: Bloomsbury, 2001.
Péan, Pierre. *L'Extrémiste: François Genoud, de Hitler à Carlos*. Paris: Fayard, 1996.
Pelt, Robert Jan van. *The Case for Auschwitz: Evidence from the Irving Trial*. Bloomington: Indiana University Press, 2002.
Perry, Marvin, and Frederick M. Schweitzer. *Antisemitism: Myth and Hate from Antiquity to the Present*. New York: Palgrave, 2002.
Poliakov, Léon. *The History of Anti-Semitism: From Voltaire to Wagner*. Philadelphia: University of Pennsylvania Press, 2003.
———. *The History of Anti-Semitism: Suicide Europe, 1870–1933*. Philadelphia: University of Pennsylvania Press, 2003.
Praeger, Dennis, and Joseph Telushkin. Rev. ed. *Why the Jews? The Reason for Antisemitism*. New York: Touchstone, 2003.
Pressac, Jean-Claude. *Auschwitz: Technique and Operation of the Gas Chambers*. New York: The Beate Klarsfeld Foundation, 1989.
Proctor, Robert N. *Racial Hygiene: Medicine under the Nazis*. Cambridge, MA: Harvard University Press, 1988.
Rees, Laurence. *Auschwitz: A New History*. New York: Public Affairs, 2005.
Reitlinger, Gerald. *The Final Solution: The Attempt to Exterminate the Jews of Europe, 1939–1945*. New York: Perpetual Book, 1961.
Rembiszewski, Sarah. *The Final Lie: Holocaust Denial in Germany: A Second Generation Denier as a Test Case*. Tel Aviv, Israel: Tel Aviv University, 1996.
———. *The "Rudolf-Report: A "Scientific Landslide?"* Tel Aviv, Israel: Tel Aviv University, 1994.
Rhodes, Richard. *Masters of Death: The SS-Einsatzgruppen and the Invention of the Holocaust*. New York: Knopf, 2002.
Ribuffo, Leo P. *The Old Christian Right: The Protestant Far Right from the Depression to the Cold War*. Philadelphia: Temple University Press, 1983.
Riesse, Volker. *Die Anfänge der Vernichtung "lebensunwerten Lebens" in den Reichgauen Danzig-Westpressen und Wartheland 1939/40*. Frankfurt, Germany: Peter Lang, 1995.
Roseman, Mark. *The Wannsee Conference and the Final Solution: A Reconsideration*. New York: Metropolitan Books, 2002.

Rosenbaum, Ron. *Explaining Hitler: The Search for the Origins of His Evil* New York: Random House, 1998.

Rothchild, Sylvia, ed. *Voices from the Holocaust.* New York: New American Library, 1981.

Rubenstein, Richard L. *Approaches to Auschwitz: The Holocaust and Its Legacy.* Rev. ed. Louisville, KY: Westminister John Knox Press, 2003.

Rousso, Henry. *Le Dossier Lyon III: Le rapport sur le racisme et le négationnisme à l'université Jean-Moulin.* Paris: Fayard, 2003.

Schafft, Gretchen E. *From Racism to Genocide: Anthropology in the Third Reich.* (Urbana: University of Illinois Press, 2004.

Schleunes, Karl A. *The Twisted Road to Auschwitz: Nazi Policy Toward German Jews, 1933–1939.* Urbana: University of Illinois Press, 1990.

Schmidt, Michael. *The New Reich: Violent Extremism in Unified Germany and Beyond.* New York: Pantheon Books, 1993.

Schwarz, Gudren. *Die Nationalsozialistischen Lager.* Frankfurt, Germany: Campus, 1990.

Segel, Benjamin W. *A Lie and a Libel: The History of the Protocols of the Elders of Zion.* Lincoln: University of Nebraska Press, 1995.

Segev, Tom. *Soldiers of Evil: The Commandants of the Nazi Concentration Camps.* New York: McGraw-Hill, 1987.

Seidel, Gill. *The Holocaust Denial: Antisemitism, Racism and the New Right.* Leeds, UK: Beyond the Pale Collective, 1986.

Shafir, Michael. *Between Denial and "Comparative Trivialization": Holocaust Negationism in Post-Communist East Central Europe.* Jerusalem, Israel: SICSA, 2002.

Shapiro, Shelly. *Truth Prevails: Demolishing Holocaust Denial: the End of "The Leuchter Report."* New York: Beate Klarsfeld Foundation, 1990.

Shermer, Michael, and Alex Grobman. *Denying History: Who Says the Holocaust Never Happened and Why Do They Say It?* Berkeley: University of California Press, 2000.

Sofsky, Wolfgang. *The Order of Terror: The Concentration Camp.* Princeton, NJ: Princeton University Press, 1997.

State of Israel, Ministry of Justice, *The Trial of Adolf Eichmann: Record of Proceedings in the District Court of Jerusalem, 1992, 5 vols.*

Steinweis, Alan E. *Studying the Jew: Scholarly Antisemitism in Nazi Germany.* (Cambridge, MA: Harvard University Press, 2006.

Stern, Fritz. *The Politics of Cultural Despair: A Study in the Rise of the Germanic Ideology.* Garden City, NY: Anchor Books, 1965.

Stern, Kenneth S. *Holocaust Denial.* New York: American Jewish Committee, 1993.

Strong, Donald. *Organized Anti-Semitism in America.* Westport, CT: Greenwood Press, 1941.

Taylor, Kate, ed. *Holocaust Denial: The David Irving Trial and International Revisionism.* London: Searchlight Educational Trust, 2000.

Timmerman, Kenneth R. *Preachers of Hate: Islam and the War on America.* New York: Three Rivers Press, 2004.

Todorov, Tzvetan. *Facing the Extreme: Moral Life in the Concentration Camps.* New York: Henry Hold, 1996.

Traverso, Enzo. *The Jews and Germany: From the 'Judeao-German Symbiosis' to the Memory of Auschwitz* Lincoln: University of Nebraska Press, 1995.

Traverso, Enzo. *The Origins of Nazi Violence.* New York: New Press, 2003.

Tull, Charles J. *Father Coughlin and the New Deal.* Syracuse, NY: Syracuse University Press, 1965.

Tusa, Ann, and John Tusa. *The Nuremberg Trial.* New York: Atheneum, 1984.

Vidal-Naquet, Pierre. *Assassins of Memory: Essay on the Denial of the Holocaust.* New York: Columbia University Press, 1992.

Vidal-Naquet, Pierre. *Holocaust Denial in France: Analysis of a Unique Phenomenon.* Tel Aviv, Israel: Tel Aviv University, 1994.

Volovici, Leon. *Antisemitism in Post-Communist Eastern Europe: A Marginal or Central Issue?* Jerusalem, Israel: SICSA, 1994.

Von Lang, Jochen. *Eichmann Interrogated: Transcripts from the Archives of the Israeli Police.* New York: Da Capo Press, 1999.

Walendy, Udo. *Auschwitz im IG-Farben Prozess—Holocaust Dokumente?* Vlotho, Germany: Verlag für Volkstum and Zeitgeschichtsforschung, 1981.

Wallace, Max. *The American Axis: Henry Ford, Charles Lindbergh, and the Rise of the Third Reich.* New York: St. Martin's Press, 2003.

Wardi, Charlotte. *Le genocide dans la fiction remanesque.* Paris: Presses Universitaires de France, 1988.

Weikart, Richard. *From Darwin to Hitler: Evolutionary Ethics, Eugenics, and Racism in Germany.* New York: Palgrave, 2004.

Weiss, John. *Ideology of Death: Why the Holocaust Happened in Germany.* Chicago: Elephant Paperbacks, 1996.

Westermann, Edward B. *Hitler's Police Battalions: Enforcing Racial War in the East.* Lawrence: University of Kansas Press, 2005.

Wistrich, Robert S. *Antisemitism: The Longest Hatred.* (New York: Schocken Books, 1991).

———. *Anti-Zionism and Antisemitism in the Contemporary World.* Washington Square: New York University Press, 1990.

———. *Hitler and the Holocaust.* New York: Modern Library, 2003.

Wyman, David S., ed. *The World Reacts to the Holocaust.* Baltimore, MD: The Johns Hopkins University Press, 1996.

Zimmerman, John C. *Holocaust Denial: Demographics, Testimonies and Ideologies.* Lanham, MD: University Press of America, 2000.

HOLOCAUST DENIAL LITERATURE

App, Austin. *The Six Million Swindle: Blackmailing the German People for Hard Marks with Fabricated Corpses.* Tacoma Park, MD: Boniface Press, 1973.

Ball, John C. *Air Photo Evidence.* Delta, British Columbia: Ball Resource Services, 1992.

Butz, Arthur R. *The Hoax of the Twentieth Century: The Case Against the Presumed Extermination of European Jewry.* Newport Beach, CA: Institute of Historical Review, 1992.

Carrel, Alexis. *Man the Unknown.* New York: Harper, 1935.

Christophersen, Thies. *Auschwitz: A Personal Account*. Rev. ed. Reedy, WV: Liberty Bell Publications, 1979.

Duke, David. *Jewish Supremacism: My Awakening to the Jewish Question*. Mandeville, LA: Free Speech Press, 2003.

Faurisson, Robert. *Mémoire en defense: contre ceux qui m'accuse de falsifier l'histoire: la question des chambres à gaz*. Paris: La Vieille Taupe, 1980.

Ford, Henry, Sr. *The International Jew: The World's Foremost Problem*. Honolulu, HI: University Press of the Pacific, 2003.

Hitler, Adolf. *Mein Kampf*. Boston: Houghton Mifflin, 1943.

Hoggan, David. *The Myth of the Six Million*. Newport Beach, CA: Noontide Press, 1969.

Irving, David. *Hitler's War*. New York: Avon Books, 1991.

Leuchter, Fred A. *The Leuchter Report: The End of a Myth: Auschwitz, Birkenau, and Majdanek, Poland by an Execution Equipment Expert*. Toronto, Canada: Samisdat Publishers, 1988.

Leuchter, Fred A., Robert Faurisson, and Germar Rudolf. *The Leuchter Reports: Critical Edition*. Chicago: Theses and Dissertations Press, 2005.

Mattogno, Carlo. *Auschwitz: The End of a Legend: A Critique of J. C. Pressac*. Chicago: Theses and Dissertation Press, 2003.

Rassinier, Paul. *The Holocaust and the Lies of Ulysses*. Costa Mesa, CA: The Institute for Historical Review, 1978.

Ross, Malcolm. *Web of Deceit*. Moncton, Canada: Stronghold Publishing, 1978.

Sanning, Walter (pseudo.). *The Dissolution of European Jewry*. Torrance, CA: Institute for Historical Review, 1983.

Smith, Bradley R. *Confessions of a Holocaust Revisionist, Part 1*. Los Angeles: Prima Facie, 1988.

Stäglich, Wilhelm. *Auschwitz Myth: A Judge Looks at the Evidence*. Torrance, CA: Institute for Historical Review, 1986.

Thion, Serge. *Vérité historique ou vérité politique? La dossier de l'affaire Faurisson. La question des chambers à gaz*. Paris: La Veille Taupe, 1980.

Tudjman, Franjo. *Wastelands—Historical Truth*. 2nd ed. Zagreb, Croatia: Matica hrvatska, 1989.

Weinberg, Gerhard L., ed. *Hitler's Second Book: The Unpublished Sequel to Mein Kampf*. New York: Enigma Books, 2006.

Yockey, Francis Parker. *Imperium: The Philosophy of History and Politics*. Newport Beach, CA: Noontide Press, 2000.

Index

German Red Cross, 108
German Society for Racial Hygiene, 24
German-Soviet Pact (1939), 85
German steel mill (Ruhr area), 119
Germany: antisemitic movement,
   16–21; Category I and Category II
   concentration camps in, 62, eugenics
   movement, 23–24; euthanasia
   program, 39–43; Hitler believed
   Jews were a danger to, 32–33; laws
   against Holocaust denial, 2, 103,
   183; outside influences promoting
   Holocaust denial in, 114–15;
   sterilization program, 38–39; target
   of Zündel's Holocaust denial
   materials, 194–95; Töben's legal
   problems in Germany, 224; trial of
   Zündel, 198;
*Germany Past and Present
   (Deutschland in Geschichte und
   Gengenwart)* (journal), 160
Gerstein, Kurt, 96–97
*The Gerstein Report—Anatomy of a
   Fraud* (pamphlet), 127–28
Gestapo, 36, 85, 157
*Giant with Feet of Clay: Raul Hilberg
   and His Standard Work on the
   "Holocaust"* (Riese auf Tönernen
   Füssen. Raul Hilberg und sein
   Standardwerk über den Holocaust),
   134
Gibson, Hutton, 234
Gibson, Joye, 234
Gibson, Mel, 234
Gleick, Edith, 177
Glendale, California, 151
Globke, Hans, 35–36
Globocnik, Odilo, 50–51, 63, 72;
   commander of Operation Reinhard,
   63, 72; Himmler's orders, 72; report
   to Hitler, 50–51
Gmurczyk, Adam, 138
Gobineau, Arthur de, 14, 17
Goddard, Henry Herbert, 38
Goebbels, Joseph, 36, 45–46, 50, 122,
   134
*Goebbels: Mastermind of the Third
   Reich* (Irving), 122

Goedsche, Hermann, 16
Goldensohn, Leon, 68; Interviews with
   Höss, 68
Goldschmidt's College (University of
   London), 169
Goldstein, Israel, 215
Goldwater, Barry, 164
Gollnisch, Bruno, 92, 99
Google, 235
Gorbachev government, 137
Göring, Hermann, 36–37, 48, 60
Grabert, Herbert, 104
Grabert publishing house, 104, 161
Graf, Jürgen, 133–135, 217; active in
   Institute for Historical Review, 166;
   collaboration with Mattogno, 128,
   134; sanctuary in Iran, 217
Grafeneck medical facility, 40
Graham, Jonathan, 223
Graml, Hermann, 33, 54, 157; critique
   of Hoggan's book, 157
Grant, Madison, 22, 30, 32; Hitler's
   reading of his works, 30
Granville, Ohio, 153
Graves, Philip, 20
Grawitz, Ernst-Robert, 66
Gray, Charles, 123
Great Britain, 113, 118, 123, 153, 204,
   234
Great Depression, 83, 145, 222
Great Holocaust Trial, The (Hoffman)
   177
Greater Romania (Romania Mare)
   (newspaper), 140
Greatest Taboo of Postwar World
   History, The: There Were No Nazi
   Gas Chambers," 231
Green, Richard J., 80
Griaznoff, Daniel, 226
Griffin, Nick, 124–26
Grimstad, William, 184, 214
Grobman, Alex, 117
Grouès, Henri Antoine. *See* Pierre,
   Abbé
Ground-penetrating radar (GPR), 225
Group for the Research and Study for a
   European Civilization (Groupement
   de recherche et d'études pour la

Iraq, 223
Irish Republican Army, 201
Iron Curtain, 80
Irvine, California, 105, 115
Irvine Marriott Hotel, 236
Irving, David, 119–24; attitude toward
    Hitler, 123; author of *The Leuchter
    Report*, 110; denial role in
    Germany, 114; famous media-star–
    type Holocaust denier, 2; friendship
    with Butler, 222; libel trial against
    Lipstadt, 123–24; May 1992
    Munich trial, 113; relationship with
    David Duke, 124, 184; speaker's
    circuit, 166; testimony at Zündel
    trial, 197
Irving-Lipstadt trial, 123–24, 226–28
Islamic Center (Geneva, Switzerland),
    133
Isolationist movement, 146
Israel: beneficiary of Holocaust lie, 93–
    95, 100–1, 106, 184, 230; hatred of
    by Muslim world, 211–12;
    Holocaust denial as way to
    attack/deny legitimacy of/, 1–2;
    Mossad (Israeli intelligence service),
    173, move to Europe proposal by
    Ahmadinejad, 216
Israel, Julius, 203
*The Israeli Holocaust against the
    Palestinians* (Hoffman), 178
Italian Fascism, 79
Italy, 79, 127–128
Itzig, Veitel (book character), 18

Jäckel, Eberhard, 4, 44, 48, 119; attack
    on Irving's scholarship, 119
Janzon, David, 129
Japan, 230
Japs Ate My Gall Bladder (Porter), 175
Jasenovac concentration camp, 139
Jaspers, Karl, 79
Je suis partout (journal), 88
Jeddah, Saudi Arabia, 215
Jehovah's Witnesses, 174
Jekelius, Dr., 120
Jesuit High School, 170
Jewish Defense League (JDL), 176

*Jewish Economic Strategy for 1992,
    The* (Uno), 230
Jewish France (La France juive)
    (Drumont), 14
*The Jewish Question as a Question of
    Race, Custom and Culture. A World
    Political Response (Die Judenfrage
    als Racen-, Sitten- und Culturfrage.
    Mit einer Weltgeschichlichen
    Antwort)*, 13
*Jewish Religion: Its Influence Today,
    The. See The Plot against
    Christianity*
*Jewish Supremacism: My Awakening
    to the Jewish Question* (Duke),
    132, 184
Jewish veterans, 34
*The Jewish War against the German
    People* (pamphlet), 104, 184
*Jewishness in Music (Das Judentum in
    der Musik)* (Wagner), 17
Jews: antisemitism toward, 6, 13; Arab
    attacks against Jews, 212–13, 216,
    219, Babi Yar, 54, 64; beginning of
    gassing, 69; blamed for World War
    II, 89, 148; comments on
    extermination by Hans Frank, 63; in
    concentration camps/forced labor
    camps/death camps, 59, 61, 63,
    escape from Einsatzgruppen, 65;
    estimates of Holocaust deaths, 3,
    11–12, 62, 116, 118, 124, 139, 141,
    154, 213, 215; Finnish Jews, 50;
    growing resentment of, 17–20, 28;
    Himmler's attitude of, 59; Hitler's
    attitude of, 28–34, 36–37, 40, 49,
    120; Hitler's views on Jewish
    emigration, 47; Holocaust denial to
    further hatred of/as weapon against,
    3–4, Leuchter's criticism, 181;
    Liebenfels's attitude of, 23; Nazi
    government legislation, 34–37; no
    major outcry against killing of, 64;
    Nuremberg Laws, 35; Operation
    Reinhard, 62; rebellion at Sobidor,
    73; Renouf anti-Jewish remarks,
    227; Sanning's projected Jewish
    population, 161; and sterilization,

Proctor, Robert N., 42
Profession Neo-Nazi (Beruf Neonazi) (film), 111
*Protocols of the Learned Elders of Zion, The*15–16, 20–21; advocacy by Butler, 222; advocacy by Töben, 224; belief in Muslim world, 213; Hitler's belief, 29–30; relationship with Russian secret service, 15
Prussian army, 19
Prussian Yearbook (Preussische Jahrbücher), 19
"Psychology in the Novel of Marivaux" ("La Psychologie dans le roman de Marivaux"), 92
"Public State in Revisionism, The," 147

Queensland University of Technology, 226

Rabat, Morocco, 128
Rachkovsky, Pyotr Ivanovich, 16; relationship with *The Protocols of the Learned Elders of Zion*, 16;
Racial biology, 25
Racial Characteristics of the German People, The (Rassekunde des deutschen Volkes) (Günther), 24
Racial Characteristics of the Jewish People, The (Rassenkunde des jüdischen Volkes), 24
Racial hygiene, 24, 37–38
Racial negative eugenics, 30, 37
Radio Islam, 129, 215; founder Rami, 129
Radio Islam Web site, 219
Radio Maryja, 139
Raes, Roeland, 130
Raisko labor camp, 107
Rami, Ahmed, 129–30, 133, 141, 166, 213, 215; association with Institute for Historical Review, 133; failed coup attempt, 129
Rampart Journal, 147
Rassinier, Paul, 84–87; Harry Elmer Barnes influenced by, 146; leadership of French Holocaust

Denial Movement, 87; writings of converted Germar Rudolf, 112
Ratajczak, Dariusz, 139
Ratcliffe, Alexander, 117
Rath, Ernst vom, 36
Al-Rauf, Hisham Abd, 217–18
Rauschning, Hermann, 30, 32, 46
Raven, Greg, 167
Ravensbrück concentration camp, 66
Ravishing the Women of Conquered Europe (App), 154
Real Holocaust, The: The Attack on Unborn Children and Life Itself (Ross), 202
Real Politics Party (Stronnictwo Polityki Realnem), 138
Red Army Faction, 115
Red Cross, 62
Red Deer, Canada, 199, 201
Red Pattern of World Conquest, The (Butler), 222
Reed College, 157
Reich, Walter, 80
Reich Chancellery, 42, 63
Reich Citizenship Law, 35
Reich Criminal Police Ofiice, 41
Reich Institute for the History of the New Germany (Reichsinstitut für Geschichte des Neuen Deutschlands), 104
Reich Ministry of Economics, 36
Reich Security Head Office, 67, 74
Reich Supreme Court (Reichsgericht), 34
Reitlinger, Gerald, 11
Remer, Otto Ernst, 105–6, 112–13; belief in *The Protocols of the Learned Elders of Zion*, 108; honors from Hitler, 105; influence on Germar Rudolf, 112
Remer Dispatch (Remer Despeche), 106
Remscheid, Germany, 112
Renan, Ernest, 13
Renouf, Francis "Frank the Bank," 226
Renouf, Michèle, 124, 225–26; follower of Irving, 225–26

Republic Broadcasting Network, 173
Republic of Ireland, 148
Republic of Malta, 135
Republican Party (American), 165
Republican Party (Republicaner Partei), 112
Research Institute for Contemporary History (Zeitgeschichtliche Forschungsstelle), 105
Revealing the Evils of Modern Globalism (Uno), 231
Review of the History of Fascism (Revue d'Histoire de Fascisme) (journal), 91
"Review of the Holocaust: Global Vision" (conference, Tehran, Iran), 94
Revisionist, The: Journal for Critical Historical Inquiry (journal), 172, 207
Revisionist Bibliography: A Select Bibliography of Revisionist Books Dealing with the Two World Wars and Their Aftermaths (Stimely), 174
Revolutionary Communist Party, 175
Reynouard, Vincent, 98, 175
Rhodes University, 229
Ribbentrop, Joachim von, 104
Ribuffo, Leo P., 21
Rich, Evelyn, 184
Right: The National Journal of Forward-Looking Americanism (journal), 164
The Right to Death (Das Recht auf den Tod) (Jost), 39
Rimland, Ingrid, 190, 197; running Zündelsite, 197; wife of Zündel, 197
Rittenhouse, E. Stanley, 187, 189–90
Riverside Military Academy, 183
Robert, Alain, 90–91
Rockefeller Institute for Medical Research, 39
Rockwell, George Lincoln, 152–53; adoption of Holocaust denial, 152; fascination with Hitler, 152
Rockwell, George (Doc) Lovejoy, 152
Rocky Mountain House High School, 199

Romania, 140, 20
Rome, Italy, 127
Roosevelt, Franklin Delano, 5, 146, 149–50, 164
Roper, Trevor, 110
Roques, Henri, 96–98, 111; attack on credibility of Gerstein, 96; revocation of dissertation, 98
Rosarito, Mexico, 171
Rosenberg, Alfred, 31, 55
Ross, Malcolm, 3, 202; on abortion, 202; impact of *Web of Deceit,* 202
Rousso, Henry, 84, 99; investigation of Lyon III, 99
Rousset, David, 85
Royal Air Force (RAF), 119
Royal Academy of Dancing, 226
Royal Courts of Justice, 227
Royal Dutch Shell Oil Company, 183
Rozett, Robert, 11
Rubber, 107
Rubin, Irv, 174
Rudolf, Germar, 2, 106, 111–12, 205, 224; association with Otto Ernst Remer, 112
Rudolf Report: Export Report on Chemical and Technical Aspects of the 'Gas Chambers' of Auschwitz (Rudolf Gutachten über die Bildung und Nachweisbarkeit von Cyanidverbinden in den Gaskammern von Auschwitz), 112–13
Ruhr (Germany), 119
Rumboli, Russia, 65
The Rune (journal), 125
Russia: antisemitism in, 14–16; Holocaust denial in, 136–38, 140, 141; Jews fled from, 17, 20
Russian antisemitism, 14–16
Russian archives, 11
Russian Revolution, 31
Russian secret service (Okhrana), 15

SA. *See* Sturmabteilung
Saba, Abdullah Ibn, 211

About the Author

STEPHEN E. ATKINS is the curator for The Robert L. Dawson French Collection at the Cushing Library and Adjunct Professor of History at Texas A&M University. His numerous published works include *Encyclopedia of Modern American Extremists and Extremist Groups* (Oryx, 2002), *Historical Encyclopedia of Atomic Energy* (Greenwood, 2000), which was awarded *Booklist* Editors' Choice Award for 2000, and *Terrorism: A Handbook* (1992).